CRIMINOLOGICAL THEORY

THIRD EDITION

CRIMINOLOGICAL THEORY

Frank P. Williams III
California State University, San Bernardino

Marilyn D. McShane
Northern Arizona University

Prentice Hall
Upper Saddle River, New Jersey 07458

Library of Congress Cataloging-in-Publication Data
WILLIAMS, FRANKLIN P. III (date)
    Criminological theory/FRANKLIN P. WILLIAMS III and MARILYN D.
McSHANE—3rd ed.
        p.   cm.
    Includes bibliographical references and index.
    ISBN 0-13-602103-4
    1. Criminology.   I. Marilyn D. McShane [date]. II. Title.
HV6018.W48   1999
364.2—dc21   98-17373

Editorial Director: *Charlyce Jones Owen*
Editor in Chief: *Nancy Roberts*
Acquisitions Editor: *John Chillingworth*
Managing Editor: *Sharon Chambliss*
Marketing Manager: *Christopher DeJohn*
Production Editor: *Edie Riker*
Cover Director: *Jayne Conte*
Buyer: *Mary Ann Gloriande*

This book was set in 10/12 Palatino by East End Publishing Services
and was printed and bound by Courier Companies, Inc. The cover was
printed by Courier Companies, Inc.

© 1999, 1994, 1988 by Prentice-Hall, Inc.
Simon & Schuster / A Viacom Company
Upper Saddle River, New Jersey 07458

Printed in the United States of America

10   9   8   7   6   5   4   3   2

ISBN 0-13-602103-4

ISBN 0-13-602103-4

Prentice-Hall International (UK) Limited, *London*
Prentice-Hall of Australia Pty. Limited, *Sydney*
Prentice-Hall Canada Inc., *Toronto*
Prentice-Hall Hispanoamericana, S.A., *Mexico*
Prentice-Hall of India Private Limited, *New Delhi*
Prentice-Hall of Japan, Inc., *Tokyo*
Simon & Schuster Asia Pte. Ltd., *Singapore*
Editora Prentice-Hall do Brasil, Ltda., *Rio de Janeiro*

CONTENTS

PREFACE

As its title implies, this book is about the major sociological theories of crime. While there are other approaches to the study of crime, since the 1920s criminology has been oriented toward sociology. There are, however, some comments on biological and psychological theories of crime and delinquency in the chapter on Positivism. Those comments have been expanded, in response to instructors' requests. However, we still intend the book to be representative of what criminological theory has *been*, because a course in criminological theory is mainly a course in history.

When we first developed the concept of this text, we wanted to provide undergraduates with a brief but clear description of the most popular criminological theories. We continue to hear from students and colleagues who have used the first two editions that many graduate students find the text valuable as a primer or as a study guide in their theory classes. With this in mind, we have expanded the chapter bibliographies so that they may prove useful to the graduate student writing a research paper.

As before we have included an update of current theory. The intent of the first edition was to focus on traditional theories, and we only briefly mentioned contemporary versions in the concluding chapter. In this third edition of the book, two new chapters have been added to update students on current perspectives. The first (Chapter 12) covers rational theories, and the second (Chapter 13) discusses gender-based theories of crime. Those perspectives were previously covered in a single chapter along with the general theory of crime (self-control theory). We have moved the latter section to the end of Chapter 10 on social control theory.

The basic format of the first two editions has been retained in most chapters. We include a discussion of the social and intellectual heritage of the theory, highlight and explain the perspective and major concepts of the theory, and summarize and list the theory's major points. The lists of major points are intended to clarify earlier commentary and to demonstrate the logical connections among the various elements of each theory. The chapter summaries may also serve as review material for examinations. Graduate students may find the major points helpful in determining the background assumptions of the theories, comparing theories, and locating hypotheses for empirical testing.

As in the earlier editions, we attempt in most chapters to provide a classification of the theoretical perspective. These areas of the book continue to draw the most discussion. In one sense, we find this appropriate. There are so many methods of classifying theories that it is inevitable instructors and others who use the text find some conflict with their own positions. Rather than hide such conflicts, we believe it is more instructive to bring them out into the open for students. Thus, we continue to provide theory classifications and encourage instructors to tell students how their approaches differ from ours.

As always, we welcome any feedback on the book. The numerous versions of each theory make critical commentary inevitable. Since this book is designed primarily to be *used,* we invite readers, students, and teachers alike to provide us with their ideas on how to make it even more useful.

We feel very fortunate that we were able to acquire firsthand the comments and advice of some of the original authors of the theories. Our gratitude and appreciation are due to Freda Adler, Ron Akers, Al Cohen, Ray Jeffery, the late Ed Lemert, Walter Miller, Lloyd Ohlin, and Austin Turk for their comments and guidance. Special thanks to those who reviewed the manuscript: Bruce A. Jacobs, University of Missouri–St. Louis; Scot B. Boeringer, Appalachian State University; and Steven Messner, SUNY–Albany. Special thanks are also in order to those who used the text in their classes and provided us commentary, or otherwise helped with their ideas and thoughts. In a more general sense, we acknowledge our debts springing from the discussions we have had over the years with Ron Akers, Austin Turk, Leslie Wilkins, Sy Dinitz, Al Reiss, Gil Geis, Hal Pepinsky, Jeff Ferrell, and a large number of very bright students and colleagues. And to Richard Quinney, we are once again grateful to the Lone Ranger.

Frank P. Williams III
Marilyn D. McShane

1

INTRODUCTION

INTRODUCTION TO THEORY

Most people immediately rebel when threatened with their first exposure to theory. This seems to happen because they think of theory as something abstract and not really applicable to the "real world." What they don't understand is that we all use theory; theory is part of everyday life. When you see a dark cloud in the sky and say that it is going to rain, you have just expressed a theory. To be sure, it is a relatively simple theory, but it does express the relationships among clouds in general, clouds that are dark, and the falling of drops of water from the sky. Theories can be very simple or very complex, depending upon the number and types of relationships expressed by them. A more complex theory of rain would be that, under certain circumstances, surface water evaporates and rises into the atmosphere. Certain atmospheric conditions cause the water to condense, first into "clouds" and ultimately into drops of rain. The complexity in this version of a theory of rain is in specifying the conditions and processes involved in evaporation and condensation.

Theories can also be concrete or abstract. Theories about rain tend to be concrete, even if complex. Theories about simple behaviors such as throwing a ball through a window also tend to be concrete. Abstract theories, however, are difficult to tie directly to reality. For instance, Einstein's theory of relativity is an abstract concept. We have difficulty in directly testing the concept that time gets slower the faster one travels, and certainly we cannot test velocities beyond the speed of light. Similarly, theories about the effect of social structure on crime rates are abstract. Social structure is an invented concept (we doubt that you have ever *seen* a social structure), and crime rates are a mathematical concept derived from dividing the number of crimes by some population size.

The most important thing about theories is that we need them to live. True, we don't really need a theory of relativity, or a theory of criminal behavior, to get along in life. But we do need the many theories we have learned about our environment. Imagine what life would be like if you could never generalize about things, if every time you saw a cloud you had to get wet to conclude that it was going to rain. And suppose you could not assume that a door represents a way to enter a building. Theories, then, are really generalizations of a sort; they explain how two or more events are related to each other and the conditions under which the relationship takes place. For example, the statement that seat belts reduce deaths in automobile accidents expresses a relationship between two events. The seat belts alone will not reduce deaths, however. There must be a condition that they be worn (we could also add that the seat belts have to be installed properly, worn correctly, etc.).

The way we express these generalizations, or think about things, depends on the form of knowledge we are using at the time. We know things through experience (often referred to as "empirical knowledge"), intuition, common sense, or science, or because someone important to us (or even an important book) has told us so. The causes of crime, for instance, are assumed to be "known" by everyone. They include broken homes, lack of religion, hanging around with the wrong crowd, poor upbringing, and so forth. While you probably don't think of these explanations as theories, they all are. At the same time, they are not good theories because they are too simplistic. If they were correct, then everyone whose life has these causes would be criminal (or delinquent), and, of course, we know that is not true. Even more important is the fact such theories also imply the reverse; that is, people who are raised in a good family environment, who are religious, and who associate with the right people will *not do* anything criminal (or delinquent). This is not true, either, since self-report studies (Short and Nye, 1958; Reiss and Rhodes, 1961; Akers, 1964; Gold, 1970) tell us that most young people at one time or another do things that are against the law.

The problem with most of our day-to-day theories is they are often illogical or they are the product of selective observations. They may work some of the time and even often enough to be used as a general rule-of-thumb for making decisions. But when we need to be accurate or more careful about making policies, these theories will fail us. Human behavior is complex, and any simplistic theory will be incorrect. Therefore, theories about crime and criminals tend to be complex theories and are based on what we know (or in the case of older theories, what was known at the time) from research on crime and criminals. As a rule, they reflect systematic observation and careful logic.

The sheer variety of behavior defined as criminal also presents a problem. When we use the term "crime," the reference is often to a wide range of illegal behavior. The individual criminal acts, though, may have very little in common except that someone, at some time, disliked each of them enough to have a law passed against them (of course, sometimes the reverse occurs and criminal behaviors are made legal again). Murder and petty theft, for example, have about as much in common as a rock and an orange.

There is an even greater problem. Criminal behavior may be merely one of a variety of similar behaviors. For instance, if we argue that some criminal behavior is thrill-seeking behavior, then a theory that predicts behavior on that basis must also include legal behavior. Carrying out a crime for thrills would be no more likely than someone going bunge-jumping, skydiving, or hang-gliding. From this perspective, a thrill-seeking behavior might be relatively predictable while one of those behaviors, crime, remains relatively unpredictable. Thus, theories of crime and criminal behavior must encompass a wide range of human activity. For this reason, some criminologists advocate limiting theories to specific criminal acts or harmful behaviors.

How can these theories be used? Our answer is that everyone already uses them, although most people do not know they are doing so. Police departments have designed their activities around some of the theoretical explanations. Each day judges hand down sentences based on their understanding of the character of the defendant and the environment in which the defendant lives. Jurors decide whether to give the death penalty based on their assumptions about the future dangerousness of the defendant. Probation officers send their clients to treatment programs to improve the clients' work skills or to resolve their use of drugs or alcohol. Prison authorities attempt to instill discipline, teach proper work habits, and deter inmates from future criminality. Finally, as reflected in the media, the public seems to attribute criminal behavior to such things as drug use, a depressed economy, poor family life, and the influence of bad friends. Criminological theory, then, is really a part of everyday life.

WHAT IS GOOD THEORY?

Since usually more than one theory purports to explain criminality at any given time, how do we know which one is best? In fact, how can we tell what is good theory in general? The most common answer is that a good theory is one that *can be tested* and that best *fits the evidence of research* (Blalock, 1969; Gibbs, 1972; Dubin, 1978; Akers, 1997). This makes sense, because our theories are scientific and should already be based on research evidence. In fact, these criteria are derived from the natural sciences, where they are used as the standard for good theory. There is really no difference between the natural and social sciences in determining good theory. There are, however, measurement problems in the social sciences, because some variables, such as social class, cannot be accurately measured as can distance, time, or hardness, and the like. Under these generally accepted criteria, if the theory is not testable or if the evidence does not support the theory, then the theory is not a good one. Unfortunately, the issue is not that simple.

Suppose, for a moment, that Einstein had lived and had proposed his theory of relativity two centuries before he did. It would not have been testable at that time, nor would the theory have fit the research evidence. Obviously, his theory would not have been considered a good theory at that time. Therefore, as changes in research evidence and the ability to measure and test occur, so do the common criteria for a good theory. In other words, it sometimes takes a while before our ability to measure and produce evidence catches up with a theory. Until that time, the theory may appear to be a "bad" one because evidence will not be available to support it. This means we might discard theories that are really good ones because our measuring capabilities cannot yet adequately test them and provide the necessary support. Therefore, as our measuring capabilities and techniques change, we may need to reexamine and retest theories to see if new research evidence provides a better fit. Of one thing we can be sure, however, if there is no current way to measure something, it is unlikely to appear in a theory—regardless of how important that something might be.

Another concern with testing is the use of a single approach to measure theoretical concepts. If one uses only one measure, and that measure is not a good one or does not adequately represent the theoretical concept, the theory may be rejected (even though, the theory may be valid). A similar problem arises when a theory is affirmed by a single test approach or measure. What is being measured may generate an erroneous result, but if the measurement is done the same way time after time the result will always the same, thereby creating the false impression of consistently valid results. Multiple methods and measures are always better ways of testing than any single approach.

If our approach to assessing a theory is based on measuring and testing, we refer to it as **quantitative** validation. A different approach, one that focuses on the substance of a theory, is called **qualitative** validation. It is these qualitative criteria that help us resolve the problem of time-specific and measurement-specific evidence. They include such factors as *logical soundness, the ability to make sense out of several conflicting positions,* and even *the degree to which the theory may sensitize people to things they otherwise would not see.* While these criteria are not often mentioned, they are no less important for the utility of a theory than quantitative tests are. Most theories of criminology do not do well on the criterion of empirical testing.[1] On the other hand, almost all the theories made sense out of things that had been puzzling people before, and they sensitized criminologists to new and important ways of looking at the phenomena of crime. Let's explore these qualitative criteria more closely.

---

1. Of course, as the previous discussion suggests, the problem with "fitting" the research evidence may be as much with the way we test and measure as it is with the theory itself. However, we are certainly not taking the position that all criminological theories are simply ahead of their time and merely waiting for research capabilities to "catch up" to them.

Logical soundness means that the theory does not propose illogical relationships and that it is internally consistent. One of the most common logic problems is that of time order, in which an event that occurs after another event is assumed to have caused the first event. For instance, if we ask marijuana users about the chance of being arrested for drug use, they will probably tell us that the probability of arrest is low. We might then think that people use marijuana because they think they have very little chance of being arrested (i.e, they are not deterred). In reality, however, a low estimate of the chance of arrest is really a reflection of the fact that they have used marijuana many times and have not been arrested. The low estimate of being arrested, then, came after the drug use and could not have caused it. In a more general example of logical soundness, if someone examined evidence that criminals in an institution for the criminally insane have irrational thinking patterns and then proposed that irrational thinking causes criminal behavior, the theory would be illogical. Very few criminals are insane, and those who are placed in insane institutions are different by their very nature. Actually, if the theory were correct, the author of the theory has demonstrated irrational thinking, and we would expect him or her to become a criminal! In another example, criminologists DeFleur and Quinney (1966) even used a special form of logic called "set theory" to analyze the logical soundness of one of the more popular theories of criminal behavior (they found that it was, indeed, internally consistent).

The ability to make sense out of several conflicting positions means that when evidence seems to indicate that there are two or more opposing facts, a theory that can reconcile those facts is a good one and is better than having different theories to account for each fact. Differential association theory (Chapter 5), for instance, brings together the concepts of disorganized social areas and organized interaction in small, intimate groups and makes sense out of differing crime rates among various groups of people. As another example, official crime statistics and self-report studies (asking people what they have done) suggest two different pictures of "the criminal." Labeling theory (Chapter 8) makes sense of both forms of evidence by pointing out that official statistics give a picture only of those who have been reacted to and that self-report information gives a picture of those who are officially criminal as well as those who have not yet been caught. A noted philosopher and historian of science, Thomas Kuhn (1970), has said that accepted new theories almost always make sense out of conflicting evidence that older theories cannot explain.

Sensitizing ability refers to focusing people's attention on a new, or even forgotten, direction of inquiry, or perhaps suggesting a different way of looking at and interpreting a fact they already know. Sometimes we concentrate so hard on a particular direction for explaining crime that we need to be reminded that there are other directions as well. One value of a sensitizing theory is that it serves to reacquaint criminologists with other facets of the problem. Using labeling theory again to illustrate, theorists in the 1950s were so focused on lower-class, urban, male, gang delinquents that all delinquency seemed to be a product of those kids. Labeling sensitized criminology to the importance of asking who gets reacted to and how we react to them. This served to remind criminologists that certain types of people are more likely to be closely observed and arrested for their behavior. In other words, labeling theory sensitized criminologists to the fact that criminality is due as much to how we react to people as it is to their personal characteristics. Thus, there was another explanation for urban, minority, male delinquency than the strain and stress of social structure.

Finally, one other qualitative criterion for a "good" theory is worthy of discussion. This criterion is very different from the others, and, it should be used with a great deal of caution. This one is *popularity*. Simply put, if a theory becomes popular with criminologists, then by definition it seems to be a "good" theory. The problem here is that popularity comes from a variety of factors, some of which have little to do with any of the other criteria mentioned. For instance, a theory can simply echo our gut-level feelings about the causes of crime, and we would tend to give it credence regardless of its logical soundness and empirical support. In fact, it is just this problem that we must watch for. The notion that something must be correct because it seems correct is one of the biggest mistakes that laypeople make about theories. Nevertheless, popularity must be included as one of the criteria for determining a "good" theory because many criminological theories do not meet the testability requirement very well yet were, and still are, very popular.

Good theory, then, is logically constructed, is based on the evidence at hand, and is supported by subsequent research. It also makes sense out of various facts and serves to make us aware of the surrounding circumstances of the phenomenon it is attempting to explain. In making your assessment of how valid a theory seems to be, keep in mind the problems associated with each of these criteria and be flexible in making your final judgment.

KINDS OF THEORY

One distinction needs to be made before engaging in a discussion about kinds of theories. There are two general forms of theory, unit theory and metatheory (see Wagner, 1984). By and large, this is a book about unit theories. **Unit theories** emphasize a particular problem (such as crime and delinquency) and make testable assertions about that problem. **Metatheories**, on the other hand, are rarely testable and are best viewed as ways of looking at and interpreting reality. In another sense, they can be seen as "theories about theories." They discuss the kinds of concepts that should be used, the general approach to using those concepts, and the way unit theories should be constructed. As an example, a criminological metatheory might specify that explanations for criminal behavior should emphasize social concepts rather than psychological and biological ones, and that social class should be used as the dominant variable. Furthermore, our metatheoretical example might specify that only official statistics should be used as appropriate evidence for unit theories. While there is an occasional discussion about metatheory in contemporary criminology, when the word "theory" is used, in most cases a unit theory is meant. Therefore, we drop the term "unit" and simply use "theory." Any reference to a metatheory will use the full term.

There are different varieties of theory, but there is no single, accepted scheme that describes the kinds of theory. As if the problem of understanding the various theories were not difficult enough, attempts by various writers to group them by some simple differences have, ironically, made matters worse by making those differences appear to be the most important characteristics of the theories. Nevertheless, categorizing and classifying theories is a necessary endeavor.

Because theories are complex and because the threads from which they are woven are not always self-evident, theories can be classified in many ways. Students of criminology will read one textbook and think that they know the theories pretty well; then they look at another textbook, find theories classified differently, and end up confused. In fact, almost every criminology textbook offers a somewhat different twist to classifying theories. Gibbons and Krohn (1986) use a system of biological, psychological, and social theories (although they devote most of their coverage to social perspectives). Another common scheme is the use of various forms of sociological and social-psychological categories (Nettler, 1974; Kornhauser, 1978; Orcutt, 1983; Reid, 1985). Others use a variety of broad approaches with numerous subcategories (Hagan, 1986; Sheley, 1991). With all these different approaches, students may begin to feel that their instructor does not know the subject unless he or she uses a classification scheme that matches their textbook. Clearly, the classification of theories has done as much as anything to muddy the theoretical waters for beginning students. It has also been a problem for some of the more experienced criminologists.

Since these classifications exist, however, they must be dealt with. It should be noted that no classification is *real*, because the world does not exist in black and white. There are many factors to consider, and the result is a forcing of theories into one category or the other when they might not fit any category very well. The end result is almost always an artificial scheme of classification (Williams, 1984). In addition, by "changing" the classification of theories, a theory may be viewed in a way its author never intended. Regardless, and even though it may sound strange to say so, such diversity is probably good. The reason for categorizing theories is to establish similarities and differences among them. If many different categorizations are being used, it means that the theories are rich enough to defy simple classification and therefore they contain many valuable nuances, concepts, and ideas.

We discuss three different methods for categorizing theories. Hopefully, they will assist those new to criminology in understanding the relationships and connections among the various theories. At the same time, a warning is in order: treat each classification scheme as nothing more than an attempt to highlight similarities and differences. These schemes are not to be used as the last word in grouping, or establishing types of, theories.

Levels of Abstraction

As we have already noted, some theories are more abstract than others. The most abstract can be called **macrotheories.** Macrotheories are broad in their scope and perhaps are best characterized as those that *explain social structure and its effects.* They paint a picture of the way the world works, fit the structure of society into that picture, and suggest how crime is related to that structure. Macrotheories focus on rates of crime (called "epidemiology") rather than on criminals and their behavior. Macrotheories are simply not interested in individual behavior. Examples of macrotheory are anomie and conflict theories.

Other, more concrete, theories can be referred to as **microtheories.** These theories are based on the assumption that a particular way of characterizing society is best; that characterization is then used directly to *explain how people become criminals* (called "etiology"). The focus may be on specific groups of people (but usually *small* groups) or on the individual. Likewise, microtheories may range from purely social to purely psychological to purely biological. In any case, they tell us how people become criminal. Microtheories are not interested in social structure and crime rates. Examples of microtheory are social control and social learning theories.

Finally, as is the case with any classification scheme, there are theories that do not fit neatly into either of the two categories and are "in-between." We will call these **bridging theories.** These theories attempt to tell us both *how social structure comes about and how people become criminal.* In fact, bridging theories are often both epidemiological (explaining differing rates of crime) and etiological (explaining criminal behavior itself). Examples of bridging theory are subculture theory and differential opportunity theory. Depending on the way in which they are viewed, or the direction of emphasis a writer finds in the theory, bridging theories can be classified as either macrotheories or microtheories. Doing so establishes one focus of the theory as more dominant than the other.

Levels of Explanation

These three general forms of theories can be further examined on the basis of their focus of explanation. What, for instance, is a theory attempting to explain: social structure in general, classes of people in society, small groups, or individual criminality? This problem is referred to as the **level of explanation** of a theory, or what the theory attempts to explain. Most theories cannot be directly compared with each other because they do not focus directly on the same subject.

Theories are often said to compete with each other in best accounting for crime and criminals. It should make sense that, in most instances, this is really not the case. Some theories explain how social events give rise to crime in society but do not attempt to explain how particular individuals become criminals; others do the opposite. Some explain the social factors important in creating criminality; others explain the psychological factors; still others the internal biological factors. Further, some theories attempt to account for *crime* as a social phenomenon, while many focus directly on *criminals* and their behavior. Obviously, these various theories are not in competition because they apply to different levels of the crime-and-criminals problem.

Unfortunately, criminology has done little thus far to integrate these various explanatory levels (but Pearson and Weiner, 1985, and Elliott et al., 1985, have tried). And, except for Williams's (1998) critical incident metatheory, there is no metatheory that puts them all together in a coherent fashion. The problem of which level a theory explains has not yet been generally recognized in criminology, although some people are beginning to do so (e.g., Short, 1985). For those beginning the study of criminological theory, however, the idea of levels of explanation is crucial because it helps to make sense out of the differences among theories. A good understanding of the area each theory deals with will help you grasp what the theorists were writing about.

Other Common Classification Schemes

The more popular classification schemes usually have two mutually exclusive categories, or dichotomies. One of the oldest of the classification schemes is **classical** and **positive**. The names come from two schools of thought in the eighteenth and nineteenth centuries (and the subject of Chapters 2 and 3). Classical theories focus on legal statutes, governmental structures, and the rights of humans. A classical orientation to a theory suggests that the theory is less concerned about traditional scientific notions of testability and more about the essence of the human condition. Positivist theories focus on pathology in criminal behavior, on treatment, and on the correction of criminality within individuals. Positivism also derives from the use of the scientific method to study phenomena. In that sense, most of today's theories are positivist ones.

Another common scheme is to separate theories into those of **structure** and those of **process**. Structural theories are those that focus on the way society is organized and its effect on behavior. Some of these are also referred to as *strain theories* (a term popularized by Travis Hirschi, 1969, and Ruth Kornhauser, 1978) because of their assumption that a disorganized society creates strain that leads to deviant behavior. Process theories attempt to explain how people become criminal. While it is sometimes difficult to classify theories in this scheme, the major orientation is on the starting point

of the theory. As a rule, a structural theory does not emphasize the individual criminal and a processual theory does not emphasize social structure.
These two forms correspond closely to the macrotheories and microtheories
we have already discussed.

The final major classification approach is that of **consensus** and **conflict,** sometimes referred to as the "old" and the "new" criminology (Gibbs,
1966). Consensus theories are those based on the assumption that there is
agreement among people in a society. At the least, they assume that members of a society hold common values. Conflict theories, on the other hand,
are based on the assumption that disagreement is common and people hold
conflicting values. Most conflict theories also take account of differences
among social classes. Since any society may have agreement and conflict at
the same time, the crux is not whether agreement exists but whether it *originally* existed. A conflict theorist may discuss a society in agreement (Marx's
false consciousness), or a consensus theorist may explain how conflict exists
(Cohen's delinquent subculture). Thus, this scheme is somewhat like the
chicken-and-egg controversy: one simply believes that either conflict or consensus is more natural to society and asserts that humans are naturally oriented toward one or the other.

SOCIAL CONTEXT AND THEORY

The final approach to understanding theory lies in an examination of social
history. Writers commonly discuss theories in the abstract, especially in
introductory textbooks. Because they do, it may seem that the theorist sits in
isolation, inventing and creating his or her new theory. Nothing could be
further from the truth. Just as there are people who have helped mold your
thoughts and views of the world, so there are for the theorist. Indeed, it
should be clear that any important influence in your life will leave its mark
on the way you perceive the world. Your college courses, for instance, are
designed to do exactly that. Your parents also provided important attitudes
and viewpoints for you. Moreover, just as you respond to the latest fads and
social events, so does the theorist. In short, those who create theories are
probably as susceptible as you are to influences in their lives. Criminological
theorists are practicing social scientists and may be even more sensitive to
social movements and trends than most of us. As a result, no theory can
really be understood and appreciated without an awareness of the context
within which it was created.

Further, each theorist makes certain assumptions about the way the
world really is, the nature of humans, and the value of particular concepts
(an unspoken metatheory). Gouldner (1970) argues that these assumptions
so severely affect the direction of theorizing that entire areas of evidence and
thought can be ignored. For this reason, the effect of assumptions can be
seen as similar to blinders on a horse: you can see only what is right in front
of you, everything else might as well not exist. If a theorist's assumptions

were spelled out, this might not represent a major problem because you could see what was included and what was omitted. Unfortunately, assumptions are not always obvious, and even the theorist may not be aware of them. Therefore, to better understand any theory, we must find ways to determine what the assumptions of that theory are. One of the best ways of doing this is to examine the context within which the theory was created.

Context has two major forms, **social** and **intellectual.** Both are handy terms for identifying areas of influence on an individual. Social context refers to the world about us: the ways people in a society are thinking, the things they are doing, the events taking place, the fads and fashions that are popular, and even the way society is structured. For example, right after the Second World War, it would have been difficult for people in the United States to criticize either the nation or the government; there was a general feeling of satisfaction with ourselves and a relative agreement about how good our values were. During the early 1970s, the opposite was common; people were uncertain about government, their lives, and their values. In both times, a theorist would have been affected by the events of the time and written into the theory some of the contemporary ideas (Williams, 1981).

The second form of context, the intellectual, refers to the personal influence of teachers, friends, family, and colleagues. Sometimes that influence extends to people whom the theorist has never even met; but the theorist has read their work and been impressed with what they had to say. For this reason, many people have been said to follow in the footsteps of their teachers. The major criminological theorists have undeniably done some "footstep following," but at the same time, their theories are popular at least in part because these theorists were also creative.

SUMMARY

One commentator on social thought (Nisbet, 1966) has noted that it is possible to discuss theory in terms of specific schools (classifying periods of time), ideas or concepts themselves (such as anomie), or *dramatis personae* (the major theorists). We contend that to appreciate and understand theory it is necessary to look at all these. Because any review of theories is in reality a history of social thought, a combination of factors needs to be taken into account. The ideas should be followed from theory to theory, the various classifications examined to see how they overlap and how they differ, and the contexts analyzed to gain a feel for the assumptions made by the theorists. Therefore, each of the following chapters examines the social and intellectual context before discussing the theory. After the theoretical presentation, the classification schemes explored in this chapter are applied to the theory.

We contend that theory is to be used, not read, memorized, and filed away for future recital. Ideas and concepts are not anyone's exclusive property; they should be rethought, reworked, and applied where needed. No one theory takes in a complete view of crime and criminals, much less a complete view of the world. For this reason, theories should be merged and integrated to form new approaches to the problems before us. And theories should be flexible enough that citizens, police officers, and judges, as well as criminologists, can use them to understand crime and criminals in our society. This doesn't mean, however, that theories of crime and criminal behavior should be simple ones. Indeed, reality is complex so we should assume that the reasons for criminal behavior are, too.

Finally, we want to caution readers that the simple presentation of each of the theories in this book cannot capture the richness of those theories. In the interest of those being exposed to theory for the first time, we have emphasized simplicity and straightforward presentation. Each of the theories is much more complex, vastly more interesting, and has many more nuances than our presentation suggests. Students should read the original works to gain a real appreciation for the theories. Anthologies are also available with the original works or excerpts from them (see, e.g., Williams and McShane's *Criminology Theory: Selected Classic Readings*, 2nd ed.).

SUGGESTED READINGS

For those who are interested in a more comprehensive, or in some cases an alternative, treatment of criminological theory, we suggest the following:

AKERS, RONALD L. (1997). *Criminological Theories: Introduction and Evaluation.* Los Angeles: Roxbury.

CULLEN, FRANCIS T. (1983). *Rethinking Crime and Deviance Theory: The Emergence of a Structuring Tradition.* Totowa, NJ: Rowman and Allanheld.

DAVIS, NANETTE J. (1975). *Sociological Constructions of Deviance.* Dubuque, IA: Brown.

FARRELL, RONALD A., and VICTORIA L. SWIGERT (1982). *Deviance and Social Control.* Glenview, IL: Scott, Foresman.

GIBBONS, DON C. (1979). *The Criminological Enterprise: Theories and Perspectives.* Englewood Cliffs, NJ: Prentice Hall.

———— (1994). *Talking about Crime and Criminals: Problems and Issues in Theory Development in Criminology.* Englewood Cliffs, NJ: Prentice Hall.

LILLY, J. ROBERT, FRANCIS T. CULLEN, and RICHARD A. BALL (1995). *Criminological Theory: Context and Consequences*, 2nd ed. Newbury Park, CA: Sage.

MARTIN, RANDY, ROBERT J. MUTCHNICK, and TIMOTHY W. AUSTIN (1990). *Criminological Thought: Pioneers, Past and Present.* New York: Macmillan.

TAYLOR, IAN, PAUL WALTON, and JOCK YOUNG (1973). *The New Criminology: For a Social Theory of Deviance.* London: Routledge and Kegan Paul.

VOLD, GEORGE B., and THOMAS J. BERNARD (1986). *Theoretical Criminology*, 3rd ed. New York: Oxford University Press.

BIBLIOGRAPHY

AKERS, RONALD L. (1964). "Socio-economic status and delinquent behavior: A retest." *Journal of Research in Crime and Delinquency* 1:38–46.

———— (1997). *Criminological Theories: Introduction and Evaluation*, 2nd ed. Los Angeles: Roxbury.

BLALOCK, HUBERT M. (1969). *Theory Construction*. Englewood Cliffs, NJ: Prentice Hall.

DeFLEUR, MELVIN L., and RICHARD QUINNEY (1966). "A reformulation of Sutherland's differential association theory and a strategy for empirical verification." *Journal of Research in Crime and Delinquency* 3: 1–22.

DUBIN, ROBERT (1978). *Theory Building*, rev. ed. New York: Free Press.

ELLIOTT, DELBERT S., DAVID HUIZINGA, and SUZANNE S. AGETON (1985). *Explaining Delinquency and Drug Use*. Beverly Hills: Sage.

GIBBONS, DON C., and MARVIN D. KROHN (1986). *Delinquent Behavior*, 4th ed. Englewood Cliffs, NJ: Prentice Hall.

GIBBS, JACK P. (1966). "Conceptions of deviant behavior: The old and the new." *Pacific Sociological Review* 9: 9–14.

———— (1972). *Sociological Theory Construction*. Hinsdale, IL: Dryden.

GOLD, MARTIN (1970). *Delinquent Behavior in an American City*. Belmont, CA: Brooks/Cole.

GOULDNER, ALVIN W. (1970). *The Coming Crisis of Western Sociology*. New York: Basic Books.

HAGAN, FRANK E. (1986). *Introduction to Criminology: Theories, Methods, and Criminal Behavior*. Chicago: Nelson Hall.

HIRSCHI, TRAVIS (1969). *Causes of Delinquency*. Berkeley: University of California Press.

KORNHAUSER, RUTH R. (1978). *Social Sources of Delinquency*. Chicago: University of Chicago Press.

KUHN, THOMAS (1970). *The Structure of Scientific Revolutions*, 2nd ed. Chicago: University of Chicago Press.

MORRISON, WAYNE (1995). *Theoretical Criminology: From Modernity to Post-Modernism*. London, UK: Cavendish.

NETTLER, GWYNN (1974). *Explaining Crime*. New York: McGraw-Hill.

NISBET, ROBERT A. (1966). *The Sociological Tradition*. New York: Basic Books.

ORCUTT, JAMES D. (1983). *Analyzing Deviance*. Homewood, IL: Dorsey Press.

PEARSON, FRANK S., and NEIL A. WEINER (1985). "Toward an integration of criminological theories." *Journal of Criminal Law and Criminology* 76: 116–150.

REID, SUE TITUS (1985). *Crime and Criminology*, 4th ed. New York: Holt, Rinehart and Winston.

REISS, ABERT J., JR., and A. LEWIS RHODES (1961). "The distribution of juvenile delinquency in the social class structure." *American Sociological Review* 26: 720–732.

RITZER, GEORGE (1975). *Sociology: A Multiple Paradigm Science*. Boston: Allyn and Bacon.

SHELEY, JOSEPH F. (1991). *Criminology: A Contemporary Handbook*. Belmont, CA: Wadsworth.

SHORT, JAMES F., JR. (1985). "The level of explanation problem in criminology." In R. F. Meier, ed., *Theoretical Methods in Criminology*, 51–72. Beverly Hills, CA: Sage.

SHORT, JAMES F., JR., and F. IVAN NYE (1958). "Extent of unrecorded juvenile delinquency: Tentative conclusions." *Journal of Criminal Law, Criminology, and Police Science* 49: 296–302.

WAGNER, DAVID G. (1984). *The Growth of Sociological Theories*. Beverly Hills, CA: Sage.

WILLIAMS, FRANK P., III (1981). "The sociology of criminological theory: Paradigm or fad." In G. F. Jensen, ed., *Sociology of Delinquency: Current Issues*, 20–28. Beverly Hills, CA: Sage.

———— (1984). "The demise of the criminological imagination: A critique of recent criminology." *Justice Quarterly* 1: 91–106.

———— (1998). *Imagining Criminology: An Alternative Paradigm*. New York: Garland.

WILLIAMS, FRANK P., III, and MARILYN D. McSHANE (1998). *Criminology Theory: Selected Classic Readings*, 2nd ed. Cincinnati, OH: Anderson.

2

THE CLASSICAL SCHOOL

INTRODUCTION

The particular conceptions of crime and criminal justice that emerged in the eighteenth century are collectively known as the Classical School of criminology. The name derives from common references to that entire period of time as the "Classical period." The term "criminology" is a misnomer since there was no criminology as we now know it until the late nineteenth century. Nonetheless, the term is commonly used because the period gave rise to some of the basic ideas for the operation of a criminal justice system and the processing of criminals. It also provided the first broadly understood theory of criminal behavior. Criminology is the study of crime and criminals, with some study of lawmaking included. The Classical School was not interested in studying criminals *per se*, so it gained its association with criminology through its focus on lawmaking and legal processing.

Two writers of this period, Cesare Beccaria (1738–1794) and Jeremy Bentham (1748–1832), wrote the best-known works, and they are considered to have had the most influence. In their writings they opposed the arbitrary and capricious nature of the criminal justice systems of the time. They proposed that both the law and the administration of justice should be based on rationality and human rights, neither of which was then commonly applied.

Among the major ideas that descend from this school are the concepts of humans as free-willed, rational beings; utilitarianism (the greatest good for the greatest number); civil rights and due process of law; rules of evidence and testimony; determinate sentencing; and deterrence. C. Ray Jeffery (1956, 1972), speaking of classical criminology, emphasizes the school's focus on a legal definition of crime rather than on a concern with criminal behavior. In addition, both the Declaration of Independence and the U. S. Constitution reflect the concerns of the Classical movement. Because of this, most of our law is classical in nature.

THE HERITAGE OF THE SCHOOL

The Social Heritage

The eighteenth century was a period of major change. The old aristocracy was being called into question, both for its claims to natural superiority and for its corrupt political practices. A new and soon-to-be powerful middle class was rising from the profits of mercantilism and the beginnings of the Industrial Revolution. Societies were becoming urbanized. Traditional conceptions of property and ownership were also being disrupted. For example, enclosure movements, the practice of claiming sole use of and fencing off previously open lands, deprived the common people of what had been their traditional right—to use the land and its resources (such as game and firewood). These changes placed stress on the poor and created a resentment that affected the agricultural and rural power base of the aristocracy.

At the same time, an emphasis on commonalities among people served to minimize national differences. With this, the rule of the Church and the aristocracy was seriously threatened. The rise of the Protestant ethic allowed people to expect success for hard work in this world and not in some Church-promised afterlife. Before this time, the common person simply had to accept his or her lot in life. The Protestant ethic promised that hard work would result in an improvement in one's life and led people to expect a direct connection between hard work and success.

Certain powerful families attempted to gain the support of the middle class in a relatively successful effort to establish dominance over the thrones of Europe. These ruling families were known as monarchies. For instance, German nobility ruled in England, Poland, Russia, and Sweden. All of this led to the emergence of a new and highly volatile political system. The aristocracy found itself besieged by both the monarchies and the emerging middle class, and its hold on the reins of power began to loosen.

The Classical period was, in many areas of life, an era of great thought and expression. In close proximity to the time when people were reading Beccaria's great treatise, *On Crimes and Punishments* (1764), J. S. Bach had composed and performed; the young colonies were about to erupt into the

American Revolution; and the Declaration of Independence, the U. S. Constitution, and the Bill of Rights were written.

Writers of the Classical period examined not only human nature but social conditions as well. In the late 1700s, John Howard wrote *The State of the Prisons of England and Wales,* Immanuel Kant produced his great essay *Foundations of the Metaphysics of Morals,* and Bentham introduced his *An Introduction to the Principles of Morals and Legislation.* Revolutions took place in both the American colonies and in France.

The judicial system was also marked by changes. Founded on the religious structures of the Middle Ages, law was mainly the product of judicial interpretation and caprice (Maestro, 1942). The accused often faced secret accusations, torture, and private trials; arbitrary and overly harsh sanctions were often applied to the convicted (Barnes, 1930). Generally, there were few written laws, and existing law was applied primarily to those who were not of the aristocracy. In fact, law was often used as a political tool to suppress those who spoke out against the aristocracy or the Church. Indeed, the Spanish Inquisition of the late fifteenth century and the Italian Roman Inquisition of the early sixteenth century testified to the vigorous use of law in the defense of Church and state.

The Intellectual Heritage

The prevailing ideas of the eighteenth century were those of reform. A group of philosophers called the Naturalists believed experience and observation could determine much about the world, especially when fortified by the human ability to reason. They rebelled against the authority of the Church and emphasized an order to things that was separate from religious revelation. Morals, ethics, and responsibilities became major topics of discussion. The application of science to the physical world had begun to reveal "truths," and people were certain that the same effort brought to bear on moral and political questions would yield similar fruit.

The major explanation for human behavior was **hedonism.** Basically, it was assumed that people would automatically attempt to maximize pleasure and minimize pain. According to Bentham (1789:29), the value of any pleasure or pain would be determined by its intensity, duration, and certainty. This theory of behavior became the basis for the concept of deterrence. Bentham's elaboration on deterrence is the essence of today's rational perspectives.

One of the major new philosophical viewpoints rested on so-called natural human rights and justified the existence of government as a **social contract** between the state and its citizens (see, e.g., the work of John Locke). This justification came close to reversing the previous political belief that people existed to serve the government and, instead, made service to the people the rationale for government. Under this social contract, a person surrendered to the authority of the state only the amount of freedom necessary to ensure protection of the rights of other citizens. Although it was not really new, the idea of a social contract between people and their government served the needs of the new middle class.

Growing specialization in trade and industry required more services such as roads, ports, municipal services, and policing, and the government made an ideal provider of those services. The increasing secularization of society, in turn, fit in well with both the social contract conception of a rational human and the rising middle class. Secularism immediately suggested reforms in institutions, which was all to the benefit of the new classes.

Finally, an emphasis on **human dignity,** stemming from the Enlightenment, was characteristic of the period. A humanistic current of thought, chiefly from England and France, aroused the young intellectuals of the day. Those works that expressly influenced Beccaria were Montesquieu's *The Spirit of the Laws* (1748) and the various pamphlets and letters of Voltaire (Maestro, 1942:17–18). In addition to Beccaria and Montesquieu, such writers and thinkers as Hume, Montaigne, Rousseau, Helvetius, Diderot, and Condorcet were the new champions of the common people and produced eloquent writings glorifying *people* rather than the Church or state. Accompanying this growth of interest in humanity came a concern with improving social conditions, making possible the rise of the social sciences.

THE PERSPECTIVE OF THE SCHOOL

The Classical School, then, generally gave us a humanistic conception of how law and criminal justice systems should be constructed. It did not give rise to theories of criminal behavior; instead, a prevailing assumption of hedonism was used as a theory of human nature and was incorporated into the rationale for building legal structures. Crime and **law** were its focus, not criminal behavior (although they assumed rationality, hedonism, and deterrence). Law was to protect the rights of both society and individual, and its chief purpose was to deter criminal behavior. Therefore, classical law emphasized moral responsibility and the duty of citizens to consider fully the consequences of behavior before they acted. This thinking, of course, required a conception of humans as possessing free will and a rational nature. Indeed, rationality was critical to the classical position. Any individual should be able to weigh the pleasure to be gained in an illegal behavior against the punishment (pain) decreed by law and subsequently to decide against the act.

The role of punishment, according to Bentham, in itself was evil and should be used only to exclude some greater evil (1789:170). Thus, the only justification for punishment was **deterrence.** The Classical School saw two forms of deterrence: a specific or individual form, and a general or societal form. *Specific* deterrence applied to the individual who committed an offense. The idea was to apply just enough pain to offset the amount of pleasure gained from the offense. In fact, many suggested that punishments should be restricted to the same degree of pain as the degree of pleasure gained from the offense. They saw punishment in excess of this calculated amount as unnecessary, for it put the state in the position of despot. *General* deterrence, on the other hand, was to apply to other potential offenders by showing them that a punished individual would not gain from his or her offense. Through watching, or otherwise knowing about, an individual receiving punishment for committing an offense, others would learn that such behavior is not profitable and thus would not commit similar acts.

These theorists saw three components to deterrence: celerity, certainty, and severity. *Celerity* is the speed with which a punishment is applied. Theoretically, at least, the closer in time a punishment is to the act, the better the result. Therefore, if an undesirable act is punished immediately, the individual would most likely be deterred. *Certainty* is the concept of making a punishment sure to happen whenever an undesirable act is committed. Classical theorists believed if every undesirable act were sure to be punished then any rational person would immediately see the lack of profit in such actions. *Severity* is the amount of pain to be inflicted on those who do harmful acts. The greater the potential severity, the more a rational person should avoid doing harm. Thus, our system of criminal punishments is set up to match severity with the harm of an offense. Finally, it is clear that Beccaria and Bentham saw deterrence as most likely to occur when celerity and certainty were maximized (swift and certain punishment). Severity, on the other hand, was viewed as less important and only something to be used when celerity and certainty were diminished. There was also danger in relying on severity—punishments that are too severe are likely to make the citizenry view government as despotic and become unruly. Our system of government has, because of the concern for the citizenry's civil rights, made severity important because of the justice system's lengthy process and a seeming uncertainty of being arrested.

According to the thought of the Classical School, the criminal justice system should respect the rights of all people. Since government drew its authority from the social contract, all individuals were equal before the law. This meant the operation of criminal justice had to be aboveboard, **due process** of law had to be followed, evidence had to be obtained from facts, and equality had to be maintained. It was proposed all punishments be specified by law, thus limiting judicial discretion. Scholars such as Beccaria suspected judges of following personal whim and not the law when determining guilt. He wanted the discretion of judges limited and the process of conviction and sentencing fully spelled out by law. In response to those who argued that exactly the same treatment of all offenders would result in inequities, Becarria said some inequities would certainly result, but not the overburdening inequity of the old system (Beccaria, 1764:16).

Like Beccaria, Bentham argued against great judicial discretion but saw the need to allow for some forms of decreased rationality among offenders. Punishments, he added, should not be inflicted if they are groundless, ineffective (i.e., administered to a person who was drunk or insane at the time of the offense), unprofitable, or needless. Bentham, a writer trained in the law, sought the systematic organization of legal procedures. He divided offenses into classes and types, distinguishing between private and public wrongs, crimes against person and against property, and violations of trust. In addition, he created what he called the "felicific calculus," an elaborate schedule of punishments designed to take into account a combination of pleasure, pain, and mitigating circumstances. This latter endeavor reflected one of the major problems of the Classical School: how to calculate the exact degree of punishment needed to offset the gain from criminal behavior. Bentham also recognized the problems that occur when lesser offenses are punished more severely than serious offenses. Indeed, these problems continue to plague us today, as judges and legislatures seek to find appropriate sentences for various crimes. The major difference seems to be that today's legislators have little of Bentham's understanding of how deterrence works and escalate sentences for lesser offenses at whim (or in response to special interest groups of voters).

Beccaria specifically decried the use of torture to elicit confessions and supported time limits on case preparation for both the defense and the prosecution. This is another example of these theorists' conviction that swiftness of punishment, not its severity, is the strength of its deterrent value. Beccaria was also opposed to the imprisonment of those not yet convicted of crimes. Languishing in the filthy, disease-ridden prisons, many of the accused died even before being tried, a situation repugnant to the humanitarian as well as to the rational thinker of the time. The writings of Beccaria and John Howard, who toured prisons and jails and described their conditions, inspired sweeping reforms of prison conditions and incarceration practices.[1]

Finally, members of the Classical School were generally opposed to capital punishment. Beccaria argued that no citizen has the right to take his or her own life and, therefore, citizens could not give this right to the state under the social contract. Moreover, if the state can take a life, where is the profit in allowing the state to govern for us? Capital punishment was, as a result, not part of the state's base of authority. Using a more pragmatic approach to capital punishment, Bentham pointed out that the death penalty might tend to make members of a jury exercise leniency out of humane motives, therefore subverting the law. Using this same line of reasoning, he also thought witnesses might perjure themselves out of the same

---

1. There is some contention about the importance of Beccaria's work. Philip Jenkins (1984) argues that it was Beccaria's "conservative" bent that provided the support for the essay. Similarly, Graeme Newman and Pietro Marongiu (1990) hold that Beccaria's work is vastly overrated today. They suggest that all the ideas in his essay were present in others' works, from which Beccaria liberally borrowed. Piers Beirne (1991, 1993, 1994) also argues there was no real classical school and that Beccaria has been continuously misinterpreted by scholars. Other critics have noted that the very processes and behaviors Beccaria objected to were being reformed both before and as he wrote.

humane motives. In short, by being humane, jurors in capital cases could spread a message that it is acceptable to ignore the law. Thus, he thought capital punishment was simply not worth the potential havoc it could create for the justice system and law.

The impact of the Classical School may be seen in the results of the French and American revolutions. Both embraced the equality of people, the right to life and liberty, fairness in the administration of justice, and restrictions on the actions of the state. Criminal law in the United States is largely classical, with its strong emphasis on individual responsibility for actions and on due process of law. In our contemporary criminal justice system, not until the sentencing stage is there a move away from the classical emphasis, with some sentences designed to "treat" the offender. Even here the current trend is toward a more punitive form of sentencing.

CLASSIFICATION OF THE SCHOOL

Since the Classical School was, in reality, a movement designed to reform society, it was both conflict-oriented and structural. The *conflict* classification derives from the fact that philosophers and scholars of this era saw human nature as needing to be restricted and controlled. They believed that people were basically self-interested and, without restraint, would act in ways that conflict with the interests of others. Proponents of these versions of human nature simply could not accept the idea of individuals naturally being in a state of consensus or agreement with each other. The promotion of social contract forms of government is an example of the way in which Classical theorists felt societies could most humanely control their citizens and their governments. In addition, the majority of their ideas were at odds with existing political and legal structures, and their reforms were aimed at existing social arrangements. The new philosophy of the common people was in conflict with religious and economic systems, the old governmental structure, and forms of knowledge based on religious revelation.

We classify the Classical School as predominantly *structural* because it emphasizes the effect of societal institutions on people in general. The theorists' main concern focused on the way governments make law and how law affects the rights of citizens. The fact that the Classical School was interested in the legislation of criminal law and in the criminal justice system, rather than in criminal behavior, is characteristic of a fully structural approach. Indeed, since most of the "criminological" theories of the period were political theories, the Classical School was predominantly *macrotheoretical* in its orientation.

There is also a processual and microtheoretical side to the Classical School. Some argue that the Classical School should be categorized as processual because of its emphasis on the rational, and hedonistic, behavior of individuals. Indeed, the justification for punishment and the construction of criminal law were based on showing a rational person that there would

---

AN EXAMPLE OF CLASSICAL THOUGHT

(Excerpts from the Virginia Bill of Rights, adopted June 12, 1776)

SECTION 1. That all men are by nature equally free and independent, and have certain inherent rights, of which, when they enter into a state of society, they cannot, by any compact, deprive or divest their posterity; namely, the enjoyment of life and liberty, with the means of acquiring and possessing property, and pursuing and obtaining happiness and safety.

SECTION 2. That all power is vested in, and consequently derived from, the people; that magistrates are their trustees and servants. . . .

SECTION 3. That government is, or ought to be, instituted for the common benefit, protection, and security of the people, nation or community; of all the various modes and forms of government, that is best which is capable of producing the greatest degree of happiness and safety. . . .

SECTION 4. That no man, or set of men, are entitled to exclusive or separate emoluments or privileges from the community. . . .

SECTION 8. That in all capital or criminal prosecutions a man hath a right to demand the cause and nature of his accusation, to be confronted with the accusers and witnesses, to call for evidence in his favor, and to a speedy trial by an impartial jury of twelve men of his vicinage, without whose unanimous consent he cannot be found guilty; nor can he be compelled to give evidence against himself; that no man be deprived of his liberty, except by the law of the land or the judgment of his peers.

---

be no profit in transgressing on the rights of others. The entire Classical legal structure is founded on the concept of a rational person and responsibility for one's own actions. Clearly, the Classical School had something to say about the process of committing crime and why crime takes place. It is also true, however, that every theoretical position begins with (often unstated) assumptions about human nature. Those assumptions form a foundation for theories but do not constitute the essence of a theory. Therefore, we believe that the rational pursuit of pleasure is best seen as an assumption rather than the real focus of Classical theory. Those who focus on the writings of Jeremy Bentham are more likely to see a microtheoretical, and processual, focus to the school.

SUMMARY

The Classical School is characterized by (1) an emphasis on free will choices and human rationality, (2) a view of behavior as hedonistic, (3) a focus on morality and responsibility, (4) a concern with political structure and the way in which government deals with its citizens, and (5) a concern for the basic rights of all people. These generic ideas and concerns were applied to criminal justice to produce concepts such as deterrence, civil rights, and due process of law; but it is the general characteristics, not the specific ones of criminal justice, that contain the essence of Classical thought.

Major Points of the School

1. People exist in a world with free will and make their own rational choices, although they have a natural tendency toward self-interest and pleasure.
2. People have certain natural rights, among them life, liberty, and ownership of property.
3. Governments are created by the citizens of a state to protect these rights, and they exist as a social contract between those who govern and those who are governed.
4. Citizens give up only the portion of their natural rights that is necessary for the state to regulate society for the benefit of all and to protect society against the natural self-interest of individuals.
5. To ensure civil rights, legislators enact law that both defines the procedures by which transgressions will be handled and specifies the exact behaviors that make up those transgressions. This law specifies the process for determining guilt and the punishment to be meted out to those found guilty.
6. Crime consists of a transgression against the social contract; therefore, crime is a moral offense against society.
7. Punishment is justified only to preserve the social contract. Therefore, the purpose of punishment is to prevent future transgressions by deterring socially harmful behavior. Only that amount of punishment necessary to offset the gains of harmful behavior is justified.
8. All people are equal in their rights and should be treated equally before the law.

EPILOGUE: CURRENT DIRECTIONS AND POLICY IMPLICATIONS

The Classical School still has a dominant effect on today's criminal justice system policies. Most Western nations still adhere to most of the Classical inventions under due process of law and the rights of individuals, largely because these concepts are imbedded in various constitutions. Two of the major concepts of the Classical School, deterrence and rationality, are still alive and well.

Deterrence has had two separate rebirths over the last two decades. In the first, the public, in moving toward a more conservative and punitive mode, has embraced the concept of deterrence and clamored for harsher sentences. The assumption, of course, is that tougher sentences will deter would-be criminals from committing crimes and make those caught and convicted reconsider their behavior. Deterrence has been the favored approach to the crimes of drunken driving and drug dealing. One of the problems with deterring criminals is that our criminal justice system does not proceed quickly. The federal system and many states have attempted to solve this by enacting speedy trial laws.

In the second renewal of interest in deterrence, many scholars have been engaged in research to see if deterrence works. Three of the favorite research topics have been the death penalty, drunken driving, and drug use. At this point, the evidence points to a short-term effect for drunken driving, probably no effect for the death penalty, and little if any effect for drug use. There is still much controversy over the proper way to test for the effects of deterrence, and the jury is still out on most of the issues (Ross and LaFree, 1986). However, it should be noted the vast majority of deterrence research has failed to find any substantial deterrent effect for legal sanctions. In the face of this evidence, contemporary legislatures and the public continue to act as if deterrence were alive and well, and the primary factor in keeping crime in check.

Researchers have also recognized that legal punishments do not stand alone, and some have argued for a version of deterrence combining both legal and informal punishment systems. In fact, the usual direction is to combine deterrence with concepts from social control theories (Chapter 10). Social learning theory (Chapter 11) can also be interpreted as a close cousin of deterrence because it includes punishment as one of the stimuli involved in the learning process. When legal deterrence is combined with informal social controls the research results usually show only a slight effect attributable to legal deterrence. Informal controls seem to have a stronger effect on individuals, particularly when the informal controls include shaming.

The public and the government have virtually embraced the notion of a rational criminal. This makes it easier to blame the offender for all aspects of a crime, rather than share some of that blame with society for creating conditions that force some people into crime. If it is an individual's decision to commit crime, then he or she is morally responsible and deserves to be punished. The great advantage of this reasoning is that we do not have to do anything other than punish while the individual is in our control. Thus, rehabilitation and skill-training are no longer a part of what a prison must do. In addition, we do not have to engage in expensive social programs to improve conditions that create crime, nor do we have to engage in even more expensive social reform. An assumption that individuals make fully rational decisions to engage in criminal behavior can save a lot of money. If this assumption is incorrect, however, these savings may be short-term ones. A failure to rectify social conditions, if they are also important, will simply make matters worse and over the long-term will cost much more in increased crime, suffering, and deterioration of neighborhoods.

Criminologists have also granted a good deal of popularity to the concept of rational offenders. We now have rational choice theories (Chapter 12) and theories of punishment called "just deserts." The rational choice theories generally suggest a connection between opportunities for offending, the environmental conditions at the time, and the readiness of the offender to engage in the offense. That is, they assert that, given the situation and the circumstances, offenders make informed decisions to commit crimes. Just deserts punishment theory returns to the Classical concept of retribution and argues that because offenders make the choice to offend, punishment is deserved. The "just" portion of the theory restates the classical notion of equitable punishment—no more or less punishment than what is required to correct the harm from the crime.

One might argue that the theoretical strands of the Classical School have become a little weak by now. The ideas of human nature and rationales of how to treat people, on which much of current policy and conceptual activity is based, are simply part of our culture. The reason that these ideas are part of our culture, however, is that the Classical School is responsible for their being there. For example, some judges have publicly questioned recent sentencing guidelines (which propose mandatory sentences for drug users) as unfair. In another case, the issue of cruel punishment is today's latest topic, with questions surrounding the use of hanging, gas, the electric chair, and lethal injection as forms of capital punishment. Not only is classical criminology still around, but it also may be safe to say that some two-hundred-year-old ideas are among our latest policy and theoretical notions. We are still engaged in debates about those ideas.

BIBLIOGRAPHY

ALDARONDO, ETIONY (1996). "Cessation and persistence of wife assault: A longitudinal analysis." *American Journal of Orthopsychiatry* 66: 141–151.

ANDENAES, JOHANNES (1966). "The general preventive effects of punishment." *University of Pennsylvania Law Review* 114: 949–983.

ANDERSON, LINDA S., THEODORE G. CHIRICOS, and GORDON P. WALDO (1977). "Formal and informal sanctions: A comparison of deterrent effects." *Social Problems* 25: 103–114.

ATKINSON, CHARLES (1905). *Jeremy Bentham: His Life and Work*. Westport, CT: Greenwood. (Reprinted 1970.)

AUSTIN, JAMES, and JOHN IRWIN (1993). *Does Imprisonment Reduce Crime? A Critique of "Voodoo" Criminology*. San Francisco: National Council on Crime and Delinquency.

BABUS, MARC, JOSEPH PERKOVICH, and VINCENT SCHIRALDI (1995). *Big Time for Petty Crime: The Story of Petty Theft Offenders in California*. San Francisco: Center on Juvenile and Criminal Justice.

BAILEY, WILLIAM C. (1978). "Deterrence and the death penalty for murders in Utah: A time series analysis." *Journal of Contemporary Law* 5: 1–20.

——— (1990). "Murder, capital punishment, and television: Execution publicity and homicide rates." *American Sociological Review* 55: 628–633.

BAILEY, WILLIAM C., and RUTH D. PETERSON (1989). "Murder and capital punishment: A monthly time-series analysis of execution publicity." *American Sociological Review* 54: 722–743.

BARNES, HARRY E. (1930). *The Story of Punishment: A Record of Man's Inhumanity to Man*. Boston: Stratford.

BECCARIA, CESARE (1764). *On Crimes and Punishments*. Trans. Henry Paolucci. Indianapolis, IN: Bobbs-Merrill. (Reprinted 1963.)

BEDAU, HUGO A., ed. (1967). *The Death Penalty in America*. Chicago: Aldine.

BEDAU, HUGO A. (1997). *The Death Penalty in America: Current Controversies*. New York: Oxford University Press.

BEIRNE, PIERS (1991). "Inventing criminology: The `science of man' in Cesare Beccaria's *Dei Delitti e Delle Pene* (1764)." *Criminology* 29: 777–820.

——— (1993). *Inventing Criminology: Essays on the Rise of "Homo Criminalis."* Albany, NY: State University of New York Press.

——— (1994). *The Origins and Growth of Criminology: Essays in Intellectual History, 1760–1945*. Aldershot, UK: Dartmouth.

BELLAMY, RICHARD, ed. (1995). *Beccaria: On Crimes and Punishments and Other Writings*. Cambridge: Cambridge University Press.

BENSON, BRUCE, L., ILJOONG KIM, and DAVID W. RASMUSSEN (1994). "Estimating deterrence effects: A public choice perspective on the economics of crime literature." *Southern Economic Journal* 61: 161–168.

BENTHAM, JEREMY (1789). *An Introduction to the Principles of Morals and Legislation*. New York: Kegan Paul (Reprinted 1948.)

——— (1830). *The Rationale of Punishment*. London: Robert Heward.

——— (1905). *Theory of Legislation*. London: Kegan Paul.

——— (1995). *The Panopticon Writings*. Ed. and introduced by Miran Bozovic. London, UK: Verso.

BERK, RICHARD A., ALEC CAMPBELL, RUTH KLAP, and BRUCE WESTERN (1992). "The deterrent effect of arrest in incidents of domestic violence: A Bayesian analysis of four field experiments." *American Sociological Review* 57: 698–708.

BERK, RICHARD A., and PHYLLIS J. NEWTON (1985). "Does arrest really deter wife battery? An effort to replicate the findings of the Minneapolis Spouse Abuse Experiment." *American Sociological Review* 50: 253–262.

BLUMSTEIN, ALFRED, JACQUELINE COHEN, and DANIEL NAGIN, eds. (1978). *Deterrence and Incapacitation: Estimating the Effects of Criminal Sanctions on Crime Rates*. Washington, DC: National Academy of Sciences.

BOWERS, WILLIAM (1974). *Executions in America*. Lexington, MA: Heath.

——— (1984). *Legal Homicide: Death as Punishment in America, 1864–1982*. Boston: Northeastern University Press.

BOWERS, WILLIAM, and GLENN PIERCE (1975). "The illusion of deterrence in Isaac Ehrlich's research in capital punishment." *Yale Law Journal* 85(2): 187–208.

BRIER, S. S., and STEVEN E. FEINBERG (1980). "Recent econometric modeling of crime and punishment: Support for the deterrence hypothesis?" *Evaluation Review* 4: 147–191.

BURKETT, STEVEN R., and DAVID A. WARD (1993). "A note on perceptual deterrence, religiously based moral condemnation, and social control." *Criminology* 31: 119–134.

BUZAWA, EVE S. and CARL G. BUZAWA, eds. (1996). *Do Arrests and Restraining Orders Work?* Thousand Oaks, CA: Sage.

CANELA-CACHO, JOSE A., ALFRED BLUMSTEIN, and JACQUELINE COHEN (1997). "Relationship between the offending frequency of imprisoned and free offenders." *Criminology* 35: 133–175.

CHIRICOS, THEODORE G., and GORDON P. WALDO (1970). "Punishment and crime: An examination of some empirical evidence." *Social Problems* 18: 200–217.

CORMAN, HOPE, and NACI H. MOCAN (1996). "A time-series analysis of crime and drug use in New York City." NBER Working Paper, #5463. Cambridge, MA: National Bureau of Economic Research.

DECKER, SCOTT H., and CAROL W. KOHFELD (1988). "Capital punishment and executions in the Lone Star State: A deterrence study." *Criminal Justice Research Bulletin* 3(12): 1–6.

————— (1990). "The deterrent effect of capital punishment in the five most active execution states: A time series analysis." *Criminal Justice Review* 15: 173–191.

DECKER, SCOTT H., RICHARD WRIGHT, and ROBERT LOGIE (1993). "Perceptual deterrence among active residential burglars: A research note." *Criminology* 31: 135–147.

DELUCA, HENRY R., THOMAS J. MILLER, and CARL F. WIEDEMANN (1991). "Punishment vs. rehabilitation: A proposal for revising sentencing practices." *Federal Probation* 55 (3): 37–45.

DINWIDDY, JOHN R. (1989). *Bentham*. New York: Oxford University Press.

DUFF, ANTHONY, and DAVID GARLAND, eds. (1994). *A Reader on Punishment*. Oxford, UK: Oxford University Press.

DUFF, R. A. (1996). "Penal communications: Recent work in the philosophy of punishment." In Michael Tonry, ed., *Crime and Justice: A Review of Research*, vol. 20, 1–97. Chicago, IL: University of Chicago Press.

DUNDES, LAUREN (1994). "Punishing parents to deter delinquency: A realistic remedy?" *American Journal of Police* 13: 113–133.

DUNFORD, FRANKLYN, DAVID HUIZINGA, and DELBERT S. ELLIOTT (1990). "The role of arrest in domestic assault: The Omaha Experiment." *Criminology* 28: 183–206.

EHRLICH, ISAAC (1975). "The deterrent effect of capital punishment: A question of life and death." *American Economic Review* 65: 397–416.

EIDE, ERLING (1994). *Economics of Crime: Deterrence and the Rational Offender*. North Holland, Neth: Elsevier.

ELIS, LORI A., and SALLY S. SIMPSON (1995). "Informal sanction threats and corporate crime: Additive versus multiplicative models." *Journal of Research in Crime and Delinquency* 32: 399–424.

ESPY, M. WATT, JR. (1980). "Capital punishment and deterrence: What the statistics cannot show." *Crime and Delinquency* 26: 537–544.

FAGAN, JEFFREY (1996). *The Criminalization of Domestic Violence: Promises and Limits*. Washington, DC: U.S. National Institute of Justice.

FINCKENAUER, JAMES O. (1988). "Public support for the death penalty: Retribution as just deserts or retribution as revenge?" *Justice Quarterly* 5: 81–100.

FOX, JAMES A. (1977). "The identification and estimation of deterrence: An evaluation of Yunker's model." *Journal of Behavioral Economics* 2: 225–242.

GARTIN, PATRICK R. (1995). "Examining differential officer effects in the Minneapolis Domestic Violence Experiment." *American Journal of Police* 14: 93–110.

GEERKEN, MICHAEL R., and WALTER R. GOVE (1975). "Deterrence: Some theoretical considerations." *Law and Society Review* 9: 497–513.

————— (1977). "Deterrence, overload, and incapacitation: An empirical evaluation." *Social Forces* 56: 424–447.

GEIS, GILBERT (1955). "Jeremy Bentham," *Journal of Criminal Law, Criminology, and Police Science* 46: 159–171.

GERTZ, MARC G., and LEROY C. GOULD (1995). "Fear of punishment and the willingness to engage in criminal behavior: A research note." *Journal of Criminal Justice* 23: 377–384.

GIBBS, JACK P. (1968). "Crime, punishment and deterrence." *Southwest Social Science Quarterly* 48: 515–530.

————— (1975). *Crime, Punishment and Deterrence*. New York: Elsevier.

GLUECK, SHELDON (1965). "Beccaria and criminal justice." *Harvard Law School Bulletin* (January).

GODFREY, MICHAEL J., and VINCENT SCHIRALDI (1995). *How Have Homicide Rates Been Affected by California's Death Penalty?* San Francisco: Center on Juvenile and Criminal Justice.

GRASMICK, HAROLD G., and ROBERT J. BURSIK, JR. (1990). "Conscience, significant others, and rational choice: Extending the deterrence model." *Law and Society Review* 24: 837–861.

GRASMICK, HAROLD G., ROBERT J. BURSIK, JR., and BRUCE J. ARNEKLEV (1993). "Reduction in drunk driving as a response to increased threats of shame, embarrassment, and legal sanctions." *Criminology* 31: 41–67.

GRASMICK, HAROLD G., ELIZABETH DAVENPORT, MITCHELL CHAMLIN, and ROBERT J. BURSIK, JR. (1992). "Protestant fundamentalism and the retributive doctrine of punishment." *Criminology* 30: 21–45.

GRASMICK, HAROLD G., and DONALD E. GREEN (1980). "Legal punishment, social disapproval and internalization as inhibitors of illegal behavior." *Journal of Criminal Law and Criminology* 71: 325–335.

Gray, Tara (1994). "Using cost-benefit analysis to measure rehabilitation and special deterrence." *Journal of Criminal Justice* 22: 569–575.

GREEN, DONALD E. (1989). "Past behavior as a measure of actual future behavior: An unresolved issue in perceptual deterrence research." *Journal of Criminal Law and Criminology* 80: 781–804.

GREEN, GARY S. (1985). "General deterrence and television cable crime: A field experiment in social control." *Criminology* 23: 629–645.

HAGAN, JOHN (1982). *Deterrence Reconsidered: Methodological Innovations.* Berkeley, CA: Sage.

HAMILTON, V. LEE, and STEVE RYTINA (1980). "Social consensus on norms of justice: Should the punishment fit the crime?" *American Journal of Sociology* 85: 1117–1144.

HARRIES, KEITH, AND DERRAL CHEATWOOD (1997). *The Geography of Execution: The Capital Punishment Quagmire in America.* Lanham, MD: Rowman and Littlefield.

HART, H. L. A. (1982). *Essays on Bentham.* Oxford: Clarendon Press.

HOWARD, JOHN (1777). *The State of the Prisons of England and Wales.* London: J. M. Dent. (Reprinted 1929.)

JACOBS, BRUCE A. (1996a). "Crack dealers' apprehension avoidance techniques: A case of restrictive deterrence." *Justice Quarterly* 13: 359–381.

——— (1996b). "Crack dealers and restrictive deterrence: Identifying narcs." *Criminology* 34: 409–431.

JEFFERY, C. RAY (1956). "The structure of American criminological thinking." *Journal of Criminal Law, Criminology, and Police Science* 46: 658–672.

——— (1972). "The historical development of criminology." In Hermann Mannheim, ed., *Pioneers in Criminology,* 2nd ed., 458–498. Montclair, NJ: Patterson Smith.

JENKINS, PHILIP (1984). "Varieties of enlightenment criminology." *British Journal of Criminology* 24: 112–130.

JOO-HEE, JONG, SHELDON EKLAND-OLSON, AND WILLIAM R. KELLY (1995). "Recidivism among paroled property offenders released during a period of prison reform." *Criminology* 33: 389–410.

KANT, IMMANUEL (1785). *Foundations of the Metaphysics of Morals.* New York: Bobbs-Merrill. (Reprinted 1959.)

KING, DAVID R. (1978). "The brutalizing effect: Execution publicity and the incidence of homicide in South Carolina." *Social Forces* 57: 683–687.

KLEIN, L., B. FORST, and V. FILATOV (1978). "The deterrent effect of capital punishment: An assessment of the estimates." In A. Blumstein, J. Cohen, and D. Nagin, eds., *Deterrence and Incapacitation: Estimating the Effects of Criminal Sanctions on Crime Rates,* 336–360. Washington, DC: National Academy of Sciences.

KOPER, CHRISTOPHER S. (1995). "Just enough police presence: Reducing crime and disorderly behavior by optimizing patrol time in crime hot spots." *Justice Quarterly* 12: 649–672.

LANGBEIN, JOHN H. (1976). *Torture and the Law of Proof: Europe and England in the Ancient Regime.* Chicago: University of Chicago Press.

LANZA-KADUCE, LONN (1988). "Perceptual deterrence and drinking and driving among college students." *Criminology* 26: 321–341.

LEMPERT, RICHARD O. (1981). "Desert and deterrence: An assessment of the moral bases of the case for capital punishment." *Michigan Law Review* 79: 1202.

―――― (1983). "The effect of executions on homicides." *Crime and Delinquency* 29: 88–115.

LEVITT, STEVEN D. (1995). *Why Do Increased Arrest Rates Appear to Reduce Crime: Deterrence, Incapacitation, or Measurement Error?* Cambridge, MA: National Bureau of Economic Research.

LEWIS, DONALD E. (1986). "The general deterrent effect of longer sentences." *British Journal of Criminology* 26: 47–62.

LIVINGSTON, EDWARD (1873). *The Complete Works of Edward Livingston on Criminal Jurisprudence.* Montclair, NJ: Patterson Smith. (Reprinted 1968.)

LOCKE, JOHN (1690). *Treatise of Civil Government and a Letter Concerning Toleration.* New York: D. Appleton-Century. (Reprinted 1937.)

LOGAN, CHARLES H. (1975). "Arrest rates and deterrence." *Social Science Quarterly* 56: 376–389.

LOTT, JOHN R., JR., and DAVID B. MUSTARD (1996). *Crime, Deterrence, and Right-to-Carry Concealed Handguns.* Chicago, IL: University of Chicago Press.

―――― (1997). "Crime, deterrence, and right-to-carry concealed handguns." *Journal of Legal Studies* 26: 1–68.

MACK, MARY P. (1963). *Jeremy Bentham.* New York: Columbia University Press.

MAESTRO, MARCELLO T. (1942). *Voltaire and Beccaria as Reformers of Criminal Law.* New York: Columbia University Press.

―――― (1973). *Cesare Beccaria and the Origins of Penal Reform.* Philadelphia: Temple University Press.

MAKKAI, TONI, and JOHN BRAITHWAITE (1994). "The dialectics of corporate deterrence." *Journal of Research in Crime and Delinquency* 31: 347–373.

MALTZ, MICHAEL D. (1996). "From Poisson to the present: Applying operations research to problems of crime and justice." *Journal of Quantitative Criminology* 12: 3–61.

MANNHEIM, HERMANN, ed. (1973). *Pioneers in Criminology,* 2nd ed. Montclair, NJ: Patterson Smith.

MARVEL, THOMAS B., and CARLISLE E. MOODY (1995). "The impact of enhanced prison terms for felonies committed with guns." *Criminology* 33: 247–281.

―――― (1996). "Determinate sentencing and abolishing parole: The long-term impacts on prisons and crime." *Criminology* 34: 107–128.

MCDOWALL, DAVID, ALAN LIZOTTE, and BRIAN WIERSEMA (1991). "General deterrence through civilian gun ownership." *Criminology* 29: 541–559.

MCFARLAND, SAM G. (1983). "Is capital punishment a short-term deterrent to homicide? A study of the effects of four recent American executions." *Journal of Criminal Law and Criminology* 74: 1014–1030.

MCGAHEY, RICHARD (1980). "Dr. Ehrlich's magic bullet: Econometric theory, econometrics, and the death penalty." *Crime and Delinquency* 26: 43–55.

MINOR, WILLIAM M., and JOSEPH HARRY (1982). "Deterrent and experiential effects in perceptual deterrence research: A replication and extension." *Journal of Research in Crime and Delinquency* 19: 190–203.

MONACHESI, ELIO D. (1955). "Cesare Beccaria." *Journal of Criminal Law, Criminology, and Police Science* 46: 439–449.

MONTESQUIEU, CHARLES LOUIS DE SECONDAT (1721). *The Persian Letters.* New York: Bobbs-Merrill. (Reprinted 1964.)

―――― (1748). *The Spirit of the Laws.* 2 vols. London: G. Bell. (Reprinted in English, 1878.)

MUELLER, GERHARD O. (1990). "Whose prophet is Cesare Beccaria? An essay on the origins of criminological theory." In William S. Laufer and Freda Adler, eds., *Advances in Criminological Theory* vol. 2, 1–14. New Brunswick, NJ: Transaction.

NAGIN, DANIEL S., and RAYMOND PATERNOSTER (1991). "The preventive effects of the perceived risk of arrest: Testing an expanded conception of deterrence." *Criminology* 29: 561–585.

NEWMAN, GRAEME, and PIETRO MARONGIU (1990). "Penological reform and the myth of Beccaria." *Criminology* 28: 325–346.

PARKER, JERRY, and HAROLD G. GRASMICK (1979). "Linking actual and perceived certainty of punishment." *Criminology* 17: 366–379.

PARKER, ROBERT N., and M. D. SMITH (1979). "Deterrence, poverty, and type of homicide." *American Journal of Sociology* 85: 614–624.

PATE, ANTONY M., and EDWIN E. HAMILTON (1992). "Formal and informal deterrents to domestic violence: The Dade County Spouse Assault Experiment." *American Sociological Review* 57: 691–697.

PATERNOSTER, RAYMOND, and LEEANN IOVANNI (1986). "The deterrent effect of perceived severity: A reexamination." *Social Forces* 64: 751–777.

PATERNOSTER, RAYMOND, and DANIEL S. NAGIN (1994). "Personal capital and social control: The deterrence implications of a theory of individual differences in criminal offending." *Criminology* 32: 581–606.

PATERNOSTER, RAYMOND, and ALEX PIQUERO (1995). "Reconceptualizing deterrence: An empirical test of personal and vicarious experiences." *Journal of Research in Crime and Delinquency* 32: 251–286.

PATERNOSTER, RAYMOND, LINDA E. SALTZMAN, GORDON P. WALDO, and THEODORE G. CHIRICOS (1983a). "Assessments of risk and behavioral experience: An exploratory study of change." *Criminology* 23: 417–433.

——— (1983b). "Perceived risk and social control: Do sanctions really deter?" *Law and Society Review* 17: 457–479.

PATERNOSTER, RAYMOND, and SALLY SIMPSON (1996). "Sanction threats and appeals to morality: Testing a rational choice model of corporate crime." *Law and Society Review* 30: 549–583.

PETERSON, RUTH D., and WILLIAM C. BAILEY (1991). "Felony murder and capital punishment: An examination of the deterrence question." *Criminology* 29: 367–395.

PHILLIPS, DAVID P. (1980). "The deterrent effect of capital punishment: New evidence on an old controversy." *American Journal of Sociology* 86: 139–148.

PHILLIPSON, COLEMAN (1923). *Three Criminal Law Reformers: Beccaria, Bentham and Romilly.* Montclair, NJ: Patterson Smith. (Reprinted 1972.)

PILIAVIN, IRVING, ROSEMARY GARTNER, CRAIG THORNTON, and ROSS MATSUEDA (1986). "Crime, deterrence, and rational choice." *American Sociological Review* 51: 101–119.

RANKIN, JOSEPH H., and EDWARD WELLS (1982). "The social context of deterrence." *Sociology and Social Research* 67: 18–39.

ROGERS, PATRICE N. (1995). *The General Deterrent Impact of California's 0.08% Blood Alcohol Concentration Limit and Administrative per se License Suspension Laws.* Sacramento: California Department of Motor Vehicles.

ROSHIER, BOB (1989). *Controlling Crime: The Classical Perspective in Criminology.* Chicago: Lyceum Books.

ROSS, H. LAURENCE (1975). "The Scandinavian myth: The effectiveness of drinking-and-driving legislation in Sweden and Norway." *Journal of Legal Studies* 4: 285–310.

——— (1977). "Deterrence regained: The Cheshire constabulary's breathalizer blitz." *Journal of Legal Studies* 6: 241–249.

——— (1982). *Deterring the Drinking Driver: Legal Policy and Social Control.* Lexington, MA: Lexington Books.

ROSS, H. LAURENCE, and HANS KLETTE (1995). "Abandonment of mandatory jail for impaired drivers in Norway and Sweden." *Accident Analysis and Prevention* 27: 151–157.

Ross, H. LAURENCE, and GARY D. LAFREE (1986). "Deterrence in criminology and social policy." In N. J. Smelser and D. R. Gerstein, eds., *Behavioral and Social Science: Fifty Years of Discovery*, 129–153. Washington, DC: National Academy Press.

SALTZMAN, LINDA E., RAYMOND PATERNOSTER, GORDON P. WALDO, and THEODORE G. CHIRICOS (1982). "Deterrent and experiential effects: The problem of causal order in perceptual deterrence research." *Journal of Research in Crime and Delinquency* 19: 172–189.

SELLIN, THORSTEN (1959). *The Death Penalty*. Philadelphia: American Law Institute.

——— (1967). *Capital Punishment*. New York: Harper and Row.

——— (1980). *The Penalty of Death*. Beverly Hills, CA: Sage.

SEMPLE, JANET (1993). *Bentham's Prison: A Study of the Panopticon Penitentiary*. Oxford, UK: Clarendon.

SHERMAN, LAWRENCE W., and RICHARD A. BERK (1984). "The specific deterrent effects of arrest for domestic assault." *American Sociological* Review 49: 261–272.

SHERMAN, LAWRENCE W., and DENNIS P. ROGAN (1995a). "Deterrent effects of police raids on crack houses: A randomized controlled experiment." *Justice Quarterly* 12: 755–781.

——— (1995b). "Effects of gun seizures on gun violence: 'Hot spots' patrol in Kansas City." *Justice Quarterly* 12: 673–693.

SHERMAN, LAWRENCE W., JANELL SCHMIDT, DENNIS ROGAN, PATRICK GARTIN, ELLEN COHN, DEAN COLLINS, and ANTHONY BACICH (1991). "From initial deterrence to long-term escalation: Short custody arrest for poverty ghetto domestic violence." *Criminology* 29: 821–850.

SHERMAN, LAWRENCE W., and DAVID WEISBURD (1995). "General deterrent effects of police patrol in crime 'hot spots': A randomized, controlled trial." *Justice Quarterly* 12: 625–648.

SILBERMAN, MATTHEW (1976). "Toward a theory of criminal deterrence." *American Sociological Review* 41: 442–461.

SINGER, RICHARD (1979). *Just Deserts: Sentencing Based on Equality and Desert*. Cambridge, MA: Ballinger.

SMITH, DOUGLAS A., and PATRICK GARTIN (1989). "Specifying specific deterrence: The influence of arrest on future criminal activity." *American Sociological Review* 54: 94–106.

SNORTUM, JOHN R. (1984). "Controlling the alcohol-impaired driver in Scandinavia and the United States: Simple deterrence and beyond." *Journal of Criminal Justice* 12: 131–148.

STACK, STEVEN (1987). "Publicized executions and homicide, 1950–1980." *American Sociological Review* 52: 532–540.

——— (1994). "Execution publicity and homicide in Georgia." *American Journal of Criminal Justice* 18: 25–39.

SYLVESTER, SAWYER (1972). *The Heritage of Modern Criminology*. Cambridge, MA: Schenkman.

TAUCHEN, HELEN, ANN D. WITTE, and HARRIET GRIESINGER (1994). "Criminal deterrence: Revisiting the issue with a birth cohort." *Review of Economics and Statistics* 76: 399–412.

THOMSON, EARNIE (1997). "Deterrence versus brutalization: The case of Arizona." *Homicide Studies* 1: 110–128.

TITTLE, CHARLES R. (1969). "Crime rates and legal sanctions." *Social Problems* 16: 409–423.

TITTLE, CHARLES R., AND ALLAN ROWE (1973). "Moral appeal, sanction threat, and deviance: An experimental test." *Social Problems* 20: 488–498.

TOLNAY, STEWART E., and GLENN DEANE (1996). "Vicarious violence: Spatial effects on Southern lynchings, 1890–1919." *American Journal of Sociology* 102: 788–815.

TRAUB, STUART H. (1996). "Battling employee crime: A review of corporate strategies and programs." *Crime and Delinquency* 42: 244–256.

TRIVIZAS, EUGENE, and PHILIP T. SMITH (1997). "The deterrent effect of terrorist incidents on the rates of luggage theft in railway and underground stations." *British Journal of Criminology* 37: 63–74.

TUNNELL, KENNETH D. (1990). "Choosing crime: Close your eyes and take your chances." *Justice Quarterly* 7: 673–690.

UNITED NATIONS, CENTRO NAZIONALE DI PREVENZIONE E DIFESA SOCIALE, eds. (1990). *Cesare Beccaria and Modern Criminal Policy.* Milan, Italy: Giuffre Editore.

VAN DEN HAAG, ERNEST (1969). "On deterrence and the death penalty." *Journal of Criminal Law, Criminology, and Police Science* 60: 141–147.

VENEZIANO, CAROL, and LOUIS VENEZIANO (1995). "Reasons for refraining from criminal activity." *American Journal of Criminal Justice* 19: 185–196.

——— (1996). "Factors accounting for not engaging in illegal acts in relationship to type of crime." *Journal of Crime and Justice* 19: 167–178.

VINCENT, BARBARA S., and PAUL J. HOFER (1994). *The Consequences of Mandatory Minimum Prison Terms: A Summary of Recent Findings.* Washington, DC: U.S. Government Printing Office.

VOLTAIRE, FRANÇOIS MARIE AROUET DE (1973). *The Selected Letters of Voltaire.* Trans. Richard A. Brooks. New York: New York University Press.

WALDO, GORDON P., and THEODORE G. CHIRICOS (1972). "Perceived penal sanction and self-reported criminality: A neglected approach to deterrence research." *Social Problems* 19: 522–540.

WALDORF, DAN, and SHEIGLA MURPHY (1995). "Perceived risks and criminal justice pressures on middle class cocaine sellers." *Journal of Drug Issues* 25: 11–32.

WEISBURD, DAVID, and LORRAINE GREEM (1995). "Policing drug hot spots: The Jersey City Drug Market Analysis experiment." *Justice Quarterly* 12: 711–735.

WEISBURD, DAVID, ELIN WARING, and ELLEN CHAYET (1995). "Specific deterrence in a sample of offenders convicted of white-collar crimes." *Criminology* 33: 587–607.

WICHARAYA, TAMASAK (1995). *Simple Theory, Hard Reality: The Impact of Sentencing Reforms on Courts, Prisons, and Crime.* Albany, NY: State University of New York Press.

WIERSMA, ERIC (1996). "Commercial burglars in the Netherlands: Reasoning decision-makers?" *International Journal of Risk Security and Crime Prevention* 1: 217–225.

WILLIAMS, FRANK P., III (1985). "Deterrence and social control: Rethinking the relationship." *Journal of Criminal Justice* 13: 141–151.

WILLIAMS, FRANK P. III, and E. LYNN WHITE (1986). "Legislative actions against drunken driving: An assessment with additional evidence on the open container." *Criminal Justice Policy Review* 1: 286–304.

WILLIAMS, KIRK R., and RICHARD HAWKINS (1986). "Perceptual research on general deterrence: A critical review." *Law and Society Review* 20: 545–572.

YOUNG, DAVID (1983). "Cesare Beccaria: Utilitarian or retributivist." *Journal of Criminal Justice* 11: 317–326.

YUNKER, J. A. (1976). "Is the death penalty a deterrent to homicide? Some time series evidence." *Journal of Behavioral Economics* 1(2): 422–427.

ZIMRING, FRANK E., and GORDON J. HAWKINS (1971). "The legal threat as an instrument of social change." *Journal of Social Issues* 27: 33–48.

——— (1973). *Deterrence: The Legal Threat in Crime Control.* Chicago: University of Chicago Press.

3

THE POSITIVE SCHOOL

INTRODUCTION

While the champions of the Classical period were writers and philosophers, the Positivists were more likely to be scientists, mathematicians, doctors, and astronomers. While the Classical reformers sought to modernize and civilize the system within which they lived, the Positivists reached out to order and explain the world around them. The earlier concentration on building a moral and fair system of justice and government was thus displaced by the scientific exploration and discovery of other aspects of life.

Although the Classicalists believed that humans possess a rational mind and thus have free will to choose good over evil, the Positivists saw behavior as determined by its biological, psychological, and social traits. The primary characteristics of positivist criminological thought are a deterministic view of the world, a focus on criminal behavior instead of on legal issues such as rights, and the prevention of crime through the treatment and rehabilitation of offenders.

The use of scientific research techniques was common to those who studied criminals from a positivist perspective. In scientific analyses, data were collected to describe and explain different types of individuals as well as different social conditions. The theory of evolution, proposed by naturalists and anthropologists, formed a basis for the study of human behavior and, more specifically, of criminal behavior.

Most criminological texts limit their consideration of the Positive School to the work of three Italian writers and thus create confusion among students when the term "positivism" is applied to later and broader theories. This chapter focuses on positivism as a more general approach and delves into the essence of what positivism *is*. In this way, one gains a more general understanding of positivism than the theories of a few people, and one that goes beyond the biological emphasis usually associated with the Positive School. In reality, positivism is a philosophical system that emphasizes the "positive" application of science to knowledge production. Therefore, the Positive School is an all-encompassing scientific perspective.

THE HERITAGE OF THE SCHOOL

The Social Heritage

The years near the turn of the twentieth century were alive with invention and discovery. Science became a major tool of scholars, and the world experienced a revolution in knowledge that brought countless changes to everyday life. Advanced communications put once-separate cultures in close contact. The Statue of Liberty was unveiled, the Eiffel Tower was completed, Henrik Ibsen wrote, Giuseppe Verdi composed, and Vincent Van Gogh painted. The automobile, the airplane, the phonograph, and electric lighting were introduced. Medicine embraced science, and researchers discovered germs and how to combat them. Sigmund Freud developed psychoanalysis, and Albert Einstein pronounced his theory of relativity.

Central to the creations of the nineteenth and early twentieth centuries was the application of science to problems of everyday life. Perhaps as never before, a method of gaining knowledge was almost deified. With the great strides made by the application of science to industry, it was to be expected that those concerned with human affairs would have a vision of perfecting humanity through scientific study.

Of great importance was the transformation of the agriculturally based aristocracies of the eighteenth century into complex, industrialized, urban societies. The French and American revolutions helped foster a new climate in which the concerns of the Classical School could be addressed. People became less concerned with their governments than previously was the case and focused more attention on social, rather than on political, problems. David Rothman (1971:59–62), for example, points out that Americans saw crime as the product of inequities in British colonial rule and expected crime to be reduced with the institution of the new democracy. When crime rates failed to drop, Americans were forced to acknowledge that crime might have other bases in human behavior.

The Intellectual Heritage

Although some see little connection between the Classical and Positivist schools, it was the Classical reaffirmation that people could develop and verify their own knowledge that led to the widespread use of science in the Positivist era. Among the various intellectual influences in this direction was the rise of a (positive) philosophy that underscored the importance of tested and systematized experience rather than pure speculation, or meta-physics. Humans were seen as responsible for their own destinies, and they were fully capable of adapting their own behaviors and social institutions to create a society that would fulfill those destinies.

A second important ingredient in the rise of positivist criminology was the concept of evolution that emerged even before the writing of Charles Darwin. Evolution became a standard form of thinking about subjects, pop-ularized to the extent that human societies were seen as evolving. Western societies represented the pinnacle of human accomplishment, and all else was less evolved. Criminals were viewed as individuals who were not as fully evolved as more civilized people. Leonard Savitz (1972:viii) even sug-gests that this evolutionary perspective contributed to the development of a racist view of criminality.

A final influence on positivist criminology was the emergence of anthropology. Still in its infancy as an academic discipline, anthropology presented evidence of other societies as being more "primitive." The chief purveyors of this evidence were missionaries and colonial administrators who were not well trained in the art of observation. Failing to look deeply into the societies they reported on, they assumed that complex organization would resemble their own European societies. Failing to find European-style social organization, they concluded that other societies were less evolved, more primitive, and closer to original human nature. Their obser-vations were then used by other disciplines and incorporated into social sci-ence theories of how societies develop and why humans behave as they do.

THE PERSPECTIVE OF THE SCHOOL

Positivism itself is more accurately called a philosophy than a theory. Even as a philosophy, there are several varieties of positivism. Abraham Kaplan (1968:389) identifies two major forms. The first is a product of eighteenth-century Enlightenment philosophy, with its emphasis on the importance of reason and experience. The second is a twentieth-century version known as "Logical Positivism," with a close association with mathematical reasoning and formal models of thought. Many today also associate positivism with various forms of statistical analysis. Within sociology alone, there have been several different understandings about the meaning of positivism (Half-penny, 1982). One important underpinning of almost any form of positivism is an interest in classifying (or establishing categories for) any subject of interest.

Many criminologists use the term "positivism" to mean an approach that studies human behavior through the use of the traditional scientific method. The focus is on **systematic observation** and the **accumulation of evidence** and **objective fact** within a **deductive framework** (moving from the general to the specific). Positivists, then, may study behavior from a bio-logical, a psychological, or a sociological perspective. The point is not the perspective from which the study is done, but the assumptions that underlie the methodology for doing the study.

Comte and the Methodology of Positivism

Much of the system of analysis that constitutes sociological positivism today was developed by Auguste Comte, a nineteenth-century French philosopher and social scientist who is credited with being the father of sociology. His approach to the study of social phenomena included an insistence on testable hypotheses, the use of comparative methods, the careful classification of societies, a systematic approach to the study of social history, and the study of abnormality as a means to understanding normality (Fletcher, 1975:ix–xi). Comte's work, among that of others, prompted scientific studies of human social behavior.

Early Nineteenth-Century Positivist Work

Perhaps the earliest of positivistically oriented work on the subject of crime was that of two statisticians, Adolphe Quetelet of Belgium and Andre Guerry of France, in the 1820s and 1830s. Each examined the **social statistics** that were available in some European countries as if they were data from the physical sciences. Quetelet, for instance, applied probability theory to these data to produce a concept of the "average person," and then extended this concept to a study of crime rates. Among other things, he found variations in crime rates by climate and season and observed the same age and sex differences we find today among criminals (Quetelet, 1831).

Other early work was largely that of biologists and anatomists who studied the human body in hopes of establishing some relationship between it and human behavior. Some of this work distinctly predates any of the usual claims to the founding of criminology. A physiognomist of the sixteenth century, J. Baptiste della Porte, related characteristics of the body to criminality (Schafer, 1976:38). In the early nineteenth century, phrenologists measured and studied the shape of the head in an attempt to determine the relationship between brain and behavior. The chief practitioners of **phrenology**, Franz Joseph Gall and Johann Gaspar Spurzheim, believed that the characteristics of the brain are mirrored in bumps on the skull. They and their followers set about documenting the relationship between these bumps and behavior, especially abnormal behavior. For a short period in the 1830s, the United States even had a journal devoted to the science of phrenology.

The Italian Positivists

The beginnings of criminological positivism are usually traced (although with questionable accuracy, as we have mentioned) to the work of three Italian thinkers, Cesare Lombroso, Enrico Ferri, and Raffaele Garofalo.

Lombroso, often called the father of modern criminology, was a surgeon who conducted systematic observations and measurements of soldiers, criminals, the insane, and the general population. The descriptive data he painstakingly collected represented the use of an experimental method in "legal" medicine that was similar to criminal anthropology. Trying to account for mental and physical differences, he pointed out that criminals have multiple physical abnormalities of an **atavistic** (subhuman or primitive) or **degenerative** nature. These physical inferiorities characterized a biological throwback that Lombroso called the **born criminal.** He also reported that criminals manifest traits of sensory impairment; a lack of moral sense, particularly the absence of remorse; and the use of slang and tattoos.

In accord with the positivist tendency to categorize traits, Lombroso distinguished other types of criminals: the insane criminal, the epileptic criminal, and the occasional criminal, who for no biological reason but by the influence of circumstances or surroundings was drawn to crime. This classification scheme was later modified by Ferri, one of Lombroso's students, to include the born criminal, those who committed crimes of passion, and the habitual criminal. Lombroso quickly embraced the "born criminal" term because it fit his previous description of the major cause of criminality. Later in life, he acknowledged his numerous critics and included social and economic factors in his list of causes of crime. He continued to insist, however, that these other causes were secondary in nature to biological factors.

Enrico Ferri's conception of criminal causality went beyond that of his teacher. While responsible for the born criminal term that Lombroso used, he introduced other important causal factors into Italian Positivism. According to Ferri, crime was caused by a number of factors including physical (race, geographics, temperature, and climate), anthropological (age, sex, organic, and psychological), and "social factors" such as customs, religion, economics, and population density.

Also building on the work of Lombroso was Raffaele Garofalo, who, perhaps most of all, was skeptical about biological explanations of criminal behavior. Garofalo believed that civilized people have certain basic sentiments about the values of human life and property; absence of these sentiments indicates a lack of concern for fellow humans. Finding a combination of environmental, circumstantial, and organic reasons for criminal behavior, he termed such behavior psychic or moral "anomaly," a deficiency of altruistic sensibility. He assumed that this psychic variation, which he carefully distinguished from insanity or mental illness, is more frequent among members of "certain inferior races" (Allen, 1972). In essence, he believed that certain people are morally less developed than others. Garofalo also commented on the legalistic nature of definitions of crime, believing that these definitions limit them in application and situation. Instead, he formulated the more universal notion of **natural crime,** by which he referred to acts that all civilized societies would readily recognize as offensive.

EXCERPT FROM LOMBROSO'S *CRIME: ITS CAUSES AND REMEDIES*

Atavism

The born criminal shows in a proportion reaching 33% numerous specific characteristics that are almost always atavistic. . . .(C)haracteristics presented by savage races are very often found among born criminals. Such, for example, are: . . . low cranial capacity; retreating forehead; highly developed frontal sinuses; . . . the thickness of the bones of the skull; . . . prognathism; obliquity of the orbits; greater pigmentation of the skin; tufted and crispy hair; and large ears. To these we may add . . . anomalies of the ear; . . . great agility; relative insensibility to pain; dullness of the sense of touch; great visual acuteness; ability to recover quickly from wounds; blunted affections; precocity as to sensual pleasures; greater resemblance between tho soxos; greater incorrigibility of the woman; laziness; absence of remorse; impulsiveness; physiopsychic excitability; and especially improvidence, which sometimes appears as courage and again as recklessness changing to cowardice. Besides these there is great vanity; a passion for gambling and alcoholic drinks; violent but fleeting passions; superstition; extraordinary sensitiveness with regard to one's own personality; and a special conception of God and morality. Unexpected analogies are met even in small details, as, for example the improvised rules of criminal gangs; . . . the custom of tattooing, the not uncommon cruelty of their games; the excessive use of gestures . . .

Twentieth-Century Positivism

Following the work of the Italian Positivists, a good deal of effort was expended in the biological area. The family histories of criminals were examined and criminal **heredity** traced to certain ancestors (Dugdale, 1877; Goddard, 1913; Goring, 1913; Estabrook, 1916). Richard Dugdale's study of six generations of the Juke family was used to infer that criminal (and antisocial) behavior is inherited. He was able to trace a number of criminals, prostitutes, and paupers in the family line, all derived from the original criminal father. Intelligence tests were developed by Alfred Binet and subsequently used to explain criminality through the concept of inherited **feeblemindedness,** or lack of intelligence (Goddard, 1914; Burt, 1925). Henry Goddard's well-known study of the Kallikak family was similar to that of Dugdale's. He matched the histories of two family lines produced by a soldier (from a well-to-do family) in the Revolutionary War. One lineage derived from a liaison with a "feebleminded" barmaid, the other from marriage to an honorable Quaker woman. Goddard traced numerous antisocial, deviant, and criminal offspring from the liaison with the barmaid and "none" from the marriage. The obvious implication was that feeblemindedness was inherited and a cause of criminality.

Other hereditary factors were considered through the examination of twins (Lange, 1919), general body types (Kretschmer, 1926; Hooten, 1939; Sheldon, 1949; Glueck and Glueck, 1950), and even endocrinology (Schlapp and Smith, 1928). The **body type** theories suggest that certain physical features result in a propensity to crime. The most quoted of this work is that of William Sheldon, who proposed three categories of a combination of body types and personality temperaments that he called **somatotypes.** An *ecto-morph* is a person who is small-boned, lean, and frail, with a sensitive and introverted (shy) personality. A *mesomorph* is a person of muscular, larger-boned body build with an aggressive, action-oriented, outgoing (extro-verted) personality. The third type, an *endomorph,* has a rather soft and fat build with a relaxed, jovial, and extroverted personality. Sheldon found that delinquents were most often of the mesomorph body type. Strains of the body type/temperament approach are continued more recently in the work of Juan Cortes and Florence Gatti (1972).

The twin research is perhaps the most interesting of the genetic stud-ies. In this form of research the behavior of identical twins (who have identi-cal genetic heritage) is compared. Fraternal twins (who have a different genetic heritage just like any two siblings) have also been used. The reason-ing is that if one twin is criminal, then the other also should be criminal. Johannes Lange's study of prisoner twins and their noninstitutionalized counterparts found a high degree of **concordance** (both twins had engaged in criminal behavior). Identical twins produce concordant results in a higher proportion than do fraternal twins. Several other studies have produced similar results (for reviews of this research see Cortes and Gatti, 1972; Dal-gaard and Kringlen, 1976; Christiansen, 1977b; and Ellis, 1982). The question that remains unanswered, however, is the effect of environment in creating likeness among twins. Comparable studies of adopted siblings have also been undertaken (Crowe, 1972; Schulsinger, 1972; Hutchings and Mednick, 1977). The logic is that if genetic theories hold true, the children should behave more like their biological parents than their adoptive parents. To some extent this was found to be the case.

Much of the literature on psychological influences on behavior has been the result of the ground-breaking work of Sigmund Freud. While Freud himself said little about crime, other psychiatrists have examined the effect of **unconscious conflict** on criminal behavior (Aichhorn, 1925; Abra-hamsen, 1944; Friedlander, 1947). Perhaps the most notable work has been that of William Healy (1915; Alexander and Healy, 1935; and with Bronner, 1936). Healy and other psychiatric workers examined juveniles in a psychi-atric institution (which he directed) and after numerous sessions determined that each juvenile had experienced **emotional trauma** at some point in life. For comparison, the brothers and sisters of the delinquents were then briefly interviewed, and very little evidence of emotional trauma was found in their histories. Healy concluded that emotional trauma is responsible for creating psychological conflicts that lead to delinquent behavior.

Other approaches have included the examination of personality differences, as with the Minnesota Multiphasic Personality Inventory (a complex personality test), and of psychopathic personalities (Hathaway and Monachesi, 1953). The MMPI contains a psychopathic personality subscale that was created by finding questions to which institutionalized delinquents gave uniformly different answers (i.e., scored higher) than "normal" juveniles. Subsequent researchers have found that institutionalized juveniles almost always score higher on the psychopathic personality subscale of the MMPI than normal juveniles do, thereby justifying psychopathy as a cause of delinquency. There is, of course, a certain irony in this research because the scale was created from questions on which the delinquents originally scored higher.

On the sociological side, some early positivistic approaches encompassed both explanations of individual behavior and rates of behavior in society. The notion that behavior, including criminal acts, involves a process of **imitating** others was proposed by Gabriel Tarde (1890). He theorized that there is short-term behavior (fashion) and long-term behavior (custom). People who are socially inferior imitate those who are superior and copy their behavior. Thus, the use of a new and unusual technique for murder (as for instance the now-famous Tylenol poisonings or so-called copy-cat killings) would spread. Tarde also suggested that as population becomes more dense, behavior will be oriented more toward fashion than toward custom. On the statistical side, the ecological studies begun by Guerry and Quetelet blossomed into a sociological criminology that set out to investigate the effect of social structure on crime. Since the 1920s, the American tradition of criminology has used the positivist technique of analyzing population data and crime rates as well as the systematic study of criminal behavior.

CLASSIFICATION OF THE SCHOOL

The Positive School is characterized by a *consensus* perspective. All the theories developed under its mantle assume the existence of a core set of values in society that can be used to determine and treat deviance. Positivists did not question the validity of their categories of harmful acts or the desirability of treating people. In fact, their assumption of consensus was so strong that they rarely ever questioned their own actions, even when "exterminating" groups of people designated as socially harmful. Other than the consensus perspective, the wide range of positivist theories makes any attempt at categorizing them very difficult. Positivist theories can be either structural or processual, so no definitive classification is possible. However, we can state that sociological theories have, as a rule, been *structurally oriented* and *macrotheoretical*, while biological and psychological theories have been *processual* and *microtheoretical*.

COMPARISON OF CLASSICAL AND POSITIVE SCHOOLS

Point	Classical School	Positive School
View of human nature	Hedonistic; free-willed rationality, morally responsible for own behavior.	Malleable; determined by biological, psychological, and social environment; no moral responsibility; consensus-oriented.
View of justice system	Social contract; exists to protect society; due process and concern with civil rights; restrictions on system.	Scientific treatment system to cure pathologies and rehabilitate offenders; no concern with civil rights.
Form of law	Statutory law; exact specification of illegal acts and sanctions.	Social law; illegal acts defined by analogy; scientific experts determine social harm and proper form of treatment.
Purpose of sentencing	Punishment for deterrence; sentences are determinate (fixed length).	Treatment and reform; sentences are indeterminate (variable length until cured).
Criminological experts	Philosophers; social reformers.	Scientists; treatment experts.

SUMMARY

The work of the Positive School, diverse as it was, represented the first real concern with studying the behavior of the criminal. Embracing the scientific method, Positivists took a deterministic stance toward behavior and left behind the Classical School's insistence that humans are rational beings with free will. In the process, the notion of punishment for deterrence began to make less sense. If an individual's behavior were not predicated on rational decisions, then how could that individual be deterred? The thing to do, obviously, was to find those factors that cause the criminal behavior and remove (or treat) them. Further, it would be useful to be able to predict which individuals would be likely to become criminal and to treat them before they could harm themselves and society.

Positivists left behind the legal focus and concerns of the Classical School. In fact, for them the only reasonable definition of criminality was a social one. Legality simply got in the way of treatment because behavioral categories did not necessarily fit legal categories. If behaviors were socially undesirable, the individuals exhibiting them should be treated and returned to normalcy. Civil rights were of no concern if the real purpose of treatment was that of help. After all, how can one object to being helped; when a physician treats us, do we feel our civil rights have been violated? Thus, early Positivists reasoned that criminals have no need to object when they are being treated by correctional experts.

Finally, positivism, as we have seen, is represented not only by biological theories of causality but by psychological and sociological theories as well. In fact, most of the theories of criminology throughout the 1950s were positivistic in nature. As a general perspective, then, positivism has had an enormous effect on the way criminological theories have been constructed and the way that research has been conducted.

Major Points of the School

1. Humans live in a world in which cause and effect operate. Attributes of that world exhibit order and can be uncovered through systematic observation.
2. Social problems, such as crime, can be remedied by means of a systematic study of human behavior. Through the application of science, human existence is perfectible, or at the least the human condition can be made better.
3. Criminal behavior is a product of abnormalities. These abnormalities may be within the person, or they may exist as external social forces.
4. Abnormal features can be found through comparison with those that are normal.
5. Once abnormalities are found, it is the duty of criminology to assist in their correction. Abnormalities should be treated and the criminal reformed.
6. Treatment is desirable both for the individual, so that he or she may become normal, and for society, so that members of society are protected from harm.
7. The purpose of sanctions against criminals is, then, not to punish but to provide for treatment.

EPILOGUE: CURRENT DIRECTIONS AND POLICY IMPLICATIONS

The more conservative attitudes of the mid 1970s through the 1990s gave rise to an assumption of consensus in values, favoring the reemergence of nonsocial theories. A major impetus was that American society was doubtful of the value of reform and rehabilitation and had no desire to pay for the massive social programs suggested by existing social theories. Thus, theories that cast the blame for crime on something more intrinsic were received favorably. A renewed interest in biological/biochemical and psychological theories of crime ensued.

Biology

Work in the biology of crime continues with research by Karl Christiansen (1977a), Sarnoff Mednick and associates (1977, 1987; Hutchings and Mednick, 1977; Kirkegaard-Sorensen and Mednick, 1977), the biosocial theorizing of C. Ray Jeffery (1977, 1989a), and recent defense provided by James

Q. Wilson and Richard Herrnstein (1985). Mednick's work, referred to as a **biosocial theory,** is an excellent example of the orientation of modern biological theorists. He views the biological characteristics of an individual as only one part in the equation of behavior—other parts are the physical and social environment. Mednick assumes that all individuals must learn to control natural urges toward antisocial and criminal behavior. This learning takes place in the family and with peer groups and is based on the punishment of undesirable behaviors. The punishment response is mediated by the autonomic (involuntary) nervous system. If the reaction is short-lived, the individual is said to have rewarded himself or herself, and criminal behavior is inhibited. However, a slow physiological recovery from punishment (and fear of it) does little to teach the individual to refrain from undesirable behavior. Mednick views criminals as having slow autonomic-nervous-system responses to stimuli.

As part of an ongoing series of writings, C. Ray Jeffery also offers an interdisciplinary biosocial theory of criminal behavior in *Advances in Criminological Theory* (1989a) and a criminology text (1989b). His perspective is that sociological, psychological, and biological characteristics should be seen as interacting together in a systems model to produce criminal behavior. Three basic systems produce the total organism: genetics, brain structure and function, and learning (1989a:72–73). He posits that individuals are born with particular biological (genetic) and psychological characteristics that not only may predispose but may actually cause certain forms of behavior. This "nature" is independent of the socialization process present in the social environment. There is, however, a good deal of interplay between nature and nurture through the physical environment and the feedback mechanisms that exist in human biochemical systems. For example, Jeffery notes that poverty translates to a certain type of diet and exposure to pollutants. The resulting nutrients and chemicals are transformed by the biochemical system into neurochemical compounds within the brain. Thus, poverty indirectly leads to behavioral differences (and, potentially, criminal behavior) through the interaction of individual and environment. Jeffery's general scheme can be summed up in an equation he provides (1989a:73):

$$Genetics \leftrightarrow Brain \leftrightarrow Behavior\ (Learning/Personality)$$
$$\updownarrow \qquad\quad \updownarrow$$
$$Environment$$

In a controversial book, *Crime and Human Nature* (1985), Wilson and Herrnstein offer a similar biosocial version of the causes of street crime. They combine genetic factors with psychological dispositions and personality traits, drug usage, and socialization factors. Their final explanation of crime not only leans heavily toward individual human nature but also has a deterrence-like component: an offender makes a decision that the potential gain from crime will outweigh any possible punishment. Thus, Wilson and

Herrnstein's criminals are born with and, throughout their life continue to gain, predispositions toward crime, but it is ultimately the criminal's own decision to commit an act that is important.

Another approach to biological effects is work on **intelligence** and crime. Also referred to as mental deficiency, intelligence has been implicated in criminality for a long time. The "feeblemindedness" work of Dugdale, Goddard, and Goring is discredited today, however. Most criminologists see intelligence not as a cause of crime but as a predisposing factor in decisions to commit crime, but they do not discuss it very often. Recent interest in intelligence is based on a controversial position, taken in the late 1960s, that intelligence is genetically based and that differences in IQ can be used to explain different criminal propensities between races (see Shockley, 1967; Jensen, 1969). One criminologist, Robert Gordon (1986), uses the position to argue that IQ is the best predictor of delinquency rates among various groups. In 1977, criminologists Travis Hirschi and Michael Hindelang published an article that reviewed studies on IQ and delinquency. They found that, as a predictor of delinquency, IQ is at least as good as any of the other major social variables. Further, they noted that IQ is also strongly related to social class and race. Because delinquency is viewed as the province of lower-class, minority youths, this relationship implies that lower-class, minority delinquents have lower IQs. Responding to the IQ and delinquency position, Scott Menard and Barbara Morse (1984) argue that IQ is merely one of the ways in which juveniles are disadvantaged in American society. They see the societal and institutional response to these disadvantages as the real causal agent in delinquent behavior. Critics of IQ tests have noted that the way in which the tests are constructed provides advantages to those who are middle class and white. Moreover, they argue that the tests do not measure innate intelligence but rather some other ability, such as facility in language or cultural concepts.

Finally, newer gene-based evolutionary theories are no longer postulating that genetic structures directly affect behavior. Because behavior is complex, these theories assume that genetic effects are indirect. They view the role of genes as affecting brain functioning, which governs behavior. Learning theories may be used in specifying how brain functioning is translated into behavior or there may be a propensity toward certain forms of learning. Even socialization may be affected by propensities toward such things as psychological or physiological traits, antisocial behaviors, and so on. These factors, then, influence how an individual will react in certain settings and make criminal behavior more or less probable.

Psychology

Recent psychological work argues that there may be a **"criminal personality,"** or a different thinking pattern among criminals. Samuel Yochelson, a psychiatrist, and Stanton Samenow, a clinical psychologist, in a widely publicized study (1976), reintroduced the case for a criminal personality. After thorough case studies of between 230 and 270 inmates at St. Elizabeth's Hospital for the criminally insane in Washington, D.C., Yochelson and Samenow pronounced that the causes of crime are not social, economic, or psychological inner conflicts. Instead, they claimed that all criminals are born with abnormal thinking patterns that affect their ability to make decisions.[1] This "criminal personality" seeks excitement, has an inordinately high opinion of self, is exploitative and selfish, manipulates others, is amoral, and so forth. An attack on the criminal's self-image tends to produce a violent reaction. All in all, Yochelson and Samenow claimed to have found fifty-two different criminal thinking patterns. The theoretical position that all criminals have different thinking patterns was popular in federal government circles for a while.

Cognitive Theory

The best example of psychologically based cognitive theory is one proposed by Glenn Walters and Thomas White (1989a). In a 1989 critique, Walters said that criminology had not adequately recognized the role of cognition in the individual. His point is that social and environmental conditions serve to limit individual options rather than determine behavior. If social and environmental factors are a backdrop for choice, then behavior can be seen as patterned by these factors while individual rationality determines the *form* of patterned activity. In short, "life conditions place effected [*sic*] individuals at increased (or decreased) risk for later criminality" (Walters, 1989:v).

Walters and White jointly argue that criminal behavior is the product of faulty, irrational thinking and deny that environmental factors determine criminal behavior, except for limiting options. Focusing on career criminals, Walters and White point out that these individuals are characterized in most, if not all, of their interactions by irresponsibility, self-indulgence, interpersonal intrusiveness, and social rule breaking. Lifestyle criminals appear to have similar thought patterns to those of early adolescents and, thus, have little conception of responsibility and self-discipline. The arrested development of the cognition process, regardless of whether the source is constitutional or environmental, tends to set these individuals up for failure. This failure applies not only to criminal situations but also to a wide range of common situations, such as school, work, and home.

Locating eight "primitive cognitive characteristics," Walters and White examined the thinking patterns of lifestyle criminals and found that from an

1. One of the major problems of this study is that Yochelson and Samenow overgeneralized the evidence. While there is little disagreement with the position that the criminally *insane* have different thinking patterns, Yochelson and Samenow did not perform similar studies on criminals who were *not* insane. Therefore, they can say nothing about "normal" criminals and certainly nothing about *all* criminals.

early age these individuals present chronic management problems. Because of their adolescent-like motives, lifestyle criminals rationalize their behavior and are preoccupied with short-term hedonism, which is destructive in the long run. Finally, Walters and White argue that lifestyle criminals direct their behavior toward "losing in dramatic and destructive ways" (1989a:8). In consistently choosing self-interested and hedonistic alternatives, criminals perpetuate their behavior.

Personality Dimensions

Another approach to the personality issue has been generated by Hans Eysenck (1977, 1989, with Gudjonnson 1990). His theory is that there are three major **personality dimensions:** *psychoticism, extroversion,* and *neuroti cism.* Criminality generally is correlated with high degrees of all three, although certain types of crime may be correlated differently. Where age is concerned, the younger offender is more likely to have high levels of extroversion than neuroticism. Older offenders, on the other hand, exhibit higher levels of neuroticism. In all age groups, psychoticism is always important. Eysenck documents these relationships across various studies and countries and notes that "antisocial" traits (smoking, legal or illegal drug use) as well as criminality are correlated with these personalities. Finally, he connects these personality traits with the development of a conscience through a learning process called **conditioning** and a high need for external stimulation. Criminals condition poorly and as a result are slow to develop an effective conscience.

Learning Theory

A final popular psychological approach to criminal behavior is through **learning theory,** particularly social learning theory. Developed by Albert Bandura (1973), the perspective adds to B. F. Skinner's operant learning theory by including imitation and modeling of behavior. That is, social learning asserts that we learn by watching others receive rewards and punishments for certain forms of behavior. We then imitate or model those behaviors that are rewarded. This theory has been heavily used in studies of aggression, family violence, and the effect of television in encouraging aggression. There is some evidence that such behavior is indeed learned from others. Criminology picked up social learning theory in the 1960s, and we examine that approach in Chapter 11.

Policy Implications

Positivist theories, old and new, are full of policy implications. Because of the theoretical emphases on treatment and pathology, they are often the backbone of social reform programs. They have even been used to argue that people are innately different and uncorrectable, thus lending themselves to extreme strategies of social reform, such as Hitler's genocide programs.

Because the biological versions have not been very popular in the past half century, until recently there have been few biologically oriented crime policies. Perhaps the closest the United States has gotten to these policies in the past several decades is the war on drugs. Not only has drug use been viewed as a major cause of crime by at least two presidential administrations, but the implicit suggestion is that neurochemical compounds (drugs) cause people to behave in ways that they would not normally behave. That is, crime is a product of the effect of drugs on human physiology and neurological systems. Thus, in the fight against crime, there is no need to implement expensive social reform policies; we merely need to eliminate drugs and crime rates will drastically decrease.

Psychological perspectives have found much more favor with policymakers as a standard approach to criminal behavior. Indeed, they have become a routine part of our criminal justice system. As a matter of course, sentenced individuals are required to attend treatment sessions of various sorts. Offenders on probation receive diagnostic tests to determine what forms of counseling and treatment they need. Such services are now being offered to victims of crimes as well. The newer forms of psychological theories, especially cognitive approaches, have been received with favor by policymakers. Cognitive theory dwells on the differences in thinking patterns between "normal" and criminal individuals, thus contributing to the assumption that criminal behavior is a result of some thinking failure of the individual. This has been translated into "bad people bring on their own bad behavior and simply deserve to be punished for their own decisions." In short, policymakers see punishment as the way to impress on bad individuals that their thinking needs correcting; no treatment programs are needed. Psychologists, however, have generally not subscribed to the no-treatment philosophy and have created techniques designed to teach offenders how to think rationally and realistically (see, for example, MacPhail, 1989).

Sociological versions of positivist theory have been the cornerstone of many of our crime policies for the past thirty years. We examine most of these under the various sociologically based theories in the coming chapters. An example or two, however, may assist in understanding their utility. Exemplified by the Great Society programs of the 1960s, reforms were instituted to provide greater opportunities to those who were socially disadvantaged. The assumption was that increased opportunities would reduce the social strain producing crime. These programs resulted in educational programs such as Project Head Start and in job-training programs such as the Job Corps and Comprehensive Employee Training Act (CETA). More recently, social control theories have led to renewed emphasis on the importance of school and family in the fight against crime. The "family values" issue of the 1992 presidential campaign can be seen, in part, as an extension of this perspective.

BIBLIOGRAPHY

ABRAHAMSEN, DAVID (1944). *Crime and the Human Mind.* New York: Columbia University Press.

AICHHORN, AUGUST (1925). *Wayward Youth.* New York: Viking. (Reprinted 1935.)

ALEXANDER, FRANZ, and WILLIAM HEALY (1935). *Roots of Crime.* New York: Knopf.

ALLEN, FRANCIS A. (1972). "Raffaele Garofalo." In Hermann Mannheim, ed., *Pioneers in Criminology,* 2nd ed, 318–340. Montclair, NJ: Patterson Smith.

ANDREWS, D. A., and J. S. WORMITH (1989). "Personality and crime: Knowledge destruction and construction in criminology." *Justice Quarterly* 6: 289–309.

ANGENENT, HUUB, and ANTON DEMAN (1996). *Background Factors of Juvenile Delinquency.* New York: Peter Lang.

BANDURA, ALBERT (1973). *Aggression: A Social Learning Approach.* Englewood Cliffs, NJ: Prentice Hall.

BEIRNE, PIERS (1987a). "Adolphe Quetelet and the origins of positivist criminology." *American Journal of Sociology* 92: 1140–1169.

——— (1987b). "Between classicism and positivism: Crime and penalty in the writings of Gabriel Tarde." *Criminology* 25: 785–819.

——— (1988). "Heredity versus environment: A reconsideration of Charles Goring's 'The English Convict' (1913)." *British Journal of Criminology* 28: 315–339.

BLACKBURNE, R. (1986). "Patterns of personality deviation among violent offenders: Replication and extension of an empirical taxonomy." *British Journal of Criminology* 26: 254–269.

BOCK, GREGORY R., and JAMIE A. GOODE, eds. (1996). *Genetics of Criminal and Antisocial Behaviour.* Chichester, UK: John Wiley.

BOHMAN, M., C. R. CLONINGER, S. SIGVARDSSON, and A. L. VON KNORRING (1982). "Predisposition to petty criminality in Swedish adoptees: I. Genetic and environmental heterogeneity." *Archives of General Psychiatry* 41: 872–878.

BOOTH, ALAN, and D. WAYNE OSGOOD (1993). "The influence of testosterone on deviance in adulthood: Assessing and explaining the relationship." *Criminology* 31: 93–117.

BRENNAN, P. A., and SARNOFF A. MEDNICK (1993). "Genetic perspectives on crime." *Acta Psychiatrica Scandinavia* 370: 19–26.

BROOKS, JOHN H., and JOHN R. REDDON (1996). "Serum testosterone in violent and nonviolent young offenders." *Journal of Clinical Psychology* 52: 475–483.

BRYCE-SMITH, D., and H. A. WALDRON (1974). "Lead, behavior, and criminality." *Ecologist* 4: 367–377.

BURT, CYRIL (1925). *The Young Delinquent.* New York: Appleton.

CAREY, GREGORY (1992). "Twin imitation for antisocial behavior: Implications for genetic and family environment research." *Journal of Abnormal Psychology* 101: 18–25.

CHRISTIANSEN, KARL O. (1968). Threshold of tolerance in various population groups illustrated by results from a Danish criminological twin study. In A. V. S. de Reuck and R. Porter, eds., *CIBA Foundation Symposium on the Mentally Abnormal Offender,* 107–116. London: I. and J. Churchill.

——— (1970). "Crime in a Danish twin population." *Acta Genetical Medical Gemellologial* 19: 323–326.

——— (1977a). "A preliminary study of criminality among twins." In S. A. Mednick and K. O. Christiansen, eds., *Biosocial Bases of Criminal Behavior,* 89–108. New York: Gardner.

——— (1977b). "A review of studies of criminality among twins." In S. A. Mednick and K. O. Christiansen, eds., *Biosocial Bases of Criminal Behavior,* 45–88. New York: Gardner.

COMTE, AUGUSTE (1853). *The Positive Philosophy of Auguste Comte.* 2 vols. Trans. Harriet Martineau. London: Chapman.

CORTES, JUAN, with FLORENCE M. GATTI (1972). *Delinquency and Crime, a Biopsychosocial Approach: Empirical, Theoretical and Practical Aspects of Criminal Behavior.* New York: Seminar Press.

CROWE, RAYMOND R. (1972). "The adopted offspring of women criminal offenders: A study of their arrest records." *Archives of General Psychiatry* 27: 600–603.

——— (1974). "An adoption study of anti-social personality." *Archives of General Psychiatry* 31: 785–791.

DALGAARD, ODD STEPHEN, and EINAR KRINGLEN (1976). "A Norwegian twin study of criminality." *British Journal of Criminology* 16: 213–232.

DALTON, KATHARINA (1961). "Menstruation and crime." *British Medical Journal* 2: 1752–1753.

——— (1964). *The Premenstrual Syndrome.* Springfield, IL: Charles C. Thomas.

DARWIN, CHARLES (1859). *The Origin of Species.* Cambridge, MA: Harvard University Press. (Reprinted 1964.)

DENNO, DEBORAH W. (1988). "Human biology and criminal responsibility: Free will or free ride?" *University of Pennsylvania Law Review* 137(2): 615–671.

D'ORBAN, P. T., and J. DALTON (1980). "Violent crime and the menstrual cycle." *Psychological Medicine* 10: 353–359.

DRIVER, EDWIN A. (1972). "Charles Buckman Goring." In Hermann Mannheim, ed., *Pioneers in Criminology*, 2nd ed., 429–442. Montclair, NJ: Patterson Smith.

DUGDALE, RICHARD L. (1877). *The Jukes: A Study in Crime, Pauperism, Disease, and Heredity.* New York: Putnam's.

DURKHEIM, EMILE (1893). *The Division of Labor in Society.* Trans. George Simpson. New York: Macmillan. (Reprinted 1933.)

ELLIS, LEE (1982). "Genetics and criminal behavior: Evidence through the end of the 1970s." *Criminology* 20: 43–66.

——— (1985). "Genetic influences and crime." In F. H. Marsh and J. Katz, eds., *Biology, Crime and Ethics: A Study of Biological Explanations for Criminal Behavior*, 65–92. Cincinnati, OH: Anderson.

ELLIS, LEE, and ANTHONY WALSH (1997). "Gene-based evolutionary theories in criminology." *Criminology* 35: 229–276.

ESTABROOK, ARTHUR (1916). *The Jukes in 1915.* Washington, DC: Carnegie Institute.

EYSENCK, HANS J. (1977). *Crime and Personality.* London: Routledge and Kegan Paul.

——— (1989). "Personality and criminality: A dispositional analysis." In W. S. Laufer and F. Adler, eds., *Advances in Criminological Theory*, vol. 1, 89–110. New Brunswick, NJ: Transaction.

——— (1996). "Personality and crime: Where do we stand?" *Psychology Crime and Law* 2 (3): 143–152.

EYSENCK, HANS J., and GISLI H. GUDJONNSON (1990). *The Causes and Cures of Crime.* New York: Plenum.

FARRINGTON, DAVID P., GEOFFREY C. BARNES, and SANDRA LAMBERT (1996). "The concentration of offending in families." *Legal and Criminological Psychology* 1: 47–63.

FELDMAN, M. PHILIP (1978). *Criminal Behavior: A Psychological Analysis.* New York: Wiley.

FERRACUTI, STEFANO (1996). "Cesare Lombroso (1835–1907)." *Journal of Forensic Psychiatry* 7: 130–149.

FERRI, ENRICO (1881). *Criminal Sociology.* Trans. Joseph Killey and John Lisle. Boston: Little, Brown. (Reprinted 1917.)

FISHBEIN, DIANA H. (1990). "Biological perspectives in criminology." *Criminology* 28: 27–72.

FISHBEIN, DIANA H., and SUSAN PEASE (1988). "The effects of diet on behavior: Implications for criminology and corrections." *Research on Corrections* 1: 1–45.

FLETCHER, RONALD (1975). "Introduction." In Kenneth Thompson, *Auguste Comte: The Foundation of Sociology*, ix–xi. New York: Halsted.

FORDE, R. A. (1978). "Twin studies, inheritance and criminality." *British Journal of Criminology* 18: 71–74.

FOX, RICHARD S. (1971). "The XYY offender: A modern myth?" *Journal of Criminal Law, Criminology, and Police Science* 62: 59–73.

FRIEDLANDER, KATE (1947). *The Psychoanalytic Approach to Juvenile Delinquency.* London: Kegan Paul, Trench and Trubner.

GABRIELLI, WILLIAM F., and SARNOFF A. MEDNICK (1983). "Genetic correlates of criminal behavior. "*American Behavioral Scientist* 27: 59–71.

GAROFALO, RAFFAELE (1885). *Criminology.* Trans. Robert W. Millar. Boston: Little, Brown. (Reprinted 1914.)

GLUECK, SHELDON, and ELEANOR T. GLUECK (1950). *Unraveling Juvenile Delinquency.* New York: Commonwealth Fund.

——— (1956). *Physique and Delinquency.* New York: Harper and Row.

——— (1974). *Of Delinquency and Crime.* Springfield, IL:Charles C. Thomas.

GODDARD, HENRY H. (1913). *The Kallikak Family: A Study in the Heredity of Feeblemindedness.* New York: Macmillan.

——— (1914). *Feeblemindedness: Its Causes and Consequences.* New York: Macmillan.

GOLDEN, CHARLES J., MICHELE L. JACKSON, and ANGELA PETRSON-ROHNE (1996). "Neuropsychological correlates of violence and aggression: A review of the clinical literature." *Aggression and Violent Behavior* 1: 3–25.

GORDON, ROBERT A. (1986). "Scientific justification and the race-IQ-delinquency model." In T. Hartnagel and R. Silverman, eds., *Critique and Explanation: Essays in Honor of Gwynne Nettler*, 91–131. New Brunswick, NJ: Transaction.

GORING, CHARLES B. (1913). *The English Convict.* London: H.M. Stationery Office.

GOTTFREDSON, MICHAEL R., and TRAVIS HIRSCHI, eds. (1987). *Positive Criminology.* Newbury Park, CA: Sage.

GRAHAM, KATHRYN, GAIL SCHMIDT, and KELLY GILLIS (1996). "Circumstances when drinking leads to aggression: An overview of research findings." *Contemporary Drug Problems* 23: 493–557.

GUERRY, ANDRE M. (1833). *Essai Sur la Statistique Morale.* Paris.

HALFPENNY, PETER (1982). *Positivism and Sociology: Explaining Social Life.* Boston: Allen and Unwin.

HARRY, B., and C. BLACER (1987). "Menstruation and crime: A critical review of the literature from the clinical criminology perspective." *Behavioral Sciences and the Law* 5: 307–322.

HATHAWAY, STARKE R., and ELIO D. MONACHESI (1953). *Analyzing and Predicting Juvenile Delinquency with the MMPI.* Minneapolis, MN: University of Minnesota Press.

——— (1963). *Adolescent Personality and Behavior: MMPI Patterns of Normal, Delinquent, Dropout and Other Outcomes.* Minneapolis, MN: University of Minneapolis Press.

HEALY, WILLIAM (1915). *The Individual Delinquent.* Boston: Little, Brown.

HEALY, WILLIAM, and AUGUSTA BRONNER (1936). *New Light on Delinquency and Its Treatment.* New Haven, CT: Yale University Press.

HEILBURN, ALFRED B. JR. (1996). *Criminal Dangerousness and the Risk of Violence.* Lanham, MD: University Press of America.

HEIMER, KAREN (1997). "Socioeconomic status, subcultural definitions, and violent delinquency." *Social Forces* 75: 799–834.

HELFGOTT, JACQUELINE B. (1997). "The relationship between unconscious defensive process and conscious cognitive style in psychopaths." *Criminal Justice and Behavior* 24: 278–293.

HILLBRAND, MARC, and NATHANIEL J. PALLONE, eds. (1994). "Special edition: The psychobiology of aggression: engines, measurement, control." *Journal of Offender Rehabilitation* 21 (3/4): 1–243.

HIRSCHI, TRAVIS, and MICHAEL J. HINDELANG (1977). "Intelligence and delinquency: A revisionist view." *American Journal of Sociology* 42: 571–587.

HOOTON, EARNEST A. (1939). *The American Criminal: An Anthropological Study*, vol. 1. Cambridge, MA: Harvard University Press.

HORNEY, JULIE (1978). "Menstrual cycles and criminal responsibility." *Law and Human Behavior* 2: 25–38.

HUTCHINGS, BARRY, and SARNOFF A. MEDNICK (1977). "Criminality in adoptees and their adoptive and biological parents: A pilot study." In S.A. Mednick and K.O. Christiansen, eds., *Biosocial Bases of Criminal Behavior*, 127–141. New York: Gardner.

JACOBS, P. A., M. BRUNTON, M. M. MELVILLE, R. P. BRITTAIN, and W. McCLEMONT (1965). "Aggressive behavior, mental sub-normality, and the XYY male." *Nature* 108: 1351–1352.

JEFFERY, C. RAY (1977). *Crime Prevention through Environmental Design*, rev. ed. Beverly Hills, CA: Sage.

——— (1979). *Biology and Crime*. Beverly Hills: Sage.

——— (1989a). "An Interdisciplinary Theory of Criminal Behavior." In W. S. Laufer and F. Adler, eds., *Advances in Criminological Theory*, vol. 1, 69–87. New Brunswick, NJ: Transaction.

——— (1989b). *Criminology: An Interdisciplinary Approach*. Englewood Cliffs, NJ: Prentice Hall.

JEFFREY, C. RAY, and DIANE L. ZAHM (1993). "Crime prevention through environmental design, opportunity theory, and rational choice models." *Advances in Criminological Theory* 5: 323–350.

JENSEN, ARTHUR R. (1969). "How much can we boost IQ and scholastic achievement?" *Harvard Educational Review* 39: 1–123.

KAPLAN, ABRAHAM (1968). "Positivism." In David L. Sills, ed., *International Encyclopedia of the Social Sciences*, vol. 12, 389–395. New York: Macmillan.

KATZ, ROGER C., and JOE MARQUETTE (1996). "Psychosocial characteristics of young violent offenders: A comparative study." *Criminal Behaviour and Mental Health* 6: 339–348.

KELLER, O. J. (1980). "The criminal personality of Lombroso revisited." *Federal Probation* 44 (1): 37–43.

KIRKEGAARD-SORENSEN, LIS, and SARNOFF A. MEDNICK (1977). "A prospective study of predictors of criminality: A description of registered criminality in high-risk and low-risk families." In S. A. Mednick and K. O. Christiansen, eds., *Biosocial Bases of Criminal Behaviors*, 229–243. New York: Gardner.

KRETSCHMER, ERNST (1926). *Physique and Character*. Trans. W. J. H. Sprott. New York: Harcourt and Brace.

LANGE, JOHANNES (1919). *Crime and Destiny*. Trans. Charlotte Haldane. New York: Charles Boni. (Reprinted 1930.)

LAUB, JOHN H., and ROBERT J. SAMPSON (1988). "Unraveling families and delinquency: A reanalysis of the Gluecks' data." *Criminology* 26: 355–380.

LEWIS, D. O., J. H. PINCUS, M. FELDMAN, L. JACKSON, and B. BARD (1986). "Psychiatric, neurological, and psychoeducational characteristics of 15 death row inmates in the United States." *American Journal of Psychiatry* 14: 838–845.

LOEBER, R., and T. DISHION (1983). "Early predictors of male delinquency: A review." *Psychological Bulletin* 94: 68–99.

LOEHLIN, J. C., and R. C. NICHOLS (1976). *Heredity, Environment, and Personality: A Study of 850 Sets of Twins*. Austin: University of Texas Press.

LOMBROSO, CESARE (1876). *L'Uomo Delinquente* (The Criminal Man). Milan: Hoepli.

——— (1918). *Crime: Its Causes and Remedies*. Trans. Henry P. Horton. Boston: Little, Brown.

LOMBROSO-FERRERO, GINA (1911). *Criminal Man*. Montclair, NJ: Patterson Smith. (Reprinted 1972.)

LYKKEN, DAVID T. (1995). *The Antisocial Personalities*. Hillsdale, NJ: Lawrence Erlbaum Associates.

MACPHAIL, DANIEL D. (1989). "The moral education approach in treating adult inmates." *Criminal Justice and Behavior* 16: 81–97.

MARK, VERNON, and FRANK ERVIN (1970). *Violence and the Brain*. New York: Harper and Row.

MARSH, FRANK H., and JANET KATZ, eds. (1985). *Biology, Crime and Ethics: A Study of Biological Explanations for Criminal Behavior*. Cincinnati, OH: Anderson.

McCORD, JOAN (1991). "The cycle of crime and socialization practices." *Journal of Criminal Law and Criminology* 82: 211–228.

McCORD, WILLIAM, and JOAN McCORD (1956). *Psychopathy and Delinquency*. New York: Wiley.

——— (1964). *The Psychopath: An Essay on the Criminal Mind*. Princeton, NJ: Van Nostrand.

McKENRY, PATRICK C., TERESA W. JULIAN, and STEPHEN M. GAVAZZI (1995). "Toward a biopsychosocial model of domestic violence." *Journal of Marriage and the Family* 57: 307–320.

MEDNICK, SARNOFF A. (1977). "A biosocial theory of the learning of law-abiding behavior." In S. A. Mednick and K. O. Christiansen, eds., *Biosocial Bases of Criminal Behavior*, 1–9. New York: Gardner.

MEDNICK, SARNOFF A., and KARL O. CHRISTIANSEN, eds. (1977). *Biosocial Bases of Criminal Behavior*. New York: Gardner.

MEDNICK, SARNOFF A., WILLIAM F. GABRIELLI, JR., and BARRY HUTCHINGS (1984). "Genetic influences in criminal convictions: Evidence from an adoption cohort." *Science* 224: 891–893.

——— (1987). "Genetic factors in the etiology of criminal behavior." In S. A. Mednick, T. L. Moffitt, and S. Stack, eds., *The Causes of Crime: New Biological Approaches*, 74–91. Cambridge: Cambridge University Press.

MEDNICK, SARNOFF A., TERRI E. MOFFITT, and SUSAN STACK, eds. (1987). *The Causes of Crime: New Biological Approaches*. Cambridge: Cambridge University Press.

MEDNICK, SARNOFF A., and JAN VOLAVKA (1980). "Biology and crime." In N. Morris and M. Tonry, eds., *Crime and Justice: An Annual Review of Research*, 85–159. Chicago: University of Chicago Press.

MEDNICK, SARNOFF A., JAN VOLAVKA, WILLIAM F. GABRIELLI, JR., and TURAN M. ITIL (1981). "EEG as a predictor of antisocial behavior." *Criminology* 19: 219–229.

MEGARGEE, EDWIN I. (1982). "Psychological determinants and correlates of criminal violence." In M. E. Wolfgang and N. A. Weiner, eds., *Criminal Violence*, 81–170. Beverly Hills, CA: Sage.

MENARD, SCOTT, and BARBARA J. MORSE (1984). "A structuralist critique of the IQ-delinquency hypothesis: Theory and evidence." *American Journal of Sociology* 89: 1347–1378.

MINER, MICHAEL H., and S. MARGRETTA DWYER (1997). "The psychosocial development of sex offenders: Differences between exhibitionists, child molesters, and incest offenders." *International Journal of Offender Therapy and Comparative Criminology* 41: 36–44.

MOIR, ANNE, and DAVID JESSEL (1995). *A Mind to Crime: The Controversial Link between the Mind and Criminal Behavior*. London, UK: Michael Joseph.

MONACHESI, ELIO D., and STARKE R. HATHAWAY (1969). "The personality of delinquents." In J. N. Butcher, ed., *MMPI: Research Development and Clinical Applications*, 207–219. New York: McGraw-Hill.

MONAHAN, JOHN, and STEPHANIE SPLANE (1980). "Psychological approaches to criminal behavior." In E. Bittner and S. I. Messenger, eds., *Criminology Review Yearbook*, vol. 2, 17–47. San Francisco: Sage.

MORAN, RICHARD (1978). "Biomedical research and the politics of crime control: A historical perspective." *Contemporary Crises* 2: 335–357.

MURCHISON, CARL (1926). *Criminal Intelligence.* Worcester, MA: Clark University Press.

NEGRIER-DORMONT, LYGIA, (1994). "Criminology: Foundations and efficacity." *International Criminal Police Review* 49 (450): 10–15.

PALLONE, NATHANIEL J., and JAMES J. HENNESSY (1996). *Tinder-box Criminal Aggression: Neuropsychology, Demography, Phenomenology.* New Brunswick, NJ: Transaction.

PIHL, R. O., F. ERVIN, G. PELLETIER, W. DIEKEL, and W. STRAIN (1987). "Hair element content of violent criminals." *Canadian Journal of Psychiatry* 27: 533.

POPE-HARRISON, G. L., JR., ELENA M. KOURL, and KENNETH F. POWELL (1996). "Anabolic-androgenic steroid use among 133 prisoners." *Comprehensive Psychiatry* 37: 322–327.

QUETELET, ADOLPHE (1831). *Research on the Propensity for Crime at Different Ages.* Trans. Sawyer F. Sylvester. Cincinnati, OH: Anderson. (Reprinted 1984.)

RAINE, ADRIAN (1993). *The Psychopathology of Crime: Criminal Behavior as a Clinical Disorder.* San Diego: Academic Press.

REISS, ALBERT J., JR., KLAUS A. MICZEK, and JEFFERY A. ROTH, eds. (1994). *Understanding and Preventing Violence.* Vol 2: *Biobehavioral Influences.* Washington, DC: National Academy Press.

RENNEVILLE, MARC (1994). "Criminal anthropology in France." *Criminologie* 27: 185–209.

RENNIE, YSABEL (1978). "The positivist revolution." In Y. Rennie, *The Search for Criminal Man,* 67–78. Lexington, MA: Lexington.

ROSANOFF, AARON J., LEVA M. HANDY, and ISABEL AVIS ROSANOFF (1934). "Criminality and delinquency in twins." *Journal of Criminal Law and Criminology* 24: 923–934.

ROTHMAN, DAVID (1971). *The Discovery of the Asylum: Social Order and Disorder in the New Republic.* Boston: Little, Brown.

ROWE, DAVID C. (1983). "Biometrical genetic models of self-reported delinquent behavior: A twin study." *Behavior Genetics* 13: 473–489.

——— (1986). "Genetic and environmental components of antisocial behavior: A study of 256 twin pairs." *Criminology* 24: 513–532.

ROWE, DAVID C., and CHESTER L. BRITT, III (1991). "Developmental explanations of delinquent behavior among siblings: Common factor vs. transmission mechanisms." *Journal of Quantitative Criminology* 7: 315–332.

ROWE, DAVID C., and D. WAYNE OSGOOD (1984). "Heredity and sociological theories of delinquency: A reconsideration." *American Sociological Review* 49: 526–540.

ROWE, DAVID C., and J. L. RODGERS (1989). "Behavioral genetics, adolescent deviance, and `d': Contributions and issues." In G. R. Adams, R. Montemayor, and T. P. Gullotta, eds., *Biology of Adolescent Behavior and Development,* 38–67. Newbury Park, CA: Sage.

RUSHTON, J. PHILIPPE (1995). "Race and crime: An international dilemma." *Society* 32: 37–41.

SAVITZ, LEONARD D. (1972). "Introduction to the reprint edition." In Gina Lombroso-Ferrero, *Criminal Man: According to the Classification of Cesare Lombroso,* reprint ed., v–xx. Montclair, NJ: Patterson Smith.

SAVITZ, LEONARD D., STANLEY H. TURNER, and TOBY DICKMAN (1977). "The origins of scientific criminology: Franz Joseph Gall as the first criminologist." In R. F. Meier, ed., *Theory in Criminology,* 41–56. Beverly Hills, CA: Sage.

SCHAFER, STEPHEN (1976). *Introduction to Criminology.* Reston, VA: Reston.

SCHLAPP, MAX G., and EDWARD H. SMITH (1928). *The New Criminology.* New York: Boni and Liveright.

SCHLESINGER, LOUIS B. , ed. (1996). *Explorations in Criminal Psychopathology: Clinical Syndromes with Forensic Implications.* Springfield, IL: Charles C. Thomas.

SCHOENTHALER, STEPHEN (1982). "Diet and crime: An empirical examination of the value of nutrition in the control and treatment of incarcerated juvenile offenders." *International Journal of Biosocial Research* 4: 25–39.

SCHUESSLER, KARL F., and DONALD R. CRESSEY (1953). "Personality characteristics of criminals." *American Journal of Sociology* 55: 166–176.

SCHULSINGER, FINI (1972). "Psychopathy, heredity and environment." *International Journal of Mental Health* 1: 190–206.

SELLIN, THORSTEN (1968). "Enrico Ferri: Pioneer in criminology." In S. Grupp, ed., *The Positive School of Criminology: Three Lectures by Enrico Ferri*, iii–xvi. Pittsburgh: University of Pittsburgh Press.

———— (1972). "Enrico Ferri." In Hermann Mannheim, ed., *Pioneers in Criminology*, 2nd ed., 361–384. Montclair, NJ: Patterson Smith.

SHAH, SALEEM A., and LOREN H. ROTH (1974). "Biological and psychophysiological factors in criminality." In D. Glaser, ed., *Handbook of Criminology*, 101–173. Chicago: Rand McNally.

SHELDON, WILLIAM H. (1949). *Varieties of Delinquent Youth: An Introduction to Constitutional Psychiatry*. New York: Harper and Row.

SHOCKLEY, WILLIAM (1967). "A `try simplest cases' approach to the heredity-poverty-crime problem." *Proceedings of the National Academy of Sciences* 57: 1767–1774.

TARDE, GABRIEL (1890). *Penal Philosophy*. Trans. Rapelje Howell. Boston: Little, Brown. (Reprinted 1912.)

VOLAKVA, JAN (1995). *Neurobiology of Violence*. Washington, DC: American Psychiatric Press.

WALDO, GORDON P., and SIMON DINITZ (1967). "Personality attributes of the criminal: An analysis of research studies, 1950–1965." *Journal of Research in Crime and Delinquency* 4: 185–202.

WALSH, ANTHONY (1995). "Genetic and cytogenetic intersex anomalies: Can they help us to understand gender differences in deviant behavior? " *International Journal of Offender Therapy and Comparative Criminology* 39: 151–166.

WALTERS, GLENN D. (1989). "Putting more thought into criminology." *International Journal of Offender Therapy and Comparative Criminology* 30: v–vii.

———— (1990). *The Criminal Lifestyle*. Beverly Hills, CA: Sage.

———— (1992). "A meta-analysis of the gene-crime relationship." *Criminology* 4: 595–610.

———— (1995). "The psychological inventory of criminal thinking styles. Part I: Potential influences of personality, work environment, and occupational role." *Criminal Justice and Behavior* 22: 307–325.

WALTERS, GLENN D., and THOMAS W. WHITE (1989a). "The thinking criminal: A cognitive model of lifestyle criminality." *Criminal Justice Research Bulletin* 4: 1–10.

———— (1989b). "Heredity and crime: Bad genes or bad research?" *Criminology* 27:455–486.

———— (1991). "Attachment and social bonding in maximum and minimum security prisons." *American Journal of Criminal Justice* 16(1):1–15.

WHITE, JENNIFER L., TERRIE E. MOFFITT, FELTON EARLS, LEE ROBINS, and PHIL A. SILVA (1990). "How early can we tell? Predictors of childhood conduct disorder and adolescent delinquency." *Criminology* 28: 507–533.

WILSON, JAMES Q., and RICHARD J. HERRNSTEIN (1985). *Crime and Human Nature*. New York: Simon and Schuster.

WOLFGANG, MARVIN E. (1972). "Cesare Lombroso." In Hermann Mannheim, ed., *Pioneers in Criminology*, 2nd ed., 232–291. Montclair, NJ: Patterson Smith.

YOCHELSON, SAMUEL, and STANTON E. SAMENOW (1976). *The Criminal Personality*. Vol. 1: *A Profile for Change*. New York: Jason Aronson.

———— (1977). *The Criminal Personality*. Vol. 2: *The Change Process*. New York: Jason Aronson.

4

THE CHICAGO SCHOOL

INTRODUCTION

The University of Chicago established the first department of sociology in 1892, and through the mid-twentieth century it was one of the dominant forces in American sociological thought. The diverse group of scholars associated with the department were collectively referred to as the "Chicago School" of sociology and criminology. Although we focus on their work in criminology, many of the major themes running through their studies are also found in the related fields of social psychology and urban sociology.

One recurrent theme of the school is that human behavior is developed and changed by the social and physical environment of the person rather than by genetic structure. As David Matza (1969) wrote, it was assumed people are complex creatures who are capable of great diversity in their lifestyles. In support of this view, the Chicago School scholars considered the community to be a major influence on human behavior. They believed a city is a natural human environment, "a microcosm of the human universe."

The methods by which the Chicago School studied the individual and the city were in themselves contributions to sociology and criminology. Developing an *empirical sociology*, researchers moved beyond social philosophy and armchair theory and began to study individuals in their social environment. At the same time, they examined people in the aggregate and as individuals. The *life history* provided a method of reaching deeply into the cumulative factors and events shaping the lives of individuals. However, the *ecological study* technique allowed them to transcend individuality and, through the collection of social data, gain a sense of the characteristics of large groups of people. Combining the information gathered from individual cases with population statistics, the Chicago School thereby constructed a framework that has been the basis for most of our criminological theories ever since.

THE HERITAGE OF THE SCHOOL

The Social Heritage

Those who worked in the social sciences during the early twentieth century dealt with the development of the big cities, rapid industrialization, mass immigration, the effects of the First World War, Prohibition, the Great Depression, and more. Through it all, the members of the Chicago School looked to the city of Chicago as a source of questions and answers. Indeed, the urbanization of the nation led many scholars to believe the city was responsible for most of the problems of society.

From a small settlement of the early 1800s, Chicago grew rapidly as "cheap labor" rushed to take advantage of canal work and inexpensive land. Opportunity attracted the abundant unskilled workers necessary to encourage industrial growth. Chicago doubled its population in the three decades between 1898 and 1930 as waves of immigrants transformed the simpler fabric of small-town uniformity into complex and conflicting patterns of urban life (Cressey, 1938:59). When the limits of industrialization were reached and the displacement of workers by technology began, the demand for a large, mobile, unskilled population disappeared, leaving a tangle of social problems ranging from inadequate housing and sanitation to homelessness, juvenile gangs, and vice.

Away from their closely knit families and familiar communities, many people found that there was no one to whom they could turn in troubled times. Thousands of unemployed people—male and female, young and old—became transients to avoid burdening relatives or friends. To counter these problems, many social work organizations and relief programs emerged between 1920 and 1930. Based on an implicit faith in the value of case work and rehabilitation, they sought to employ and thus reform the troubled masses. Though much attention was focused on the needs of the poor, it was also recognized that crime seemed to be fostered in the slums. The study of the slums, the immigrants living there, and crime became politically and socially relevant (Kobrin, in Laub, 1983a:89).

Representing the last major wave of immigrants to the United States, southern and eastern Europeans received much of the blame for the nation's conditions. Among an existing population derived largely from western and northern Europe, the new immigrants were discriminated against and looked on as inferior stock. Aside from the prejudices inspired by peculiar customs and mannerisms, immigrants' loyalties were always suspect, particularly in times of war and political conflict. Children of immigrants, adapting more rapidly to the change in culture than their parents and grandparents, were often embarrassed by their families and drew away from them, forming their own support groups and gangs (Whyte, 1943).

The melting pot of the American dream was also a law-enforcement nightmare as it became apparent that city neighborhoods had few purposes or customs in common at any one time. People often felt the law was not theirs and refused to support or contribute to its enforcement. The search for a solution to these problems turned the city into a human laboratory for the new sociologists at the University of Chicago.

The Intellectual Heritage

Until the early twentieth century, American criminology had drawn from its European (Italian and English) heritage and supported popular Positivist explanations of crime, usually of the biological variety. Much of the previous research had linked feeblemindedness and hereditary factors with delinquency (Shaw and McKay, 1931:4). A change in this perspective came with the rise of cultural (rather than biological) theories of the behavior of individuals and groups.

As sociology moved into the study of crime, German influence began to take hold. As Martin Bulmer (1984:38) notes in his history of the Chicago School, the leading figures in sociology had studied in Germany and were profoundly influenced by that experience. The German approach (as well as that of the French sociologist Emile Durkheim), in contrast to the approach of the Italian Positivists, was preeminently social and cultural. At the same time, anthropology, under the leadership of Franz Boas and his students, had dedicated itself to demonstrating that human nature is almost solely a product of culture, not of biology (Edgerton, 1976). Under this general social science umbrella, the foundation was being laid for a new sociological criminology.

In addition to the substance of their work, American sociologists were trying to establish a reputation for scientific analysis in their field, to counteract the image of sociology as philosophical and speculative (Short, 1971:xii). The scientific study of social problems, especially of crime, became one way for sociologists to enhance their academic and scientific credibility. Painstakingly, they gathered facts about urban life, watching and recording the growth and structure of the developing city.

THE PERSPECTIVE OF THE SCHOOL

Methodological Contributions

Two major methods of study were employed by the Chicago School. The first was the use of **official data** (crime figures, census reports, housing and welfare records). This information was applied to geographical layouts of the city, indicating areas of high crime, truancy, and poverty. Charts and graphic portraits of social phenomena were maintained over periods of time, and the figures displayed a stability that led to a revolutionary thought in crime causation: certain areas of the city remained crime-prone even though various ethnic populations came and went.

The second method of study was the **life history.** W. I. Thomas first studied this form of folk psychology in Germany (Bulmer, 1984:36) and developed it into "ethnography" at the University of Chicago. This type of study shifted away from theoretical abstracts to the more intimate aspects of the real world. The life history or case study approach presented the social-psychological process of becoming a criminal or delinquent. Sociologists became research explorers; they met, talked with, ate with, and virtually lived with their subjects. As the everyday lives of addicts, hobos, and delinquents unfolded, the observers were invited to analyze the characters as they appeared in their natural environment, be it a slum, a street corner, or a railroad car. Borrowing the idea of studying plants and animals in their natural habitat, researchers attempted to present a human ecology, to interpret people in time and space as they naturally appear. For this reason the Chicago School was often referred to as the "Ecological School."

Ecological and Social Disorganization Theory

Perhaps as important as any other contribution of the Chicago School was the organic approach to the study of the community taken by Robert Park. Working under the assumption that the city is similar to a body with its different organs, Park sent his students out to examine the various organs, or "social worlds," of the metropolis (Farris, 1967:52). From these investigations and others, Park and Ernest Burgess produced a conception of the city as a series of distinctive concentric circles radiating from the central business district. The farther one moved away from the center of these **concentric zones,** the fewer social problems were found. The basic idea was that the growth of cities, and the location of various areas and social problems, is not random but instead is part of a pattern. Burgess's conception of the concentric zone pattern of city growth provided the foundation for later Chicago School explanations of crime and delinquency.

Using the ecological concepts of dominance, invasion, and succession from plant and animal ecology, the general theory maintained there are dominant uses of land within the zones. When those uses characteristic of an inner zone encroach on the adjacent outer zone, invasion occurs and that territory becomes less desirable. In time, the invading land uses replace the existing land uses, resulting in a new social and physical environment. In this way, the inner zone grows to include the adjacent outer zone, thus causing a ripple effect among all the zones.

The first zone was the *central business district,* with its businesses and factories but few residences. The zone next to it was referred to as the *zone of transition* because businesses and factories were encroaching on this area. This zone was not desirable as a location for residences and homes but owing to its deterioration was the cheapest place to live. Immigrants, then, usually settled into this second zone because it was inexpensive and near the factories where they could find work. As they could afford to move, they moved into the third zone, the *zone of workingmen's homes*, and were themselves replaced in the zone of transition by another wave of immigrants. Other zones radiating out from there were increasingly more expensive to live in.

Subsequent research noted that social ills seemed to follow a pattern in which the most problems were found in the first zone and progressively fewer problems were found in each succeeding zone. Clifford Shaw and Henry McKay, for instance, documented that rates of delinquency, tuberculosis, and infant mortality followed the same decreasing pattern as one moved away from the central business district. The ethnographic and life history work of the Chicago School was then, in part, devoted to explaining the effect of these ecological areas on social life.

The observations made by researchers provided a picture of the city as a place where life is superficial, people are anonymous, relationships are transitory, and kinship and friendship bonds are weak. The Chicago School saw the weakening of primary social relationships as a process of social disorganization. In turn, **social disorganization** became the primary explanation for the emergence of crime. Shaw and McKay's version of social disorganization is based on a conception of primary relationships similar to those found in a village. If relationships in the family and friendship groupings are good, neighborhoods are stable and cohesive, and people have a sense of loyalty to the area, then social organization is sound. Without these characteristics, a community or neighborhood is socially disorganized. Normal social control, which prevents crime and delinquency, cannot do its job. Robert Sampson and Byron Groves (1989) list four elements that constitute social disorganization: (1) low economic status, (2) a mixture of different ethnic groups, (3) highly mobile residents moving in and out of the area, and (4) disrupted families and broken homes. Thus, social disorganization is an explanation of the distribution of rates (or epidemiology) of crime and delinquency.

Shaw and McKay also noted that the zone of transition was more socially disorganized than other areas, primarily because of the high degree of mobility, the decaying neighborhoods, and the encroachment of the business and factory district. This was a particularly serious matter in the zone of transition because of the number of immigrants. Faced with the difficulty of maintaining primary relationships (and the difficulty of financially succeeding in a relatively class-bound society), immigrants retreated to the safety of their own native cultures. The relationship between immigrants and crime was finally seen not as a product of heredity but as a dual problem of social disorganization and of *conflict* with existing American culture.

Another contribution made by Shaw and McKay was their explanation of the process by which social disorganization affects juveniles and leads to delinquency, commonly referred to as **cultural transmission theory.** According to this theory, juveniles who live in socially disorganized areas have greater opportunities for exposure to those who espouse delinquent and criminal values. Indeed, one of the primary characteristics of those areas is that a delinquent tradition has developed. This delinquent tradition provides a way of transmitting delinquent values, as Shaw and McKay (1942:168) explain:

> The importance of the concentration of delinquents is seen most clearly when the effect is viewed in a temporal perspective. The maps representing distribution of delinquents at successive periods indicate that, year after year, decade after decade, the same areas have been characterized by these concentrations. This means that delinquent boys in these areas have contact not only with other delinquents who are their contemporaries but also with older offenders, who in turn had contact with delinquents preceding them, and so on back to the earliest history of the neighborhood. This contact means that the traditions of delinquency can be and are transmitted down through successive generations of boys, in much the same way that language and other social forms are transmitted.

In later chapters of this book, the similarity of social disorganization theory and cultural transmission theory to social control and differential association theories becomes evident. Thus, it can easily be argued that Shaw and McKay exerted a great deal of influence on the criminological theories following them.

Symbolic Interactionism

The social-psychological theory of **symbolic interactionism** has been one of the more lasting of the Chicago School's theoretical perspectives. Although the Chicago School theorists who developed it never referred to it by this name (Blumer, 1969:1), symbolic interactionism developed from a belief that human behavior is the product of purely social symbols communicated between individuals. A basic idea of symbolic interactionism is that the mind and the self are not innate but are products of the social environment. It is in the process of communicating, or symbolizing, that humans come to define both themselves and others. These symbols have meanings affecting the way we see the world. If, for example, we are introduced to a juvenile delinquent, we may not see the person but may view him or her as "the standard juvenile delinquent"; that is, we see someone who is all the things we expect a juvenile delinquent to be.

Further, we pick up our own self-concept from our perception of what others think about us. These others are not necessarily specific individuals but, often, generalized types of people (George Mead [1934] called this abstract person the "generalized other"). Thus, we create our own identities by reflection from others. W. I. Thomas's addition of situations led to the understanding that we can have many identities, or self-concepts, depending on the setting in which we find ourselves. In the school setting, one may be a student; at home, a parent; at work, an insurance salesperson; at play, the team captain; in our parents' house, a child; and so forth. Each situation demands its own role, its own identity, its own behaviors. Moreover, in social life, one may incorrectly define the situation and behave inappropriately. To paraphrase Thomas's famous saying, a proper definition of the situation is necessary for one to respond with acceptable behavior.

This recognition of the complexity and relativity of social life, with its multiplicity of required roles, gave the Chicago School an understanding of deviance. Such an understanding required the ability to view human behavior, and guidelines for that behavior, as *relative*. For the Chicago School, there were no absolutes, no set of universal rules governing human behavior. First, there are places where normal behaviors would be defined by those outside of the place as deviant, in the "hobo jungles," for example. There people engage in "deviant" behavior by correctly defining the situation and following the roles expected of them. The behavior is not, of course, deviant from the perspective of that specific setting but only from the perspective of outside society. Second, people can misdefine situations, act inappropriately, and become deviant. Here it is the misreading of the situational guidelines that leads to rule-violating behavior. For instance, at the street corner near your home you may legally make a right turn at a red light. Elsewhere, you may erroneously assume, much to your dismay when you get a ticket, that right turns are also allowed.

Symbolic interactionism, then, provided a true social origin for both self-concepts and behaviors. It also gave us a relativistic (i.e., situational) understanding of the rules and guidelines that govern behavior. The Chicago School gave criminology an appreciation of the effect of social settings and situational values on crime and deviant behavior, which served to offset the universal rule approach of the Positive School. The appearance of the labeling perspective in the criminological writing of the 1960s was directly related to this theoretical approach.

Culture Conflict

Having taken a relativistic position on human values and behavior, it was only natural for the Chicago School to recognize that conflict is common in society. Robert Park, impressed by the thoughts of a dominant German conflict sociologist, Georg Simmel, incorporated the notion of conflict as a central component of an influential sociology textbook that he wrote with Ernest Burgess (1924). Here conflict is viewed as a major social process, set in motion by the differences in values and cultures among groups of people. Louis Wirth, one of Park's students, wrote a thesis on cultural conflicts in immigrant families (1925), and a few years later (1931) wrote about the relationship of the conflict of cultures to crime and delinquency. Another graduate (and subsequently a faculty member) of the Chicago School, Edwin Sutherland, also wrote (1929) on conflicting values and how criminal behavior arises from them.

The best statement of culture conflict theory, however, came from a scholar who was not a member of the Chicago School. In his book *Culture*

Conflict and Crime (1938), Thorsten Sellin produced what is seen today as the seminal work on culture conflict. Although the book was to have been written with Sutherland as a project of the Social Science Research Council, Sellin alone completed the work. The central thesis of culture conflict, though, was borrowed from the writings and teachings of Wirth and others at the University of Chicago (Sellin, in Laub, 1983b).

Sellin's culture conflict theory revolves around the idea of **conduct norms,** or rules that govern behavior. In this sense, conduct norms are similar to W. I. Thomas's concept of definitions for behavior. According to Sellin, one is reared with cultural values about proper conduct. The content of those norms varies from culture to culture. Groups with social and political power can even use their conduct norms to control the definition of crime. Thus, the legal definition of crime is but the conduct norm for one particular social group. People come in conflict with these legal definitions of behavior accidentally or intentionally. If one's own culture approves an act but the dominant culture does not, the stage is set for criminal behavior.

Sellin suggested that there are two main forms of culture conflict. The first, called **primary conflict,** occurs when two different cultures govern behavior, for example, when someone from one culture emigrates to another cultural area. The "old" culture cannot simply be cast off, and for a while it continues to influence the person's behavior. Sellin's classic example of this involves an "Old World" family who moved to New Jersey: the daughter was seduced by a young man, and her father, following an Old World tradition, killed him to protect the family honor. The father was arrested, yet he

---

AN EXAMPLE OF PRIMARY CULTURE CONFLICT

Minors' Forced Marriages Lead to 3 Arrests

Lincoln, Neb.—An Iraqi refugee accused of forcing his 13- and 14-year-old daughters to marry men twice their age in an Islamic ceremony was jailed on child abuse charges, and the alleged husbands were charged with rape.

A university professor from Iraq and a lawyer for the so-called husbands said the three men were following Islamic tradition and did not intend to violate state law.

"It is a clash between cultural mores and U.S. law," said Terry Cannon, a lawyer for two of the alleged husbands. The recent immigrants were jailed on $50,000 bail each and could get up to 50 years in prison.

The father, a school janitor on disability, was jailed on $10,000 bail. He faces up to six months in jail and a $1,000 fine.

Nebraska requires people to be 17 or older to marry.

Source: Paul Dean, "Cultures at the Crossroads" *Los Angeles Times*, December 13, 1996: E1, E4.

could not understand why, since from his cultural perspective he had committed no crime. Another example of primary conflict is when one country conquers another and imposes its laws on the conquered people. For a while, citizens of the conquered nation run afoul of some of the new laws simply because they are not yet accustomed to the new laws.

The other form of culture conflict is called **secondary conflict.** Here, Sellin was referring to smaller cultures existing within a larger culture; the term we might use today is "subculture." People who live in a geographic area begin, over a period of time, to create their own set of values (conduct norms). While these values are not wholly different from those of the larger culture, there are enough differences to give rise to conflict. The people within an urban, center-city neighborhood, for example, may develop values leading to law breaking. The agents of the law, of course, respond from the framework of laws based on middle-class values, laws that do not allow for subcultural differences. Thus, some subcultures see gambling and prostitution as legitimate behaviors, but the larger society has usually declared them illegal. Because of their values, then, the members of such subcultures are more likely to be arrested for gambling and prostitution than are other members of society whose values are more closely represented in law.

The notion of conflict, and culture conflict, as it grew from the Chicago School, have strongly influenced American sociological criminology. In his book *Explaining Crime* (1974:141), Gwynn Nettler states that all subsequent social explanations have been based on the assumption that culture conflict is the fundamental source of crime. While his point may be arguable, the relativistic conflict approach of the Chicago School has been critical to the further development of criminology.

CLASSIFICATION OF THE SCHOOL

As diverse in its viewpoints as it was, the Chicago School still shared a few commonalities. The main thrust of its work, for instance, was *positivist* in character, albeit of a "newer" social variety. The assumption of determinism strongly characterized all the work of the school, from the initial symbolic interactionism of Mead and Thomas to the statistical work of Shaw and McKay. Further, the positivist emphasis on systematic observation and testing is clearly reflected in the work of the Chicago School. It is clear that Chicago criminologists saw pathology in the city, and they conducted their studies in an effort to learn what was wrong. Ultimately, they wanted to correct the social ills of the city, and crime and delinquency were high on their list. The Chicago School also helped create what may be the best criminological examples of using theory to develop reform and treatment programs.

It is difficult to classify the Chicago School as either structural or processual, largely because different members of the school stressed different factors in their explanations of society. Regardless of any assumptions they might have made about the structure of society (seen most clearly in the later work of Shaw and McKay [1942]), the dominant orientation was that of *process*. All those associated with the Chicago School stressed the processes involved in behavior, the ways that people come to act in response to other people, real or imagined. Even the reliance on social disorganization (in reality a structural element) was derived from a different source from that of the anomie-strain theories that followed later [see Chapter 6]. For the Chicago School, the product of social disorganization was a variety of conduct norms and behavior rules, not societal strain. These various norms result in deviance as members of different groups or subcultures apply different definitions to the situations they commonly shared. Thus, the school's focus was on the process of gaining definitions, and its underlying question was: how do individuals use their definitions of self and situation to produce behavior?

Chicago School theorists were, at heart, *consensus* theorists. This does not mean that they did not emphasize conflict—they did. The assumption, however, was that consensus, or a natural conformity to cultural lifeways, is the initial pattern of human behavior. This was demonstrated by their appreciation of diversity in human behavior, yet it was a patterned diversity, one shared by the members of the culture to which one belongs. It was only where one group came into contact with another that conflict developed. And, of course, these theorists recognized that society is made up of a variety of cultural groups; therefore, conflict is simply a fact of life.

Finally, the Chicago School produced chiefly *microtheories* (with the exception of culture conflict, which is a macrotheory). The social-psychological approach to the study of human behavior dominated almost all the work of these theorists and became the common thread that wound through the diverse positions they espoused. They focused more on the process of becoming deviant than on explaining how the structure of society affects deviant behavior. This is somewhat ironic, given that members of the Chicago School developed the study of ecological rates and prepared the evidence for most of the macrotheoretical work that followed.

SUMMARY

Although the sociological approach to studying modern problems started out as the interest of a small group of professors and students, the second generation of scholars expanded their interest into the realm of city programs and local research offices. The theoretical positions advanced by the Chicago School became the basis for much of the criminological work of the next three decades (1940s through the 1960s). The theoretical explanations that the Chicago School theorists (and their followers) gave to their research data can still be found behind many contemporary criminological theories. In short, because of its widespread influence, the Chicago School was the discipline of criminology prior to the late 1950s.

Major Points of the School

1. Humans are social creatures, and their behavior is a product of their social environment.
2. Social environments provide cultural values and definitions that govern the behavior of those who live within them.
3. Urbanization and industrialization have created communities that have a variety of competing cultures, thus breaking down older and more cohesive patterns of values.
4. This breakdown, or disorganization, of urban life has resulted in the basic institutions of family, friendship groups, and social groups becoming more impersonal.
5. As the values provided by these institutions become fragmented, several opposing definitions about proper behavior arise and come into conflict. Continued disorganization makes the potential for conflict even more likely.
6. Deviant or criminal behavior generally occurs when one behaves according to definitions that conflict with those of the dominant culture.
7. Social disorganization and social pathology are most prevalent in the center-city area, decreasing with distance from that area.
8. Crime and delinquency are transmitted by frequent contact with criminal traditions that have developed over time in disorganized areas of the city.

EPILOGUE: CURRENT DIRECTIONS
AND POLICY IMPLICATIONS

The work of the Chicago School, with its focus on cities, communities, and social organization, continued through the 1940s. After that time, two different approaches became dominant. Stressing individual deviance on the one hand, and the effect of cultural and societal structures on the other, the majority of criminologists spent their time on the theories of labeling, control, and anomie.[1] The community-based theories of the Chicago School did not disappear, however. Disciples of the Chicago School continued their work. In the late 1970s, however, the tradition gained renewed attention. The interest can probably be attributed to the emergence of victimization data. Whatever the reason, the Chicago School is still with us, with ecological/social disorganization theory currently enjoying a resurgence of popularity.

Some of the concerns of ecological criminology reappeared in the 1970s under the headings of **environmental design** and geographical criminology. Drawing from Jane Jacobs's ideas on urban renewal, C. Ray Jeffery suggested in 1969 that crime prevention should focus on changing the physical

---

1. It is not quite true to say that the Chicago School ideas fell into decline during the 1950s and 1960s. Two dominant theories, Albert Cohen's subculture theory and Richard Cloward and Lloyd Ohlin's differential opportunity theory, attempted to integrate the concepts of social disorganization and cultural transmission with anomie theory. A review of these theories can be found in Chapter 7. In addition, labeling theory is an offshoot of the Chicago School's symbolic interactionism and was the dominant theory of the 1960s. See Chapter 8 for an explanation of the relationship between symbolic interactionism and labeling theories.

environment rather than on changing the offender (something he saw as much more difficult). Oscar Newman (1972), an architect, further elaborated on environmental design with his notion of **defensible space.** Newman's idea was that any physical area would be better insulated against crime if those who live there recognize it as their territory and keep careful watch over the area. Because of the simplicity of the defensible space concept, the federal government adopted many of the architectural components into their regulations for constructing public housing. Moreover, the entire concept of environmental design generated many of today's crime prevention programs and served as the impetus for the neighborhood watch program. While Jeffery decries the emphasis on hardware, he and Newman are responsible for what may have been the main approach to crime control and prevention throughout the 1970s.

The late 1970s saw a renewed interest in the ecological and social disorganization perspective. Victimization studies, coupled with an article by Lawrence Cohen and Marcus Felson on "routine activities" (see Chapter 12), were instrumental in reviving research on the location of crime. Cohen (with others) followed this with a compex theory called "evolutionary ecology theory" (briefly discussed in Chapter 13). Not only were ecological studies popular again, but criminologists also set out to extend the ideas of Shaw and McKay (see Bursik, 1988). One of the major new directions has focused on the stability of ecological areas over time. Applying the concept of criminal careers to ecological areas, Albert Reiss, Jr., and others have begun researching and writing about **community crime careers.** Spurred by examinations of urban renewal and crime rates, this new direction asks how changes inside and outside of urban areas affect their crime rate patterns. The task now is to determine which natural social changes result in which kind of crime patterns (Kobrin and Schuerman, 1982; Bottoms and Wiles, 1986; Reiss, 1986; Schuerman and Kobrin, 1986). Others have combined environmental design, community ecological features, and criminal opportunities to explain rates of offending in areas that are identified as "hot spots" for crime.

In a perspective related to both environmental design and social disorganization, several criminologists (Hunter, 1978; Wilson and Kelling, 1982; Taylor and Gottfredson, 1986) have posited that deteriorated neighborhoods are related to social disinterest in the neighborhood (**incivility**). This in turn, creates a greater climate of fear and crime, which then results in fewer social controls and a more deteriorated neighborhood. In a similar vein, Rodney Stark (1987) presents an ecological theory that he calls *deviant places.* Stark's theory is contained in a detailed list of thirty propositions that capture much of the concept of incivility. Generally, he elaborates on the ecological theory claims of Shaw and McKay that varying neighborhood controls and structure result in varying crime rates. Moreover, Stark reiterates the Chicago School's position that "kinds-of-places" explanations are more important in understanding crime rates than "kinds-of-people" explanations. Other criminologists (Laub, 1983b; Sampson, 1985; Esbensen and Huizinga, 1990) have reported research results that lead them to believe that rather than an either-or choice between people and places, a better explanation of crime rates combines both approaches.

Concerning policy implications, the work of the Chicago School has been directly relevant. Shaw and McKay, working for the state of Illinois' Institute of Juvenile Research, implemented their theories almost from the very beginning. As Ruth Kornhauser (1978), Charles Tittle (1983), and Robert Bursik (1986) have pointed out, Shaw and McKay felt that the critical problem in social disorganization is the community's inability to regulate itself. Their long-lasting Chicago Area Project attempted to reorganize neighborhoods and provide the social organization they felt was lacking. Because Shaw and McKay felt that renewal and reorganization had to come from within, they worked to get people in the neighborhoods to institute and oversee the changes. They did this by helping create community organizations and committees, offering workers who could teach political skills, and helping the community reach out to city hall. They assisted communities in gaining political power and establishing control of their neighborhoods. Neighborhoods were encouraged to clean up the environment, and workers helped juveniles in trouble with the authorities. The projects that came out of this approach often involved the construction of recreation facilities and areas for juveniles in a community. This general approach to delinquency prevention spread widely throughout the United States and still constitutes one of the most popular solutions to delinquency (and other social problems).

In a 1986 article, Albert Reiss discusses several forms that policies derived from ecological theories may take. Generally, he notes that interventions focus on either the social structures or the social controls in the community (1986:23). Examples of such policies are those that intercede in juvenile peer groups to diminish their power and the establishment of housing regulations that distribute certain types of individuals throughout a complex, rather than grouping them. Reiss even suggests that public policies be questioned when they prevent or restrict a community from exercising control over itself. Of interest is his suggestion that impact reviews be required when proposed policies result in changes in social life, just as environmental impact reviews are now required before physical changes can take place.

In short, the ideas of the Chicago School are alive and well and probably living in your neighborhood. The "new" environmental design concepts, based on ecological evidence, are used by developers in the design and construction of subdivisions. The neighborhood convenience store has also used environmental design concepts to reduce victimization opportunities. Further, police departments have for years used a Chicago School invention called "spot maps" to help them pinpoint criminal activity. Now, the newer ecological approaches have contributed a variation on the old spot maps called "hot spot" analysis (discussed in Chapter 12). It should be evident from these remarks that the scholars of the Chicago School have provided us with a rich mixture of ideas, and we are just now beginning to tap some of them.

BIBLIOGRAPHY

ANDERSON, NELS (1923). *The Hobo*. Chicago: University of Chicago Press.

ATHENS, LONNIE H. (1980). *Violent Criminal Acts and Actors: A Symbolic Interactionist Study*. Boston: Routledge and Kegan Paul.

BACHMAN, RONET (1991). "An analysis of American Indian homicide: A test of social disorganization and economic deprivation at the reservation county level." *Journal of Research in Crime and Delinquency* 28: 456–471.

BENNETT, JAMES (1981). *Oral History and Delinquency: The Rhetoric of Criminology*. Chicago: University of Chicago Press.

BLUMER, HERBERT (1969). *Symbolic Interactionism: Perspectives and Method*. Englewood Cliffs, NJ: Prentice Hall.

BOGGS, SARAH (1965). "Urban crime patterns." *American Sociological Review* 30: 899–908.

BORIS, STEVEN B. (1979). "Stereotypes and dispositions for criminal homicide." *Criminology* 17: 139–158.

BOTTOMS, ANTHONY E., and PAUL WILES (1986). "Housing tenure and residential community crime careers in Britain." In A. Reiss and M. Tonry, eds., *Communities and Crime. Crime and Justice: A Review of Research*, vol. 8., 101–162. Chicago: University of Chicago Press.

BRANTINGHAM, PAUL J., and PATRICIA L. BRANTINGHAM (1978). "A theoretical model of crime site selection." In M. D. Krohn and R. L. Akers, eds., *Crime, Law and Sanctions*, 105–118. Beverly Hills, CA: Sage.

——— (1981). *Environmental Criminology*. Beverly Hills, CA: Sage.

BULMER, MARTIN (1984). *The Chicago School of Sociology*. Chicago: University of Chicago Press.

——— (1986). "The ecological fallacy: Its implications for social policy analysis." In M. Bulmer, ed., *Social Science and Social Policy*, 223–256. London: Allen and Unwin.

BURGESS, ERNEST W. (1925). "The growth of the city." In R. E. Park, E. W. Burgess, and Roderick D. McKenzie, eds., *The City*, 47–62. Chicago: University of Chicago Press.

BURSIK, ROBERT J., JR. (1984). "Urban dynamics and ecological studies of delinquency." *Social Forces* 63: 393–413.

——— (1986). "Ecological stability and the dynamics of delinquency." In A. Reiss and M. Tonry, eds., *Communities and Crime. Crime and Justice: A Review of Research*, vol. 8, 35–66. Chicago: University of Chicago Press.

——— (1988). "Social disorganization and theories of crime and delinquency: Problems and prospects." *Criminology* 26: 519–551.

BURSIK, ROBERT J., JR., and HAROLD G. GRASMICK (1993). *Neighborhoods and Crime: The Dimensions of Effective Community Control*. New York: Lexington Books.

BURSIK, ROBERT J., JR., and JIM WEBB (1982). "Community change and patterns of delinquency." *American Journal of Sociology* 88: 24–42.

BUTTELL, ALAN J., and WILLIAM THOMPSON (1986). "The environment of a traffic stop: A dramaturgical analysis." *American Journal of Police* 5(11): 29–44.

BYRNE, JAMES M., and ROBERT J. SAMPSON, eds. (1986). *The Social Ecology of Crime*. New York: Springer-Verlag.

CHARON, JOEL M. (1979). *Symbolic Interactionism: An Introduction, an Interpretation, an Integration*. Englewood Cliffs, NJ: Prentice Hall.

CHILTON, ROLAND J. (1964). "Continuity in delinquency area research: A comparison of studies for Baltimore, Detroit, and Indianapolis." *American Sociological Review* 29: 74–83.

COHEN, LAWRENCE E., BRYAN J. VILA, and RICHARD MACHALAK (1995). "Exppropriative crime and crime policy: An evolutionary ecological analysis." *Studies on Crime and Crime Prevention* 4: 197–219.

COOLEY, CHARLES H. (1902). *Human Nature and the Social Order.* New York: Scribner's.

——— (1909). *Social Organization.* New York: Scribner's.

COVINGTON, JEANETTE, and RALPH B. TAYLOR (1989). "Gentrification and crime: Robbery and larceny changes in appreciating Baltimore neighborhoods during the 1970s." *Urban Affairs Quarterly* 25: 142–172.

CRESSEY, PAUL F. (1938). "Population succession in Chicago: 1898–1930." *American Journal of Sociology* 44: 59–69.

CURRY, G. DAVID, and IRVING A. SPERGEL (1988). "Gang homicide, delinquency, and community." *Criminology* 26: 381–405.

D'ALLESIO, STEWART, and LISA STOLZENBERG (1990). "A crime of convenience: The environment and convenience store robbery." *Environment and Behavior* 22: 255–271.

DEFLEUR, LOIS B. (1967). "Ecological variables in the cross-cultural study of delinquency." *Social Forces* 45: 556–570.

DEFRONZO, JAMES (1996). "Welfare and burglary." *Crime and Delinquency* 42: 223–230.

EBBE, OBI N. I. (1989). "Crime and delinquency in metropolitan Lagos: A study of `crime and delinquency area' theory." *Social Forces* 67: 751–765.

EDGERTON, ROBERT (1976). *Deviance: A Cross-Cultural Perspective.* Menlo Park, CA: Cummings.

ELLIOTT, DELBERT S., WILLIAM JULIUS WILSON, DAVID HUIZINGA, ROBERT J. SAMSON, AMANDA ELLIOTT, and BRUCE RANKIN (1996). "The effects of neighborhood disadvantage on adolescent development." *Journal of Research in Crime and Delinquency* 33: 389–426.

ESBENSEN, FINN-AAGE, and DAVID HUIZINGA (1990). "Community structure and drug use: From a social disorganization perspective." *Justice Quarterly* 7: 691–709.

EVANS, DAVID J., and DAVID T. HERBERT, eds. (1989). *The Geography of Crime.* London: Routledge.

FARBER, BERNARD (1988). "The human element: Sociology at Chicago." *Sociological Perspectives* 31: 339–359.

FARRINGTON, DAVID P., ROBERT J. SAMPSON, and PER OLOF WIKSTROM, eds. (1993). *Integrating Individual and Ecological Aspects of Crime.* Stockholm: National Council on Crime Prevention

FARRIS, ROBERT E. L. (1967). *Chicago Sociology: 1920–1932.* Chicago: University of Chicago Press.

FIGLIO, ROBERT M., SIMON HAKIM, and GEORGE F. RENGERT, eds. (1986). *Metropolitan Crime Patterns.* Monsey, NY: Criminal Justice Press.

FIGUEIRA-MCDONOUGH, JOSEFINA (1991). "Community structure and delinquency: A typology." *Social Service Review* 65: 65–91.

——— (1992). "Community structure and female delinquency rates: A heuristic discussion." *Youth and Society* 24: 3–30.

FRASER, MARK W. (1996). "Aggressive behavior in childhood and early adolescence: An ecological-developmental perspective on youth violence." *Social Work* 41: 347–361.

GEORGES-ABEYIE, DANIEL E., and KEITH D. HARRIES, eds. (1980). *Crime: A Spatial Perspective.* New York: Columbia University Press.

GOLD, MARTIN (1987). "Social ecology." In Herbert C. Quay, ed., *Handbook of Juvenile Delinquency,* 62–105. New York: John Wiley.

GOTTFREDSON, DENISE C., RICHARD J. MCNEIL, III, and GARY D. GOTTFREDSON (1991). "Social area influences on delinquency: A multilevel analysis." *Journal of Research in Crime and Delinquency* 28: 197–226.

GOVE, WALTER R., and MICHAEL L. HUGHES (1980). "Reexamining the ecological fallacy: A study in which aggregate data are critical in investigating the pathological effects of living alone." *Social Forces* 58: 1157–1177.

GREENBERG, STEPHANIE, WILLIAM ROHE, and JAY R. WILLIAMS (1982). *Safe and Secure Neighborhoods: Physical Characteristics and Informal Territorial Control in High and Low Crime Neighborhoods.* Washington, DC: National Institute of Justice.

HAGEDORN, JOHN M. (1991). "Gangs, neighborhoods, and public policy." *Social Problems* 38: 529–542.

HARRIES, KEITH D. (1980). *Crime and the Environment.* Springfield, IL: Charles C. Thomas.

——— (1995). "The ecology of homicide and assault: Baltimore city and county, 1989–91." *Studies on Crime and Crime Prevention* 4: 44–60.

HEIMER, KAREN, and ROSS I. MATSUEDA (1994). "Role-taking, role commitment, and delinquency: A theory of differential social control." *American Sociological Review* 59: 365–390.

HEITGARD, JANET L., and ROBERT J. BURSIK, JR. (1987). "Extracommunity dynamics and the ecology of delinquency." *American Journal of Sociology* 92: 775–787.

HESSELING, RENE B. P. (1992). "Using data on offender mobility in ecological research." *Journal of Quantitative Criminology* 8: 95–106.

HUNTER, A. (1978). "Symbols of incivility." Paper presented at the annual meeting of the American Society of Criminology, Dallas, TX.

INGRAM, A. LEIGH (1993). "Type of place, urbanism, and delinquency: Further testing the determinist theory." *Journal of Research in Crime and Delinquency* 30: 192–212.

JACOBS, JANE (1961). *The Death and Life of Great American Cities.* New York: Vintage.

JEFFERY, C. RAY (1969). "Crime prevention and control through environmental engineering." *Criminologica* 7: 35–58.

——— (1971). *Crime Prevention through Environmental Design.* Beverly Hills, CA: Sage.

——— (1976). "Criminal behavior and the physical environment." *American Behavioral Scientist* 20: 149–174.

——— (1977). *Crime Prevention through Environmental Design,* rev. ed. Beverly Hills, CA: Sage.

JOE, KAREN A. (1995). "Delinquency in Chicago during the roaring twenties: Assembling reality in ethnography." *Journal of Gang Research* 3: 19–32.

JOHNSTONE, JOHN W. C. (1978). "Social class, social areas, and delinquency." *Sociology and Social Research* 63: 49–72.

JONASSEN, CHRISTEN T. (1971). "A re-evaluation and critique of the logic and some methods of Shaw and McKay." In H. L. Voss and D. M. Petersen, eds., *Ecology, Crime and Delinquency,* 133–145. New York: Meredith.

KAPSIS, ROBERT E. (1978). "Residential succession and delinquency: A test of Shaw and McKay's theory of cultural transmission." *Criminology* 15: 459–486.

KENNEDY, LESLIE W., ROBERT A. SILVERMAN, and DAVID R. FORDE (1991). "Homicide in urban Canada: Testing the impact of economic inequality and social disorganization." *Canadian Journal of Sociology* 16: 397–410.

KNOX, GEORGE (1981). "Social disorganization models of deviance." In G. F. Jensen, ed., *Sociology of Delinquency,* 78–92. Beverly Hills, CA: Sage.

KOBRIN, SOLOMON (1959). "The Chicago Area Project—A 25-year assessment." *Annals of the American Academy of Political and Social Science* 322: 19–29.

KOBRIN, SOLOMON, and LEO SCHUERMAN (1982). "Interaction between neighborhood change and criminal activity." Draft final report. Los Angeles: University of Southern California, Social Science Research Institute.

KORNHAUSER, RUTH R. (1978). *Social Sources of Delinquency.* Chicago: University of Chicago Press.

KPOSOWA, AUGUSTINE J., and KEVIN D. BREAULT (1993). "Reassessing the structural covariates of U.S. homicide rates: A county level study." *Sociological Focus* 26: 27–46.

LANDER, BERNARD (1954). *Understanding Delinquency.* New York: Columbia University Press.

LAUB, JOHN (1983a). "Interview with Solomon Kobrin." In John Laub, *Criminology in the Making: An Oral History,* 87–105. Boston: Northeastern University Press.

———— (1983b). "Urbanism, race, and crime." *Journal of Research in Crime and Delinquency* 20: 283–298.

LEE, BARRETT A., RALPH S. OROPESA, BARBARA J. METCH, and AVERY M. GUEST (1984). "Testing the decline-of-community thesis: Neighborhood organizations in Seattle, 1929 and 1979." *American Journal of Sociology* 89: 1161–1188.

LEE, NELLA (1995). "Culture conflict and crime in Alaskan native villages." *Journal of Criminal Justice* 23: 177–189.

LENGERMANN, PATRICIA M. (1988). "Robert E. Park and the theoretical content of Chicago sociology: 1920–1940." *Sociological Inquiry* 58: 361–377.

LEVIN, YALE, and ALFRED LINDESMITH (1937). "English ecology and criminology of the past century." *Journal of Criminal Law and Criminology* 27: 801–816.

LEWIS, J. DAVID, and RICHARD L. SMITH (1980). *American Sociology and Pragmatism: Mead, Chicago Sociology, and Symbolic Interaction.* Chicago: University of Chicago Press.

LI, LIYING (1995). "Sociological explanations of crimes in late imperial China: 1744–1903." *International Journal of Comparative and Applied Criminal Justice* 19: 107–127.

LINDSTROM, FRED B., and RONALD A. HARDERT, eds. (1988). "Kimball Young on founders of the Chicago School." *Sociological Perspectives* 31: 269–297.

LOFLAND, LYN H. (1983). "Understanding urban life: The Chicago legacy." *Urban Life* 11: 491–511.

LYNCH, JAMES P., and DAVID CANTOR (1992). "Ecological and behavioral influences on property victimization at home: Implications for opportunity theory." *Journal of Research in Crime and Delinquency* 29: 335–362.

MATZA, DAVID (1969). *Becoming Deviant.* Englewood Cliffs, NJ: Prentice Hall.

MCKAY, HENRY D. (1967). "A note on trends in rates of delinquency in certain areas in Chicago." *Juvenile Delinquency and Youth Crime,* Appendix F. Washington, DC: U.S. Government Printing Office.

MCKENZIE, RODERICK D. (1924). "The ecological approach to the study of the human community." *American Journal of Sociology* 30: 287–301.

MEAD, GEORGE H. (1934). *Mind, Self, and Society.* Charles W. Morris, ed. Chicago: University of Chicago Press.

MIETHE, TERANCE D., MICHAEL HUGHES, and DAVID MCDOWALL (1991). "Social change and crime rates: An evaluation of alternative theoretical approaches." *Social Forces* 70: 165–185.

MIETHE, TERANCE D., and ROBERT F. MEIER (1994). *Crime and Its Social Context: Toward an Integrated Theory of Offenders, Victims, and Situations.* Albany: State University of New York Press.

MILES-DOAN, REBECCA, and SUSAN KELLY (1997). "Geographic concentration of violence between intimate partners." *Public Health Reports* 112: 135–141.

MOORE, JOAN, DIEGO VIGIL, and ROBERT GARCIA (1983). "Residence and territoriality in Chicano gangs." *Social Problems* 31: 182–194.

MORASH, MERRY (1984). "Establishment of a juvenile police record: The influence of individual and peer group characteristics." *Criminology* 22: 97–111.

MORIARTY, LAURA J. (1994). "Social disorganization theory, community empower-ment, and coalition building: Exploring the linkages." *Criminal Justice Policy Review* 6: 229–240.

MORRIS, TERRENCE (1958). *The Criminal Area*. London: Kegan Paul.

MORROW, K. BRENT, and GWENDOLYN T. SORELL (1989). "Factors affecting self-esteem, depression, and negative behaviors in sexually abused female adolescents." *Journal of Marriage and the Family* 51: 677–686.

NELSON, AMANDA L., ROSEMARY D. F. BROMLEY, and COLIN J. THOMAS (1996). "The geography of shoplifting in a British city: Evidence from Cardiff." *Geoforum* 27: 409–423.

NETTLER, GWYNN (1974). *Explaining Crime*. New York: McGraw-Hill.

NEWMAN, OSCAR (1972). *Defensible Space: Crime Prevention through Urban Design*. New York: Macmillan.

OHM, ROSE MARIE (1988). "The continuing legacy of the Chicago School." *Sociological Perspectives* 31: 360–376.

PARK, ROBERT E., and ERNEST W. BURGESS (1924). *Introduction to the Science of Sociology*, 2nd ed. Chicago: University of Chicago Press.

PARK, ROBERT E., ERNEST W. BURGESS, and RODERICK D. McKENZIE, eds. (1925). *The City*. Chicago: University of Chicago Press.

PERKINS, DOUGLAS D., JOHN W. MEEKS, and RALPH B. TAYLOR (1992). "The physical environment of street blocks and resident perceptions of crime and disorder: Implications for theory and measurement." *Journal of Environmental Psychology* 12: 21–34.

PERKINS, DOUGLAS D., ABRAHAM WANDERSMAN, and RICHARD C. RICH (1993). "The physical environment of street crime: Defensible space, territoriality and inci-vilities." *Journal of Environmental Psychology* 13: 29–49.

PETEE, THOMAS A., GREGORY S. KOWLASKI, and DON W. DUFFIELD (1994). "Crime, social disorganization, and social structure: A research note on the use of interurban ecological models." *American Journal of Criminal Justice* 19: 117–132.

POGREBIN, MARK R., and ERIC D. POOLE (1990). "Culture conflict and crime in the Korean-American community." *Criminal Justice Policy Review* 4: 69–78.

QUINNEY, RICHARD (1964). "Crime, delinquency, and social areas." *Journal of Research in Crime and Delinquency* 1: 149–154.

——— (1966). "Structural characteristics, population areas, and crime rates in the United States." *Journal of Criminal Law, Criminology and Police Science* 57: 45–52.

RAHAV, GIORA (1981). "Culture conflict, urbanism, and delinquency." *Criminology* 18: 523–530.

RAUSHENBUSH, WINIFRED (1979). *Robert E. Park: Biography of a Sociologist*. Durham, NC: Duke University Press.

REISS, ALBERT J., JR., ed. (1964). *Louis Wirth on Cities and Social Life*. Chicago: University of Chicago Press.

——— (1976). "Settling the frontiers of a pioneer in American criminology: Henry McKay." In J. F. Short, Jr., ed., *Delinquency, Crime and Society*, 64–88. Chicago: University of Chicago Press.

——— (1981). "Towards a revitalization of theory and research on victimization by crime." *Journal of Criminal Law and Criminology* 72: 704–713.

——— (1986). "Why are communities important to understanding crime?" In A. Reiss and M. Tonry, eds., *Communities and Crime. Crime and Justice: A Review of Research*, vol. 8, 1–33. Chicago: University of Chicago Press.

REISS, ALBERT J., JR., and MICHAEL TONRY, eds. (1986). *Communities and Crime. Crime and Justice: A Review of Research*, vol. 8. Chicago: University of Chicago Press.

RENGERT, GEORGE, and JOHN WASILCHICK (1985). *Suburban Burglary: A Time and Place for Everything*. Springfield, IL: Charles C. Thomas.

ROBINSON, WILLIAM S. (1950). "Ecological correlations and the behavior of individuals." *American Sociological Review* 15: 351–357.

ROSENBAUM, DENNIS P., and PAUL J. LAVRAKAS (1995). "Self-reports about place: The application of survey and interview methods to the study of small areas." In J. E. Eck and D. Weisburd, eds., *Crime and Place*, 285–314. Monsey, NY: Criminal Justice Press.

SAMPSON, ROBERT J. (1985). "Structural sources of variation in race-age-specific rates of offending across major U.S. cities." *Criminology* 23: 647–673.

——— (1986a). "Crime in cities: The effects of formal and informal social control." In A. Reiss and M. Tonry, eds., *Communities and Crime. Crime and Justice: A Review of Research,* vol. 8, 271–311. Chicago: University of Chicago Press.

——— (1986b). "Neighborhood family structure and the risk of criminal victimization." In J. Byrne and R. J. Sampson, eds., *The Social Ecology of Crime,* 25–46. New York: Springer-Verlag.

——— (1992). "Family management and child development: Insights from social disorganization theory." *Advances in Criminological Theory* 3: 63–94.

SAMPSON, ROBERT J., and THOMAS C. CASTELLANO (1982). "Economic inequality and personal victimization." *British Journal of Criminology* 22: 363–385.

SAMPSON, ROBERT J., and BYRON W. GROVES (1989). "Community structure and crime: Testing social disorganization theory." *American Journal of Sociology* 94: 774–802.

SCHLOSSMAN, STEVEN, and MICHAEL SEDLAK (1983). *The Chicago Area Project Revisited.* Santa Monica, CA: Rand.

SCHMID, CALVIN F. (1960). "Urban crime areas." *American Sociological Review* 25: 527–542, 655–678.

SCHUERMAN, LEO, and SOLOMON KOBRIN (1986). "Community careers in crime." In A. Reiss and M. Tonry, eds., *Communities and Crime. Crime and Justice: A Review of Research,* vol. 8, 67–100. Chicago: University of Chicago Press.

SELLIN, THORSTEN (1938). *Culture Conflict and Crime.* New York: Social Science Research Council.

SHANNON, LYLE W. (1986). "Ecological evidence of the hardening of the inner city." In R. M. Figlio, S. Hakim, and G. F. Rengert, eds., *Metropolitan Crime Patterns,* 27–53. Monsey, NY: Criminal Justice Press.

SHAW, CLIFFORD R. (1930). *The Jackroller.* Chicago: University of Chicago Press.

——— (1931). *The Natural History of a Delinquent Career.* Chicago: University of Chicago Press.

——— (1938). *Brothers in Crime.* Chicago: University of Chicago Press.

SHAW, CLIFFORD R., and HENRY D. MCKAY (1931). *Report on the Causes of Crime .* Vol 2: *Social Factors in Juvenile Delinquency.* National Commission on Law Observance and Enforcement, Report No. 13. Washington, DC: U.S. Government Printing Office.

——— (1942). *Juvenile Delinquency in Urban Areas.* Chicago: University of Chicago Press.

SHAW, CLIFFORD R., FREDERICK M. ZORBAUGH, HENRY D. MCKAY, and LEONARD S. COTTRELL (1929). *Delinquency Areas.* Chicago: University of Chicago Press.

SHICHOR, DAVID, and MENACHEM AMIR (1979). "Some ethnic aspects of official delinquency in Israel." *California Sociologist* 2: 69–83.

SHIHADEH, EDWARD S., and DARRELL J. STEFFENSMEIER (1994). "Economic inequality, family disruption, and urban black violence: Cities as units of stratification and social control." *Social Forces* 73: 729–751.

SHORT, JAMES F., JR. (1972). "Introduction to the revised edition." In C. R. Shaw and H. D. McKay, *Juvenile Delinquency and Urban Areas,* rev. ed., xxv–liv. Chicago: University of Chicago Press.

———— ed. (1971). *The Social Fabric of the Metropolis: Contributions of the Chicago School of Urban Sociology.* Chicago: University of Chicago Press.

SHORT, JAMES F., JR., SOLOMON KOBRIN, and ANTHONY SORRENTINO (1980). "Henry D. McKay: 1899–1980." *American Sociological Association Footnotes* 8 (October): 11.

SHORT, JAMES F., JR., and FRED L. STRODTBECK (1965). *Group Process and Gang Delinquency.* Chicago: University of Chicago Press.

SIMCHA-FAGAN, ORA, and JOSEPH E. SCHWARTZ (1986). "Neighborhood and delinquency: An assessment of contextual effects." *Criminology* 24: 667–699.

SLATIN, GERALD T. (1969). "Ecological analysis of delinquency: Aggregation effects." *American Sociological Review* 34: 894–907.

SMITH, DOUGLAS A., and G. ROGER JARJOURA (1988). "Social structure and criminal victimization." *Journal of Research in Crime and Delinquency* 25: 27–52.

SNODGRASS, JON (1976). "Clifford R. Shaw and Henry D. McKay: Chicago criminologists." *British Journal of Criminology* 16: 1–19.

SORRENTINO, ANTHONY (1972). *Organizing against Crime: Redeveloping the Neighborhood.* New York: Human Sciences Press.

SPERGEL, IRVING A. (1990). "Youth gangs: Continuity and change." In M. Tonry and N. Morris, eds., *Crime and Justice: A Review of Research,* vol. 12, 171–275. Chicago: University of Chicago Press.

STACK, STEVEN (1995). "The effect of temporary residences on burglary: A test of criminal opportunity theory." *American Journal of Criminal Justice* 19: 197–214.

STAHURA, JOHN M., and C. RONALD HUFF (1986). "Crime in suburbia, 1960–1980." In R. M. Figlio, S. Hakim, and G. F. Rengert, eds., *Metropolitan Crime Patterns,* 55–71. Monsey, NY: Criminal Justice Press.

STARK, RODNEY (1987). "Deviant places: A theory of the ecology of crime." *Criminology.* 25: 893–909.

STEINMETZ, SUZANNE K. (1998). *Duty Bound: Elder Abuse and Family Care.* Newbury Park, CA: Sage

STERN, SUSAN B., and CAROLYN A. SMITH (1995). "Family processes and delinquency in an ecological context." *Social Service Review* 69: 703–731.

SUTHERLAND, EDWIN H. (1929). "Crime and the conflict process." *Journal of Juvenile Research* 13: 38–48.

SUTTLES, GERALD D. (1968). *The Social Order of the Slum: Ethnicity and Territory in the Inner City.* Chicago: University of Chicago Press.

———— (1972). *The Social Construction of Communities.* Chicago: University of Chicago Press.

TAUB, RICHARD, D. GARTH TRYLOR, and JAN D. DUNHAM (1984). *Paths of Neighborhood Change: Race and Crime in Urban America.* Chicago: University of Chicago Press.

TAYLOR RALPH (1984). "Block crime and fear: Defensible space, local social ties, and territorial functioning." *Journal of Research in Crime and Delinquency* 13: 525–542.

TAYLOR, RALPH B., and JEANETTE COVINGTON (1988). "Neighborhood changes in ecology and violence." *Criminology* 26: 553–589.

———— (1993). "Community structural change and fear of crime." *Social Problems* 40: 374–397.

TAYLOR, RALPH B., and STEPHEN D. GOTTFREDSON (1986). "Environmental design, crime and prevention: Examination of community dynamics." In A. Reiss and M. Tonry, eds., *Communities and Crime. Crime and Justice: A Review of Research,* vol. 8, 387–416. Chicago: University of Chicago Press.

TAYLOR RALPH B., STEPHEN D. GOTTFREDSON, and SIDNEY BROWER (1980). "The defensibility of defensible space: A critical review and synthetic framework for future research." In T. Hirschi and M. Gottfredson, eds., *Understanding Crime: Current Research and Theory,* 53–71. Beverly Hills, CA: Sage.

THOMAS, WILLIAM I., and FLORIAN ZNANIECKI (1918). *The Polish Peasant in Europe and America.* Chicago: University of Chicago Press.

THRASHER, FREDERICK M. (1927). *The Gang*. Chicago: University of Chicago Press.

TITTLE, CHARLES (1983). "Social class and criminal behavior: A critique of the theoretical foundation." *Social Forces* 62: 334–358.

TOBY, JACKSON (1957). "Social disorganization and stake in conformity: Complementary factors in the predatory behavior of hoodlums." *Journal of Criminal Law, Criminology and Police Science* 48: 12–17.

TOY, CALVIN (1992). "Coming out to play: Reasons to join and participate in Asian gangs." *Gang Journal* 1: 13–29.

TRIPLETT, RUTH (1993). "The conflict perspective, symbolic interactionism, and the status characteristics hypothesis." *Justice Quarterly* 10: 541–558.

TURNER, JOHNATHAN H. (1988). "The mixed legacy of the Chicago School of sociology." *Sociological Perspectives* 31: 325–338.

VILA, BRYAN (1994). "A general paradigm for understanding criminal behavior: Extending evolutionary ecological theory." *Criminology* 32: 311–359.

VILA, BRYAN J., and LAWRENCE E. COHEN (1993). "Crime as strategy: Testing an evolutionary ecological theory of expropriative crime." *American Journal of Sociology* 98: 873–912.

WALKER, JEFFERY T. (1992). *Ecology and Delinquency in 1990: A Partial Replication and Update of Shaw and McKay's Study in Little Rock, Arkansas*. Unpublished dissertation. Hunstville, TX: Sam Houston State University.

——— (1994). "Human ecology and social disorganization revisit delinquency in Little Rock." In G. Barak, ed., *Varieties of Criminology: Readings from a Dynamic Discipline*, 47–78. Westport, CT: Praeger.

WALLIS, C. P., and R. MOLLIPHANT (1967). "Delinquent areas in the county of London: Ecological factors." *British Journal of Criminology* 7: 250–284.

WATERS, ROBERT (1988). "Race and the criminal justice process: Two empirical studies on social enquiry reports and ethnic minority defendants." *British Journal of Criminology* 28: 82–94.

WEISHEIT, RALPH A., and EDWARD L. WELLS (1996). "Rural crime and justice: Implications for theory and research." *Crime and Delinquency* 42: 379–397.

WHYTE, WILLIAM F. (1943). *Street Corner Society: The Social Structure of an Italian Slum*. Chicago: University of Chicago Press.

WIKSTROM, PER-OLOF H. (1991). *Urban Crime, Criminals, and Victims: The Swedish Experience in an Anglo-American Comparative Perspective*. New York: Springer-Verlag.

WILKS, JUDITH A. (1967). "Ecological correlates of crime and delinquency." In Appendix A, President's Commission on Law Enforcement and the Administration of Justice, Task Force Report: *Crime and Its Impact: An Assessment*, 138–156. Washington, DC: U.S. Government Printing Office.

WILSON, JAMES Q., and GEORGE L. KELLING (1982). "Broken windows: The police and neighborhood safety." *Atlantic* 249: 29–38.

WIRTH, LOUIS (1925). *Culture Conflicts in the Immigrant Family*. Unpublished master's thesis, Sociology Department, University of Chicago.

——— (1931). "Culture conflict and misconduct." *Social Forces* 9: 484–492.

WITT, DAVID D. (1987). "A conflict theory of family violence." *Journal of Family Violence* 2: 291–301.

ZORBAUGH, HARVEY W. (1929). *The Gold Coast and the Slum*. Chicago: University of Chicago Press.

5

DIFFERENTIAL ASSOCIATION THEORY

INTRODUCTION

Edwin H. Sutherland presented his theory of differential association in two versions, the first in 1939 and the final version in 1947. The latter is still found in its original form in Sutherland and Donald Cressey's *Criminology* (1978, in its tenth edition and with David Luckenbill added as third author in the eleventh edition, 1992). Sutherland created a general theory of criminal behavior by insisting behavior is *learned* in a social environment. In fact, for Sutherland, all behavior is learned in much the same way. Therefore, the major difference between conforming and criminal behavior is in *what* is learned rather than in *how* it is learned.

In the 1920s and 1930s it was still common to assert crime is the result of individual biological or mental defects. In the first two editions of his *Principles of Criminology*, Sutherland criticized and rejected both of these positions and in so doing, advanced the cause of sociological criminology. Criminologist C. Ray Jeffery (1977:97) has even said criminology is allied with the discipline of sociology today because of Sutherland.

Within the sociological criminology of the period, however, multiple-factor theories were popular. Sutherland's theory provided a much less complex and more coherent approach to the cause of crime and delinquency, yet it was well grounded in existing evidence. In a sense, his work set the tone for what we study and how we study it. Thus, we gain a great heritage from Sutherland, and his theory may be the most popular criminological theory of this century.

THE HERITAGE OF THE THEORY

The Social Heritage

Many of the insights that shaped Sutherland's theory came from events of the 1920s and 1930s. The Federal Bureau of Investigation had begun to produce yearly reports of crimes known to the police, the Uniform Crime Reports, and evidence was growing that certain categories of people are more likely to be criminals than others are. Since these people matched the Chicago School ecological data, official statistics seemed to support the view that crime is a part of the sociological domain rather than of the biological or psychological disciplines.

The Great Depression also served as fertile ground for sociological observations. As the Depression began, Sutherland served for a year with the Bureau of Social Hygiene in New York. He saw that people who previously had not been criminal, or even who had not been in contact with criminals, committed criminal acts as a direct result of their impoverished situation during the Depression. Others, comparatively well off, took advantage of the economic situation and manipulated banks and stocks. All these are forms of "crime" in which Sutherland had an interest since the 1920s. Crime and other criminal behaviors were obviously not inborn or the results of feeblemindedness (a popular "intelligence" explanation of crime during the 1910s and 1920s). Criminality was the product of situation, opportunity and, of course, values.

In addition, two other events occurred that may have affected Sutherland's views on criminal behavior: Prohibition and the criminalization of drug use. A colleague at the University of Indiana, Alfred Lindesmith, was working in both of these areas and had a great deal of interaction with Sutherland. These "new" forms of crime taught the astute observer that criminality is, in part, governed by the legal environment. Individuals who engaged in behavior that was not criminal at one point could become criminals by engaging in the same behavior subsequent to the mere passage of law. The focus on crime as defined by the legal codes was important to Sutherland largely because he saw society continually evaluated conduct in terms of adherence to the law. Though many positivists of this time preferred expanded sociological (or nonlegal) interpretations of crime, Sutherland saw the practical importance of working within legal parameters.

The Intellectual Heritage

The major intellectual influences on Sutherland's thinking came from the members of the Chicago School, particularly W. I. Thomas. The editor of a collection of Sutherland's papers even comments in his introduction that "Sutherland's theory of criminal behavior . . . may be regarded as an adaptation of the interactional sociology expounded by W. I. Thomas" (Schuessler, 1973:xi). In addition, symbolic interactionist materials developed by George

Mead, Robert Park, and Ernest Burgess's conception of the city as a multifaceted organism, the ecological work of Clifford Shaw and Henry McKay, and Sutherland's association with Thorsten Sellin were crucial to the actual development of his theory. Indeed, it was while Sutherland and Sellin worked together on a project for the Social Science Research Council to make criminology more scientific that they settled on culture conflict as the orienting strategy. Sutherland's critique of the final product led him to more thoroughly focus his own ideas. Sutherland himself taught at the University of Chicago from 1930 to 1935 and, throughout his life, never went far from the Chicago area (Vold, 1951). The fact that Sutherland was born, raised, and educated in a religious, rural Midwestern setting is also said to have influenced his perspective (Schuessler, 1973:x). His father was a religious fundamentalist and stern disciplinarian who was a minister, a college professor, and a college president. Mark Gaylord and John Galliher (1988) have made a case that his father was very influential in helping develop Sutherland's critical stance toward theory and evidence.

The two chief methodologies developed by the Chicago School, the examination of statistical information and the life history, were also important to Sutherland. Using the former approach, members of the Chicago School had already shown that, as the central area of a city was subjected to succeeding waves of immigrants, the high crime rates remained in the same *location*. Since the same high rates did not follow the residents who moved out into other areas of the city, it was obvious something (values) was being transmitted that kept the crime rates high (Shaw and McKay, 1931).

In the search for the causes behind high crime rates in certain areas, several theorists proposed that the answer lay in the conflict between different cultural groups (Sutherland, 1929; Wirth, 1931; Sellin, 1938). Because the central-city area was inhabited largely by immigrants (it was the cheapest place to live and closest to the factories and businesses where they worked), culture conflict theorists suggested their values and norms were simply different from those of the general population of Chicago. The source of the high crime rates, then, was not the area itself but the way in which the immigrants had been socialized to their native or "private" cultures in contrast to American or "public" culture (Schuessler, 1973:98).

The life history approach was also practiced by Sutherland in a collection of case histories from incarcerated immigrants and in a series of interviews and contacts with a professional thief beginning in about 1930. In a book based on this work, the thief, Chic Conwell, talked about learning the trade and the apprenticeship and recognition within the almost-institutionalized profession of thieves. This was, perhaps, for Sutherland the first analysis of how a group associating itself differently, isolating and reinforcing its values, could grow out of the general culture. This was also the first appearance of the term "differential association." There is, however, some controversy over the way the term is used in *The Professional Thief*, (1937) and the theoretical usage appearing later. Our own readings and the commentaries of others (Snodgrass, 1973:4–5; Gibbons, 1979:50) suggest the earlier use of the term was much narrower than the concept Sutherland conveyed in his theory. Indeed, in a discussion of the common, but mistaken, belief that Sutherland was referring to the members of groups who kept themselves apart from others, Cressey (in Sutherland and Cressey, 1978:86) said: "This kind of error may stem from Sutherland himself, for in his work on the professional thief he used the term `differential association' to characterize the members of the behavior system, rather than to describe the process presented in the first statement of his theory, two years later."

In formulating his theory, then, Sutherland drew on three major theories from the Chicago School: ecological and cultural transmission theory, symbolic interactionism, and culture conflict theory. In doing so, he was able to make sense of both the varying crime rates in society (the culture conflict approach) and the process by which individuals became criminal (the symbolic interactionist approach). Within this context, Sutherland formulated a theory that was an attempt to explain both individual criminal behavior and the variation in group (societal) rates of crime. He had to take into account that criminal behavior is not necessarily different from conventional behavior, values are important in determining behavior, and certain locations and people are more crime-prone than others.

A final major influence on Sutherland's thinking was an important critique of criminology written in 1933 by Jerome Michael and Mortimer J. Adler (Sutherland, 1973d; Cressey, 1979). They reviewed criminology and argued it had failed to produce sufficient scientific evidence, had developed no coherent theories, and had no rigorous standards. After first defending criminology against the critique, Sutherland set out to create a theory based on rigorous scientific standards. Differential association theory was the result. In keeping with his critical stance, Sutherland revised his theory in at least three drafts between 1939 and the publication of the last version in 1947. Even that last version was not meant to be final.

THE THEORETICAL PERSPECTIVE

The first suggestion of differential association theory came in the second edition of *Principles of Criminology* (1934). There, Sutherland (1934:51–52) stated:

> First, any person can be trained to adopt and follow any pattern of behavior which he is able to execute. Second, failure to follow a prescribed pattern of behavior is due to the inconsistencies and lack of harmony in the influences which direct the individual. Third, the conflict of cultures is therefore the fundamental principle in the explanation of crime.

This statement became the basis for differential association theory, which Sutherland developed more fully. Some versions attribute the "discovery" of differential association in this preliminary statement to Henry McKay

(Sutherland, 1973b:16). Gaylord and Galliher (1988) suggest Sutherland clearly knew what he was doing and his inherent modesty led him to credit his friends.

The first full version of the theory was proposed in 1939, with the publication of the third edition of *Principles*. This version referred to systematic criminal behavior and focused equally on both cultural conflict and social disorganization and on differential association. Sutherland would later eliminate the reference to systematic criminal behavior and limit the discussion of cultural conflict. When Sutherland used the term "systematic," he meant either "criminal careers or organized criminal practices" (1939:4). It is the latter that causes the most problems of understanding. Based on his commentary in the 1939 edition of *Principles*, as well as on later sources (Cressey, 1960b:3; Sutherland, 1973b:21 22), the reference to organized criminal practices seems to have meant those behaviors with supporting definitions readily available in the community and not just organized crime as we think of it today. This interpretation is supported by his choice of the term "adventitious" for nonsystematic criminal behavior. The difference from the final version of the theory, where he dropped the term "systematic," is not so marked as it would seem. Sutherland evidently felt systematic criminal behavior includes almost all forms of criminal behavior (Cressey, 1960b:3).

DIFFERENTIAL ASSOCIATION

By the term "differential association," Sutherland meant that "the contents of the patterns presented in association" would differ from individual to individual (1939:5). Thus, he never meant mere *association* with criminals would cause criminal behavior. Instead, the content of the communications from others was given primary focus. Sutherland viewed crime as a consequence of conflicting values; that is, the individual followed culturally approved behavior that was *disapproved* (and set in law) by the larger American society. Sutherland's own summary (1939:9) of the first version is "Systematic criminal behavior is due immediately to differential association in a situation in which cultural conflicts exist, and ultimately to the social disorganization in that situation." As an individual-level explanation, differential association theory is entirely a product of the social environment surrounding individuals and the values gained from important others in that social environment.

DIFFERENTIAL SOCIAL ORGANIZATION

The first version of differential association theory clearly explained more than the process of how individuals become delinquent. It was also an epidemiological theory of the distribution of crime rates and delinquency rates in society. Sutherland used the concepts of differential social organization and culture conflict to offer an explanation of why rates vary from group to group (Reinarman and Fagan, 1988). He believed, with his mentors in the Chicago School, that culture conflict is rampant in society. This conflict, in part a product of a disorganized society separated into many groups, creates many values and interests among the different societal groups. Inevitably, many of these values come into conflict, and some of them deal with values about the law. Groups with different values about the law (and lawful behavior) come into conflict with the authorities more often, resulting in higher rates of crime and delinquency. Indeed, high rates of crime can be used as an indicator of socially disorganized areas. Moreover, as Craig Reinarman and Jeffrey Fagan point out, the probability of differential association itself (and thus the learning of definitions) is a "function of differential social organization" (1988:311).

THE FINAL VERSION OF THE THEORY

The second, and final, version of the theory was proposed in the fourth edition of *Principles* in 1947. There Sutherland expressly incorporated the notion that all behavior is learned and, unlike other theorists of the time, moved away from referring to the varied cultural perspectives as "social disorganization." He used the term "differential social organization" or "differential group organization" instead. This allowed him more clearly to apply the learning process to a broader range of American society. The final version of differential association was proposed in nine points:

1. Criminal behavior is learned.
2. Criminal behavior is learned in interaction with other persons in a process of communication.
3. The principal part of the learning of criminal behavior occurs within intimate personal groups.
4. When criminal behavior is learned, the learning includes (a) techniques of committing the crime, which are sometimes very complicated, sometimes very simple; (b) the specific direction of motives, drives, rationalizations, and attitudes.
5. The specific direction of motives and drives is learned from definitions of the legal codes as favorable or unfavorable.
6. A person becomes delinquent because of an excess of definitions favorable to violation of law over definitions unfavorable to violation of law.
7. Differential associations may vary in frequency, duration, priority, and intensity.
8. The process of learning criminal behavior by association with criminal and anticriminal patterns involves all of the mechanisms that are involved in any other learning.
9. While criminal behavior is an expression of general needs and values, it is not explained by those general needs and values, since noncriminal behavior is an expression of the same needs and values. (Edwin H. Sutherland and Donald R. Cressey, *Criminology*, 10th ed. Philadelphia: J. B. Lippincott Co., 1978, pp. 80–82. With permission.)

Generally, then, differential association theory says criminal behavior is learned in association with intimate others by interacting and communicating with those others. Two basic things are learned: the techniques for committing criminal behavior, and the definitions (values, motives, drives, rationalizations, attitudes) supporting such behavior. Sutherland stressed a *relationship* must exist; that is, the transfer of skills or values cannot be accomplished merely by reading books or watching movies. The techniques may be thought of as the "how's," or the content of an act, and the definitions as the "why's," or the reasons for doing it.

The learning of techniques is important, but Sutherland focused less on that than on the learning of definitions. Bill McCarthy (1996) has recently argued that tutelage by those already skilled in criminal methods is crucial to understanding the theory. As an example, it makes no difference what definitions a would-be criminal has about the desirability of safe-cracking if he or she is unable to break into the safe. It is also obvious that criminal tutors provide definitions favorable to breaking the law. However, as Sutherland emphasized, most criminal behaviors require nothing more than what is learned during the course of daily activity. In other words, he saw most criminal behaviors as having essentially the same techniques that one learns from conventional behavior.

Criminal behavior occurs, according to Sutherland, when there is an excess of definitions favoring criminal behavior, as opposed to those definitions favoring conventional behavior. The phrase "excess of definitions," however, does not mean a simple excess as we might think of in numbers, but instead, the *weight* of definitions as determined by the quality and intimacy of interaction with others (frequency, priority, duration, and intensity). Sutherland saw individuals as operating on a balance or ratio of potential good and bad behavioral definitions. One could become a shoplifter in the same manner as one becomes a bricklayer. The resulting behavior often may be determined not only by the persons to whom one is exposed but also by the *absence* of alternative (criminal or noncriminal) patterns to fall back on.

In short, the theory of differential association does not necessarily emphasize *who* one's associates are; rather, it focuses on the *definitions* provided by those associations. Indeed, it suggests that once the techniques of criminal behavior are learned, the values (definitions) supporting that behavior may be learned from *anyone.*

The different social organizations to which individuals belong provide the associations from which a variety of forms of behaviors, both favoring and opposing legal norms, can be learned. Thus, the term "differential association" implies that individuals as well as groups are exposed to differing associations with people who vary in the importance they attach to respect for the law or law-abiding behavior. Individuals, then, will lean toward or away from crime according to the cultural standards of their associates, especially those with whom they spend frequent and long periods of time (Schuessler, 1973).

Once certain definitions exist, an individual tends to be more suscepti- ble to similar behavioral definitions (Sutherland, 1973e). This means an indi- vidual with an excess of criminal definitions will be open to new criminal definitions. Moreover, that individual will be less receptive to anticriminal definitions. Over time, as individuals interact within different groups, their patterns of definitions toward any behavior will change. Highly organized areas will have stable patterns of associations and offer consistent defini- tions to their residents. Unorganized areas will have high mobility and a mixture of cultural groups, resulting in inconsistent definitions and a greater likelihood that the ratio of criminal to anticriminal definitions will change frequently.

CLASSIFICATION OF THE THEORY

Differential association is a *positivist* theory in that it focuses on criminals and their behavior. For Sutherland, the real questions concern criminal behavior, not how criminal law came to be or even how the criminal justice system should be changed. Because of this approach, differential associa- tion is a *microtheory* when applied to etiological issues of criminal behavior. There is clearly a macrotheoretical component to Sutherland's theory, however. The theory is based on the concepts of differential social organi- zation and culture conflict. As we have noted earlier, differential associa- tion also has a societal and group explanation of crime and delinquency that predicts differing rates of crime. That component has, until recently, been largely ignored in favor of the processual, microtheoretical aspects of the theory.

In addition, the theory is oriented toward *conflict*. Sutherland's main objective was to explain how normative and cultural conflicts influence the learning of criminal behavior (Cressey, 1979). His work thus focused on con- flicting values, not on groups or classes with conflicting interests. In this sense, then, the theory is not a contemporary conflict theory. The key to clas- sifying Sutherland's differential association as a conflict theory lies in his recognition that a large number of values or definitions exist in society, some of which are favorable to law-abiding behavior and some of which are not. This version of society does not suggest a consensus of values, and Suther- land, in fact, referred to some laws as a product of the values of certain seg- ments of society.

Finally, differential association is a theory of *process*, rather than of structure. Granted, it takes into account facts about the structure of society and even argues for a structural explanation of crime rates, but the focus of the final version of the theory is on the process of becoming criminal. That is, Sutherland emphasizes the behavior itself and the processes operating to create criminal behavior as opposed to conventional behavior. It is this area of the theory that has contributed to its classification by many criminologists as a symbolic interactionist theory.

SUMMARY

Sutherland's differential association theory remains one of the most popular theories of criminal behavior today. The late Donald Cressey carried on as a champion of the theory and as coauthor of Sutherland's textbook. The theory itself is twofold. First, it states that differential group organization explains varying crime rates and, second, differential association explains individual criminal behavior. The former has been largely ignored, since criminal behavior was the express focus of Sutherland's nine propositions.

According to this theory, criminal behavior is based on interactions we have with others and the values we receive from others during those interactions. We learn values from important people (parents, close friends, important business associates) around us. Those values either support or oppose criminal behavior. To the extent that the weight of values is against criminal behavior, we will be law-abiding. On the other hand, if the weight of values supports criminal behavior, we will commit crime. Finally, an excess of values supporting criminal behavior does not mean we will commit *any* criminal behavior, just the one(s) specifically supported by the definitions.

Major Points of the Theory

1. Criminal behavior is learned in the same way as any other behavior.
2. Learning takes place in social settings and through what the people in those settings communicate.
3. The largest part of learning takes place in communication with those who are most important to us.
4. The intimate social environment provides a setting for learning two things: the actual way to accomplish a behavior (if necessary) and the values or definitions concerning that behavior.
5. These values about certain behavior may be in opposition to the established legal codes. To the extent we receive many statements about values, the *weight* of those statements (the importance and closeness of those who convey them) is more important than the actual number of statements.
6. Criminal behavior takes place when the weight of the values concerning a particular behavior is in opposition to the legal codes.
7. The great number of groups and cultures in society makes possible the learning of different types of values or definitions. The greater the number of groups and cultures in a specific area, the greater is the likelihood of learning definitions conducive to criminal behavior.
8. Some groups in society have more values in opposition to the legal codes than others (some are more in conflict); thus, some groups have higher crime rates than others.

EPILOGUE: CURRENT DIRECTIONS
AND POLICY IMPLICATIONS

As Ross Matsueda (1988:277–278) has observed, there have been three general trends in the way differential association theory has been treated over the years. In the 1950s, the trend was to focus on delinquent subcultures as a means of transmitting definitions conducive to delinquency. This meant explaining how delinquent subcultures form, why they continue, and how they transmit delinquent definitions and values. The work of Albert Cohen, and of Richard Cloward and Lloyd Ohlin, exemplify this approach. We treat both of these perspectives in greater detail in Chapter 7.

A second trend, in the 1950s and 1960s, was to return to the Chicago School roots of the theory and explain the symbolic interactionist relationships within differential association. An allied perspective, role theory, was an obvious candidate for merger into differential association. Cressey (1954), in replying to criticisms that differential association did not apply to crimes of passion and "compulsive crimes," used symbolic interactionism and role theory as a means of extending the direct propositions of the theory. Cressey's argument was rationalizations and verbalizations exist that motivate behavior. This **"vocabulary of motives"** combines with the role an individual identifies himself or herself as playing at the moment. Because learning a vocabulary of motives is achieved in the same way as learning any other set of values, Cressey felt compulsive crimes are well within the province of differential association theory. Another criminologist, Daniel Glaser (1956), combined the theory with the symbolic interactionist concept of identification to create **differential identification.** In this approach and later adaptations, Glaser (1960, 1978) used the differential association proposition relating to intensity of associations and specified the degree and strength of identification with another person as a key ingredient in the learning of values. The stronger the identification with another person, the more likely an individual is to accept the other's values. This extended to the learning of values from those who are not direct associates of an individual, such as public figures, actors, and athletes. Because the media in Sutherland's day were not as pervasive as they are today, he rejected the idea that the media could be a source of definitions. However, if Sutherland had lived longer, it is very likely that he would have accepted Glaser's addition to his theory.

The third trend, from the mid- until the late 1960s, attempted to explain the processes involved in the learning component of differential association through the use of psychologically based social learning theories. C. Ray Jeffery (1965), Robert Burgess and Ronald Akers (1966), and later Akers (1973, 1977) were the foremost examples. The major reason for these reinterpretations of the theory lay in the popular criticism that the major concepts in differential association are untestable because of their abstract nature. We describe social learning theories in detail in Chapter 11.

Recent interest in differential association theory has focused on testing the theory's various theoretical concepts, particularly the notion of associations. Almost invariably, this research has demonstrated that an association with delinquent or criminal peers has a major effect on illegal behavior. A major criticism of this research is that we do not know which came first—the association with delinquent others or the illegal behavior itself. More recent research has begun to incorporate measures of time order (when the associations and behaviors occurred), and differential association theory appears to be supported (see, for example, the research of Tittle, Burke, and Jackson, 1986). Another direction corresponds to the renewed interest in social disorganization, as we noted in the previous chapter. Sutherland's theory, with its use of differential social organization to explain crime rates, corresponds nicely with social disorganization concerns. Now past its fiftieth birthday, differential association theory seems to be as popular as ever.

In the area of policy, Sutherland's theory has implications for treatment and even the study of alternative "types" of crime. Cressey has pointed to prison programs that could use the concept of associating with role models who provide conventional definitions for behavior. Standard conditions of both probation and parole include warnings to keep away from criminal associations. Juvenile delinquency projects invariably stress the importance of avoiding "undesirables," and school programs uniformly make use of role models for youngsters. Virtually all contemporary models of parenting suggest that parents watch and supervise their children's choice of friends.

In another area, Sutherland generated interest and research in white-collar crime, a term he is credited with inventing. He used his theory to explain how those of higher social standing learn crime in the same manner as those in the lower classes, who largely commit street crimes. In the past two decades, research in white-collar crime and theory has become a staple in criminology. Governmental concern with white-collar and corporate criminality has grown to the point where corporations often receive criminal punishments for their illegal actions. White-collar criminals, such as ex-stockbroker Michael Milken and ex-banker Charles Keating, have become common targets of government investigations and prosecution. Training programs in corporate ethics are direct offshoots of differential association theory.

BIBLIOGRAPHY

ADAMS, REED(1973). "Differential association and learning principles revisited." *Social Problems* 20: 458–470.

———— (1974). "The adequacy of differential association theory." *Journal of Research in Crime and Delinquency* 11: 1–8.

AGNEW, ROBERT (1993). "Why do they do it? An examination of the intervening mechanisms between 'social control' variables and delinquency." *Journal of Research in Crime and Delinquency* 30: 245–266.

AKERS, RONALD L. (1973). *Deviant Behavior: A Social Learning Approach.* Belmont, CA: Wadsworth.

———— (1977). *Deviant Behavior: A Social Learning Approach,* 2nd ed. Belmont, CA: Wadsworth.

———— (1985). *Deviant Behavior: A Social Learning Approach,* 3rd ed. Belmont, CA: Wadsworth.

———— (1996). "Is differential association/social learning cultural deviance theory?" *Criminology* 34: 229–247.

AKERS, RONALD L., and GANG LEE (1996). "A longitudinal test of social learning theory: Adolescent smoking." *Journal of Drug Issues* 26: 317–343.

AKERS, RONALD L., and ROSS L. MATSUEDA (1989). "Donald R. Cressey: An intellectual portrait of a criminologist." *Sociological Inquiry* 59: 423–438.

ANDREWS, D. A. (1980). "Some experimental investigations of the principles of differential association through deliberate manipulations of the structure of service systems." *American Sociological Review* 45: 448–462.

AULTMAN, MADELINE G. (1979). "Delinquency causation: A typological comparison of path models." *Journal of Criminal Law and Criminology* 70: 152–163.

BENDA, BRENT B., (1997). "An examination of a reciprocal relationship between religiosity and different forms of delinquency within a theoretical model." *Journal of Research in Crime and Delinquency* 34: 163–186.

BENDA, BRENT B., and LEANNE WHITESIDE (1995). "Testing an integrated model of delinquency using LISREL." *Journal of Social Science Research* 21: 1–32.

BRUINSMA, GERBEN J. N. (1992). "Differential association theory reconsidered: An extension and its empirical test." *Journal of Quantitative Criminology* 8: 29–49.

BURGER, WILLIAM (1993). *American Crime and Punishment: The Religious Origins of American Criminology*. Buchanan, MI: Vande Vere Publishing.

BURGESS, ROBERT L., and RONALD L. AKERS (1966). "A differential association-reinforcement theory of criminal behavior." *Social Problems* 14: 128–147.

CATALANO, RICHARD F., RICK KOSTERMAN, J. DAVID HAWKINS, MICHAEL D. NEWCOMB, and ROBERT D. ABBOTT (1996). "Modeling the etiology of adolescent substance use: A test of the social development model." *Journal of Drug Issues* 26: 429–455.

CHEUNG, YUET-WAH, and AGNES M. C. NG (1988). "Social factors in adolescent deviant behaviour in Hong Kong: An integrated theoretical approach." *International Journal of Comparative and Applied Criminal Justice* 12: 27–45.

CHIRICOS, THEODORE G. (1967). "The concept of cause: A developmental analysis of the theory of differential association." *Issues in Criminology* 3: 91–99.

CLARKE, ROBERT E. (1972). *Reference Group Theory and Delinquency*. New York: Behavioral Publications.

CLOWARD, RICHARD A., and LLOYD E. OHLIN (1960). *Delinquency and Opportunity: A Theory of Delinquent Gangs*. New York: Free Press.

COHEN, ALBERT K. (1955). *Delinquent Boys: The Culture of the Gang*. New York: Free Press.

COHEN, ALBERT K., ALFRED LINDESMITH, and KARL SCHUESSLER, eds. (1956). *The Sutherland Papers*. Terre Haute: Indiana University Press.

CRESSEY, DONALD R. (1952). "Application and verification of the differential association theory." *Journal of Criminal Law, Criminology, and Police Science* 43: 43–52.

——— (1953). *Other People's Money*. New York: Free Press.

——— (1954). "The differential association theory and compulsive crimes." *Journal of Criminal Law and Criminology* 45: 49–64.

——— (1960a). "Epidemiology and individual conduct: A case from criminology." *Pacific Sociological Review* 3: 47–58.

——— (1960b). "The theory of differential association: An introduction." *Social Problems* 8: 2–6.

——— (1964). *Delinquency, Crime and Differential Association*. The Hague, Netherlands: Martinus Nijhoff.

——— (1965). "Social psychological foundations for using criminals in the rehabilitation of criminals." *Journal of Research in Crime and Delinquency* 2: 49–59.

——— (1966). "The language of set theory and differential association." *Journal of Research in Crime and Delinquency* 3: 22–26.

——— (1968). "Culture conflict, differential association, and normative conflict." In M. E. Wolfgang, ed., *Crime and Culture*, 43–54. New York: Wiley.

———— (1972). "Role theory, differential association and compulsive crimes." In A. M. Rose, ed., *Human Behavior and Social Processes: An Interactionist Approach*, 443–467. London: Routledge and Kegan Paul.

———— (1979). "Fifty years of criminology." *Pacific Sociological Review* 22: 457–480.

DeFleur, Melvin L., and Richard Quinney (1966). "A reformulation of Sutherland's differential association theory and a strategy for empirical verification." *Journal of Research in Crime and Delinquency* 3: 1–22.

Dull, R. Thomas (1983). "Friends' use and adult drug and drinking behavior: A further test of differential association theory." *Journal of Criminal Law and Criminology* 74: 1608–1619.

Elliot, Delbert S., and Scott Menard (1992). "Delinquent friends and delinquent behavior: Temporal and developmental patterns." In J. D. Hawkins, ed., *Some Current Theories of Crime and Deviance*. New York: Springer-Verlag.

Else, John F., and Keith D. Stephenson (1974). "Vicarious expiation: A theory of prison and social reform." *Crime and Delinquency* 20: 359–372.

Empey, Lamar T. (1967). "Delinquency theory and recent research." *Journal of Research in Crime and Delinquency* 4: 28–42.

Empey, Lamar T., and Steven G. Lubeck (1971). *Explaining Delinquency: Construction, Test, and Reformation of a Sociological Theory*. Lexington, MA: Heath Lexington Books.

Ferdinand, Theodore N. (1987). "The methods of delinquency theory." *Criminology* 26: 841–862.

Galliher, John F., and Cheryl Tyree (1985). "Edwin Sutherland's research on the origins of sexual psychopath laws: An early case study of the medicalization of deviance." *Social Problems* 33: 100–113.

Gaylord, Mark S., and John Galliher (1988). *The Criminology of Edwin Sutherland*. New Brunswick, NJ: Transaction.

Geis, Gilbert (1985). "Criminological perspectives on corporate regulation: A review of recent research." In B. Fisse and P. A. French, eds., *Corrigible Corporations and Unruly Law*, 63–83. San Antonio, TX: Trinity Press.

Geis, Gilbert, and Colin Goff (1986). "Edwin H. Sutherland's *White-Collar Crime in America*: An essay in historical criminology." In L. A. Knafla, J. Cockburn, and E. Dwyer, eds., *Criminal Justice History: An International Annual*, vol. 7, 1–31. Westport, CT: Meckler.

Gibbons, Don C. (1979). *The Criminological Enterprise: Theories and Perspectives*. Englewood Cliffs, NJ: Prentice Hall.

Ginsberg, Irving J., and James R. Greenley (1978). "Competing theories of marijuana use: A longitudinal study." *Journal of Health and Social Behavior* 19: 22–34.

Giordana, Peggy C., Stephen A. Cernkovich, and Michael D. Pugh (1986). "Friendships and delinquency." *American Journal of Sociology* 91: 1170–1202.

Glaser, Daniel (1956). "Criminality theories and behavioral images." *American Journal of Sociology* 61: 433–444.

———— (1960). "Differential association and criminological prediction." *Social Problems* 8: 6–14.

———— (1962). "The differential association theory of crime." In A. M. Rose, ed., *Human Behavior and Social Process*, 425–442. Boston: Houghton Mifflin.

———— (1978). *Crime in Our Changing Society*. New York: Holt, Rinehart and Winston.

———— (1979). "A review of crime-causation theory and its application." In N. Morris and M. Tonry, eds., *Crime and Justice: An Annual Review of Research*, vol. 1, 203–238. Chicago: University of Chicago Press.

Glueck, Sheldon (1956). "Theory and fact in criminology: A criticism of differential association." *British Journal of Delinquency* 7: 92–109.

Goff, Colin (1982). *Edwin H. Sutherland and White-Collar Crime*. Unpublished doctoral diss.: University of California, Irvine.

Gold, David (1957). "On description of differential association." *American Sociological Review* 22: 448–450.

Gomme, Ian M. (1985). "Predictors of status and criminal offenses among male and female adolescents in an Ontario community." *Canadian Journal of Criminology* 27: 147–159.

Gould, Leroy C. (1969). "Juvenile entrepreneurs." *American Journal of Sociology* 74: 710–719.

Griffin, Brenda S., and Charles T. Griffin (1978). "Drug use and differential association." *Drug Forum* 1: 1–8.

Heimer, Karen, and Ross I. Matsueda (1994). "Role-taking, role commitment, and delinquency: A theory of differential social control." *American Sociological Review* 59: 365–390.

Hepburn, John R. (1976). "Testing alternative models of delinquency causation." *Journal of Criminal Law and Criminology* 67: 450–460.

Hirschi, Travis, and Michael Gottfredson (1979). "Introduction: The Sutherland tradition in criminology." In T. Hirschi and M. Gottfredson, eds., *Understanding Crime: Current Theory and Research*, 7–19. Beverly Hills, CA: Sage.

Jaquith, Susan N. (1981). "Adolescent marijuana and alcohol use: An empirical test of differential association theory." *Criminology* 19: 271–280.

Jeffery, C. Ray (1959). "An integrated theory of crime and criminal behavior." *Journal of Criminal Law, Criminology, and Police Science* 49: 533–552.

——— (1965). "Criminal behavior and learning theory." *Journal of Criminal Law, Criminology and Police Science* 54: 294–300.

——— (1977). *Crime Prevention through Environmental Design*, 2nd ed. Beverly Hills, CA: Sage.

Jensen, Gary F. (1972). "Parents, peers and delinquent action: A test of the differential association perspective." *American Journal of Sociology* 78: 562–571.

Johnson, Richard E., Anastasios C. Marcos, and Stephen J. Bahr (1987). "The role of peers in the complex etiology of adolescent drug use." *Criminology* 25: 323–340.

Junger, Marianne (1988). "Social control theory versus differential association: A test on panel data." In J. Junger-Tas and R. L. Block, eds., *Juvenile Delinquency in the Netherlands*, 71–95. Amstelveen, Netherlands: Kugler.

Krohn, Marvin D. (1974). "An investigation of the effect of parental and peer associations on marijuana use: An empirical test of differential association theory." In M. Reidel and T. Thornberry, eds., *Crime and Delinquency: Dimensions of Deviance*, 75–87. New York: Prager.

LaBouvie, Erich (1996). "Maturing out of substance use: Selection and self-correction." *Journal of Drug Issues* 26: 457–476.

Laub, John H., and Robert J. Sampson (1991). "The Sutherland-Glueck debate: On the sociology of criminological knowledge." *American Journal of Sociology* 96: 1402–1440.

Lindesmith, Alfred R. (1988). "Foreword." In M. Gaylord and J. Galliher, eds., *The Criminology of Edwin Sutherland*, ix–xiv. New Brunswick, NJ: Transaction.

Liska, Allen E. (1969). "Interpreting the causal structure of differential association theory." *Social Problems* 16: 485–492.

——— (1978). "Deviant involvement, associations and attitudes: Specifying the underlying causal structures." *Sociology and Social Research* 63: 73–88.

Makkai, Toni, and John Braithwaite (1991). "Criminological theories and regulatory compliance." *Criminology* 29: 191–217.

Marcos, Anastasios C., Stephen J. Bahr, and Richard E. Johnson (1987). "Test of a bonding/association theory of adolescent drug use." *Social Forces* 65: 135–161.

Massey, James L., and Marvin D. Krohn (1986). "A longitudinal examination of an integrated social process model of deviant behavior." *Social Forces* 65: 106–134.

MATSUEDA, ROSS L. (1982). "Testing control theory and differential association: A causal modeling approach." *American Sociological Review* 47: 489–504.

────── (1988). "The current state of differential association theory." *Crime and Delinquency* 34: 277–306.

MATSUEDA, ROSS L., and KAREN HEIMER (1987). "Race, family structure, and delinquency: A test of differential association and social control theories." *American Sociological Review* 52: 826–840.

MATTHEWS, VICTOR (1968). "Differential identification: An empirical note." *Social Problems* 15: 376–388.

McCARTHY, BILL (1996). "The attitudes and actions of others: Tutelage and Sutherland's theory of differential association." *British Journal of Criminology* 36: 135–147.

McKAY, HENRY D. (1960). "Differential association and crime prevention: Problems of utilization." *Social Problems* 8: 25–37.

MICHAEL, JEROME, and MORTIMER J. ADLER (1933). *Crime, Law, and Social Science.* New York: Harcourt, Brace.

NAESS, SIRI (1964). "Comparing theories of criminogenesis." *Journal of Research in Crime and Delinquency* 1: 171–180.

OPP, KARL-DIETER (1989). "The economics of crime and the sociology of deviant behavior: A theoretical confrontation of basic propositions." *Kyklos* 42: 405–430.

ORCUTT, JAMES D. (1987). "Differential association and marijuana use: A closer look at Sutherland (with a little help from Becker)." *Criminology* 25: 341–358.

RAYMOND, FRANK B. (1975). "A sociological view of narcotics addiction." *Crime and Delinquency* 21: 11–18.

REINARMAN, CRAIG, and JEFFREY FAGAN (1988). "Social organization and differential association: A research note from a longitudinal study of violent juvenile offenders." *Crime and Delinquency* 34: 307–327.

REISS, ALBERT J., JR., and ALBERT L. RHODES (1961). "The distribution of delinquency and social class structure." *American Sociological Review* 26: 720–732.

────── (1964). "An empirical test of differential association theory." *Journal of Research in Crime and Delinquency* 1: 5–18.

ROBIN, GERALD D. (1974). "White-collar crime and employee theft." *Crime and Delinquency* 20: 251–262.

SCHRAG, CLARENCE, and LEROY C. GOULD (1962). "Theory construction and prediction in juvenile delinquency." *Proceedings of the American Statistical Association, 1962:* 68–73.

SCHUESSLER, KARL, ed. (1973). *Edwin H. Sutherland: On Analyzing Crime.* Chicago: University of Chicago Press.

SELLIN, THORSTEN (1938). *Culture Conflict and Crime.* New York: Social Science Research Council, Bulletin 41.

SEVERY, L. J. (1973). "Exposure to deviance committed by valued peer group and family members." *Journal of Research in Crime and Delinquency* 10: 35–46.

SHAW, CLIFFORD R., and HENRY D. McKAY (1931). *Report on the Causes of Crime.* Vol. 2: *Social Factors in Juvenile Delinquency.* National Commission on Law Observance and Enforcement, Report No. 13. Washington, DC: U.S. Government Printing Office.

SHERWOOD, JOHN J. (1965). "Self identity and referent others." *Sociometry* 28: 66–81.

SHOHAM, SHLOMO, and GIORA RAHAV (1968). "Social stigma and prostitution." *British Journal of Criminology* 8: 402–412.

SHORT, JAMES F., JR. (1957). "Differential association and delinquency." *Social Problems* 4: 233–239.

────── (1958). "Differential association with delinquent friends and delinquent behavior." *Pacific Sociological Review* 1: 20–25.

——— (1960). "Differential association as a hypothesis: Problems of empirical testing." *Social Problems* 8: 14–25.

——— (1974). "Collective behavior, crime and delinquency." In D. Glaser, ed., *Handbook of Criminology*, 403–449. Chicago: Rand McNally.

——— (1979). "On the etiology of delinquent behavior." *Journal of Research in Crime and Delinquency* 16: 28–33.

SHOVER, NEAL (1972). "Structures and careers in burglary." *Journal of Criminal Law, Criminology and Police Science* 63: 540–549.

SIMONS, RONALD L., MARTIN G. MILLER, and STEPHEN M. AIGNER (1980). "Contemporary theories of deviance and female delinquency: An empirical test." *Journal of Research in Crime and Delinquency* 17: 42–57.

SMITH, DOUGLAS A., and ROBERT BRAME (1994). "On the initiation and continuation of delinquency." *Criminology* 32: 607–629.

SMITH, DOUGLAS A., and RAYMOND PATERNOSTER (1987). "The gender gap in theories of deviance: Issues and evidence." *Journal of Research in Crime and Delinquency* 24: 140–172.

SNODGRASS, JON (1972). *The American Criminological Tradition: Portraits of the Men and Ideology in a Discipline.* Unpublished doctoral diss.: University of Pennsylvania, Philadelphia.

——— (1973). "The criminologist and his criminal: The case of Edwin H. Sutherland and Broadway Jones." *Issues in Criminology* 8: 2–17.

STANFIELD, ROBERT E. (1966). "The interaction of family variables and gang variables in the aetiology of delinquency." *Social Problems* 13: 411–417.

STRATTON, JOHN R. (1967). "Differential identification and attitudes toward the law." *Social Forces* 46: 256–262.

SUTHERLAND, EDWIN H. (1926). "The biological and sociological processes." *Papers and Proceedings of the Twentieth Annual Meeting of the American Sociological Society* 20: 58–65.

——— (1929). "Crime and the conflict process." *Journal of Juvenile Research* 13: 38–48.

——— (1934). *Principles of Criminology*, 2nd ed. Philadelphia: Lippincott.

——— (1937). *The Professional Thief: By a Professional Thief.* Chicago: University of Chicago Press.

——— (1939). *Principles of Criminology*, 3rd ed. Philadelphia: Lippincott.

——— (1947). *Principles of Criminology*, 4th ed. Philadelphia: Lippincott.

——— (1949). *White Collar Crime.* New York: Dryden.

——— (1973a). "Critique of the theory." In K. Schuessler, ed., *Edwin H. Sutherland on Analyzing Crime,* 30–41. Chicago: University of Chicago Press.

——— (1973b). "Development of the theory." In K. Schuessler, ed., *Edwin H. Sutherland on Analyzing Crime,* 13–29. Chicago: University of Chicago Press.

——— (1973c). "The Michael-Adler report." In K. Schuessler, ed., *Edwin H. Sutherland on Analyzing Crime,* 229–246. Chicago: University of Chicago Press.

——— (1973d). "The prison as a criminological laboratory." In K. Schuessler, ed., *Edwin H. Sutherland on Analyzing Crime,* 247–256. Chicago: University of Chicago Press.

——— (1973e). "Susceptibility and differential association." In K. Schuessler, ed., *Edwin H. Sutherland on Analyzing Crime,* 42–43. Chicago: University of Chicago Press.

SUTHERLAND, EDWIN H., and DONALD R. CRESSEY (1978). *Criminology*, 10th ed. Philadelphia: Lippincott.

SUTHERLAND, EDWIN H., DONALD R. CRESSEY, and DAVID F. LUCKENBILL (1992). *Principles of Criminology*, Eleventh Edition. Dix Hills, New York: General Hall.

SUTHERLAND, EDWIN H., and HARVEY J. LOCKE (1936*). Twenty Thousand Homeless Men: A Study of Unemployed Men in the Chicago Shelters.* Philadelphia: Lippincott.

SUTHERLAND, EDWIN H., CLIFFORD R. SHAW, CHARLES E. GEHLKE, SHELDON GLUECK, and WARREN A. STEARNS (1932). "Housing and delinquency." In J. M Gries and J. Ford, eds., *Housing and the Community: Home Repair and Remodeling*, 13–49. Washington, DC: U. S. Government Printing Office.

TITTLE, CHARLES R., MARY JEAN BURKE, and ELTON F. JACKSON (1986). "Modeling Sutherland's theory of differential association: Toward an empirical clarification." *Social Forces* 65: 405–432.

VASOLI, ROBERT H., and DENNIS A. TERZOLA (1974). "Sutherland's professional thief." *Criminology* 12: 131–154.

VOLD, GEORGE B. (1951). "Edwin Hardin Sutherland: Sociological criminologist." *American Sociological Review* 16: 3–9.

VOLKMAN, RITA, and DONALD R. CRESSEY (1963). "Differential association and the rehabilitation of drug addicts." *American Journal of Sociology* 69: 129–142.

VOSS, HARWIN L. (1964). "Differential association and reported delinquent behavior. A replication." *Social Problems* 12: 78–85.

——— (1969). "Differential association and containment theory: A theoretical convergence." *Social Forces* 47: 381–391.

WARR, MARK (1993). "Age, peers, and delinquency." *Criminology* 31: 17–40.

WARR, MARK, and MARK STAFFORD (1991). "The influence of delinquent peers: What they think or what they do?" *Criminology* 29: 851–866.

WEINBERG, S. KIRSON (1954). "Theories of criminality and problems of prediction." *Journal of Criminal Law, Criminology and Police Science* 45: 412–429.

——— (1966). "Personality and method in the differential association theory: Comments on `A reformulation of Sutherland's differential association theory and a strategy for empirical verification.'" *Journal of Research in Crime and Delinquency* 3: 165–172.

WILLIAMS, FRANK P., III (1990). "Review of Gaylord and Galliher's *The Criminology of Edwin Sutherland*." *Criminal Justice Review* 15: 83–84.

WIRTH, LOUIS (1925). *Culture Conflicts in the Immigrant Family*. Unpublished master's thesis: Sociology Department, University of Chicago.

——— (1931). "Culture conflict and misconduct." *Social Forces* 9: 484–492.

6

ANOMIE THEORY

INTRODUCTION

Anomie is a concept closely associated with two theorists, Emile Durkheim and Robert K. Merton. When Durkheim introduced the term in his 1893 book *The Division of Labor in Society*, he used it to describe a condition of "deregulation" occurring in society. By this he meant that the general procedural rules of a society (the rules that say how people ought to behave toward each other) have broken down and that people do not know what to expect from each other. This deregulation, or normlessness, easily leads to deviant behavior. Durkheim later used the term *anomie*, in *Suicide: A Study in Sociology* (1897), to refer to a morally deregulated condition in which people have inadequate moral controls over their behavior (see Olson, 1965). Thus, a society may be anomic if people do not know when to quit striving for success, or how to treat other people along the way. Whichever of these two descriptions of anomie is used—a breakdown in either the rules of society or the moral norms—it is clear that Durkheim was talking about a disruption of normal societal conditions.

Durkheim's central thesis in *The Division of Labor in Society* was that societies evolved from a simple, nonspecialized form (mechanical) toward a complex, highly specialized form (organic). In both cases, he referred to the way in which people interact with each other and the way in which labor is carried out. In the mechanical society, people behave and think similarly and, except for a division of labor along gender lines, perform most of the same work tasks and have group-oriented goals. As a society becomes more complex, work also becomes more complex and specialized. Modern, organic societies are characterized by highly interactive sets of relationships, specialized labor, and individual goals. For example, one person's work skills are rarely sufficient to provide all that is necessary to live. People depend on each other to produce various items. The distribution of these items, once produced, is a problem. Highly complex relationships are required to distribute the products of each person's skills. This, for Durkheim, suggested that an organic society is a contractual society, and he saw almost all relationships as contractual ones. By this he meant that people are no longer tied together by bonds of kinship and friendship but, because of the impersonality of modern society, by various types of contractual bonds. The problem with such societies is that these bonds are constantly being broken (the concept of bonds reappears in our discussion of social control theories in Chapter 10). In sum, the rules governing how people in organic societies interact with each other (the contracts) are continually in flux, and social conditions are constantly in danger of disruption. When disruption occurs, we have anomie.

Anomie, then, refers to the breakdown of social norms and a condition in which those norms no longer control the activity of societal members. Without clear rules to guide them, individuals cannot find their place in society and have difficulty adjusting to the changing conditions of life. This in turn leads to dissatisfaction, frustration, conflict, and deviance. Studying France and Europe after the Industrial Revolution, Durkheim saw economic crises, forced industrialization, and commercialization as factors producing anomie. Durkheim was fairly sure that contemporary Western societies had reached such a point of complexity that they were in a constant state of anomie. Even so, he saw that a period of social disruption, such as an economic depression, would make matters worse and result in greater anomie and, of course, higher rates of crime, suicide, and deviance.

In 1938, Merton borrowed the concept of anomie to explain deviance in the United States. His concept, however, differed from that of Durkheim. Dividing social norms (or values) into two types, Merton talked of societal *goals* and the acceptable *means* for achieving those goals. In addition, he redefined anomie as a disjuncture (or split) between those goals and means as a result of the way society is structured; for example, with class distinctions. Deviance, then, could be explained as a symptom of a social structure within which "culturally defined aspirations and socially structured means" are separated from each other. Or, in other words, deviance is a product of anomie. It is Merton's treatment of anomie that we consider in this chapter.

THE HERITAGE OF THE THEORY

The Social Heritage

Like the Industrial Revolution, the Great Depression of the 1930s produced insights for sociologists. An entire generation of sociologists could observe the collapse and deregulation of social traditions and the effect this had on both individuals and the institutions of society. As did Edwin

Sutherland, Merton noted that crime was not necessarily an intrinsic part of the person, and he rejected individualistic views of pathology (Merton and Ashley-Montagu, 1940). The increasing popularity of Durkheim's discussion of anomie, when combined with the Depression, provided sociological insights into the connection between social structure and deviant behavior. Similarly, the notion of the division of labor opened up possibilities for an examination of the role of aspirations and opportunities in American society.

The importance of analyzing social structure itself became firmly grounded when the government's New Deal reform efforts focused on rearranging society. Sociologists and others found themselves moving away from the narrower applications of sociology and toward an examination of social structure as a whole (Merton, 1964:215). Given the popular belief of the time—that government was largely responsible for society's problems—Durkheim had provided social scientists with a ready-made explanation: society was simply in a state of deregulation.

Another factor affecting criminology during the 1930s was the emergence of and emphasis on the collection of demographic data (information about people). Moreover, in examining both the ecological data collected by Clifford Shaw and Henry McKay and the newly created Uniform Crime Reports, it was evident that certain segments of society were burdened with high crime rates. These were the very same segments of society in which a relatively permanent state of deregulation could be observed. An obvious explanation was that, somehow, deregulation led to deviance. Finally, the idea that social class might be a crucial sociological factor in explaining societal events was gaining popularity. Just as sociologists were viewing other behavior as being influenced by social class position (Lynd and Lynd, 1929; Dollard, 1937), it occurred to theorists that an explanation of deviance based on social class differences might be productive.

The Intellectual Heritage

Merton was influenced by two sociologists during the 1930s. He was first introduced to the concept of anomie by the work of Pitirim Sorokin, whose 1928 book *Contemporary Sociological Theories* called attention to Durkheim's use of the term "anomic suicide" (Merton, 1964:215). Perhaps even more important, Merton had studied under Talcott Parsons, whose approach to explaining social events emphasized the way society is structured. This approach became known as "structural-functionalism." As an undergraduate at Temple University, Merton had also studied under George Simpson, who was to write the popular translation of Durkheim's *Division of Labor in Society* in the 1930s (Martin, Mutchnick, and Austin, 1990). Merton, then, was well prepared to adopt Durkheim's interest in anomie.

Parsons saw society as the product of an equilibrium of forces (like a pendulum) that served to produce order. When the various components of the social structure became "unbalanced"—that is, when the pendulum swung too far to either side—society became disorganized. Durkheim's concept of anomie fit nicely into the Parsonian framework and was a major focus of Parsons's book, *The Structure of Social Action* (1937). With Simpson's translation into English of Durkheim's *Division of Labor* in 1933, the use of social structure in explaining social behavior became accepted.

Two strains of psychological/biological positivism during the 1930s also exerted an influence on Merton. Freudian psychotherapy, with its emphasis on internal conflicts, was exceedingly popular. Moreover, Earnest Hooton had created a stir with his controversial books on the biological inferiority of criminals. Merton reacted strongly to these approaches and, with anthropologist Ashley-Montagu, published a strong rebuttal to them in 1940. In sharpening criticism against the nonsociological positions, Merton more clearly focused his thoughts on the effects of social structure. In addition, Merton read some of the works of Karl Marx during the 1930s. The Marxist influence can be seen most clearly in Merton's focus on the American capitalist system's excessive attention to financial success goals.

Finally, there is the question of whether a linkage exists between Sutherland's differential association theory and Merton's anomie theory. Merton (1997:519) recently said that he views the two theories as complementary. In one sense, then, the individual-level process (the sociopsychological, in Merton's words) had already been developed by the Chicago School and its followers. What Merton wanted to explain was the missing part "how those patterns of criminal preferences and behaviors emerged in the first place." Thus, the theory of anomie was partly an avoidance of processual elements and partly a push to explain the structural components of deviance.

THE THEORETICAL PERSPECTIVE

Merton's anomie theory is, above all, a theory of deviance; that is, it does not focus on criminality. Further, Merton's conception of deviance is relatively general. When one conceives of a society that emphasizes well-structured **goals** for its members and equally structured avenues to reach those goals, deviance becomes any behavior that does not follow commonly accepted values. For example, Merton uses the term "deviance" to refer to bureaucratic behavior as well as to criminal behavior.

Merton notes that certain goals are strongly emphasized throughout society (he uses the example of financial success). Society also emphasizes (legitimizes) certain **means** to reach those goals (such as hard work, education, starting at the bottom and working one's way up). When these goals are too strongly stressed, as Merton said financial success was in the United States, the stage is set for anomie. Not everyone has equal access to the achievement of legitimate financial success, and as a result, these people may search for other, perhaps illegitimate, ways of succeeding. Because of social inequality, the approved means to reach the success goals are not readily available to certain groups in society, even though the goals are said to apply equally to all. Certain groups of people, the lower social class and minorities, for instance, may be at a disadvantage in gaining business positions that would allow them to pursue the goal of financial success. According to Merton, when this inequality exists because of the way society is structured, the social structure is anomic. Given the evidence that there are several segments of society in which legitimate avenues to success are severely restricted without a corresponding reduction in the emphasis on achievement, U.S. society seems to be in a permanent state of anomie. The individuals caught in these anomic conditions (largely the lower classes) are then faced with the strain of being unable to reconcile their aspirations with their limited opportunities. As with Durkheim's formulation of anomie, this does not mean that anomie conditions are constant. As social conditions change, thereby resulting in greater or lesser inequality, so does the degree of anomie.

We should note, however, that legitimate means are not necessarily the most efficient methods of reaching the goals. Other means, although perhaps illegitimate or de-emphasized by society, may be both available and more efficient. It is also important to keep in mind that Merton focuses on financial success only as an *example* throughout his work; he did not mean to imply that it was the only major goal that exists in American society. In fact, Merton later stated:

> The theory holds that *any* extreme emphasis upon achievement—whether this be scientific productivity, accumulation of personal wealth or, by a small stretch of the imagination, the conquests of a Don Juan—will attenuate conformity to the institutional norms governing behavior designed to achieve the particular form of "success," especially among those who are socially disadvantaged in the competitive race. It is the conflict between cultural goals and the availability of using institutional means—whatever the character of the goals—which produces a strain toward anomie. (1968:220)

The success goals themselves are not necessarily applicable to all social classes at the same time. Indeed, each class may have its own brand of success goals, and a number of different goals are possible. Rather than a reference to specific goals, Merton talks about the presence of a cultural message that legitimates upward striving and the alleged mobility that is available to all those who desire to achieve. It is then the *emphasis* on reaching the goals that becomes important. Because of this, any test of the theory that concentrates on one goal or concept of success will invariably be deficient.

The Modes of Adaptation

Merton presents five ways (modes) of adapting to strain caused by restricted access to the socially approved goals and means. If the emphasis on goals and means is maintained even in the face of a realization that the means are restricted, an individual will remain **conforming.** Most people follow this adaptation, Merton maintains; if they did not, the very existence of society would be threatened. The remaining four modes, however, represent a departure from this all-endorsing adaptation and thus are the "real" deviant modes of adaptation.

First is the case in which the emphasis on the approved goals of society is maintained while legitimate means are replaced by other, nonapproved means. This mode of adaptation, called **innovation** is the most common of the four deviant types. Interestingly, for some segments of society, innovative means may be *more efficient* in reaching a goal than the approved means for doing so. For example, instead of saving money and letting it slowly earn interest in a bank, a faster way of accumulating a lot of money is to rob the bank. The primary characteristic of innovation can also be seen in the familiar statement, "The end justifies the means."

However, when the goals themselves are rejected and the focus is shifted to the means, the mode of adaptation is that of **ritualism.** In this mode the means can become the aspirations of an individual, as when one attempts to treat a job (means) as a form of security instead of using the job as a means of achieving success. In this example, keeping the job has become the goal, resolving the frustration of unsuccessfully chasing the original goal. Ritualism can also be seen in bureaucratic behavior, in which an employee has no power to actually do anything for anyone and instead focuses on the fact that the paperwork must be correctly filled out, in three copies.

A third mode, **retreatism,** involves a rejection of *both* the goals and means. Retreatists are those individuals who opt not to be innovative and, at the same time, need to resolve their inability to reach the important goals in life. Their solution is that they simply quit trying to get ahead. This pattern is best seen as dropping out of society and is exemplified by vagrants, alcoholics, and drug addicts. In 1938, Merton saw retreatism as the least common mode of adaptation. Today, perhaps, it is more common.

The final mode of adaptation, **rebellion,** is of a different type from the other three. While those modes emphasize rejection of means or goals, or

MERTON'S TYPOLOGY OF ADAPTATIONS TO ANOMIE

		Culture Goals	*InstitutionalizedMeans*
I.	Conformity	+	+
II.	Innovation	+	-
III.	Ritualism	-	+
I.	Retreatism	-	-
V.	Rebellion	±	±

(+)signifies "acceptance," (-) signifies "elimination," and (±) signifies "rejection and substitution of new goals and standards."

both, rebellion focuses on the *substitution* of new goals and means for the original ones. Merton's conception suggests that rebellion "leads men outside the environing social structure to envisage and seek to bring into being a new, that is to say a greatly modified social structure. It presupposes alienation from reigning goals and standards" (1968:209). These individuals, then, are precisely what the term indicates: rebels and revolutionaries.

In short, Merton's anomie theory explains how social structure contributes to the creation of deviance on all levels, although the primary focus of the theory is on the lower class. Because of the societally induced disjunction (separation) between cultural aspirations and the approved methods of attaining those aspirations, the lower class is most likely to exhibit deviant, nonapproved, adaptive behavior. Merton (1997:519) summarizes anomie theory in this way:

> It holds that rates of various types of deviant behavior (not only crime) are high in a society where, as with the American Dream, the culture places a high premium on economic success and upward mobility for *all* its members, although in brute social fact large numbers of people located in the lower reaches of the social structure have severely limited access to legitimate resources for achieving those culturally induced or reinforced goals. Since the key question in this theory focuses on the socially structured sources and consequences of deviant behavior, it says next to nothing about the social mechanisms for transmitting such patterns of behavior or about the ways in which individuals' initial departures from the norms crystallize into deviant careers.

CLASSIFICATION OF THE THEORY

Anomie theory is a *positivist* theory. In contrast to positivist theories locating pathology within the individual, anomie theory locates pathology within the social structure. Merton explains how a pathological social structure (one in which there is an undue emphasis on goals, especially economic ones, without corresponding avenues of access available to all members of the society) serves to create a strain in certain segments of society and, ultimately, a push toward deviance. Because of this concern with structural strain, anomie theory is often referred to as a "strain theory" (see the discussion of strain theory later in this chapter).

The assumption of a *consensus* of values also characterizes anomie theory. American society imposes on us the "right" things to do and the "right" ways to do them. Unless there is considerable unanimity about societal goals and means, there can be no anomic condition that results in adaptations to those goals and means. In other words, adaptations or deviations would merely be alternate modes of success or achievement.

Anomie is a *structural* theory. It focuses on the way society is structured and how that structure serves to create deviance within American society. It does not, nor did Merton intend it to, specify the process by which *individuals* become deviant. Instead, anomie theory deals with the pathology of existing social structure and the subsequent forms of deviance arising in the various segments of society as a whole. In short, Merton intends to explain variations in rates of deviance (1968:186) among societal groups and not how the process of choosing among adaptations takes place. This broad scope and emphasis on explaining social structure also makes anomie theory a *macrotheory*.

Finally, and outside of our usual classification scheme, anomie theory is often called a *functionalist* theory. Functionalism presumes that it is desirable to explain a social phenomenon in terms of its effect on, and its consequences for, the social structure in which it exists. In other words, Merton uses the concepts of cultural goals and norms to explain how they serve to produce both conformity *and* deviance within the social structure.

SUMMARY

Merton's theory of anomie is still among the most influential of all criminological theories, although presented as long ago as 1938. It continues to draw commentary and research, and several modifications have been offered (Richard Cloward's [1959] addition of an illegitimate opportunity structure is probably the most important; see the discussion of differential opportunity theory in Chapter 7). Further, elements of anomie theory are, at least in part, found in more contemporary criminological theories (e.g., Hirschi, 1969:198).

Anomie theory comments on extreme emphases on cultural goals and accompanying cultural messages that assert the importance of striving for those goals. Unless the means to reach the goals are equitably distributed in society, the overemphasis on goals and inequality of means will result in socially structured and patterned rates of deviance. Groups who have the greatest access to the approved means are mostly conforming. Conversely, those groups with the least access to the means have higher rates of deviance. In U.S. society this suggests that structured inequality leads to deviance and crime, with the highest rates among the lower classes. Indeed, the theory's premise is that the lower class suffers the most anomic conditions and therefore has the highest level of involvement in deviant behavior.

Major Points of the Theory

1. Most members of society share (or are socialized into) a common system of values.
2. This common value system teaches us both the things we should strive for (cultural goals) and the most appropriate ways (societal means) to achieve those goals.
3. If the goals and the means to achieve them are not equally stressed, an anomic condition is created.
4. In a disorganized society, different degrees of access to these goals and means exist. Thus, the means are not equally distributed within a disorganized society.

5. Some societies, such as that of the United States, may place too much stress on success goals. In a disorganized society, this results in a striving toward those goals, but not enough access to the means to achieve them.
6. Without reasonable access to the socially approved means, members of society will attempt to find some way to resolve the pressure to achieve. These alternative solutions are called "modes of adaptation."
7. The various modes of adaptation are formed by combinations of accepting, rejecting, or substituting for the goals and the means.

   a. If, in the face of moral pressure, the individual continues to "accept" the value of both the goals and the means, the form of behavior exhibited will be *conforming*. This is the most common form of adaptation.
   b. If the individual accepts the goals but rejects the means to achieve them, the form of behavior will be deviant and *innovative*. Here, more available and faster ways of achieving the goals are created.
   c. If the individual sees the goals as unattainable (rejects them) but accepts the means anyway, the form of behavior will be deviant and *ritualistic*. In this case, the focus of the individual becomes the means rather than the ends.
   d. If the individual rejects both the goals and the means, the form of behavior will be deviant and *retreatist*. A person engaged in this behavior will no longer strive toward the goals and not even continue in the normal stream of life.
   e. If both the goals and the means are rejected and then substituted for, the form of behavior will be deviant and *rebelling*. This form of deviance actually rejects the way society is currently set up and attempts to create a new form of society.

EPILOGUE: CURRENT DIRECTIONS
AND POLICY IMPLICATIONS

Current Directions

As we have already noted, anomie theory remains popular, but the current tendency among criminologists is to use it in a more general form. This form is often called **strain theory.** Although Merton uses the word "strain" in his presentation, Albert K. Cohen (himself referred to as a strain theorist) argues that Travis Hirschi, in his 1969 book *Causes of Delinquency* invented the category of strain theory (Cohen, 1993). The classification was more recently given emphasis by Ruth Kornhauser (1978) in her critique of criminological theories.

This category of theories is defined by its focus on *motivation*. That is, strain theories require that people be motivated to commit criminal and delinquent acts. Without such motivation, there would be conformity. In other words, strain theories are focused on some special state of mind (or collective state of mind) such as a pathology, tension, frustration, or mental conflict. As a result, people in this state of mind "see crime as expressions, symptoms, or ways of dealing with, solving, or getting relief from whatever is troubling them" (Cohen, 1993). Such theories include psychological and psychoanalytic versions, which explain the source of these symptoms by looking at individuals and locating answers in their own situation and history.

The sociological versions of strain theory ask the question, "Where do these strains come from?" In other words, what is it about the way in which society is organized and arranged that tends to produce the conditions and circumstances that give rise to deviant behavior? Sociological strain theories also attempt to explain the origins of motivational states (and usually are concerned with the distribution of those states). They search for the origins of strain in the way society is put together or arranged; that is, in the social structure. Theories such as Merton's place the source of strain in cultural messages and social inequalities. We refer to all these approaches as *structural* strain theories.

Other than Merton's further writing and elaboration on his theory, several theorists have added to the general strain theory perspective. Most notable are Cohen (1955, 1965), Cloward (1959), and Cloward with Ohlin (1960). These extensions are examined in detail in the chapter on subculture theories (Chapter 7). Other theorists, however, have directly added to anomie theory by suggesting new categories for the modes of adaptation (Dubin, 1959; Harary, 1966). These writers were concerned with Merton's use of the substitution concept and argued that it opened the door to many more than the five modes of adaptation predicted by the scheme of accepting and rejecting the goals and means. Other criminologists have critiqued the theory and conducted studies to see if the relationships implied in the theory exist. Many have noted that the theory is wanting in support, but some (McShane and Williams, 1985; Messner, 1988; Bernard, 1987b; Burton and Cullen, 1992; Menard, 1995) have argued that much of the research on anomie theory has been done with micro-level variables dealing with individuals, rather than the more appropriate use of macro-level variables measuring characteristics of groups. As a result, the downturn of popularity for anomie theory during the 1970s is more likely the result of criminological attention turning to "newer" theories rather than any lack of supportive evidence (Lilly, Cullen, and Ball, 1989).

Aspirations and Expectations

One variety of newer work carries on the Mertonian tradition of examining disparities between aspirations and expectations. In this vein, aspirations are viewed as the ideal goals that one should strive for, whereas expectations are what the individual thinks he or she can actually achieve. The argument is that a disparity between aspirations and expectations leads to a sense of frustration and higher probabilities of deviant behavior. Typically, this approach is used for adolescents, because they have not had time to be rejected by the social system and thereby meet Merton's criteria for a shortage of means (for examples of this approach, see Liska, 1971; Farnworth and Leiber, 1989).

Relative Deprivation

Another direction suggests that the relative discrepancy between poverty and wealth is important in determining crime rates. For instance, in areas of extreme poverty or extreme wealth, we might expect to find that such conspicuous differences create more frustration and despair and, subsequently, higher crime rates. Several studies have suggested that this variation of strain theory makes sense and, indeed, does have the anticipated effect (Blau and Blau, 1982; Sampson, 1985; Messner, 1989).

Immediacy of Goals

Yet another variety of strain theory seeks to resolve one of the major criticisms of strain theory: that the goals/means formula does not explain middle-class deviance very well. While this might not be a valid criticism, Delbert Elliott and Harwin Voss (1974) added middle-class delinquency to the strain picture. They did so by focusing more on immediate goals than the long-range aspirations usually connected with strain theory. Juveniles are more likely to be concerned about their immediate goals (popularity, athletic achievement, good grades) than whether they will eventually succeed in life. Moreover, these immediate goals are not necessarily tied to social class, although middle-class juveniles are perhaps more likely to chase immediate goals that are more difficult to achieve (class president, captain of cheerleaders). When coupled with other impediments to success (physical unattractiveness, poor personality, lack of coordination, or inferior intellectual ability), the inability to achieve goals may be seen as a combination of several factors.

New Strain Theories

General strain theory: This best known of the contemporary versions of strain theory is the result of the work of Robert Agnew (1985, 1989, 1992; and White, 1992). Agnew contends that traditional strain theories look at positively valued goals. He asserts that another ingredient should be added: the avoidance of painful (or negative) situations. Just as an individual's goals can be blocked, so can the ability to avoid undesirable situations or stressful life events. For instance, a juvenile may not be able to avoid a bad family situation, drop out of school as a solution to poor grades, or even hide from peer rejection. All these situations may yield levels of frustration as high as those from blocked aspirations or immediate goals. When both positive blockage and negative avoidance are combined, the stress levels suggest that we can expect the highest rates of delinquency or deviance. Even though it is relatively new, general strain theory has already received support from a number of other research studies (Agnew and White, 1992; Paternoster and Mazerolle, 1994; Hoffman and Su, 1997).

Institutional strain theory: This second contemporary adaptation of strain theory comes from Steven Messner and Richard Rosenfeld (1994). Given the traditional Mertonian scheme—that economic sources of strain yield anomic conditions—they argue an entire level of noneconomic institutions has been omitted. A more rounded picture of structural constraints on deviance includes the contributions of such institutions as the family, schools, religion, and law. For anomie to work, not only is a disjunction of goals and means necessary, but social institutions must also be weakened. Messner and Rosenfeld posit that a dysjunction affects these institutions in such a way as to contribute to a loss of control; that is, an anomic environment weakens the family's control over its members and thus its power to curtail deviant behavior. The theory obviously incorporates concepts from control theory and provides a bridge from cultural controls (old strain versions) to more personal levels of control. As is the case with general strain theory, research has already begun to focus on this new version of strain theory.

Each of these additions to the Mertonian strain approach provide another level of explanation to the structural variables of the original perspective and demonstrate the value of relationships between cultural strain and personal factors. This acknowledgment of the complexity of strain is an important advance in combining structural factors with individual-level variables.

Policy Implications

Policy implications are easy to draw from anomie and strain theories; putting them into practice is another matter entirely. Because anomie is a macro-level theory, the proper form of policy would be aimed at modifying the social structure. Examples would include the elimination of class structures, racism, and prejudice, all of which are factors working to limit the opportunities for reaching goals. Other approaches, as we discuss in the following chapter, involve programs to provide increased job opportunities. Most clearly seen in the Depression-era work programs, many programs that aimed to increase opportunities for meaningful work were also created during the 1960s. Similarly, greater educational opportunity would be a desirable program under strain theory. California's education master plan of the 1960s, for example, gave all citizens free access to at least two years of college. Programs aimed at decreasing school dropout rates and increasing educational levels are also in keeping with the anomie tradition. From the perspective of Agnew's strain theory, a reasonable approach would be to find ways to decrease negative relationships in families, schools, and neighborhoods.

A final policy implication deserves attention. Ruth Kornhauser (1978) as well as Steve Brown, Finn Esbensen, and Gil Geis (1991) have suggested that one possible policy implementation of anomie theory would be to reduce aspirations. While they do not actually suggest that we do so, some of the possibilities are intriguing. We could, for instance, introduce a caste system in which individuals remain in the caste to which they are born, never being allowed to dream of goals beyond their reach. Or, perhaps we could mount a campaign to tell everyone that the American Dream is over. None of these things would, of course, be desirable—crime is not the worst ill in society. On the positive side though, we could attempt to restrict advertising that announces the availability of all sorts of luxury goods and our need to secure those goods to keep up with the proverbial "Jones family next door." In this sense, the advertising media might be blamed (under anomie theory) for magnifying the tensions between the haves and the have-nots.

BIBLIOGRAPHY

ABRAHAM, GARY A. (1983). "Misunderstanding the Merton thesis: A boundary dispute between history and sociology." *ISIS* 74: 368–387.

Adler, Freda, and William S. Laufer, eds. (1995). *The Legacy of Anomie Theory: Advances in Criminological Theory*, vol. 6. New Brunswick, NJ: Transaction.

AGNEW, ROBERT (1984). "Goal achievement and delinquency." *Social Forces* 64: 151–167.

———— (1985). "A revised strain theory of delinquency." *Social Forces* 64: 151–167.

———— (1987). "On `testing structural strain theories.'" *Journal of Research in Crime and Delinquency* 24: 281–286.

———— (1989). "A longitudinal test of the revised strain theory." *Journal of Quantitative Criminology* 5: 373–387.

———— (1991). "Strain and subcultural crime theory." In Joseph Sheley, ed., *Criminology: A Contemporary Handbook*, 273–292. Belmont, CA: Wadsworth.

———— (1992). "Foundation for a general strain theory of crime and delinquency." *Criminology* 30: 47–66.

———— (1993). "Why do they do it? An examination of the intervening mechanisms between 'social control' variables and delinquency." *Journal of Research in Crime and Delinquency* 30: 245–266.

———— (1994). "Delinquency and the desire for money." *Justice Quarterly* 11: 411–427.

AGNEW, ROBERT, FRANCIS T. CULLEN, VELMER S. BURTON, JR., T. DAVID EVANS, and R. GREGORY DUNAWAY (1996). "A new test of classic strain theory." *Justice Quarterly* 13: 681–704.

AGNEW, ROBERT, and D. JONES (1988). "Adapting to deprivation: An examination of inflated educational expectations." *Sociological Quarterly* 29: 315–337.

AGNEW, ROBERT, and HELENE RASKIN WHITE (1992). "An empirical test of general strain theory." *Criminology* 30: 475–499.

AKERS, RONALD, and JOHN COCHRAN (1985). "Adolescent marijuana use: A test of three theories of deviant behavior." *Deviant Behavior* 6: 323–346.

ANGELL, ROBERT C. (1962). "Preferences for moral norms in three areas." *American Journal of Sociology* 67: 650–660.

AULTMAN, MADELINE, and CHARLES WELLFORD (1979). "Towards an integrated model of delinquency causation: An empirical analysis." *Sociology and Social Research* 63: 316–327.

BALKWELL, JAMES W. (1990). "Ethnic inequality and the rate of homicide." *Social Forces* 69: 53–70.

BALL, RICHARD, and ROBERT LILLY (1971). "Juvenile delinquency in an urban county." *Criminology* 9: 69–85.

BARON, STEPHEN W., and TIMOTHY F. HARTNAGEL (1997). "Attributions, affect, and crime: Street youths' reactions to unemployment." *Criminology* 35: 409–434.

BELL, WENDELL (1957). "Anomie, social isolation and the class structure." *Sociometry* 20: 105–116.

BENNETT, RICHARD, and SANDRA BAXTER (1983). "Police personnel levels and the incidence of crime: A cross-national investigation." *Criminal Justice Review* 8: 32–40.

BERNARD, THOMAS (1984). "Control criticisms of strain theories: An assessment of theoretical and empirical adequacy." *Journal of Research in Crime and Delinquency* 21: 353–372.

—— (1987a). "Reply to Agnew." *Journal of Research in Crime and Delinquency* 24: 287–290.

—— (1987b). "Testing structural strain theories." *Journal of Research in Crime and Delinquency* 24: 262–280.

BIERSTEDT, ROBERT (1981). "Robert K. Merton." In *American Sociological Theory: A Critical History*. New York: Academic Press.

BLAU, JUDITH M., and PETER M. BLAU (1982). "The cost of inequality: Metropolitan structure and violent crime." *American Sociological Review* 47: 114–129.

BOHLKE, ROBERT H. (1961). "Social mobility, stratification inconsistency and middle class delinquency." *Social Problems* 8: 351–363.

BORDUA, DAVID J. (1958–1959). "Juvenile delinquency and `anomie': An attempt at replication." *Social Problems* 6: 230–238.

BRAITHWAITE, JOHN (1989). "Criminological theory and organizational crime." *Justice Quarterly* 6: 333–358.

BREED, WARREN (1958). "Occupational mobility and suicide among white males." *American Sociological Review* 28: 179–188.

BREZINA, TIMOTHY (1996). "Adapting to strain: An examination of delinquent coping responses." *Criminology* 34: 39–60.

BROWN, STEPHEN E., FINN-AGE ESBENSEN, and GILBERT GEIS (1991). *Criminology: Explaining Crime and Its Context*. Cincinnati, OH: Anderson.

BURGER, WILLIAM (1993). *American Crime and Punishment: The Religious Origins of American Criminology*. Buchanan, MI: Vande Vere Publishing.

BURTON, VELMER S., JR., and FRANCIS T. CULLEN (1992). "The empirical status of strain theory." *Journal of Crime and Justice* 15: 1–30.

BURTON, VELMER S., JR., FRANCIS T. CULLEN, DAVID T. EVANS, and R. GREGORY DUNAWAY (1994). "Reconsidering strain theory: Operationalization, rival theories, and adult criminality." *Journal of Quantitative Criminology* 10: 213–239.

CARMICHAEL, BENJAMIN (1990). "An exploratory study of values and attitudes of black delinquents in custody." *Journal of Crime and Justice* 13: 66–85.

CERNKOVICH, STEPHEN A. (1978). "Evaluating two models of delinquency causation: Structural theory and control theory." *Criminology* 16: 335–362.

CHAMLIN, MITCHELL B., and JOHN K. COCHRAN (1995). "Assessing Messner and Rosenfeld's institutional anomie theory: A partial test." *Criminology* 33: 411–429.

CHAPMAN, IVAN (1977). "A critique of Merton's typology of modes of individual adaptation." *Quarterly Journal of Ideology* 1: 13–18.

CHEUNG, YUET-WAH, and AGNES M. NG (1988). "Social factors in adolescent deviant behaviour in Hong Kong: An integrated theoretical approach." *International Journal of Comparative and Applied Criminal Justice* 12: 27–45.

CHILTON, ROLAND J. (1964). "Delinquency area research: Baltimore, Detroit, and Indianapolis." *American Sociological Review* 29: 71–83.

CLARK, JOHN P., and EUGENE P. WENNIGER (1962). "Socio-economic class and area as correlates of illegal behavior among juveniles." *American Sociological Review* 27: 826–834.

—— (1963). "Goal orientations and illegal behavior among juveniles." *Social Forces* 42: 49–59.

CLEMMENS, PATRICIA, and JAMES RUST (1979). "Factors in adolescent rebellious feelings." *Adolescence* 14: 159–173.

CLINARD, MARSHALL B. (1964a). *Anomie and Deviant Behavior.* New York: Free Press.

——— (1964b). "The theoretical implications of anomie and deviant behavior." In M. B. Clinard, ed., *Anomie and Deviant Behavior,* 1–56. New York: Free Press.

CLOWARD, RICHARD A. (1956). "Remarks." In H. L. Witmer and R. Kotinsky, eds., *New Perspectives for Research in Juvenile Delinquency,* 80–91. Washington, DC: U.S. Government Printing Office.

——— (1959). "Illegitimate means, anomie, and deviant behavior." *American Sociological Review* 24: 164–176.

CLOWARD, RICHARD A. and LLOYD E. OHLIN (1960). *Delinquency and Opportunity: A Theory of Delinquent Gangs.* New York: Free Press.

COHEN, ALBERT K. (1955). *Delinquent Boys: The Culture of the Gang.* New York: Free Press.

——— (1965). "The sociology of the deviant act: Anomie theory and beyond." *American Sociological Review* 30: 5–14.

——— (1993). Letter to the author (FW). January 29, 1993.

COHEN, LAWRENCE, and KENNETH LAND (1987). "Sociological positivism and the explanation of criminality." In M. R. Gottfredson and T. Hirschi, eds., *Positive Criminology.* Newbury Park, CA: Sage.

COLVIN, MARK, and JOHN PAULY (1989). "A critique of criminology: Toward an integrated structural-Marxist theory of delinquency production." *American Journal of Sociology* 89: 513–551.

CONGER, JOHN C., and WALTER B. MILLER (1966). *Personality, Social Class and Delinquency.* New York: Wiley.

COSER, LEWIS A., and ROBERT NISBET (1975). "Merton and the contemporary mind: An affectionate dialogue." In L. A. Coser, ed., *The Idea of Social Structure: Papers in Honor of Robert K. Merton,* 3–10. New York: Harcourt Brace Jovanovich.

CRESSEY, DONALD R., and WITOLD KRASSOWSKI (1958). "Inmate organization and anomie in American prisons and Soviet labor camps." *Social Problems* 5: 217–230.

CULLEN, FRANCIS T. (1988). "Were Cloward and Ohlin strain theorists?" *Journal of Research in Crime and Delinquency* 25: 214–241.

DEFRONZO, JAMES (1996). "Welfare and burglary." *Crime and Delinquency* 42: 223–230.

DESROCHES, FREDERICK (1983). "Anomie: Two theories of prison riots." *Canadian Journal of Criminology* 25: 173–190.

DOLLARD, JOHN (1937). *Caste and Class in a Southern Town.* New Haven, CT: Yale University Press.

DUBIN, ROBERT (1959). "Deviant behavior and social structure: Continuities in social theory." *American Sociological Review* 24: 147–164.

DULL, R. THOMAS (1983). "An empirical examination of the anomie theory of drug use." *Journal of Drug Education* 13: 49–62.

DURKHEIM, EMILE (1893). *The Division of Labor in Society.* New York: Free Press. (Reprinted and translated 1933.)

——— (1897). *Suicide: A Study in Sociology.* New York: Free Press. (Reprinted and translated 1951.)

EDWARDS, WILLIE J. (1992). "Predicting juvenile delinquency: A review of correlates and a confirmation by recent research based on an integrated theoretical model." *Justice Quarterly* 9: 553–583.

——— (1996). "A measurement of delinquency differences between a delinquent and nondelinquent sample: What are the implications?" *Adolescence* 31: 973–989.

ELLIOTT, DELBERT S. (1962). "Delinquency and perceived opportunity." *Sociological Inquiry* 32: 216–234.

—— (1966). "Delinquency, school attendance and dropout." *Social Problems* 13: 307–314.

ELLIOTT, DELBERT S., and HARWIN VOSS (1974). *Delinquency and Dropout.* Lexington, MA: Lexington Books.

ELLIS, DESMOND (1989). "Male abuse of a married or cohabiting female partner: The application of sociological theory to research findings." *Violence and Victims* 4: 235–255.

EMPEY, LAMAR, and STEVEN LUBECK (1971). *Explaining Delinquency: Construction, Test, and Reformation of a Sociological Theory.* Lexington, MA: Heath Lexington Books.

EPPS, EDGAR G. (1967). "Socioeconomic status, race, level of aspiration and juvenile delinquency: A limited empirical test of Merton's concept of deviation." *Phylon* 28: 16–27.

FARNWORTH, MARGARET, and MICHAEL J. LEIBER (1989). "Strain theory revisited: Economic goals, educational means, and delinquency." *American Sociological Review* 54: 263–274.

FARRELL, RONALD, and JAMES NELSON (1978). "A sequential analysis of delinquency." *International Journal of Criminology and Penology* 3: 255–268.

FERDINAND, THEODORE N. (1987). "The methods of delinquency theory." *Criminology* 25: 841–859.

FIGUIERA-MCDONOUGH, JOSEFINA (1984). "Feminism and delinquency: In search of the elusive link." *British Journal of Criminology* 24: 325–342.

—— (1986). "School context, gender, and delinquency." *Journal of Youth and Adolescence* 15: 79–98.

GALLIHER, JOHN (1971). "Training in social manipulation as a rehabilitative technique." *Crime and Delinquency* 17: 431–436.

GARFIELD, EUGENE (1977). "Robert K. Merton: Among the giants." *Current Comments* 28: 5–7.

GLASER, DANIEL, and KENT RICE (1959). "Crime, age, and employment." *American Sociological Review* 24: 679–686.

GOLD, MARTIN (1958). "Suicide, homicide, and the socialization of aggression." *American Journal of Sociology* 63: 651–661.

GOMME, IAN (1985). "Predictors of status and criminal offenses among male and female adolescents in an Ontario community." *Canadian Journal of Criminology* 27: 147–159.

GOODE, WILLIAM J. (1961). "Illegitimacy, anomie, and cultural penetration." *American Sociological Review* 26: 910–925.

GOULD, LEROY C. (1969). "Juvenile entrepreneurs." *American Journal of Sociology* 74: 710–719.

GUTTENTAG, MARCIA (1968). "The relationship of unemployment to crime and delinquency." *Journal of Social Issues* 24: 105–114.

HARARY, FRANK (1966). "Merton revisited: A new classification for deviant behavior." *American Sociological Review* 31: 693–697.

HARTNAGEL, TIMOTHY, and HARVEY KRAHN (1989). "High school dropouts, labor market success, and criminal behavior." *Youth and Society* 20: 416–444.

HASKELL, MARTIN R. (1961). "Toward a reference group theory of juvenile delinquency." *Social Problems* 8: 220–230.

HILBERT, RICHARD (1989). "Durkheim and Merton on anomie: An unexplored contrast and its derivatives." *Social Problems* 36: 242–250.

HILL, GARY, and ELIZABETH CRAWFORD (1990). "Women, race, and crime." *Criminology* 28: 601–626.

HIRSCHI, TRAVIS (1969). *Causes of Delinquency.* Berkeley: University of California Press.

HOFFMAN, JOHN P., and SUSAN S. SU (1997). "The conditional effects of stress on delinquency and drug use: A strain theory assessment of sex differences." *Journal of Research in Crime and Delinquency* 34: 46–78.

HYMAN, HERBERT H. (1953). "The value systems of the different classes: A social-psychological contribution to the analysis of stratification." In R. Bendix and S. M. Lipset, eds., *Class, Status, and Power,* 488–499. New York: Free Press.

IGA, MAMORU, and KENSHIRO OHARA (1967). "Suicide attempts of Japanese youth and Durkheim's concept of anomie: An interpretation." *Human Organization* 26: 58–68.

JAFFE, ELIEZER (1969). "Family anomie and delinquency: Development of the concept and some empirical findings." *British Journal of Criminology* 9: 376–388.

JARJOURA, G. ROGER (1996). "The conditional effect of social class on the dropout-delinquency relationship." *Journal of Research in Crime and Delinquency* 33: 232–255.

JOHNSON, ERIC A. (1993). "Crime and the Industrial Revolution: The German case." *Criminal Justice History: An International Annual* 12: 19–27.

JOHNSON, L. V., and M. MATRE (1978). "Anomie and alcohol use: Drinking patterns in Mexican-American and Anglo neighborhoods." *Journal of Studies on Alcohol* 39: 894–902.

JUNGER, MARIANNE, and WIM POLDER (1992). "Some explanations of crime among four ethnic groups in the Netherlands." *Journal of Quantitative Criminology* 8: 51–78.

KAPSIS, ROBERT (1978). "Black ghetto diversity and anomie: A socio-political view." *American Journal of Sociology* 83: 1132–1153.

KEANE, CARL (1993). "The impact of financial performance on frequency of corporate crime: A latent variable test of strain theory." *Canadian Journal of Criminology* 35: 293–308.

KILLIAS, MARTIN (1989). "Criminality among second-generation immigrants in western Europe: A review of the evidence." *Criminal Justice Review* 14: 13–42.

KINSEY, B., and L. PHILLIPS (1968). "Evaluation of anomy as a predisposing or developmental factor in alcohol addiction." *Quarterly Journal of Studies on Alcohol* 29: 892–898.

KORNHAUSER, RUTH R. (1978). *Social Sources of Delinquency.* Chicago: University of Chicago Press.

KROHN, MARVIN (1978). "A Durkheimian analysis of international crime rates." *Social Forces* 57: 654–670.

LAFREE, GARY, and KRIS A. DRASS (1996). "The effect of changes in intraracial income inequality and educational attainment on changes in arrest rates for African Americans and whites." *American Sociological Review* 61: 614–634.

LANDER, BERNARD (1954). *Toward an Understanding of Juvenile Delinquency.* New York: Columbia University Press.

LANIER, MARK M., and DAVID L. CARTER (1993). "Applying computer simulation to forecast homicide rates." *Journal of Criminal Justice* 21: 467–479.

LASKY, D., and J. ZIENGENFUSS (1979). "Anomie and drug use in high school students." *International Journal of the Addictions* 14: 861–866.

LEE, DAVID J., RICHARD S. DEFRANK, and ROBERT M. ROSE (1990). "Anomie, alcohol abuse and alcohol consumption: A prospective analysis." *Journal of Studies on Alcohol* 51: 415–420.

LEWIS, RODNEY (1973). "Toward an understanding of police anomie." *Journal of Police Science and Administration* 1: 484–490.

LI, LIYING (1995). "Sociological explanations of crimes in late imperial China: 1744–1903." *International Journal of Comparative and Applied Criminal Justice* 19: 107–127.

LILLY, J. ROBERT, FRANCIS T. CULLEN, and RICHARD A. BALL (1989). *Criminological Theory: Context and Consequences.* Newbury Park, CA: Sage.

LINDESMITH, ALFRED R., and JOHN GAGNON (1964). "Anomie and drug addiction." In M. B. Clinard, ed., *Anomie and Deviant Behavior,* 158–188. New York: Free Press.

LISKA, ALLEN (1971). "Aspirations, expectations and delinquency: Stress and additive models." *Sociological Quarterly* 12: 99–107.

LUPSHA, PETER (1969). "On theories of urban violence." *Urban Affairs Quarterly* 4: 273–296.

LYND, ROBERT S., and HELEN MERRELL LYND (1929). *Middletown: A Study in American Culture.* Harcourt, Brace and World.

MARKS, STEPHEN R. (1974). "Durkheim's theory of anomie." *American Journal of Sociology* 80: 329–363.

MARTIN, RANDY, ROBERT MUTCHNICK, and TIMOTHY AUSTIN (1990). "Robert Merton." In R. Martin, R. Mutchnick, and T. Austin, *Criminological Thought: Pioneers Past and Present,* 207–238. New York: Macmillan.

McCARTHY, BILL, and JOHN HAGAN (1992). "Mean streets: The theoretical significance of situational delinquency among homeless youths." *American Journal of Sociology* 98: 597–627.

McSHANE, MARILYN, and FRANK P. WILLIAMS III (1985). "Anomie theory and marijuana use: Clarifying the issues." *Journal of Crime and Justice* 8: 21–40.

MEIER, DOROTHY, and WENDELL BELL (1959). "Anomia and differential access to the achievement of life goals." *American Sociological Review* 26: 753–758.

MENARD, SCOTT (1995). "A developmental test of Mertonian anomie theory." *Journal of Research in Crime and Delinquency* 32: 136–174.

MERTON, ROBERT K. (1936). "The unanticipated consequences of purposive social action." *American Sociological Review* 1: 894–904.

——— (1938). "Social structure and anomie." *American Sociological Review* 3: 672–682.

——— (1957). *Social Theory and Social Structure,* rev. ed. New York: Free Press.

——— (1959). "Social conformity, deviation, and opportunity structures: A comment on the contributions of Dubin and Cloward." *American Sociological Review* 24: 177–188.

——— (1964). "Anomie, anomia, and social interactions: Contexts of deviant behavior." In M. B. Clinard, ed., *Anomie and Deviant Behavior,* 213–242. New York: Free Press.

——— (1968). *Social Theory and Social Structure,* rev. and enlarged ed. New York: Free Press.

——— (1997). "On the evolving synthesis of differential association and anomie theory: A perspective from the sociology of science." *Criminology* 35: 517–525.

MERTON, ROBERT K., and M. F. ASHLEY-MONTAGU (1940). "Crime and the anthropologist." *American Anthropologist* 42: 384–408.

MESSNER, STEVEN F. (1988). "Merton's 'Social Structure and Anomie': The road not taken." *Deviant Behavior* 9: 33–53.

——— (1989). "Economic discrimination and societal homicide rates: Further evidence on the cost of inequality." *American Sociological Review* 54: 597–611.

MESSNER, STEVEN F., and REID M. GOLDEN (1992). "Racial inequality and racially disaggregated homicide rates: An assessment of alternative theoretical explanations." *Criminology* 30: 421–445.

MESSNER, STEVEN F., and RICHARD ROSENFELD (1994). *Crime and the American Dream.* Belmont, CA: Wadsworth.

NETTLER, GWYNN (1959). "Antisocial sentiment and criminality." *American Sociological Review* 24: 202–208.

O'CONNELL, BRIAN, HERBERT HOLZMAN, and BARRY ARMANDI (1986). "Police cynicism and the modes of adaptation." *Journal of Police Science and Administration* 14: 307–313.

OGLE, ROBBIN S., DANIEL, MAIER-KATKIN, and THOMAS J. BERNARD (1995). "A theory of homicidal behavior among women." *Criminology* 33: 173–193.

OLSEN, MARVIN (1965). "Durkheim's two concepts of anomie." *Sociological Quarterly* 6: 37–44.

PALAMORE, ERDMAN B., and PHILLIP E. HAMMOND (1964). "Interacting factors in juvenile delinquency." *American Sociological Review* 29: 848–854.

PARSONS, TALCOTT (1937). *The Structure of Social Action.* New York: McGraw-Hill.

PASSAS, NIKOS (1990). "Anomie and corporate deviance." *Contemporary Crises* 14: 157–178.

PATERNOSTER, RAYMOND, and PAUL MAZEROLLE (1994). "General strain theory and delinquency: A replication and extension." *Journal of Research in Crime and Delinquency* 31: 235–263.

PHILLIPS, LORNE (1976). "An application of anomy theory to the study of alcoholism." *Journal of Studies on Alcohol* 37: 78–84.

POOLE, ERIC, and ROBERT REGOLI (1983). "Professionalism, role conflict, work alienation, and anomia: A look at prison management." *Social Science Journal* 20: 63–70.

POWELL, ELWIN H. (1958). "Occupation, status, and suicide: Toward a redefinition of anomie." *American Sociological Review* 23: 131–139.

——— (1966). "Crime as a function of anomie." *Journal of Criminal Law, Criminology and Police Science* 57: 161–171.

RANKIN, JOSEPH (1980). "School factors and delinquency: Interactions by age and sex." *Sociology and Social Research* 64: 420–434.

RAYMOND, FRANK (1975). "A sociological view of narcotics addiction." *Crime and Delinquency* 21: 11–18.

REISS, ALBERT J., JR., and ALBERT L. RHODES (1959). "Are educational norms and goals of conforming, truant, and delinquent adolescents influenced by group position in American society?" *Journal of Negro Education* (Summer): 252–267.

——— (1961). "The distribution of juvenile delinquency in the social class structure." *American Sociological Review* 26: 720–732.

——— (1963). "Status deprivation and delinquent behavior." *Sociological Quarterly* 4: 135–149.

RHODES, ALBERT L. (1964). "Anomia, aspiration, and status." *Social Forces* 42: 434–440.

ROSENBERG, BERNARD, and HARRY SILVERSTEIN (1969). *The Varieties of Delinquent Experience.* Waltham, MA: Blaisdell.

ROSENFELD, RICHARD (1989). "Robert Merton's contributions to the sociology of deviance." *Sociological Inquiry* 59: 453–466.

RUSHING, WILLIAM A. (1971). "Class culture and 'social structure and anomie.'" *American Journal of Sociology* 76: 857–872.

SAMPSON, ROBERT J. (1985). "Structural sources of variation in race-age-specific rates of offending across major U.S. cities." *Criminology* 23: 647–673.

SEEMAN, M. (1963). "Alienation and social learning in a reformatory." *American Journal of Sociology* 69: 270–284.

SHARPE, ANDREW N. (1995). "Corporate performance crime as structurally coerced action." *Australian and New Zealand Journal of Criminology* 28 (1): 73–92.

SHOHAM, SHLOMO, GIORA RAHAV, and A. KREIZLER (1970). "The measurement of movements on the conformity deviance continuum as an auxiliary tool for action-research." *Acta Criminologica* 3: 103–141.

SHORT, JAMES F., JR. (1964). "Gang delinquency and anomie." In M. B. Clinard, ed., *Anomie and Deviant Behavior,* 98–127. New York: Free Press.

SIMON, WILLIAM, and JOHN GAGNON (1976). "The anomie of affluence: A post-Mertonian conception." *American Journal of Sociology* 82: 356–378.

SIMONS, RONALD, MARTIN MILLER, and STEPHEN AIGNER (1980). "Contemporary theories of deviance and female delinquency: An empirical test." *Journal of Research in Crime and Delinquency* 17: 42–57.

SMITH, DAVID L., ROBERT DURANT, and TIMOTHY J. CARTER (1978). "Social integration, victimization, and anomia." *Criminology* 16: 395–402.

SMITH, DOUGLAS, and RAYMOND PATERNOSTER (1987). "The gender gap in theories of deviance: Issues and evidence." *Journal of Research in Crime and Delinquency* 24: 140–172.

SOROKIN, PITIRIM A. (1928). *Contemporary Sociological Theories.* New York: Harper and Brothers.

SPERGEL, IRVING (1964). *Racketville, Slumtown, Haulberg.* Chicago: University of Chicago Press.

STINCHCOMBE, ARTHUR I. (1975). "Merton's theory of social structure." In L. A. Coser, ed., *The Idea of Social Structure,* 11–13. New York: Harcourt Brace Jovanovich.

TINTO, VINCENT, ELENA PAOLILLO, and FRANCIS T. CULLEN (1978). "The social patterning of deviant behaviors in school." In *Theoretical Perspectives on School Crime,* 1386–1439. Hackensack, NJ: National Council on Crime and Delinquency.

TITTLE, CHARLES (1983). "Social class and criminal behavior: A critique of the theoretical foundation." *Social Forces* 62: 334–358.

TYGART, CLARENCE (1988). "Strain theory and public school vandalism: Academic tracking, school social status, and students' academic achievement." *Youth and Society* 20: 106–118.

WALTERS, STEPHEN (1991). "Alienation and the correctional officer: A multivariate analysis." *American Journal of Criminal Justice* 16: 50–62.

WENZ, FRIEDRICH (1979). "Self-injury behavior, economic status and the family anomie syndrome among adolescents." *Adolescence* 14: 387–398.

WILKINSON, KAREN (1985). "An investigation of the contribution of masculinity to delinquent behavior." *Sociological Forces* 18: 249–263.

WILSON, ROBERT A. (1971). "Anomie in the ghetto, a study of neighborhood type, race, and anomie." *American Journal of Sociology* 77: 66–87.

WINSLOW, ROBERT W. (1967). "Anomie and its alternatives: A self-report study of delinquency." *Sociological Quarterly* 8: 168–480.

WOOD, ARTHUR L. (1942). "Social organization and crime in small Wisconsin communities." *American Sociological Review* 7: 40–46.

YOUNG, THOMAS (1990). "Native American crime and criminal justice require criminologists' attention." *Journal of Criminal Justice Education* 1: 111–126.

ZEITZ, LEONARD, RICHARD MEDALIE, and PAUL ALEXANDER (1969). "Anomie, powerlessness, and police interrogation." *Journal of Criminal Law, Criminology, and Police Science* 60: 314–322.

7

SUBCULTURE THEORIES

INTRODUCTION

With few exceptions, criminological theories of the 1950s and early 1960s focused on juvenile delinquency. Many of the theorists set out to explain what they believed to be the most common form of delinquency: gangs. They were interested in explaining the origins of delinquent gangs and the context in which different types of gangs developed. At the same time, the cultures studied by the Chicago School began to be referred to by the new sociological term "subcultures."

Combining these two topics, criminologists began studying gang delinquency and theorizing about delinquent subcultures. In separate works, Albert K. Cohen in 1955 and Richard A. Cloward and Lloyd E. Ohlin in 1960 combined the work of the Chicago School (and Sutherland) with Merton's anomie theory. Both focused on urban, lower-class, male, gang delinquency. Other theories included Walter Miller's (1958) theory of lower-class "focal concerns" and Marvin Wolfgang and Franco Ferracuti's (1968) theory of the subculture of violence.

Because of the differences among these theories, it is difficult to characterize them as a generic subculture theory. Even characterizing them as strain theories, as some writers have done, is not accurate. Cohen has long refuted a simple strain theory characterization of his work, and Frank Cullen (1988) has recently made a cogent argument that Cloward and Ohlin were not primarily strain theorists. Therefore, this chapter is divided into three sections. After a discussion of the heritage of the theories, we examine, in turn, Cohen's theory of the delinquent subculture, Cloward and Ohlin's differential opportunity theory, and two other subculture theories, those of Miller, and Wolfgang and Ferracuti.

THE HERITAGE OF THE THEORIES

The Social Heritage

The 1950s were a time of prosperity and a tremendous rise in consumerism. The values of the middle class had proven their superiority in a massive war effort, and, consequently, for many it was difficult to conceive of anything other than the middle-class way as being "normal." It may even have been this same pride in "the American way" that helped create the climate for communist-chasing during the McCarthy years.

Along with this spirit, the right to education was seen for the first time as something all Americans shared. As a result of educational benefits provided to military veterans, college enrollment climbed, and the middle class began to expect a college education for its children. Public schooling captured the attention of America and, by the end of the 1950s, the Soviet success in putting into orbit the first satellite resulted in a call in the United States for better education in the sciences. These events ultimately led to changes in the U.S. educational system.

At the same time, the peaking urbanization of the United States was producing increasingly deteriorated central city areas. Middle-class suburbs were developing, and the first housing subdivision was built outside Philadelphia. The Supreme Court outlawed segregation, but economic and territorial boundaries were already distinct. The problems of the cities were the problems of the people who lived there, principally the lower class. Delinquency was viewed as a lower-class problem, and gangs were the most visible form of delinquency. With a clear "we–they" separation, middle-class America saw itself as superior to the lower class.

As Charles Murray (1984) notes, the dominant concepts of poverty, as translated into policy during the 1950s, tended to rely on explanations of individual behavior. The popular view was that individuals were responsible for their own situations and that the poor probably had not worked hard enough. The civil rights movement and other factors already mentioned helped recast the responsibility for poverty into a social framework. With the arrival of the 1960s, the time was ripe for a reinterpretation of the effects of poverty. Bob Lilly, Frank Cullen, and Richard Ball (1989:90) point out that the new social responsibility served to highlight Merton's theory and to emphasisze the emerging opportunity-oriented theories of Cohen, and Cloward and Ohlin.

The Intellectual Heritage

The intellectual traditions behind the theories of the 1950s included the Chicago School theories and the Mertonian conception of anomie. Scholars who were associated with the Chicago School continued their study of crime and delinquency rates and researched the relationship between community and delinquency. Edwin Sutherland, previously the dominant figure in criminology, spread the work of the Chicago School through several graduate students who had studied with him at the University of Indiana in the 1940s. These students would become prominent criminologists.

Robert Merton's theories had also become influential. His writings in sociology, and those of Talcott Parsons, had established a concern with social structure and the examination of social class differences. Within criminology, this "structural-functionalist" approach captured the imagination of theorists who sought ways to reconcile Merton's structure with the Chicago School's process.

A final major influence on the subculture theorists of the 1950s was the writing of a researcher at the Chicago Area Project, Solomon Kobrin. He and others, in examining street gangs and studying the relationships between male generations in a lower-class community, found strong ties between the political hierarchy and organized crime. These ties were so strong that Kobrin referred to them jointly as a "single controlling group" (Kobrin, in Laub, 1983b). It was from these observations that Kobrin (1951) introduced the concept of an integrated community. According to this concept, the degree of social control present within a community is dependent on how well the criminal element is organized as well as on the character of its relationship with the community's official leadership. A community that is organized and integrated has greater social control over the behavior of juveniles than a community where integration is lacking. This control exists because organized crime members reside in the community with their families. Thus, they have an interest in controlling and preventing violence in the community. Because they have power and participate in the political arena, organized crime is able to use that political power to have the police keep the streets in their neighborhood safe. In short, they want the same things for their community that you and I do. Kobrin's insights led the way to a future combination of the Mertonian and Chicago School paradigms.

COHEN'S SUBCULTURE OF DELINQUENCY

Albert K. Cohen's book, *Delinquent Boys: The Culture of the Gang* (1955), was the first attempt at solving the problem of how a delinquent subculture could begin.[1] Cohen also attempted to integrate several theoretical perspectives, including the work of Clifford Shaw and Henry McKay, Edwin Sutherland, and Robert Merton.[2] Although criticized severely (see, especially, Kit-

---

1. We would like to express our appreciation to Albert Cohen for his review and comments on the summary.

2. Most criminologists have viewed Cohen's work as a combination of the East Coast anomie tradition and the Chicago School tradition. Although this view is correct, it is curious that Cohen's book contains only one citation to Merton's work, and this is in a footnote on social disorganization, whose primary source is Shaw and McKay.

suse and Dietrick, 1959; Bordua, 1960, 1961, 1962), his work has been influential among criminologists.

After an examination of the research on juvenile delinquency, Cohen noted that delinquent behavior is most often found among lower-class males and that gang delinquency is the most common form. He also determined that gang subcultures are characterized by behavior that is **nonutilitarian, malicious,** and **negativistic.** In other words, Cohen saw in subcultural delinquency no rationale for stealing (other than seeking peer status), a delight in the discomfort of others, and an obvious attempt to flout middle-class values. The research also characterized gangs as engaged in various forms of delinquent acts (versatility), interested mainly in the present (short-run hedonism) as opposed to the future, and hostile to outsiders (group autonomy). These constitute the factors that had to be explained by a theory of the delinquent subculture.

Cohen declared that all children (indeed, all individuals) seek social **status.** However, not all children can compete equally for status. By virtue of their position in the social structure, lower-class children tend to lack both material and symbolic advantages. As long as they compete among themselves, the footing is relatively equal; it is in competition with middle-class children that those of the lower class fall short.

The first major status problems facing lower-class children are found in the school system. Not only do these children have to compete with middle-class children, but they are also evaluated by adults who use a "**middle-class measuring rod,**" a set of standards that are difficult for the lower-class child to attain. These standards include sharing, delaying gratification, setting long-range goals, and respecting others' property. All of these things intrinsically relate to being brought up with property of one's own and to having parents who know firsthand the future can be better and hard work pays off. None of these standards are necessarily self-evident to the parents of lower-class children, and they cannot be expected to lie to their children. In this competitive framework, then, lower-class children lose ground in the search for status, among both fellow students and teachers. Those who most strongly feel the loss most suffer **status-frustration.** Employing the Freudian mechanism of **reaction-formation** (a defensive mechanism to overcome anxiety) as an explanation, Cohen speculated a hostile overreaction to middle-class values may occur.

Because many lower-class children are trapped in this status-frustration, various adaptations to the middle class take place. For some, adjustment to the middle-class measuring rod results in a **collective solution** to the problem of status. This solution, Cohen suggested, also requires a change in the way status is attained. This is accomplished by jointly establishing "new norms, new criteria of status which define as meritorious the characteristics they *do* possess, the kinds of conduct of which they *are* capable" (1955:66, emphasis in original). Thus, a new cultural form, a **delinquent subculture,** is created to resolve problems of lower-class status.

It is this delinquent subculture that provides the nonutilitarian, malicious, and negativistic character of gang delinquency. Abandoning and inverting the middle-class value system, gang members can achieve status simply by doing those things they do well, such as showing toughness or standing up for themselves. As long as the need for status exists, the delinquent subculture will exist as an available solution for lower-class, male youth.

The more a frustrated lower-class youth interacts with those in the delinquent subculture, the greater is the likelihood the youth will take up the definitions and behaviors of the subculture. Cohen is really saying, then, that the strains resulting from social disorganization (or differential social organization) create a commonly shared situation for many lower-class children. Whether such children become delinquent depends on the degree and strength of their interaction with members of the delinquent subculture. Those who have frequent interaction and begin to view gang delinquents as their significant others are most likely to view the delinquent subculture as the solution to their problems.

We should also note that Cohen proposed, albeit in few words, theories of female delinquency and middle-class male delinquency. In both instances he used the concepts of status-frustration and reaction-formation to explain the form of delinquent subculture available to each group. He characterized females as frustrated by the sexual "double standard" and, through the reaction-formation process, as resolving their status-frustration by engaging in sexually-oriented delinquent behavior. Cohen viewed middle-class males, in contrast, as anxious about their "maleness" because of the child-rearing responsibilities of the mother. The reaction-formation process in this case results in a "masculine protest" against female authority, creating a middle-class male delinquent subculture. The subculture emphasizes behavior involving masculine activities, especially those revolving around the automobile, and thus leads to joy riding, "drag racing," and being "bad."

Classification of the Theory

Cohen's subculture theory is usually referred to as a *strain*, or *structural*, theory. While this is accurate, it is only partially so because while the source of the delinquent subculture is strain, the theory focuses on the process by which the subculture is created. The latter part represents the influence of the Chicago School's process orientation. This duality also makes it difficult to classify the theory as either a macrotheory or a microtheory; instead, classification as a *bridging* theory is appropriate. In this respect, Cohen borrows from strain theory an explanation of social structure and proceeds to describe how delinquent subcultures come about. He does this from a *consensus* approach, meaning that society emphasizes reaching goals in the accepted middle-class way. It is only after frustration develops from an inability to reach status goals that lower-class children find a need for alternative means. Similarly, the theory is a clear example of sociological *pos-*

itivism (as are most criminological theories). In fact, Cohen, (1955:21–48) tells us there are certain forms of behavior to be explained, and he then develops the concept of subculture as a means of understanding those behaviors. Cohen himself says (1993):

> *Delinquent Boys* is not just a strain theory and structural theory. It is also a theory that emphasizes the role of *process* and of interaction; specifically, the way in which the availability of others who are similarly circumstanced (who experience the same strain) and interaction with those others determines how the actor will deal with strain.

Major Points of the Theory

1. Members of society share a common value system that emphasizes certain values over others. In the United States, these values are closely associated with the middle class.
2. Most of these common values stress goals that result in the gaining of status; therefore, status itself becomes a generally approved goal.
3. Opportunities to reach these goals are more often available to the middle class than to the lower class.
4. Societal institutions, especially schools, reflect middle-class value-goals and use them to evaluate those who come in contact with the institution.
5. Because of their limited opportunities, lower-class youths are often evaluated unfavorably by the school system, leading to frustration in their pursuit of status.
6. Unable to gain status through the use of conventional school opportunities (grades, social standing), lower-class youths rebel (reaction-formation) against middle-class values while still keeping status as a goal.
7. Over a period of time, lower-class youths collectively create a new value system in opposition to middle-class values. The standards of this new value system are mostly anticonventional and afford the youths opportunities for gaining status.
8. This "delinquent solution" is passed on through the transmission of values from youth to youth and generation to generation, fostering an ongoing delinquent subculture that provides status for behavior that is negativistic, malicious, and nonutilitarian.

CLOWARD AND OHLIN'S DIFFERENTIAL OPPORTUNITY THEORY

The theory that became known as "differential opportunity theory" had its origins in a 1959 article by Richard Cloward. Noting Merton's anomie theory had specified only one opportunity structure, Cloward argued there is a second opportunity structure. Not only does a set of legitimate means exist to reach cultural goals, but standard illegitimate avenues exist as well (the **illegitimate opportunity structure**). This second source of opportunities became the background of the theory proposed in a book Cloward wrote with Lloyd Ohlin, *Delinquency and Opportunity: A Theory of Delinquent Gangs* (1960).[3]

---

3. We would like to express our appreciation to Lloyd Ohlin for his review and comments on the summary.

According to Cloward and Ohlin, more than one way exists for juveniles to reach their aspirations. In those urban, lower-class areas where very few legitimate opportunities are available, one can find opportunities of a different kind. Further, these opportunities are just as well established and access is just as limited as in the legitimate structure. Thus, position in society dictates the ability to participate in both conventional and criminal avenues of success.

Using the writings of Solomon Kobrin (1951) on integrated conventional and criminal activity in lower-class communities, Cloward and Ohlin aregued that the form of delinquent subculture depends on the **degree of integration** present in the community. Moreover, they suggested that in a community without a stable criminal structure, lower-class juveniles would have no greater opportunity to succeed in life through criminal avenues than they would through conventional means. There would be no criminal "business" to join and to work one's way up through the ranks, no way to learn properly a criminal trade, and no way to become a "professional." People who could work their way up through a criminal business, in contrast, could gain the wherewithal to enable them to slip over to legitimate business. In fact, this is exactly what Kobrin (1951:657) meant by community integration: leaders in legitimate and illegitimate businesses share the goal of profitability, membership in religious and social organizations, and participation in the political process. And, of course, they share the desire for safe streets in the neighborhood where they live.

Cloward and Ohlin proposed there would be three ideal types of delinquent gang subcultures: criminal, conflict, and retreatist. First, where communities are fully integrated, gangs would act almost as an apprenticeship group for adult, organized criminal concerns. In this **criminal subculture,** the primary focus would be on profit-making activities, and violence would be minimal. These subcultural gangs would practice the criminal "trades" under the loose supervision of organized crime. Gang members could participate in various gambling activities (e.g., "running numbers") or learn and participate in profit-making activities such as shoplifting, fencing, and extortion. A contemporary example of participation in illegal activities is drug distributors' use of under-aged gang members as drug carriers and dealers. If caught with drugs, under-age juveniles do not face the same penalties as adults.

Cloward and Ohlin also pointed out that criminal gangs exist where there is an integration of ages as well as legitimate and illegitimate groups. In this way they stress the learning of roles and the effect of role models on the shaping of the subcultural activities. In other words, young juveniles learn by watching and associating with older youths, who in turn learn from the adults around them. As Cloward and Ohlin explained: "Just as the middle-class youth, as a consequence of intimate relationships with, say, a banker or a businessman, may aspire to become a banker or a businessman, so the lower-class youth may be associated with and aspire to become a 'policy king'" [the extortion racket] (1960:162–163). The influence of the Chicago School's symbolic interactionist perspective, especially Suther-land's differential association theory, is obvious here.

A nonintegrated community would not only lack a well-organized and ongoing illegitimate structure but, according to Kobrin (1951:658), would also exercise very weak community control over juveniles. Thus, any gang subculture that would develop in one of these communities would exhibit unrestrained behavior. As in Cohen's delinquent subculture, the primary focus would be on gaining "respect." Violence, property damage, and unpredictable behavior would become the hallmarks of such gangs. Cloward and Ohlin called this form the **conflict subculture**. These gangs would cause trouble equally for the community's adult criminal element and for the conventional adults.

In short, a socially disorganized community tends to create a gang subculture that is equally disorganized. Transient and unstable relation-ships in the community are reflected in juvenile interactions, and relation-ships and role models between youths of different ages would be difficult to sustain. Further, the illegitimate adult role models available to juveniles tend to be individuals who are not successful criminals (compared with those in organized crime). Interaction and learning in these areas reflect the nature of the community, and stable criminal learning environments cannot be developed.

In both integrated and nonintegrated communities one can also find juveniles who have no access to either of the opportunity structures. These individuals, over time, develop what Cloward and Ohlin called a **retreatist subculture**. Their primary focus is on drugs, and their gang-related activi-ties are designed to bring them the money for their own drug use. The term for these subcultural delinquents is "double failures," juveniles who for one reason or another cannot achieve sufficient success in either the legitimate or the illegitimate world. There are two possibilities for their retreat from the other two types of subcultures (Cloward and Ohlin, 1960:181). First, they may simply have internalized prohibitions against violence or other crimi-nal activity. Second, they may have failed to achieve status (or other forms of success) in a criminal or conflict gang. One possibility for this status failure is gangs are attributed different levels of "rep," or reputation, and these juveniles may have been previous members of gangs with little status. Not all "double failures" become drug users, but they are more susceptible than others. The interaction and learning involved in the retreatist subculture is derived from older drug users teaching new drug users how to find drug sources and how to use drugs.

In sum, differential opportunity theory extends the anomie theory of Merton and adds the community-based observations of the Chicago School. Additionally, it suggests that subcultural patterns determine the form of delinquent behavior. For that matter, Cloward and Ohlin seem to suggest the real problem of understanding deviance lies in explaining how different reactions (adaptations) to strain occur and defining the context in which those reactions appear (Cullen, 1984:39–49, 1988). Differential opportunity theory, then, assumes strain in the lower class as a given and attempts to explain the existence of various forms of delinquency as adaptations to strain, based on the stability of the community and the availability of adult role models. Because of this, the theory's major focus is on the learning mechanisms available to produce the ongoing forms of delinquent subculture.

Classification of the Theory

Differential opportunity theory is usually termed a strain theory. But as with Cohen's theory, it has elements of both structure and process. In combining the strain of anomie theory and the process of the Chicago School and differential association theory (Cloward and Ohlin, 1960:x), differential opportunity theory leans more toward structure. Yet even while emphasizing the effect of one's place in the social structure, it attempts to explain the process by which the content of criminal lifestyles is transmitted. In a similar vein, this one is a *bridging theory* that leans slightly toward the macrotheoretical level. Finally the theory is both *positivistic* and *consensus-oriented.* It attempts to explain how behavior is developed and transmitted, and it assumes, with Merton, a primary emphasis on reaching cultural goals.

Major Points of the Theory

1. Members of society share a common set of values that emphasize the desirability of certain life goals, especially that of success.
2. There are standard avenues—legitimate and illegitimate—for achieving these goals.
3. These two general avenues (opportunity structures) are not equally available to all groups and classes of society.
4. Members of the middle and upper classes have primary access to the legitimate opportunity structure (business, politics), while members of the lower class have primary access to the illegitimate opportunity structure (organized crime).
5. In any urban, lower-class area, the degree of integration of these two opportunity structures determines the social organization of the community. The less the integration, the more the community is disorganized.
6. Communities with well-organized and integrated illegal opportunity structures provide learning environments for organized criminal behavior. In such communities, the male delinquent subculture takes on either of two ideal forms that are dependent on the degree of access to the illegitimate structure:
   a. When an opportunity to participate successfully in the illegitimate structure is available to young males, the subcultural gang type most commonly found will be a criminal gang. This form of gang serves as a training ground for the form of illegitimate activity found in the community.

    b. When opportunities for joining the illegitimate structure are as limited as are those for joining the legitimate structure, the most common form of subcultural gang will be a retreatist gang. Here the gang members are basically withdrawn from the community (they are "double failures"), and they solve their problem of access to drugs.

7. Disorganized communities exert weak social controls and create disorganized gang subcultures. When young males are deprived of both legitimate and criminal opportunities, the common form of gang subculture will be a conflict gang. Such gangs engage in violence and destructive acts against both opportunity structures.

OTHER SUBCULTURE THEORIES

Miller's Lower-class Focal Concerns

After Cohen's work in 1955, Walter B. Miller (1958) examined lower-class areas in Boston and came to different conclusions.[4] As an anthropologist, Miller was familiar with ethnography, a research technique based on the direct observation of social groups in their natural settings. Using this approach, he concluded that middle-class values were less important to gang delinquency than Cohen and others thought. Thus, Miller's theoretical perspective stressed differences in social-class lifestyles to a greater degree than did the consensus models of Cohen and of Cloward and Ohlin.

Miller saw a society composed of different social groups or classes, each with a subculture resembling those of other groups in some respects and differing in others. Miller used the concept of **focal concern** rather than value to describe the things important to subcultures. Focal concerns are features or aspects of a subculture that require constant attention and care, as, for example, motherhood in the female subculture. Behavior related to focal concerns, such as the "trouble" concern in lower-class subculture, can be either valued or disvalued, depending on the situation and the people involved.

The lower class, as an integral part of the larger society, shares many characteristics and concerns with other social classes. At the same time, the lower class also has distinctive features that differ significantly from those of the middle and upper classes. The legal system of the United States and the norms it incorporates conform more closely to the official standards of middle- and upper-class people than to those of lower-class people. As a result, certain common behaviors, viewed as entirely appropriate by some lower-class subcultures, routinely violate official moral or legal codes.

In common with other class subcultures, lower-class subcultures provide models for appropriate male and female behavior. They illustrate and

4. We would like to express our appreciation to Walter Miller for his review and comments on the summary.

teach those traits, skills, and characteristics needed for successful social and occupational performance in lower-class life. That is, they contribute necessary values and behaviors for a lifestyle in which low-skilled labor is common. Criminal behavior in lower-class communities, as in other communities, approximates the general characteristics of noncriminal behavior. For instance, legitimate financial and accounting skills that play a vital role in middle-class life equip people to engage in crimes such as embezzlement. Similarly, characteristics such as risk taking, physical courage, and the machismo ethic are not only important for many lower-class occupational roles but they also prepare people to engage in violent crimes such as robbery and assault.

Miller tried to characterize the richness and complexity of lower-class subcultures in a shorthand fashion. He did this by describing a set of focal concerns that underlie the reasons and motivations for common forms of lower-class behavior. Most lower-class crime and delinquency result primarily from efforts to conform to lower-class subcultural standards rather than a deliberate flouting of middle-class standards (Cohen's perspective). Miller described six focal concerns characterizing the subcultures of low-skilled laboring populations in the United States: trouble, toughness, smartness, excitement, fate, and autonomy. **Trouble** represents a commitment to law-violating behavior or "being a problem" to other people. **Toughness** is "machismo" and being fearless, brave, and daring. Characteristics of **smartness** include being cunning, living by one's wits, and deceiving and "conning" others. **Excitement** means living for thrills, doing dangerous things, and taking risks. Fortune and luck are part of the focal concern of **fate**. Finally, **autonomy** signifies independence—not having to rely on others as well as rejecting authority.

These concerns play a role in the commission of activities that may be legal or illegal, depending on the circumstances. In lower-class subcultures, incentives for engaging in crime are generally stronger, and incentives for avoiding crime are weaker than in the other classes. However, while illegal forms of behavior are generally more common among lower-class youth than among youth in higher social classes, only a very small portion of behavior by lower-class youth is illegal.

In many lower-class households, Miller observes, children are raised without the active participation of a male acting as a father. The absence of fathers creates a special problem for male children trying to learn appropriate adult male behavior. Youth gangs serve as one important device for accommodating this problem. Gangs provide a learning environment intensely focused on male qualities and abilities admired in lower-class communities: toughness, street-smartness, fighting ability, defeating rival groups by force and craft, earning respect by courage, and risk taking. Criminal activity often represents a highly effective means of achieving these goals. Gang membership also provides valuable psychological benefits, such as a sense of belonging and an opportunity to gain prestige and respect, which are difficult for lower-class youth to achieve in the context of family or school.

From Miller's viewpoint, then, the behavior of lower-class gang members is consistent with the special set of concerns, valued qualities, and life goals characteristic of many American lower-class communities. Miller (1958:19) summarizes this by saying "the dominant component of the motivation of 'delinquent' behavior engaged in by members of lower class [street] corner groups involves a positive effort to achieve states, conditions, or qualities valued with the actor's most significant cultural milieu." Illegal practices, such as gang fighting and robbery, customarily undertaken by male gang members result in part from efforts to achieve qualities and conditions seen as appropriate adult male behavior in their own communities. However often such behavior violates the law, it is seldom seen as abnormal within this subcultural context.

Major Points of the Theory

1. Society is composed of different social classes whose lifestyles or subcultures have both common and differing features.
2. The subcultures of the lower, middle, and upper classes differ in significant respects from one another.
3. Because the dominant culture is the middle class, the existence of different values often bring the lower class into conflict with the dominant culture.
4. Lower-class values serve to create young male behaviors that are delinquent by middle-class standards but that are normal and useful in lower-class life.
5. Lower-class subcultures place special emphasis on a set of issues or "focal concerns" that influence customary behavior. These include trouble, toughness, smartness, excitement, fate, and autonomy.
6. Many lower-class males are raised in fatherless households. Learning behavior and attitudes appropriate to adult male roles thus poses special problems.
7. Youth gangs provide a context for learning important elements of adult male roles for many lower-class youth. Gangs also provide psychological benefits such as a sense of belonging, opportunities for gaining prestige, and enhanced self-esteem.
8. Gang crime that seriously victimizes the larger community is in part a byproduct of efforts by lower-class youth to attain goals valued within their subcultural milieu.

Wolfgang and Ferracuti's Subculture of Violence

The last of the major subcultural theories was developed in 1967, by Marvin Wolfgang and Franco Ferracuti. Their work was substantively different from the other subculture theories, perhaps because it was developed almost a decade after delinquent-subculture theories and criminology had developed new concerns. Derived from Wolfgang's earlier study of homicide (1958), their subculture theory attempted to integrate a wide range of disciplinary approaches to understanding deviant behavior. As they expressly state, the idea of a subculture of violence was derived from a combination of theories (1967:314). From the sociological perspective they included culture conflict, differential association, and theories on culture, social, and personality systems. From psychology they chose theories on learning, conditioning, developmental socialization, and differential identification. Finally, they also incorporated findings from research on criminal homicide and other assaultive crimes.

Their theory may be summarized as follows: though members of a subculture hold values different from those of the central society, it is important to realize they are not totally different from or in total conflict with the greater society of which they are a part. Those in the subculture of violence learn a willingness to resort to violence and share a favorable attitude toward the use of violence. This attitude, though possible to hold at any age, is most common in groups ranging from late adolescence to middle age. Persons who commit violent crimes but are not identified by any link to a subculture are distinctly more pathological and display more guilt and anxiety about their behavior than do members of the subculture.

SUMMARY

Along with anomie theory, subculture theories dominated criminology during the 1950s and the early 1960s. Interestingly, the primary authors (Cohen, and Cloward and Ohlin) had training in both the Chicago School tradition and Merton's anomie approach. Thus, the main approach was that of reconciling these two schools.

Even though these theorists focused on gang delinquency, the concept of subculture was the real problem to be explained. For Cohen it was the question of how a subculture could develop; for Cloward and Ohlin it was the attempt to explain the form a subculture might take. In each case, they assumed Merton was correct, certain groups of people were disadvantaged in the great chase for success, and the problem was to explain resulting deviant behavior. Miller saw the same overall subculture picture as the other theorists but explained the delinquent subculture as a culture by itself, with its own lifestyles, values, and concerns. For Miller there was no need to use strain to explain the creation of a set of values in opposition to the conventional ones. Wolfgang and Ferracuti were less interested in explaining the existence of subcultures than in outlining what those subcultures provide to their members. They assumed subcultures provide definitions for behavior that, once learned, result in their members' greater willingness to use violence.

Taken together, subculture theories provide explanations of how groups of individuals develop similar values and rationales for behavior. They differ in explaining the way in which the subcultures develop, but they all use the existence of subcultures to explain different forms of delinquency or crime. Moreover, they all locate the process of becoming delinquent or criminal in the subcultural environment.

EPILOGUE: CURRENT DIRECTIONS AND POLICY IMPLICATIONS

Current Directions

Except for the subculture of violence perspective, subculture theories are, at heart, based on a relationship between the lower-class and delinquency or crime. Criticisms of the class-delinquency-crime connection emerged when self-report studies became popular in the early 1960s (these studies asked juveniles to "self-report" their own delinquent acts). Many of the studies found only weak class-delinquency relationships, but they also focused on less serious types of delinquency. Later, Charles Tittle, Wayne Villemez, and Douglas Smith (1978) reviewed the research literature and suggested that the class-crime relationship was a myth. Others, such as John Braithwaite (1981), disagreed, arguing that there was a "myth of classlessness." Of these criticisms, the self-report studies had the most impact because their popularity closely followed the dominant subcultural theories. In all probability, the issue of the class-delinquency relationship is not yet settled. As Steve Brown (1985) and David Brownfield (1986) have noted, not only are research measures of class and crime poorly constructed, but the critics fail to take into consideration that subculture theories do not necessarily predict high crime rates for the entire lower class. A part of the lower class is known as the "underclass." The underclass has even fewer opportunities and may be more involved in crime than the rest of the lower class. This group constitutes the real test of subculture theories.

Other modifications to subcultural theories have been presented. Gresham Sykes and David Matza (1957) critiqued Cohen's conception of lower-class gang values as the opposite of middle-class values. They argued that lower-class juveniles do not need opposite values to commit delinquent acts. All that is necessary is a series of rationalizations or "**neutralizations**" to overcome conventional values (see Chapter 10 on social control theory for more on the techniques of neutralization). Sykes and Matza also proposed that other respectable values, called "**subterranean values,**" are present in the larger culture. It is not necessary one pursue the hard-working, always aspiring, set of dominant values. Subterranean values emphasize the worth of seeking fun or tolerating certain kinds of conflict or violence. Thus, juveniles at all class levels may share the alleged anti-middle-class values of Cohen's lower-class gang delinquents. Cohen, with James Short (1958), responded that the description of delinquency presented in *Delinquent Boys* was a "**parent**" delinquent subculture. By this they referred to a more extensive form of subculture, one with a general set of values and with behaviors that were not specialized. Other subcultures, specializing in various types of behaviors, were formed from this parent subculture. Short and his colleagues later demonstrated there was indeed evidence to suggest that a generic form of parent subculture existed and that more specialized forms of gangs and delinquent behaviors developed from it.

Other criminologists, such as Lewis Yablonsky (1959, 1962), have suggested that theories need to account for less cohesive groups and more poorly organized behavior than subcultural theories posit. Yablonsky proposed that, other than a central leader, other members might not be so strongly attached to the gang. He called these loosely formed gangs "**near groups.**" He also theorized the leader was a psychotic type who instigated the others to engage in delinquent behavior.

The most widely known attempt to incorporate subculture concepts after the 1960s is referred to as the "**Southernness hypothesis**" (Hackney, 1969; Gastil, 1971). An extension of the subculture of violence thesis, the Southernness hypothesis reflects an effort to understand the distribution of homicide rates. The theory, which attempts to explain why the southern region of the United States has a higher homicide rate than other regions, argues that the region shares a subculture in which males are more ready to use violence to settle arguments. In short, the theory speculates as a part of their cultural background, those who live in the southern United States learn a willingness and readiness to use violence. Research on the issue has yet to come to a definitive conclusion, and some critics argue that no such subculture exists.

Another subcultural explanation for crime has been proposed by Claude Fischer (1975). Fischer's theory holds that the size of a place (the number of people living there) has a direct effect on participation in deviant behavior. The larger the place, the more deviant behavior is expected to occur. He links size with the variety, number, and intensity of subcultures and the presence of subcultures with deviant behavior. In one sense, Fischer's theory is related to the Chicago School's emphasis on cities and their attendant evils. However, he extends urbanness theory by suggesting that the size of the city operates through an increasing variety of subcultures to generate deviance.

On a final note, subcultural perspectives have recently been integrated into several attempts to explain delinquency and crime. The most popular of these include the work of Delbert Elliott and colleagues (1979, 1985), Herman and Julia Schwendinger (1985), and Braithwaite (1989a, 1989b). (These perspectives are discussed in the section on integrative theories in Chapter 14.)

Policy Implications

Subculture theories proved to have important policy implications because they offered hope to a new generation of liberal-thinking people. The Kennedy and Johnson presidential administrations took the subcultural theory promise of restructuring society to heart and attempted to implement the major concepts of opportunity theory. They spent millions of dollars in the Great Society and War on Poverty efforts, most notably in such programs as the Peace Corps, the Job Corps, the Comprehensive Employee Training Act (CETA), and Project Head Start. Attorney General Robert Kennedy took the differential opportunity thesis and "adopted it as the blueprint for the federal response to crime during his brother's administration" (Brown, Esbensen, and Geis, 1991:320). Lloyd Ohlin even served in a post at the Department of Health, Education, and Welfare with the job of redesigning federal delinquency prevention efforts.

The most famous of the 1960s subcultural projects was the **Mobilization for Youth (MFY)** Project in New York City, under the directorship of Richard Cloward. Designed to increase educational and job opportunities for youths in deprived communities, MFY had a $12 million budget. Part-time jobs and schoolbooks were provided, but providing better life opportunities was more difficult to accomplish. Recognizing this, MFY borrowed some of the ideas of the old Chicago Area Project and assisted in organizing the communities involved in the program. The main goal was to spur political action on behalf of the communities. MFY served as the central point for organizing strikes and protests, and for wielding the community's political power. Even today the political remnants of MFY exist in New York City, much to the chagrin of the city's political leaders. Unfortunately, however, even a project on the scope of MFY, with its large budget, was not enough to implement the theoretical concepts successfully. Restructuring society, even in small areas, proved to be too great a task. Critiques of the project are available, but there is no consensus on the extent of its success (Moynihan, 1969; Pfohl, 1985).

Several delinquency projects have also been grounded in the concepts of subculture theories. The Silverlake and Provo experiments (Empey and Lubeck, 1971; Empey and Erickson, 1972) were based on the idea that groups of delinquents, under the guidance of an adult counselor, can assist each other to become more conventional. The usual term is "guided group interaction." These delinquency treatment projects attempt to change delinquents' subculture, or milieu, to make it more conducive to conventional definitions of behavior. These and other similar projects used peer pressure, staff guidance, and group meetings to facilitate nondelinquent values and goals.

School-based projects to alleviate the effects of lower-class subcultural environments are common. Many such programs have been created since the 1960s to help children do better and stay in school. Project Head Start is the most widely known of these programs. It was designed to reduce the difficulties encountered by underprivileged children entering school by offering them some of the same advantages given to middle-class children in private kindergartens and preschools. According to the subcultural thesis, a better-prepared child will do better in school, feel less deprivation, and be more likely to accept conventional values.

BIBLIOGRAPHY

Agnew, Robert (1990). "The origins of delinquent events: An examination of offender accounts." *Journal of Research in Crime and Delinquency* 27: 267–294.

ALISSI, ALBERT (1970). "Delinquent subcultures in neighborhood settings: A social system perspective." *Journal of Research in Crime and Delinquency* 7: 46–57.

ALLEN, H. D., and WILLIAM B. BANKSTON (1981). "Another look at the southern culture of violence hypothesis: The case of Louisiana." *Southern Studies* 20: 55–66.

ANDERSON, CRAIG A., and KATHRYN B. ANDERSON (1996). "Violent crime rate studies in philosophical context: A destructive testing approach to heat and southern culture of violence effects." *Journal of Personality and Social Psychology* 70: 740–756.

BANKSTON, WILLIAM B., and H. D. ALLEN (1980). "Rural social areas and patterns of homicide: An analysis of lethal violence in Louisiana." *Rural Sociology* 45: 223–237.

BARON, STEPHEN W., and DAVID B. TINDALL (1993). "Network structure and delinquent attitudes within a juvenile gang." *Social Networks* 15: 255–273.

BARTOLLAS, CLEMENS, STUART MILLER, and SIMON DINITZ (1976). "The 'booty bandit': A social role in a juvenile institution." *Journal of Homosexuality* 1: 203–212.

BENNETT, RICHARD, and PETER BASIOTIS (1991). "Structural correlates of juvenile property crime: A cross-national, time-series analysis." *Journal of Research in Crime and Delinquency* 28: 262–287.

BERNARD, THOMAS J. (1990). "Angry aggression among the 'truly disadvantaged.'" *Criminology* 28: 73–96.

BLAU, PETER, and REID M. GOLDEN (1986). "Metropolitan structure and criminal violence." *Sociological Quarterly* 27: 15–26.

BLOCH, HERBERT, A., and ARTHUR NIEDERHOFFER (1958). *The Gang*. New York: Philosophical Library.

BOOKIN-WEINER, HEDY, and RUTH HOROWITZ (1983). "The end of the youth gang: Fad or fact?" *Criminology* 21: 585–602.

BORDUA, DAVID J. (1960). *Sociological Theories and Their Implications for Juvenile Delinquency*. Facts and Facets, no. 2. Washington, DC: U.S. Government Printing Office.

——— (1961). "Delinquent subcultures: Sociological interpretations of gang delinquency." *Annals of the American Academy of Political and Social Science* 338: 119–136.

——— (1962). "Some comments on theories of group delinquency." *Sociological Inquiry* 32: 245–260.

BOYER, DEBRA (1989). "Male prostitution and homosexual identity." *Journal of Homosexuality* 17: 151–184.

BRAITHWAITE, JOHN (1981). "The myth of social class criminality reconsidered." *American Sociological Review* 46: 37–57.

——— (1989a). *Crime, Shame and Reintegration*. New York: Cambridge University Press.

——— (1989b). "Criminological theory and organizational crime." *Justice Quarterly* 6: 333–358.

BROWN, MARJORIE (1979). "Teenage prostitution." *Adolescence* 14: 665–680.

BROWN, STEPHEN E. (1985). "The class-delinquency hypothesis and juvenile justice system bias." *Sociological Inquiry* 55: 213–223.

BROWN, STEPHEN E., FINN-AAGE ESBENSEN, and GILBERT GEIS (1991). *Criminology: Explaining Crime and Its Context*. Cincinnati, OH: Anderson.

BROWNFIELD, DAVID H. (1986). "Social class and violent behavior." *Criminology* 24: 421–438.

——— (1987). "A reassessment of cultural deviance theory: The use of underclass measures." *Deviant Behavior* 8: 343–359.

BURGER, WILLIAM (1993). *American Crime and Punishment: The Religious Origins of American Criminology*. Buchanan, MI: Vande Vere Publishing.

CAMPBELL, ANNE (1984). *The Girls in the Gang: A Report from New York City*. New York: Basil Blackwell.

CAMPBELL, ANNE, and STEVEN MUNCER (1989). "Them and us: A comparison of the cultural context of American gangs and British subcultures." *Deviant Behavior* 10: 271–288.

CAO, LIQUN, ANTHONY ADAMS, and VICKIE J. JENSEN (1997). "A test of the black subculture of violence thesis: A research note." *Criminology* 35: 367–379.

CHEATWOOD, DERRAL, MARGARET A. ZAHN, and CAROLYN REBECCA BLOCK (1991). "Homicide research and the Wolfgang tradition." *Journal of Crime and Justice* 14: 1–95.

CHIN, KO-LIN (1990). *Chinese Subculture and Criminality: Non-traditional Crime Groups in America.* Westport, CT: Greenwood Press.

CLINARD, MARSHALL B., and DANIEL J. ABBOTT (1973) *Crime in Developing Countries: A Comparative Perspective.* New York: Wiley.

CLOWARD, RICHARD A. (1959). "Illegitimate means, anomie, and deviant behavior." *American Sociological Review* 24: 164–176.

CLOWARD, RICHARD A., and LLOYD E. OHLIN (1960). *Delinquency and Opportunity: A Theory of Delinquent Gangs.* New York: Free Press.

COHEN, ALBERT K. (1955). *Delinquent Boys: The Culture of the Gang.* New York: Free Press.

——— (1965). "The sociology of the deviant act: Anomie theory and beyond." *American Sociological Review* 30: 5–14.

——— (1993). Letter to the author (FW), January 29, 1993.

COHEN, ALBERT K., and JAMES F. SHORT, JR. (1958). "Research on delinquent subcultures." *Journal of Social Issues* 14: 20–37.

COVINGTON, JEANNETTE (1987). "Addict attitudes toward legalization of heroin." *Contemporary Drug Problems* 14: 315–340.

CROMWELL, PAUL F. (1970). "Slang usage in the addict subculture." *Crime and Delinquency* 16: 75–78.

CULLEN, FRANCIS T. (1984). *Rethinking Crime and Deviance Theory: The Emergence of a Structuring Tradition.* Totowa, NJ: Rowman and Allanheld.

——— (1988). "Were Cloward and Ohlin strain theorists?" *Journal of Research in Crime and Delinquency* 25: 214–241.

CURTIS, LYNN A. (1975). *Violence, Race, and Culture.* Lexington, MA. Lexington Books.

DATESMAN, SUSAN, FRANK SCARPITTI, and RICHARD STEPHENSON (1975). "Female delinquency: An application of self and opportunity theories." *Journal of Research in Crime and Delinquency* 12: 107–123.

DAVID, PEDRO R., and JOSEPH W. SCOTT (1973). "A cross-cultural comparison of juvenile offenders, offenses, due processes, and societies: The cases of Toledo, Ohio, and Rosario, Argentina." *Criminology* 11: 183–205.

DEFLEUR, LOIS (1969). "Alternative strategies for the development of delinquency theories applicable to other cultures." *Social Problems* 17: 30–39.

——— (1970). *Delinquency in Argentina: A Study of Cordoba's Youth.* Pullman: Washington State University Press.

DIXON, JO, and ALAN J. LIZOTTE (1987). "Gun ownership and the 'southern subculture of violence.'" *American Journal of Sociology* 93: 383–405.

DOERNER, WILLIAM G. (1975). "A regional analysis of homicide rates in the United States." *Criminology* 13: 90–101.

——— (1978). "The index of southernness revisited: The influence of wherefrom upon whodunit." *Criminology* 16: 47–66.

DONNERMEYER, JOSEPH, and HOWARD PHILLIPS (1984). "Vandals and vandalism in the USA: A rural perspective." In C. Levy-Leboyer, ed., *Vandalism: Behaviour and Motivations,* 149–160. Amsterdam, Netherlands: North-Holland.

DORN, DEAN S. (1968). "Self-concept, alienation, and anxiety in a contraculture and subculture: A research report." *Journal of Criminal Law, Criminology, and Police Science* 59: 531–535.

DOWNES, DAVID M. (1966). *The Delinquent Solution: A Study in Subcultural Theory.* New York: Free Press.

ELLIOTT, DELBERT S., SUZANNE S. AGETON, and RACHELLE J. CANTER (1979). "An integrated theoretical perspective on delinquent behavior." *Journal of Research on Crime and Delinquency* 16: 3–27.

ELLIOTT, DELBERT S., DAVID HUIZINGA, and SUZANNE S. AGETON (1985). *Explaining Delinquency and Drug Use.* Beverly Hills, CA: Sage.

ELLIOTT, DELBERT S., and HARWIN L. VOSS (1974). *Delinquency and Dropout.* Lexington, MA: Lexington Books.

ELLISON, CHRISTOPHER (1991a). "An eye for an eye? A note on the southern subculture of violence thesis." *Social Forces* 69: 1222–1239.

——— (1991b). "Southern culture and firearms ownership." *Social Science Quarterly* 72: 267–283.

EMPEY, LAMAR T., and MAYNARD L. ERICKSON (1972). *The Provo Experiment: Evaluating Community Control of Delinquency.* Lexington, MA: Lexington.

EMPEY, LAMAR T., and STEVEN G. LUBECK (1971). *Explaining Delinquency: Construction, Test, and Reformation of a Sociological Theory.* Lexington, MA: Heath Lexington Books.

ERLANGER, HOWARD S. (1974). "The empirical status of the subculture of violence thesis." *Social Problems* 22: 280–292.

——— (1975). "Is there a 'subculture of violence' in the South?" *Journal of Criminal Law and Criminology* 66: 483–490.

FAGAN, JEFFREY, ELIZABETH PIPER, and MELINDA MOORE (1986). "Violent delinquents and urban youth." *Criminology* 24: 439–471.

FAUPEL, CHARLES (1988). "Heroin use, crime and employment status." *Journal of Drug Issues* 18: 467–479.

FAUPEL, CHARLES, and CARL KLOCKARS (1987). "Drugs-crime connections: Elaborations from the life histories of hard-core heroin addicts." *Social Problems* 34: 54–68.

FELSON, RICHARD B., ALLEN E. LISKA, SCOTT J. SOUTH, and THOMAS L. MCNULTY (1994). "The subculture of violence and delinquency: Individual vs. school context effects." *Social Forces* 73: 155–73.

FERRACUTI, FRANCO, and MARVIN E. WOLFGANG (1973). *Psychological Testing of the Subculture of Violence.* Rome, Italy: Bulzoni.

FISCHER, CLAUDE S. (1975). "Toward a subcultural theory of urbanism." *American Journal of Sociology* 80: 1309–1341.

FISHER, ROY (1970). "Borstal recall delinquency and the Cloward-Ohlin theory of criminal subcultures." *British Journal of Criminology* 10: 52–63.

FORSYTH, CRAIG J., and THOMAS A. MARCKESE (1993). "Thrills and skills: A sociological analysis of poaching." *Deviant Behavior* 14: 157–172.

FRUMKIN, R. M., RONALD COWAN, and JAMES DAVIS (1969). "Drug use in a midwest sample of metropolitan hinterland high school students." *Corrective Psychiatry and Journal of Social Therapy* 15: 8–13.

GASTIL, RAYMOND D. (1971). "Homicide and a regional culture of violence." *American Sociological Review* 36: 412–417.

GAZAN, HAROLD (1968). "The informal system: An agent of change in juvenile rehabilitation." *Crime and Delinquency* 14: 340–345.

GEBERTH, VERNON (1978). "The quarterkids." *Law and Order* 26: 30–43.

HACKNEY, STEVEN (1969). "Southern violence." *American Historical Review* 74: 906–925.

HARRIS, MARY G. (1988). *Cholas: Latino Girls and Gangs.* New York: AMS Press.

HASKELL, MARTIN (1960–1961). "Toward a reference group theory of juvenile delinquency." *Social Problems* 8: 220–230.

HAWKINS, DARNELL F. (1984). "Black and white differentials: Alternative to an inadequate theory." *Criminal Justice and Behavior* 10: 407–440.

HINDELANG, MICHAEL J. (1979). "Race and involvement in common law personal crimes." *American Sociological Review* 43: 93–109.

HOROWITZ, RUTH, and GARY SCHWARTZ (1974). "Honor, normative ambiguity and gang violence." *American Sociological Review* 39: 238–251.

HUFF-CORZINE, LIN, JAY CORZINE, and DAVID C. MOORE (1986). "Southern exposure: Deciphering the South's influence on homicide rates." *Social Forces* 64: 906–924.

JENKINS, PHILIP (1990). "Sharing murder: Understanding group serial homicide." *Journal of Crime and Justice* 12: 125–148.

JOHNSON, RICHARD E. (1980). "Social class and delinquent behavior." *Criminology* 18: 86–93.

JOHNSTONE, JOHN W. C. (1978). "Social class, social areas and delinquency." *Sociology and Social Research* 63: 49–72.

——(1983). "Recruitment to a youth gang." *Youth and Society* 14: 281–300.

KELLY, DELOS, and R. W. BALCH (1971). "Social origins and school failure: A reexamination of Cohen's theory of working-class delinquency." *Pacific Sociological Review* 14: 413–430.

KENNEDY, LESLIE W., and STEPHEN W. BARON (1993). "Routine activities and a subculture of violence: A study of violence on the street." *Journal of Research in Crime and Delinquency* 30: 88–112.

KITSUSE, JOHN I., and DAVID C. DIETRICK (1959). "*Delinquent Boys*: A critique." *American Sociological Review* 24: 208–215.

KLEIN, MALCOLM W., ed. (1967). *Juvenile Gangs in Context: Theory, Research and Action.* Englewood Cliffs, NJ: Prentice Hall.

—— (1971). *Street Gangs and Street Workers.* Englewood Cliffs, NJ: Prentice Hall.

KOBRIN, SOLOMON (1951). "The conflict of values in delinquency areas." *American Sociological Review* 16: 653–661.

KOWALSKI, GREGORY S., R. L. DITTMANN, and W. L. BUNG (1990). "Spatial distribution of criminal offenses by states." *Journal of Research in Crime and Delinquency* 17: 4–25.

KOWALSKI, GREGORY S., CHARLES E. FAUPEL, and P. D. STARR. (1987). "Urbanism and suicide: A study of American counties." *Social Forces* 66: 85–101.

KOWALSKI, GREGORY S., and THOMAS A. PETEE (1991). "Sunbelt effects on homicide rates." *Sociology and Social Research* 75: 73–79.

KPOSOWA, AUGUSTINE J., and KEVIN D. BREAULT (1993). "Reassessing the structural covariates of U.S. homicide rates: A county level study." *Sociological Focus* 26: 27–46.

KPOSOWA, AUGUSTINE J., KEVIN D. BREAULT, and BEATRICE M. HARRISON (1995). "Reassessing the structural covariates of violent and property crimes in the USA: A county level analysis." *British Journal of Sociology* 46: 79–105.

KVARACEUS, WILLIAM C. (1966). *Anxious Youth: Dynamics of Delinquency.* New York: Merrill.

KVARACEUS, WILLIAM C., and WALTER C. MILLER (1959). *Delinquent Behavior: Culture and the Individual.* National Educational Association. Washington, DC: U.S. Government Printing Office.

LAFREE, GARY, KRISS A. DRASS, and PATRICK O'DAY (1992). "Race and crime in postwar America: Determinants of African-American and white rates, 1957–1988." *Criminology* 30: 157–185.

LAND, KENNETH, PATRICIA MCCALL, and LAWRENCE COHEN (1990). "Structural covariates of homicide rates: Are there any invariances across time and social space?" *American Journal of Sociology* 95: 922–963.

LANDAU, SIMHA (1975). "Pathologies among homicide offenders: Some cultural profiles." *British Journal of Criminology* 15: 157–166.

LANE, ROGER (1986). *Roots of Violence in Black Philadelphia,1860–1900.* Cambridge, MA: Harvard University Press.

LANIER, MARK M., and DAVID L. CARTER (1993). "Applying computer simulation to forecast homicide rates." *Journal of Criminal Justice* 21: 467–479.

LAUB, JOHN H. (1983a). "Interview with Albert K. Cohen." In J. Laub *Criminology in the Making: An Oral History,* 182–203. Boston: Northeastern University Press.

———— (1983b). "Interview with Solomon Kobrin." In J. Laub, *Criminology in the Making: An Oral History,* 87–105. Boston: Northeastern University Press.

———— (1983c). "Interview with Lloyd E. Ohlin." In J. Laub, *Criminology in the Making: An Oral History,* 204—224. Boston: Northeastern University Press.

LERMAN, PAUL (1967). "Argot, symbolic deviance, and subcultural delinquency." *American Sociological Review* 32: 209–224.

LESIEUR, HENRY, and JOSEPH SHELEY (1987). "Illegal appended enterprises: Selling the lines." *Social Problems* 34: 249–260.

LESTER, DAVID (1978). "A study of civilian-caused murders of police officers." *International Journal of Criminology and Penology* 6: 373–378.

LILLY, J. ROBERT, FRANCIS T. CULLEN, and RICHARD A. BALL (1989). *Criminological Theory: Context and Consequences.* Newbury Park, CA: Sage.

LOFTIN, COLIN, and ROBERT H. HILL (1974). "Regional subculture and homicide." *American Sociological Review* 39: 714–724.

LOMBARDO, ROBERT M., and ARTHUR J. LURIGIO (1995). "The neighborhood's role in recruiting and perpetuating membership in street crews: The case of the Chicago outfit." In Jay Albanese, ed., *Contemporary Issues in Organized Crime,* 87–110. Monsey, NY: Criminal Justice Press.

LOTTIER, S. (1938). "Criminal offenses in sectional regions." *Journal of Criminal Law and Criminology* 29: 329–344.

MAKKAI, TONI, and JOHN BRAITHWAITE (1991). "Criminological theories and regulatory compliance." *Criminology* 29: 191–220.

MARCUS, A. M. (1975). "The asocial personality: A classification." *Canadian Journal of Criminology and Corrections* 17: 94–98.

MARTIN, RANDY, ROBERT MUTCHNICK, and TIMOTHY AUSTIN (1990a). "Albert Cohen." In R. Martin, R. Mutchnick, and T. Austin, *Criminological Thought: Pioneers Past and Present,* 239–260. New York: Macmillan.

———— (1990b). "Lloyd Ohlin." In R. Martin, R. Mutchnick, and T. Austin, *Criminological Thought: Pioneers Past and Present,* 261–298. New York: Macmillan.

MASON, ROBERT, and LYLE CALVIN (1978). "A study of admitted income tax evasion." *Law and Society Review* 3: 73–89.

MATHEWS, FREDERICK (1989). *Familiar Strangers: A Study of Adolescent Prostitution,* rev. ed. Ontario: Central Toronto Youth Services.

MATZA, DAVID, and GRESHAM M. SYKES (1961). "Juvenile delinquency and subterranean values." *American Sociological Review* 26: 712–719.

MAXSON, CHERYL, MARGARET GORDON, and MALCOLM KLEIN (1985). "Differences between gang and nongang homicides." *Criminology* 23: 201–216.

McCARTHY, JOHN, OMER GALLE, and WILLIAM ZIMMERN (1975). "Population density, social structure, and interpersonal violence." *American Behavioral Scientist* 18: 771–791.

McKANNA, CLARE V., JR. (1995). "Alcohol, handguns, and homicide in the American West: A tale of three counties, 1880–1920." *Western Legal History* 8: 455–482.

MEGARGEE, EDWIN, and ROY GOLDEN (1973). "Parental attitudes of psychopathic and subcultural delinquents." *Criminology* 10: 427–439.

MESSNER, STEVEN F. (1983a). "Regional and racial effects on the urban homicide rate: The subculture of violence revisited." *American Journal of Sociology* 88: 997–1007.

———— (1983b). "Regional differences in the economic correlates of the urban homicide rates: Some evidence on the importance of context." *Criminology* 21: 477–488.

MESSNER, STEVEN F., and S. J. SOUTH (1986). "Economic deprivation, opportunity structure, and robbery victimization: Intra- and interracial patterns." *Social Forces* 64: 975–991.

MICHALOWSKI, RAYMOND (1975). "Violence in the road: The crime of vehicular homicide." *Journal of Research in Crime and Delinquency* 12: 30–43.

MILLER, JEROME (1970). "Research and theory in middle-class delinquency." *British Journal of Criminology* 10: 33–51.

MILLER, WALTER B. (1958). "Lower-class culture as a generating milieu of gang delinquency." *Journal of Social Issues* 14: 5–19.

——— (1959a). "Implications of lower class culture for social work." *Social Service Review* 33: 219–236.

——— (1959b). "Preventive work with street corner gangs: Boston delinquency project." *Annals of the American Academy of Political and Social Science* 322: 97–106.

——— (1962). "The impact of a total-community delinquency control project." *Social Problems* 10: 168–191.

MORAN, RICHARD (1971). "Criminal homicide: External restraint and subculture of violence." *Criminology* 8: 357–374.

MOYNIHAN, DANIEL P. (1969). *Maximum Feasible Misunderstanding: Community Action in the War on Poverty.* New York: Free Press.

MURRAY, CHARLES (1984). *Losing Ground: American Social Policy, 1950–1980.* New York: Basic Books.

NATIONAL INSTITUTE OF JUSTICE (1981). *Employment and Crime: A Review of Theories and Research.* Washington DC: U.S. Government Printing Office.

NEAPOLITAN, JERRY (1994). "Poverty and property crime: The moderating effects of population size and concentration." *Sociological Spectrum* 14: 181–191.

O'DONNELL, J. (1967). "The rise and decline of a subculture." *Social Problems* 15: 73–84.

OHLIN, LLOYD (1968). "The effect of social change on crime and law enforcement." *Notre Dame Lawyer* 43: 834–846.

PALACIOS, WILSON R. (1996). "Side by side: An ethnographic study of a Miami gang." *Journal of Gang Research* 4: 27–38.

PALMORE, ERDMAN B., and PHILLIP E. HAMMOND (1964). "Interacting factors in juvenile delinquency." *American Sociological Review* 29: 848–854.

PARKER, ROBERT N. (1989). "Poverty, subculture of violence, and type of homicide." *Social Forces* 67: 983–1007.

——— (1993). "Alcohol and theories of homicide." In F. Adler and W. S. Laufer, eds., *New Directions in Criminological Theory,* 113–141. New Brunswick, NJ: Transaction.

PARKER, ROBERT N., and ALLISON TOTH (1990). "Family, intimacy, and homicide: A macrosocial approach." *Violence and Victims* 5: 195–210.

PFOHL, STEPHEN J. (1985). *Images of Deviance and Social Control: A Sociological History.* New York: McGraw-Hill.

POLK, KENNETH, DEAN FREASE, and F. LYNN RICHMOND (1974). "Social class, school experience, and delinquency. *Criminology* 12: 84–96.

POLSKY, NED (1967). *Hustlers, Beats, and Others.* Chicago: Aldine.

QUICKER, JOHN C. (1973). "A consideration of the relationship of 'punitiveness' to delinquency as developed in opportunity theory." *Journal of Criminal Law and Criminology* 64: 333–338.

RHODES, ALBERT L., and ALBERT J. REISS, JR. (1969). "Apathy, truancy and delinquency as an adaptation to school failure." *Social Forces* 48: 12–22.

RICE, TOM W., and CAROLYN R. GOLDMAN (1994). "Another look at the subculture of violence thesis: Who murders whom and under what circumstances." *Sociological Spectrum* 14: 371–384.

ROBIN, GERALD D. (1964). "Gang member delinquency: Its extent, sequence and typology." *Journal of Criminal Law, Criminology and Police Science* 55: 59–69.

Rodman, Hyman (1963). "The lower-class value stretch." *Social Forces* 42: 205–215.

Roebuck, Julian B., and Komanduri S. Murty (1996). *The Southern Subculture of Drinking and Driving: A Generalized Deviance Model for the Southern White Male.* New York: Garland.

Rothstein, Edward (1962). "Attributes related to high school status: A comparison of perceptions of delinquent and non-delinquent boys." *Social Problems* 10: 75–83.

Sampson, Robert J. (1985). "Race and criminal violence: Demographically disaggregated analysis of urban homicide." *Crime and Delinquency* 31: 47–82.

Schrac, Clarence C. (1962). "Delinquency and opportunity: Analysis of a theory." *Sociology and Social Research* 46: 167–175.

—— (1969). "Critical analysis of sociological theories." In *Crimes of Violence, U.S. National Commission on the Causes and Prevention of Violence,* 1241–1289. Task Force on Individual Acts of Violence, vol. 13. Washington, DC: U.S. Government Printing Office.

Schwendinger, Herman, and Julia S. Schwendinger (1985). *Adolescent Subcultures and Delinquency.* New York: Praeger.

Sherif, Muzafer, and C. W. Sherif (1964). *Reference Groups: Explorations into Conformity and Deviation of Adolescents.* New York: Harper and Row.

—— (1967). "Group processes and collective interaction in delinquent activities." *Journal of Research in Crime and Delinquency* 4: 43–62.

Shick, J. Fred, David Smith, and Frederick Meyers (1968). "Use of marijuana in the Haight-Ashbury subculture." *Journal of Psychedelic Drugs* 2: 49–66.

Shoemaker, Donald, and J. Sherwood Williams (1987). "The subculture of violence and ethnicity." *Journal of Criminal Justice* 15: 461–472.

Short, James F., Jr. (1965). "Perceived opportunities, gang membership, and delinquency." *American Sociological Review* 30: 56–67.

—— (1974). "Youth, gangs, and society: Micro- and macrosociological processes." *Sociological Quarterly* 15: 3–19.

——, ed. (1968). *Gang Delinquency and Delinquent Subcultures.* New York: Harper and Row.

Short, James F., Jr., and Fred L. Strodtbeck, eds. (1965). *Group Process and Gang Delinquency.* Chicago: University of Chicago Press.

Short, James F., Jr., Ray A. Tennyson, and Kenneth I. Howard (1965). "Behavior dimensions of gang delinquency." In J. Short and F. Strodtbeck, eds., *Group Process and Gang Delinquency,* 77–101. Chicago: University of Chicago Press.

Short, James F., Jr., and Herbert Yahraes (1971). "Delinquent gangs: An answer to the needs of the socially disabled." In *The Mental Health of the Child,* 384–394. U.S. National Institute of Mental Health. Washington, DC: U.S. Government Printing Office.

Siegel, Larry J., Spencer A. Rathus, and Carol Ann Ruppert (1973). "Values and delinquent youth: An empirical re-examination of theories of delinquency." *British Journal of Criminology* 13: 237–244.

Simcha-Fagan, Ora, and Joseph Schwartz (1986). "Neighborhood and delinquency: An assessment of contextual effects." *Criminology* 24: 667–703.

Simons, Ronald, and Phyllis Gray (1989). "Perceived blocked opportunity as an explanation of delinquency among lower-class black males: A research note." *Journal of Research in Crime and Delinquency* 26: 90–101.

Singer, Simon I. (1986). "Victims of serious violence and their criminal behavior: Subcultural theory and beyond." *Violence and Victims* 1: 61–70.

Smith, Michael (1979). "Hockey violence: A test of the violent subculture hypothesis." *Social Problems* 27: 235–247.

Spergel, Irving (1961). "An exploratory research in delinquent subcultures." *Social Service Review* 35: 33–47.

———— (1963). "Male young adult criminality, deviant values and differential opportunities in two lower class Negro neighborhoods." *Social Problems* 10: 237–250.

———— (1964). *Racketville, Slumtown, Haulburg*. Chicago: University of Chicago Press.

———— (1967). "Deviant patterns and opportunities of pre-adolescent Negro boys in three Chicago neighborhoods." In M. Klein, ed., *Juvenile Gangs in Context: Theory, Research and Action*, 38–54. Englewood Cliffs, NJ: Prentice Hall.

STEFFENSMEIER, DARRELL J. (1980). "Sex differences in patterns of adult crime, 1965–1977: A review and assessment." *Social Forces* 58: 1080–1108.

STEFFENSMEIER, DARRELL J., and MILES D. HARER (1991). "Did crime rise or fall during the Reagan presidency? The effects of an aging U.S. population on the nation's crime rate." *Journal of Research in Crime and Delinquency* 28: 330–359.

SYKES, GRESHAM M., and DAVID MATZA (1957). "Techniques of neutralization: A theory of delinquency." *American Sociological Review* 22: 664–670.

TAYLOR, CARL S. (1989). *Dangerous Society*. East Lansing: Michigan State University Press.

TITTLE, CHARLES R. (1989). "Urbanness and unconventional behavior: A partial test of Claude Fischer's subcultural theory." *Criminology* 27: 273–306.

TITTLE, CHARLES R., WAYNE J. VILLEMEZ, and DOUGLAS A. SMITH (1978). "The myth of social class and criminality: An empirical assessment of the empirical evidence." *American Sociological Review* 43: 643–656.

TOY, CALVIN (1993). "A short history of Asian gangs in San Francisco." *Justice Quarterly* 9: 647–665.

TUNNELL, KENNETH D., and TERRY C. COX (1995). "Applying a subculture of violence thesis to an ongoing criminal lifestyle." *Deviant Behavior* 16: 373–389.

TYGART, C. E. (1991). "Juvenile delinquency and number of children in a family: Some empirical and theoretical updates." *Youth and Society* 22: 525–536.

WATSON, J. MARK (1980). "Outlaw motorcyclists: An outgrowth of lower class cultural concerns." *Deviant Behavior* 2: 31–48.

WEISBURG, KELLY (1985). *Children of the Night: A Study of Adolescent Prostitution*. Lexington, MA: Lexington Books.

WOLF, DANIEL (1991). *The Rebels: A Brotherhood of Outlaw Bikers*. Toronto: University of Toronto Press.

WOLFGANG, MARVIN E. (1958). *Patterns in Criminal Homicide*. Philadelphia: University of Pennsylvania Press.

———— (1970). *Youth and Violence*. U.S. Youth Development and Delinquency Prevention Administration. Washington, DC: U.S. Government Printing Office.

WOLFGANG, MARVIN E., and FRANCO FERRACUTI (1967). *The Subculture of Violence: Towards an Integrated Theory in Criminology*. London: Tavistock.

———— (1968). "Violence, U.S.A. riots and crime." *Crime and Delinquency* 14: 289–305.

YABLONSKY, LEWIS (1959). "The delinquent gang as near group." *Social Problems* 7: 108–117.

———— (1962). *The Violent Gang*. New York: Macmillan.

8

LABELING THEORY

INTRODUCTION

In the early 1960s a different approach to criminological theory was taken. Although it was an offshoot of older theories, labeling theory asked questions about crime and criminals from a new perspective, challenging previous definitions of deviance. Those associated with labeling argued earlier theories had placed too great a reliance on the individual deviant and neglected the variety of ways people could *react* to deviance. This message was important enough that the position became known as the *societal reaction school*.

By de-emphasizing the criminal, labeling came close to the old Classical School in its concern for the action of official agencies, as well as the making and application of law. The theory also spurred interest in the way these agencies operate, so for a while criminology was intensely interested in investigating the criminal justice process. Perhaps equally important, labeling sensitized criminology to the relativity of its subject matter and the middle-class values it had used to study criminals.

Labeling suggested criminologists had overemphasized the original deviant act as well as the character of the deviant. Noting definitions of crime change from time to time and from place to place, labeling theorists questioned the pervasive notion that because crime is bad, those who commit crime must also be bad and a criminal act is naturally bad. The same examples we gave for culture conflict apply to labeling. If something is not a crime in one country, but one commits that act in a second country, has the individual suddenly become "bad," or is a different criminal law the "cause" of the crime?

Some criminologists have debated the content of labeling theory, insisting it is not a theory but instead a sensitizing perspective. This point has considerable merit, especially since those most important in the development of the position do not refer to themselves as labeling theorists; in fact, there would appear to be no identifiable labeling theorists. Further, since it is an offshoot of symbolic interactionism, labeling may not be new. In truth, though, labeling has as much right to be called a theory as do most of the other approaches discussed in this book. Labeling makes logical causal statements and generates propositions for testing (see Wellford, 1975), which is perhaps more than some other criminological theories can claim. Whether it is a theory or perspective is not critical, because labeling has had a profound impact on criminology and on the study of deviance in general.

THE HERITAGE OF THE THEORY

The Social Heritage

At the end of the 1950s society was becoming conscious of racial inequality, segregation, and civil rights. The issue of underprivileged members of society became a real one. Civil rights protests and demonstrations were commonplace. African-Americans protested their treatment in restaurants, theaters, buses, and college admission. Education itself became the center of much of the civil rights movement. While equality did not come quickly, white society grew more conscious of its treatment of minority groups.

Social changes of this magnitude were bound to influence social thinkers. Educators began examining ways to create classless schools. The Supreme Court handed down several important civil rights decisions. New programs were instituted in the juvenile justice system with an avowed purpose of diverting juveniles before they were stigmatized with the label "delinquent." In short, the time was ripe for sociologists and criminologists to extend their theorizing about the effects of social class and minority status on those who came into contact with the criminal justice system.

The popularity of labeling theory, once it had been proposed, was enhanced by the social atmosphere promoted by the Kennedy and Johnson administrations: the Great Society where all would be equal. Social scientists embraced plans to make quality education more equally available to all, to increase opportunities, and to overcome the previous stigma associated with being a member of a minority group. Even as the country moved through the decade of the 1960s and became more critical of the prospect of government bringing equality to society, labeling seemed to be a natural answer to the question of why certain people were more frequently stigmatized. Indeed, with mistrust of government growing during the late 1960s and early 1970s, labeling was one way to critique and explain the abuses of power.

The Intellectual Heritage

The intellectual heritage of labeling reflected the Chicago School's symbolic interactionism. The teaching and writing of both George Herbert Mead and W. I. Thomas at the University of Chicago had influenced several creative people. Their students, some of whom returned to teach at Chicago, continued to spread the symbolic interactionist approach. A group of graduate students at Chicago during the late 1940s and early 1950s applied the approach to several areas of deviance. One of these students, Howard S. Becker, was to become the person most strongly identified with labeling.

In addition to the teachers of the Chicago School, their students and writings introduced others to the concept of symbolic interactionism. One of the first contributors to labeling, Edwin Lemert, took a symbolic interactionist approach and applied it to social pathologies, including stuttering among West Coast Indians. Lemert taught this approach to his students, some of whom would become important advocates of the new societal reaction school.

Bob Lilly, Frank Cullen, and Richard Ball (1989) suggest Robert Merton's (1968) concept of the "self-fulfilling prophecy" was also an important ingredient in the popularity of labeling. Just by its presence, a false label can easily become the truth for those ready to believe it.

The late 1950s also precipitated a methodological innovation in the measurement of deviance with the rise of self-report studies (questionnaires and interviews with juveniles who reported on their own delinquent behavior). Although earlier researchers had asked young people about their delinquent acts, it was the systematic work of James Short and F. Ivan Nye (1958) that began the comparison of admitted delinquent activity with official statistics. Their work suggested that official statistics such as Uniform Crime Reports and juvenile court records did not accurately portray those who commit delinquent acts. The differences in findings between self-report studies and official statistics suggested the portrait of an "official" delinquent might be, in part, a result of the kind of person who came to the attention of the authorities. This implied reaction by authorities rather than actual deviance might explain the disproportionate number of lower-class youths in the various delinquency statistics. The subsequent attempts to replicate the Short and Nye study also served to keep the topic current.

THE THEORETICAL PERSPECTIVE

Early Labeling Theory Literature

Many criminologists trace labeling theory to Frank Tannenbaum's 1938 book *Crime and the Community*. The "dramatization of evil," as Tannenbaum called it, suggested deviant behavior was not so much a product of the deviant's lack of adjustment to society as it was the fact he or she had adjusted to a special group. Thus, criminal behavior is a product of ". . . the conflict between a group and the community at large" (1938:8), where there are two opposing definitions of appropriate behavior. Tannenbaum wrote a "tag" becomes attached when a child is caught in delinquent activity. The tag identifies the child as a delinquent, may change the child's self-image, and causes people to react to the tag, not the child. Thus, his argument was that the process of tagging criminals or delinquents actually helps create delinquency and criminality (1938:19–20).

Definition of Crime

Labeling theory required a different orientation to deviance than that of previous theories. Noting other definitions depend on statistical, pathological, or relativistic views of deviance, Becker pointed out none of them does justice to the reality of deviance (1963:3–18). He saw that deviance can often be in the eye of the beholder because members of various groups have different conceptions of what is right and proper in certain situations.

Further, there must be a reaction to the act. That is, deviance must be discovered by some group that does not share a belief in the appropriateness of the behavior, and it must subsequently be called deviance. To the extent law reflects the values of that group, the behavior is labeled crime and the perpetrator a criminal. For advocates of labeling theory, this distinction is important because it emphasizes those who engage in criminal behavior are not synonymous with those who are labeled criminal. Thus, the question of "Why do people become criminal?" becomes "How do people get reacted to as being deviant?" (Becker, in Debro, 1970:167).

The notorious Rodney King beating in Los Angeles is a good example of differential group definitions and reaction. The police defined their use of force as reasonable because they were "defending themselves" and attempting to exercise control. As revealed at the first trial, King was defined as a threat and not under control if he moved. It did not matter how much movement was involved. Apparently, the police officers were able to convince the jury to use their definition of when a suspect is "under control." Others who saw the videotape saw King's minimal movement as an effort to protect

---

BECKER'S TYPES OF DEVIANT BEHAVIOR

	Obedient Behavior	*Rule-breaking Behavior*
Perceived as Deviant	Falsely Accused	Pure Deviant
Not Perceived as Deviant	Conforming	Secret Deviant

Source: Howard S. Becker, *Outsiders: Studies in the Sociology of Deviance* (New York: Free Press, 1963) 20.

himself and the police as committing a crime under color of authority. In short, whether the police actions were defined as a crime or not depended on the reaction of the audience. The acts themselves were not in question, only the interpretation was.

Studying the Reactors

Becker's interest in organizations and careers was in large part responsible for his defining deviance from outside the actor (those who are reacted to). The point he made was that, while sociologists ordinarily begin their study of other occupations by insisting the entire organization be examined, the study of crime focused only on the criminal. The remainder of the "crime organization" (the social audience and the criminal justice system) was ignored in favor of an isolated criminal. Becker noted he was merely following the occupational sociology approach: "I approached deviance as the study of people whose occupation, one might say, was either crime or catching criminals" (Becker, in Debro, 1970:166).

This concern of labeling gained impetus through the influential work of John Kitsuse and Aaron Cicourel (1963). They questioned the way criminologists use official statistics, especially the Uniform Crime Reports, in determining the amount of criminality in society. Their point was official statistics may not represent levels of criminality as well as they reflect the behavior of those who take the reports of crime and compile the statistics. They suggested official statistics were a better measure of who the police, and others, react to by arresting and initiating the criminal process.

Labeling as a Result of Societal Reaction

The labeling approach to deviance can be broken down into two parts: the problem of explaining how and why certain individuals get labeled, and the effect of the label on subsequent deviant behavior (Orcutt, 1973; Gove, 1975). The former view of labeling is really that of asking what causes the label; thus, the label is a dependent variable whose existence must be explained. The classic statement of this focus is Becker's:

> *Social groups create deviance by making the rules whose infraction constitutes deviance,* and by applying those rules to particular people and labeling them as outsiders. From this point of view, deviance is *not* a quality of the act the person commits, but rather a consequence of the application by others of rules and sanctions to an "offender." The deviant is one to whom that label has successfully been applied; deviant behavior is behavior that people so label [emphasis in original]. (1963:9)

By the *creation* of deviance, Becker meant rules, circumstances, characteristics of the individual, and reactions of those in the "audience" serve to separate those acts that are "deviant" from those that are not, even though they may appear as identical behaviors. It is not even necessary the behavior exist; what is important is the reactors believe in its existence. Thus, it is the *reaction* to behavior that creates deviance. The problem is to explain how *outsiders,* as Becker referred to deviants, are chosen and labeled.

The Rodney King incident is also an excellent illustration of the point that no act is required for the audience to react as if a deviant act had taken place. For the police officers, even though King might not have been moving to get up and threaten them, it appears they *thought* he was. Therefore, they acted as if an act had happened. Those who saw the videotape probably saw little motion on the part of King, and for them, the actions of the officers, and not King, were interpreted as deviant. Moreover, because the officers believed King was on PCP, they reacted as if he was (later drug tests revealed no evidence to sustain that belief) One question to be asked is why the officers attributed PCP use to King. The labeling answer is King fit the stereotype of people the police believe to be drug users.

As another example of this phenomenon, try to remember if you have ever been accused of something you didn't do. That you had not done anything didn't matter; what mattered was someone else reacted as if you had. Obviously, then, deviance is "in the eye of the beholder."

To explore this problem, Becker added to his discussion a typology of types of deviant behavior (1963:19–22). He considered whether a particular behavior was conforming or deviant and whether the reactors perceived the behavior as conforming or deviant. The resulting four types of deviant behavior were called falsely accused, pure deviant, conforming, and secret deviant. **Falsely accused** acts are those that either did not exist or were actually conforming, but the audience reacted as if the acts were deviant. Both **pure deviant** and **conforming** acts are those in which the perception matched the reality of the act. Finally, **secret deviant** acts are those in which deviance had indeed occurred but the audience either ignored the acts or had not reacted as if they were deviant. Becker believed secret deviant acts are quite common. As important as these four types of deviance are, even more critical is the possibility characteristics of people have something to do with which of the types would be used.

This approach to deviance meant several facts about criminals needed explaining in a completely new way. Those who were arrested were, of course, predominantly lower class, urban, young, and male. The new societal reaction school wanted to know why official agents reacted to these people more often than others. Their answers, exemplified by the earlier work of Garfinkel (1956), suggested some common factors are at work. The likelihood of reaction was greater if an individual were less socially powerful (age, social class), a member of a group with different values from the dominant group, or relatively isolated. Labeling theorists set about the process of determining how and why these types of people came to the attention of others.

Labeling as a Cause of Deviance

Labeling advocates were also concerned with the effect of labels on the person who is labeled. This aspect of labeling treats the label as an independent variable, a causal agent, which then creates deviant behavior. There are two ways in which this may take place: (1) the label may catch the attention of the labeling audience, causing the audience to watch and continue the labeling of the individual; or (2) the label may be internalized by the individual and lead to an acceptance of a deviant self concept. Either of these processes may amplify the deviance (Wilkins, 1965) and create a *career deviant.*

Among the problems a label creates is a subsequent reaction. Individuals who have been labeled become more visible in the sense that people are more aware of them. This awareness often causes them to be watched more closely and, thus, a second and third discovery of deviant behavior is even more likely than the first time. Especially important is that those who are in deviance-processing occupations (criminal justice agencies) closely watch individuals once they have come to the attention of their agency. In a sense, those labeled are the clientele of the criminal justice system, and, like any other good business, the system keeps close tabs on its customers. It is difficult for those once labeled, such as probationers, parolees, or ex-offenders, to escape the attention of this audience, and subsequent behavior is likely to be identified and relabeled.

When the original label is more likely to be distributed among those with lower-class characteristics, this attention serves to reinforce the image of those individuals as deviants. People who are identified as "deviants" then have fewer chances to make good in the conventional world. This means conventional avenues to success are often cut off, and illegal means may become the only way left open. Thus, labeling advocates argue the lower class bears the brunt of the labeling process and is kept deviant through relabeling.

As an example, it appears one reason some people commit crime is because they have very few legitimate opportunities available to them to get a job, make money, and buy the things advertised on television. Young African-American males in many central cities of the United States have unemployment rates of 40 to 50 percent. There are few jobs, and no one will hire them. After being previously caught for committing a couple of thefts, one individual is arrested again and receives a prison sentence. In the overcrowded prison, there is little to do except work in the license plate factory. After being released, the individual's opportunities for legitimate work have certainly not increased and have probably decreased. Employers who would not hire the individual before are even less likely to do so now. In short, there may be little for the individual to turn to except crime.

A study by Richard Schwartz and Jerome Skolnick (1962) illustrates the criminogenic effect of a criminal label. They conducted a field experiment to examine the effect of a criminal court record on the employability of an unskilled worker. Four employment folders were constructed with identical applications except for a record of criminal involvement. As Schwartz and Skolnick explain it:

> The four folders differed only in the applicant's reported record of criminal court involvement. The first folder indicated the applicant had been convicted and sentenced for assault; the second, he had been tried for assault and acquitted; the third, also tried for assault and acquitted, but with a letter from the judge certifying the finding of not guilty and reaffirming the legal presumption of innocence. The fourth folder made no mention of any criminal record. (1962:134)

Twenty-five of each of the folders were created. These folders were presented by an employment agent to one hundred people hiring for resort hotel jobs in the Catskills. Reactions by the hotel employers were placed in one of two categories: a willingness to consider the applicant in any way, and those who made no response or refused to consider the applicant. The results were only one employer expressed further interest in the convicted folder, three in the tried-but-acquitted folder, six in the tried-and-acquitted-with-letter folder, and nine in the no-criminal-record folder. While there are problems with the study, the labeling implications are clear: not only does a criminal record help reduce employment opportunities but any suggestion of criminal involvement may have a similar effect.

At this point we should add labeling is not all negative. The discussions of labeling in criminology are about negative effects because of the subject matter—crime and delinquency. Positive labeling also exists. Indeed, positive labels are actively pursued by all of us. Right now you are pursuing a number of positive labels, and one is probably a college degree. In other words, you are seeking a college degree for the status it provides and the image it projects to other people. Indeed, life is designed around labels.

The second form of labeling effect is best reflected in what Lemert (1951) called **secondary deviance**.[1] This concept suggests that, in addition to audience reaction, there is the possibility an individual will react to the label. In this instance, Lemert assumes the individual does not identify the initial act (primary deviance) as an important part of his or her self-image. People vary in their vulnerability or sensitivity to the reaction of others. If the original self-image is not strong enough, the labeled person may come to accept the image offered by others and change the self-image accordingly. The more often a person is labeled, the more likely it is this change will take place.

Feedback is important to the process by which a new self concept is internalized. Lemert describes the road to secondary deviance as follows:

> (1) primary deviation; (2) societal penalties; (3) further primary deviation; (4) stronger penalties and rejections; (5) further deviation, perhaps with hostilities and resentments beginning to focus upon those doing the penalizing; (6) crisis reached in the tolerance quotient, expressed in formal action by the community stigmatizing of the deviant; (7) strengthening of the deviant conduct as a

---

1. We would like to express our appreciation to the late Edwin Lemert for his review and comments on the summary.

reaction to the stigmatizing and penalties; (8) ultimate acceptance of deviant social status and efforts of adjustment on the basis of the associated role. (1951:77)

In a sense, then, secondary deviance is gained through a trading back and forth until the labeled person finally accepts the label as a real identity. This often results in the person's joining a deviant subculture with further deviance being the product of the subcultural lifestyle. That is, future forms of deviant behavior are a product of the new role itself. Deviance in its secondary form is quite literally *created* by the labeling process.

A good example of secondary deviance is the case of a juvenile who gets caught trying a minor illegal drug, such as marijuana. The juvenile is labeled "a drug user." If he or she is caught again, even though the use is experimental, the "drug user" label begins to stick, and others start to treat the juvenile as if he or she is a "druggie." Faced with being rejected by others, the juvenile may accept that definition and begin to associate with drug users. At the point the juvenile joins a drug subculture and accepts an identity as a drug user, secondary deviance comes into play. All deviant behaviors that would not have occurred, but for the presence of the label and the changed self-concept, are behaviors that are secondary to the primary, experimental drug use. Labeling theorists argue this secondary deviance would not have occurred had it not been for the labeling process. Therefore, some criminologists (Schur, 1973) have suggested the best approach to reducing juvenile delinquency, and subsequent criminal behavior, is to do nothing when delinquent acts are discovered.

Master Status and Retrospective Interpretation

Two other important labeling concepts are those of master status and retrospective interpretation. **Master status,** as developed by Everett Hughes (1945) and Becker (1963), conveys the notion that there are central traits to people's identities blinding us to their other characteristics. These traits can be separated into those statuses that are almost always the prime characteristics (master status) of a person and those that are important but secondary (auxiliary status) traits. Examples of common master statuses are one's sex, jobs (as priest, as physician), and some forms of deviance (homosexuality). Where deviance is concerned, "criminal" is usually a master status. This makes it difficult for a person once labeled a criminal to be perceived as someone who may be trustworthy, even though the criminal act may have been an isolated one in the person's life.

Years ago, in a tour of a jail, we saw an excellent example of the effect of master status. A group of perhaps a dozen citizens was being escorted on a tour of a new jail facility. The jail officer, showing his knowledge of the inmates, was sharing tidbits of information about them as the group moved along the walkway between the cells. He would point to an inmate and say, "Joe, here, is a car thief—we caught him about two weeks ago driving a stolen Lincoln." The group would make a few comments among themselves and move along. Toward the end of the walkway, the jail officer pointed to a rather small man sitting in the back of his cell and said, "This fellow's an axe murderer." Almost as if choreographed, the group took a collective step away from the cell. Obviously, they were reacting to the fictional person created by the label, not to the real person who sat in that cell. The axe murderer turned out to be an accountant who lost control when he returned home one day and found his spouse in bed with another man. His act of violence was probably the only one he would ever commit in his life, yet he was now saddled forever with the master status of "axe murderer." All those who are convicted of crimes share to some degree the problem of master status and the restrictions imposed by the stereotype of what a criminal is and does.

Retrospective interpretation provides us with an idea of how identities can be reconstructed to fit a new label. Since the term "criminal" conveys a master status, it is difficult for people to understand how such a central fact about a person's character was not there before the criminal act and the labeling. To resolve this inconsistency, a process of reexamination takes place, and past events and behavior are reinterpreted to fit the new identity. Thus, we think back to the past and see a criminal there all the time. Retrospective interpretation not only applies to people around the labeled person but also to an official agency's reinterpretion of the person's records.

We practice retrospective interpretation all the time. Imagine a school teacher who has just seen a young child who came to school with a serious bruise. She asks the child what happened and is told the father hit the child with a baseball bat. What the teacher doesn't know is the child and the father didn't see each other, and in taking the bat out of a closet, the child got in the way. Following guidelines the teacher reports the incident to authorities, who go to the house. No one is home, a neighbor down the street asks why the police are there, and they tell him they are investigating a report of child abuse. At that point, the neighbor searches his memory and announces he knew it all along. He heard the father yelling at the child once and had seen the child with torn clothing. Obviously, he felt child abuse was taking place the entire time, and the neighbor tells the police he believes the father has abused the child before. This example is a typical retrospective interpretation. The neighbor feels the police wouldn't be there unless something was wrong, therefore the "child abuser" label offered by the police is accepted, and previous events are reconstructed to fit the new label.

CLASSIFICATION OF THE THEORY

Because labeling can be viewed as both an effect and a cause (societal reaction and secondary deviance), there are two forms of labeling. Perhaps nowhere is the lack of a coherent theory more noticeable than in the attempt to classify labeling. Thus, we first provide a classification for the main thrust of labeling and then note any variation for other parts of the theory.

Labeling theory is predominantly a *processual* theory because of its concern with the way labeling takes place. It does, however, have some elements of structure in its discussion of the types of individuals most likely to be labeled. Similarly, labeling is largely a *classical* theory in its emphasis on crime, law, and processing rather than on criminal behavior. While it is true classical theory is normally a structural approach, labeling clearly is less interested in the criminal act than in the rules and guidelines for reaction to that act. The individual comes into focus only when attention turns to the effects of the labeling process. Lemert's version of secondary deviance suggests a return to positivist concepts with his explanation of how the labeling process causes subsequent deviant behavior. Here, the focus is once more on the individual actor.

Other classifications are more straightforward. Labeling is clearly a variation of *conflict* assumptions rather than being consensus-oriented. From its refusal to treat definitions of crime as universal, to its approach to explaining how reactions are distributed in society, the theory embodies cultural pluralism and value conflict. Finally, labeling is a *microtheory*. It focuses on the effects of societal reaction to the individual's behavior. Even when there is discussion of the way in which authorities react to deviance, the emphasis is on the process of labeling individuals instead of on explaining how social structure creates labels.

SUMMARY

Labeling theory is a combination of several theoretical threads. With its heritage in symbolic interactionism and a divergent group of theorists, the core essence of labeling is hard to find. At least two main thrusts are present. First, there is the concept of societal reaction. This component treats the problem of differences in reaction to deviance and focuses on the meaning of deviance to the audience. Second, there is the issue of secondary deviance, the problem of what a label means, and does, to the person labeled. Both of these thrusts are compatible, yet they seem to suggest entirely different theoretical approaches.

The effect of labeling theory on criminology has been substantial. Perhaps most important, it caused criminologists to question the middle-class values they were using in their descriptions of deviance and criminality. Researchers began a critical examination of criminal justice agencies and the way in which those agencies process individuals. The need to study deviant subjects *as part of humanity*, rather than as mere objects (Matza, 1969), also began to impress itself on criminologists. Even such criminal justice movements as diversion owe a direct debt to the work of those involved in the labeling movement. Finally, labeling was the precursor of conflict theories and, thus, in one fashion or another, occupied criminology for more than a decade.

Major Points of the Theory

1. Society is characterized by multiple values with differing degrees of overlap.
2. The quality of any individual behavior is determined only by the application of values. The identification of a behavior as deviant occurs through a reaction to that behavior.
3. Deviance is a quality of the reaction and is not intrinsic to the behavior itself. If there is no reaction, there is no deviance.
4. Once behavior is perceived by a social audience and labeled deviant, the individual who engaged in that behavior is also labeled deviant.
5. The process of reacting and labeling is more likely when those labeled are less socially powerful than their audience is. Thus, deviance is more commonly ascribed to the less-powerful in society.
6. Reactors (individuals, social groups, law enforcement agencies) tend to observe more closely those whom they have identified as deviants and therefore find even more deviance in those persons. Subsequent acts are reacted to more quickly and the label more firmly affixed.
7. The audience views an individual, once labeled, as being what the label says he or she is. A person labeled as a criminal is perceived to be first and foremost a criminal; other attributes that are not covered by the label may be ignored.
8. In addition to "becoming" a deviant for the audience, an individual may begin to accept the label as a self-identity. Acceptance of the label depends on the strength of the individual's original self-concept and the force of the labeling process.
9. A change in self-concept results in an internalization of the deviant character, with all its attributes.
10. Further deviant behavior (secondary deviance) is a product of living and acting within the role of the deviant label, often as a part of a deviant subculture.

EPILOGUE: CURRENT DIRECTIONS AND POLICY IMPLICATIONS

Current Directions

Labeling ideas have been incorporated into criminology as standard observations. Even so, additions and clarifications have been made to the earlier literature. Edwin Schur (1971), for instance, points out there are three "audiences" who react to deviance. First, the *significant-other* audience is a very important informal group because its members are those whom the individual is most likely to feel are influential. These people have substantial informal labeling power. Second, the *social-control-agency* audience is primarily made up of authorities. Not only do these people have formal labeling power, but they can also adversely affect the life of the individual. The final group is the *society-at-large* audience. These people are primarily important as a group with the ability to define good and bad and to stir the authorities into action. Schur adds each of these groups can have subgroups that have particular interests and, therefore, may be more important to some labeling processes than to others. Another source of labeling Schur might have added to the list is self-labeling. Some individuals are so socialized that their "conscience" provides an important source of their own labels. To a varying degree, probably all of us are capable of self-labeling.

We should also note labeling has been heavily criticized, and some criminologists (Hirschi, 1975; Wellford, 1975; Gove, 1976) have suggested it has little evidence to back it up. These critiques are based primarily on the adequacy of research on labeling theory, and as with other theories we have discussed, there is some question whether the research has adequately tested labeling. Other criminologists, such as Solomon Kobrin (1976), have criticized labeling for being too simplistic. In truth, there has been no complete statement of labeling, and the lists of propositions and statements are mostly derived from sketches put together by the critics themselves. Labeling is potentially quite complex once one realizes it was meant as only one side of the deviance coin, the other side being the factors that go into creating the original act. Societal reaction by itself is exceedingly complex, and we have not yet fully introduced its intricacies into our studies of labeling (Sampson, 1986; Link, et al., 1987).

One of the best arguments for labeling is that the concept of labeling (not just negative labeling) is an important part of our lives. Another way to view labels is to call them "categories." By using categories for things, we do not have to deal with individual objects or events; instead, we can treat them as a type of object or event and react accordingly. Imagine the problems that would occur if you had to treat each chair, food, or person you encountered as a specific and separate object. Our brains (and those of other organisms) are probably designed to identify objects as members of categories to reduce the strain that would otherwise result. Labeling seems to come naturally—the question is *how* we categorize people and events and *what effect* that categorization process has on the way we view and act toward people.

Some theorists have been working on more complex versions of labeling theory. Responding to the problem that the theory does not handle *mala in se* crimes (naturally bad behavior) very well, Gary LaFree (1981) has attempted to update labeling in this direction. Others (Scheff, 1988; Grasmick, Bursik, and Kinsey, 1991; Grasmick, Bursik, and Arneklev, 1993; Braithwaite, 1989) have begun to focus on **shaming,** an obvious extension of labeling. While also found in the deterrence literature, shaming reflects the effect of self-labeling (or self-stigmatizing) or the effect of labeling-stigmatizing by others. The concept of shaming is quite old, having been the basis of many older forms of punishment (the stocks, the "scarlet letter"). The most elaborate of these perspectives, that of Braithwaite, is more fully discussed in Chapter 14.

Another extension of labeling has been suggested by Dario Melossi (1985) in what he refers to as a "grounded labeling theory." Heeding a major criticism of critical theories, that there are no usable (or likely) policies to be generated from them, Melossi suggested that critical theorists return to their roots in labeling. In so doing, he proposed an integrated approach in which the motivation of an actor had to be set in the historical context of a society.

The combination attempts to explain an act taking place for specific reasons and a reaction based on the audience's contemporary understanding of both the actor and his or her place in society. Further, the audience's place in society is also crucial. To illustrate, lower-class individuals might commit an act out of frustration with their lack of ability to succeed in society. The reaction to their acts is governed by the degree of threat to existing society represented by both the acts and the actors, and the necessity at that particular time and place to do something about the situation. If threat and situation necessity are high, the audience will react strongly to the individual.

Finally, Joseph Gusfield (1981) has attempted to integrate labeling as a force in the maintenance of existing social order. Using four types of labels, he examined each for its effect on social order. The first label, **sick deviants,** is given to those who are believed to have no control over their behavior and whose acts are so deviant no normal person would have done them (such as mass murderers). Gusfield views this label as reinforcing social order by emphasizing the true abnormality of such behavior. The second label, **repentant deviants,** also reinforces social order. People so labeled are those who have been defined as deviant and are now apologetic for their actions. Such persons are characterized by their volunteer work with other deviants and by membership in such organizations as Alcoholics Anonymous. Social order is reinforced by their public and obvious remorse over their previous behavior. **Cynical deviants** constitute the third label. These people exhibit an awareness of the deviant nature of their behavior but don't care and exhibit no remorse. Common criminals are frequently seen as this type. Cynical deviants are a threat to the social order precisely because they flout rules and laws. The last label is **enemy deviants.** These people not only believe nothing is wrong with their behavior, but they also believe the rules of society are incorrect. Their obvious threat to social order is based on a combination of their flouting the rules and their attempts to convert others to their beliefs. What we do to people as we react to their deviance, then, depends on the type of label we give them.

While no great resurrection of labeling theory is about to occur, it is evident the concepts and ideas of labeling are being revived in a number of ways. Several theorists have used labeling concepts in integrated theories (see Edwards, 1992, and Hayes, 1997, for characteristic examples). The labeling suggestions about who gets processed by the criminal justice system and the harshness of sanctions have never really been out of fashion. Researchers have consistently examined these "extra legal" variables to explain differences in arrests, prosecutions, and sentencing. Of all these ideas, the most promising appears to be Braithwaite's reinvestigation of shaming.

Policy Implications

As was the case with strain theories, it is easy to produce policy statements from labeling theory. Indeed, concepts from labeling theory were used to create major changes in policy, especially in the juvenile justice system. Policy implications fall within four general areas: diversion, due process, decriminalization, and deinstitutionalization (Empey, 1982:409; Lilly, Cullen and Ball, 1989:131–135).

The first policy area, *diversion*, is a direct product of labeling's contention that labels can cause future problems, therefore they should be avoided if at all possible. If stigma is assigned to children because they are processed by the juvenile justice system, the obvious answer is to avoid processing them. In other words, divert them from the system. During the 1970s, diversion programs sprang up everywhere, perhaps because of overcrowding in the system's facilities. Children who would have been brought into the juvenile system were placed into informal programs outside of the system. The idea was to avoid records, stigmatizing labels such as "juvenile delinquent," and making the children seem different. If it worked, the diversion movement would reduce future delinquencies and adult criminality. Most of the diversions were for less serious acts of delinquency, and rarely were they used for delinquents who were persistent offenders.

Unfortunately, most of the evidence indicates diversion did not reduce labeling (the children simply received a different label), and the use of diversion seemed to increase the number of children brought into the control network (Dunford, 1977; Blomberg, 1980; Austin and Krisberg, 1981). Indeed, the diversion programs were said to have created a "net-widening" effect— a larger net was being cast over undesirable juvenile behavior. Children who would have been dismissed from the system were now being placed in diversion. Some studies (e.g., Esbensen, 1984), however, found diversion was being honestly practiced, removing children who really would have been processed by the system. Nonetheless, as Arnold Binder and Gilbert Geis (1984) observed, regardless of the honesty of diversion, the system cannot now do without the programs because it cannot otherwise absorb the cost and numbers of juveniles currently being diverted.

Due process, or the problem of differential processing, is another by-product of labeling. Because labeling was concerned that characteristics of individuals might create different reactions, it was obvious those characteristics might influence formal processing. Critics (see Schur, 1973) of the juvenile justice system of the 1960s charged that the justice being dispensed "in the best interests of the child" resulted in unpredictable and discriminatory practices. Thus, they wanted the same legal protections in juvenile systems that were found in adult criminal systems. Due process became a rallying cry, and by the mid 1970s most juvenile court proceedings were governed by due process considerations.

Where decriminalization is concerned, juveniles were not the only focus. The early *decriminalization* movements centered on status offenders (juveniles who committed an act that, had they been an adult, would not have been illegal). Status offenders were brought before the juvenile court for offenses such as running away, staying out too late, and engaging in sexual behaviors. By bringing these children into the juvenile system, even into detention facilities, criminologists argued the children were not only being stigmatized but were learning truly delinquent behavior from those with whom they were placed. In the resulting "correction" of the system, status offenders were generally removed from the juvenile justice system and handed over to social agencies.

Juveniles were not the only ones affected by the decriminalization movement, however. Criminologists, particularly Edwin Schur (1965; with Bedau, 1974), argued victimless crimes should not be a part of the criminal justice system. Some forms of so-called victimless crimes were indeed removed. By the mid 1970s, most jurisdictions had begun to place drunken and disorderly offenders in alcohol treatment facilities rather than in jail. Another example can be found in drug offenses. For instance, marijuana use has been the focus of a decriminalization movement for more than twenty years. This doesn't mean the advocates of this position all want to legalize marijuana use; decriminalization literally means to remove it from the criminal law. Advocates argue that other forms of social sanctions may serve just as well to control drug use.

Finally, labeling was behind *deinstitutionalization* policies (see Schur, 1973; Scull, 1977). The prolonged warehousing of the mentally ill was declared inhumane during the late 1960s. Except for the most serious of cases, mental patients were released from institutions and placed in community outpatient facilities. There was no great upsurge of mental health problems, and the idea is a standard one today. Concerning the juvenile justice system, an even grander experiment was undertaken in Massachusetts. Jerome Miller, the director of the juvenile institutions, decided the institutions were doing more harm to their wards than good. As a result, he ordered all the juvenile institutions closed. The predictions of dire results, as with the release of mental patients, again appears to have been unfounded (Miller, 1991).

Labeling theory has clearly been quite popular at the policy level. Those in today's criminal justice system, and particularly those in the juvenile justice system, routinely worry about the implications of labeling. Some criminologists have even suggested that just as labeling is a critical component of punishment, delabeling should also be undertaken. That is, we need a "coming-out ceremony" in which the previous bad label is exchanged for a new, good one (or at least a neutral one). Along these lines John Braithwaite's reintegrative labeling approach contains theoretical notions that assist the process of returning an offender to the community. In this way, we might be able use a label to assist in punishment, yet diminish the problems associated with reaction to the label once punishment is over. Moreover, we have still to explore the policy implications of the emerging emphasis on shaming.

BIBLIOGRAPHY

ABELSON, ELAINE (1989). *When Ladies Go a-Thieving: Middle-Class Shoplifters in the Victorian Department Store.* New York: Oxford University Press.

AGETON, SUZANNE, and DELBERT S. ELLIOTT (1974). "The effect of legal processing on delinquent orientation." *Social Problems* 22: 87–100.

AKERS, RONALD L. (1968). "Problems in the sociology of deviance." *Social Forces* 46: 455–465.

ALBONETTI, CELESTA A. (1992). "Charge reduction: An analysis of prosecutorial discretion in burglary and robbery cases." *Journal of Quantitative Criminology* 8: 317–333.

AL-TALIB, NADHIM I., and CHRISTINE GRIFFIN (1994). "Labelling effect on adolescents' self-concept." *International Journal of Offender Therapy and Comparative Criminology* 38: 47–57.

ANDERSON, DENNIS B., and DONALD F. SCHOEN (1985). "Diversion programs: Effects of stigmatization on juvenile/status offenders." *Juvenile and Family Court Journal* 36: 13–25.

AULTMAN, MADELINE, and CHARLES WELLFORD (1979). "Towards an integrated model of delinquency causation: An empirical analysis." *Sociology and Social Research* 63: 316–327.

AUSTIN, JAMES, and BARRY KRISBERG (1981). "Wider, stronger, and different nets: The dialectics of criminal justice reform." *Journal of Research in Crime and Delinquency* 18: 165–196.

BANKSTON, CARL L., III, and STEPHEN J. CALDAS (1996). "Adolescents and deviance in a Vietnamese American community: A theoretical synthesis." *Deviant Behavior* 17: 159–181.

BARTUSCH, DAWN J., and ROSS L. MATSUEDA (1996). "Gender, reflected appraisals, and labeling: A cross-group test of an interactionist theory of delinquency." *Social Forces* 75: 145–176.

BAZEMORE, GORDON (1985). "Delinquent reform and the labeling perspective." *Criminal Justice and Behavior* 12: 131–169.

BECKER, HOWARD S. (1953). "Becoming a marijuana user." *American Journal of Sociology* 59: 236–242.

——— (1963). *Outsiders: Studies in the Sociology of Deviance.* New York: Free Press.

———, ed. (1964). *The Other Side.* New York: Free Press.

——— (1973). "Labeling theory reconsidered." In S. Messinger, S. Halleck, P. Lerman, N. Morris, P. V. Murphy, and M. E. Wolfgang, eds., *The Aldine Crime and Justice Annual—1973*, 3–32. Chicago: Aldine.

BENNETT, TREVOR (1979). "The social distribution of criminal labels: Police 'proaction' or 'reaction'?" *British Journal of Criminology* 19: 134–145.

BERNSTEIN, ILENE N., EDWARD KICK, JAN LEUNG, and BARBARA SCHULZ (1977). "Charge reduction: An intermediary stage in the process of labelling criminal defendants." *Social Forces* 56: 362–384.

BINDER, ARNOLD, and GILBERT GEIS (1984). "Ad populum argumentation in criminology: Juvenile diversion as rhetoric." *Crime and Delinquency* 30: 624–647.

BLOMBERG, THOMAS G. (1977). "Diversion and accelerated social control." *Journal of Criminal Law and Criminology* 68: 274–282.

——— (1980). "Widening the net: An anomaly in the evaluation of diversion programs." In M. W. Klein and K. S. Teilman, eds., *Handbook of Criminal Justice Evaluation*, 572–595. Beverly Hills, CA: Sage.

BRAITHWAITE, JOHN (1989). "Criminological theory and organizational crime." *Justice Quarterly* 6: 333–358.

BROWN, WALN K. (1990). "Juvenile probation department experiences compared by adult outcome." *Journal of Offender Counseling, Services and Rehabilitation* 15: 109–116.

BUSTAMANTE, JORGE A. (1972). "The 'wetback' as deviant: An application of labeling theory." *American Journal of Sociology* 77: 706–718.

CHAMBLISS, WILLIAM J. (1973). "The Saints and the Roughnecks." *Society* 11: 24–31.

CHARLES, MICHAEL (1986). *Policing the Streets.* Springfield, IL: Charles C. Thomas.

CHEATWOOD, DERRAL (1986). "The contributions of labeling studies to criminology." *Journal of Crime and Justice* 9: 111–137.

CHEN, HUEY-TSYH (1991). "Dropping in and dropping out: Judicial decisionmaking in the disposition of felony arrests." *Journal of Criminal Justice* 19: 1–18.

CHEUNG, YUET-WAH, and M. C. AGNES (1988). "Social factors in adolescent deviant behaviour in Hong Kong: An integrated theoretical approach." *International Journal of Comparative and Applied Criminal Justice* 12: 27–45.

CHIRICOS, THEODORE, PHILIP JACKSON, and GORDON WALDO (1972). "Inequality in the imposition of a criminal label." *Social Problems* 19: 553–572.

COFFEE, JOHN C. (1972). "Privacy versus parens patriae: The role of police records in the sentencing and surveillance of juveniles." *Cornell Law Review* 57: 571–620.

COHEN, BRUCE J., and ARTHUR VENER (1968). "Self-concept modification and total correctional institutions." *Journal of Correctional Education* 20: 8–11, 14, 16, 17, 24.

COHEN, LAWRENCE E., and RODNEY STARK (1974). "Discriminatory labeling and the five-finger discount: An empirical analysis of differential shoplifting dispositions." *Journal of Research in Crime and Delinquency* 11: 25–39.

COHEN, STANLEY (1973). "Protest, unrest and delinquency: Convergences in labels and behavior." *International Journal of Criminology and Penology* 1: 117–128.

CONOVER, PATRICK W. (1976). "A reassessment of labeling theory: A constructive response to criticism." In L. A. Coser and O. N. Larsen, eds., *Uses of Controversy in Sociology,* 228–243. New York: Free Press.

CORLEY, CHARLES, STEPHEN CERNKOVICH, and PEGGY GIORDANO (1989). "Sex and the likelihood of sanction." *Journal of Criminal Law and Criminology* 80: 540–556.

COVINGTON, JEANETTE (1984). "Insulation from labelling: Deviant defenses in treatment." *Criminology* 22: 619–643.

CULLEN, FRANCIS T., and JOHN B. CULLEN (1978). *Toward a Paradigm of Labeling Theory.* Lincoln: University of Nebraska.

CURRIE, ELLIOT P. (1968). "Crime without criminals: Witchcraft and its control in Renaissance Europe." *Law and Society Review* 3: 7–32.

DAVIS, NANETTE J. (1972). "Labeling theory in deviance research: A critique and reconsideration." *Sociological Quarterly* 13: 447–474.

DEAN, DOUGLAS G. (1982). "The impact of a juvenile awareness program on select personality traits of male clients." *Journal of Offender Counseling, Services and Rehabilitation* 6: 73–85.

DEBRO, JULIUS (1970). "Dialogue with Howard S. Becker." *Issues in Criminology* 5: 159–179.

DELAMATER, JOHN (1968). "On the nature of deviance." *Social Forces* 46: 445–455.

DOTTER, DANIEL L., and JULIAN B. ROEBUCK (1988). "The labeling approach re-examined: Interactionism and the components of deviance." *Deviant Behavior* 9: 19–32.

DOWNS, WILLIAM R., and JOAN ROBERTSON (1990). "Referral for treatment among adolescent alcohol and drug abusers." *Journal of Research in Crime and Delinquency* 27: 190–209.

DUNFORD, FRANKLYN W. (1977). "Police diversion: An illusion." *Criminology* 15: 335–352.

EDWARDS, WILLIE J. (1992). "Predicting juvenile delinquency: A review of correlates and a confirmation by recent research based on an integrated theoretical model." *Justice Quarterly* 9: 553–583.

EMPEY, LAMAR T. (1982). *American Delinquency.* Chicago: Dorsey Press.

ERIKSON, KAI T. (1962). "Notes on the sociology of deviance." *Social Problems* 9: 307–314.

———— (1966). *Wayward Puritans.* New York: Wiley.

ESBENSEN, FINN-AAGE (1984). "Net-widening? Yes and no: Diversion impact assessed through a systems process rates analysis." In S. Decker, ed., *Juvenile Justice Policy: Analyzing Trends and Outcomes,* 115–128. Beverly Hills, CA: Sage.

ESSES, VICTORIA, and CHRISTOPHER WEBSTER (1988). "Physical attractiveness, dangerousness, and the Canadian Criminal Code." *Journal of Applied Social Psychology* 18: 1017–1031.

FARRELL, RONALD A., and JAMES F. NELSON (1978). "A sequential analysis of delinquency." *International Journal of Criminology and Penology* 6: 255–268.

FARRINGTON, DAVID P. (1977). "The effects of public labelling." *British Journal of Criminology* 17: 112–125.

FARRINGTON, DAVID P., S. G. OSBORN, and D. J. WEST (1978). "The persistence of labelling effects." *British Journal of Criminology* 18: 277–284.

FAUST, FREDERIC L. (1973). "Delinquency labeling: Its consequences and implications." *Crime and Delinquency* 19: 41–48.

FINESTONE, HAROLD (1976). *Victims of Change: Juvenile Delinquents in American Society.* Westport, CT: Greenwood.

FISHER, SETHARD (1972). "Stigma and deviant careers in school." *Social Problems* 20: 78–83.

FISHMAN, GIDEON (1976). "The paradoxical effect of labeling." *International Journal of Criminology and Penology* 4: 1–7.

FLEMING, THOMAS, and L. A. VISANO, eds. (1983). *Deviant Designations: Crime, Law and Deviance in Canada.* Toronto: Butterworths.

FOSTER, JACK D., SIMON DINITZ, and WALTER C. RECKLESS (1972). "Perceptions of stigma following public intervention for delinquent behavior." *Social Problems* 20: 202–209.

FRAZIER, CHARLES E., and JOHN K. COCHRAN (1986). "Official intervention, diversion from the juvenile justice system, and dynamics of human services work: Effects of a reform goal based on labeling theory." *Crime and Delinquency* 32: 157–176.

FREASE, DEAN E. (1972). "The schools, self-concept and juvenile delinquency." *British Journal of Criminology* 12: 133–146.

GARFINKEL, HAROLD (1956). "Conditions of successful degradation ceremonies." *American Journal of Sociology* 61: 420–424.

GIBBS, JACK P. (1966). "Conceptions of deviant behavior: The old and the new." *Pacific Sociological Review* 9: 9–14.

GIBBS, JACK P., and MAYNARD L. ERICKSON (1975). "Major developments in the sociological study of deviance." *Annual Review of Sociology* 1: 21–42.

GIBBS, LEONARD E. (1974). "The effects of juvenile legal procedures on juvenile offenders' self-attitudes." *Journal of Research in Crime and Delinquency* 11: 51–55.

GOFFMAN, ERVING (1959a). "The moral career of the mental patient." *Psychiatry: Journal for the Study of Interpersonal Processes* 22: 123–135.

———— (1959b). *The Presentation of Self in Everyday Life.* Garden City, NY: Doubleday Anchor Books.

———— (1963). *Stigma: Notes on the Management of Spoiled Identity.* Englewood Cliffs, NJ: Prentice Hall.

GOODE, ERICH (1975). "On behalf of labeling theory." *Social Problems* 22: 570–583.

GOUGH, AIDAN, R., and MARY ANN GRILLI (1972). "The unruly child and the law: Toward a focus on the family." *Juvenile Justice* 23: 9–12.

GOVE, WALTER R. (1970). "Societal reaction as an explanation of mental illness: An evaluation." *American Sociological Review* 35: 873–884.

———, ed. (1975). *The Labelling of Deviance: Evaluating a Perspective.* New York: Halsted.

——— (1976). "Deviant behavior, social intervention, and labeling theory." In L. A. Coser and O. N. Larsen, eds., *Uses of Controversy in Sociology*, 219–227. New York: Free Press.

——— (1980). "The labeling perspective: An overview." In W. R. Gove, ed., *The Labelling of Deviance: Evaluating a Perspective*, 2nd ed., 9–32. Beverly Hills, CA: Sage.

GRASMICK, HAROLD G., ROBERT J. BURSIK, JR., and BRUCE J. ARNEKLEV (1993). "Reduction in drunk driving as a response to increased threats of shame, embarrassment, and legal sanctions." *Criminology* 31: 41–67.

GRASMICK, HAROLD G., ROBERT J. BURSIK, JR., and KARYL A. KINSEY (1991). "Shame and embarrassment as deterrents to noncompliance with the law: The case of an antilittering campaign." *Environment and Behavior* 23: 233–251.

GUSFIELD, JOSEPH (1981). *The Culture of Public Problems: Drinking, Driving, and the Symbolic Order.* Chicago: University of Chicago Press.

HAGAN, JOHN (1972). "The labelling perspective, the delinquent, and the police: A review of the literature." *Canadian Journal of Criminology and Corrections* 14: 150–165.

——— (1973). "Labelling and deviance: A case study in the 'sociology of the interesting.'" *Social Problems* 20: 447–458.

HAGAN, JOHN, and ALBERTO PALLONI (1990). "The social reproduction of a criminal class in working-class London, circa 1950–1980." *American Journal of Sociology* 96: 265–299.

HARRIS, A. R. (1975). "Imprisonment and expected value of criminal choice: A specification and test of aspects of the labeling perspective." *American Sociological Review* 40: 71–87.

HAYES, HENNESSEY D. (1997). "Using integrated theory to explain the movement into juvenile delinquency." *Deviant Behavior* 18: 161–184.

HENSHEL, RICHARD, and ROBERT A. SILVERMAN, eds. (1975). *Perception in Criminology.* New York: Columbia University Press.

HEPBURN, JOHN R. (1978). "Race and the decision to arrest: An analysis of warrants issued." *Journal of Research in Crime and Delinquency* 15: 54–73.

HIRSCHI, TRAVIS (1975). "Labeling theory and juvenile delinquency: An assessment of the evidence." In W. R. Gove, ed., *The Labelling of Deviance: Evaluating a Perspective*, 181–201. New York: Halsted.

HOMANT, ROBERT J., and DANIEL KENNEDY (1982). "Attitudes toward ex-offenders: A comparison of social stigmas." *Journal of Criminal Justice* 10: 383–392.

HUGHES, EVERETT C. (1945). "Dilemmas and contradictions of status." *American Journal of Sociology* 50: 353–359.

HUSSENSTAMM, F. K. (1975). "Bumper stickers and the cops." In D. J. Steffensmeier and R. M. Terry, eds., *Examining Deviance Experimentally: Selected Readings*, 251–255. Port Washington, NY: Alfred.

INCIARDI, JAMES A. (1972). "Visibility, societal reaction, and criminal behavior." *Criminology* 10: 217–233.

JAYEWARDENE, C. H. S., and F. E. MCWATT (1984). "The police and the female delinquent." *Canadian Police College Journal* 8: 203–217.

JENSEN, GARY F. (1980). "Labeling the identity." *Criminology* 18: 121–129.

KAPLAN, HOWARD B., and KELLY R. DAMPHOUSSE (1997). "Negative social sanctions, self-derogation, and deviant behavior: Main and interactive effects in longitudinal perspective." *Deviant Behavior* 18: 1–26.

KAPLAN, HOWARD B., and ROBERT J. JOHNSON (1991). "Negative social sanctions and juvenile delinquency: Effects of labeling in a model of deviant behavior." *Social Science Quarterly* 71: 98–122.

KATZ, JACK (1972). "Deviance, charisma, and rule-defined behavior." *Social Problems* 20: 186–202.

KEANE, CARL, A. R. GILLIS, and JOHN HAGAN (1989). "Deterrence and amplification of juvenile delinquency by police contact: The importance of gender and risk-orientation." *British Journal of Criminology* 29: 336–352.

KELLEY, THOMAS (1983). "Status offenders can be different: A comparative study of delinquent careers." *Crime and Delinquency* 29: 365–380.

KEMPF, KIMBERLY, and ROY AUSTIN (1986). "Older and more recent evidence on racial discrimination in sentencing." *Journal of Quantitative Criminology* 2: 29–48.

KIJEWSKI, KRISTINA J. (1983). "The effect of the decision to charge upon subsequent delinquent behavior." *Canadian Journal of Criminology* 25: 201–208.

KITSUSE, JOHN (1962). "Societal reaction to deviance: Problems of theory and method." *Social Problems* 9: 247–256.

KITSUSE, JOHN, and AARON V. CICOUREL (1963). "A note on the use of official statistics." *Social Problems* 11: 131–139.

KLEIN, MALCOLM W. (1974). "Labeling, deterrence, and recidivism: A study of police dispositions of juvenile offenders." *Social Problems* 22: 292–303.

——— (1986). "Labeling theory and delinquency policy: An experimental test." *Criminal Justice and Behavior* 13: 47–79.

KLEIN, MALCOLM W., KATHERINE S. TEILMAN, J. A. STYLES, S. B. LINCOLN, and S. LABIN-ROSENSWEIG (1976). "The explosion of police diversion programs." In M. W. Klein, ed., *The Juvenile Justice System*, 101–119. Beverly Hills, CA: Sage.

KLEMKE, LLOYD W. (1978). "Does apprehension for shoplifting amplify or terminate shoplifting activity?" *Law and Society Review* 12: 391–403.

KOBRIN, SOLOMON (1976). "The labeling approach: Problems and limits." In J. F. Short, ed., *Delinquency, Crime, and Society*, 239–253. Chicago: University of Chicago Press.

KOTARBA, J. (1980). "Labeling theory and everyday deviance." In J. Douglas, ed., *Introduction to the Sociologies of Everyday Life*, 82–112. Boston: Allyn and Bacon.

LAFREE, GARY D. (1981). "Official reactions to social problems: Police decisions in sexual assault cases." *Social Problems* 28: 582–594.

LAURITSEN, JANET L., and F. DAVIS QUINET-KENNA (1995). "Repeat victimization among adolescents and young adults." *Journal of Quantitative Criminology* 11: 143–166.

LEFTON, MARK, JAMES K. SKIPPER, and CHARLES H. McCAGHY (1968). *Approaches to Deviance: Theories, Concepts, and Research Findings*. New York: Appleton-Century-Crofts.

LEMERT, EDWIN M. (1951). *Social Pathology: A Systematic Approach to the Theory of Sociopathic Behavior*. New York: McGraw-Hill.

——— (1967). *Human Deviance, Social Problems and Social Control*. Englewood Cliffs, NJ: Prentice Hall.

——— (1971). *Instead of Court: Diversion in Juvenile Justice*. National Institute of Mental Health. Center for Studies of Crime and Delinquency, Public Health Service Publication No. 2127. Washington, DC: U.S. Government Printing Office.

——— (1972). *Human Deviance, Social Problems and Social Control*, 2nd ed. Englewood Cliffs, NJ: Prentice Hall.

——— (1974). "Beyond Mead: The societal reaction to deviance." *Social Problems* 21: 457–468.

—— (1981). "Diversion in juvenile justice: What hath been wrought." *Journal of Research in Crime and Delinquency* 18: 34–46.

LEUNG, KWOK, and SING LAU (1989). "Effects of self-concept and perceived disapproval of delinquent behavior in school children." *Journal of Youth and Adolescence* 18: 345–359.

LIAZOS, ALEXANDER (1972). "The poverty of the sociology of deviance: Nuts, sluts, and perverts." *Social Problems* 20: 103–120.

LILLY, J. ROBERT, FRANCIS T. CULLEN, and RICHARD A. BALL (1989). *Criminological Theory: Context and Consequences.* Newbury Park, CA: Sage.

LINK, BRUCE G. (1987). "Understanding labeling effects in the area of mental disorders: An assessment of the effects of expectations of rejection." *American Sociological Review* 52: 96–112.

LINK, BRUCE G., FRANCIS T. CULLEN, JAMES FRANK, and JOHN F. WOZNIAK (1987). "The social rejection of former mental patients: Understanding why labels matter." *American Journal of Sociology* 92: 1461–1500.

LINK, BRUCE G., FRANCIS T. CULLEN, ELMER STRUENING, PATRICK SHROUT, and BRUCE DOHREWEND (1989). "A modified labeling theory approach to mental disorders: An empirical assessment." *American Sociological Review* 64: 400–423.

LOFLAND, JOHN (1969). *Deviance and Identity.* Englewood Cliffs, NJ: Prentice Hall.

MAHONEY, ANNE R. (1974). "The effect of labeling upon youths in the juvenile justice system: A review of the evidence." *Law and Society Review* 8: 583–614.

MANKOFF, MILTON (1971). "Societal reaction and career deviance: A critical analysis." *Sociological Quarterly* 12: 204–218.

MANNING, PETER K. (1973). "Survey essay on deviance." *Contemporary Sociology* 2: 123–128.

MARGOLIN, LESLIE (1992). "Deviance on record: Techniques for labeling child abusers in official documents." *Social Problems* 39: 58–70.

MARTIN, RANDY, ROBERT MUTCHNICK, and TIMOTHY AUSTIN (1990a). "Erving Goffman." In R. Martin, R. Mutchnick, and T. Austin, *Criminological Thought: Pioneers Past and Present*, 321–347. New York: Macmillan.

—— (1990b). "Howard Saul Becker." In R. Martin, R. Mutchnick, and T. Austin, *Criminological Thought: Pioneers Past and Present*, 349–378. New York: Macmillan.

MATSUEDA, ROSS L. (1992). "Reflected appraisals, parental labeling, and delinquency: Specifying a symbolic interactionist theory." *American Journal of Sociology* 97: 1577–1611.

MATZA, DAVID (1969). *Becoming Deviant.* New York: Prentice Hall.

McBARNET, DOREEN (1991). "Whiter than white collar crime: Tax, fraud insurance and the management of stigma." *British Journal of Sociology* 42: 323–344.

McCORMICK, ALBERT E. (1977). "Rule enforcement and moral indignation: Some observations on the effects of criminal antitrust convictions upon societal reaction processes." *Social Problems* 25: 30–39.

McLORG, PENELOPE A., and DIANE E. TAUB (1987). "Anorexia nervosa and bulimia: The development of deviant identities." *Deviant Behavior* 8: 177–189.

MELOSSI, DARIO (1985). "Overcoming the crisis in critical criminology: Toward a grounded labeling theory." *Criminology* 23: 193–208.

MERTON, ROBERT K. (1968). *Social Theory and Social Structure*, rev. ed. New York: Free Press.

MILLER, JEROME G. (1991). *Last One over the Wall: The Massachusetts Experiment in Closing Reform Schools.* Columbus: Ohio State University Press.

NEWMAN, GRAEME (1974). "Acts, actors, and reactions to deviance." *Sociology and Social Research* 58: 434–440.

NEWTON, CHARLES, and RANDALL G. SHELDEN (1975). "The delinquent label and its effects on future behavior: An empirical test of Lemert's levels of deviance." *International Journal of Criminology and Penology* 3: 229–241.

OPP, KARL-DIETER (1989). "The economics of crime and the sociology of deviant behavior: A theoretical confrontation of basic propositions." *Kyklos* 42: 405–430.

ORCUTT, JAMES D. (1973). "Societal reaction and the response to deviation in small groups." *Social Forces* 52: 259–267.

OSBORNE, LYNNE (1974). "Beyond stigma theory: A literary approach." *Issues in Criminology* 9: 71–90.

PALAMARA, FRANCES, FRANCIS T. CULLEN, and JOANNE GERSTEN (1986). "The effect of police and mental health intervention on juvenile deviance: Specifying contingencies in the impact of formal reaction." *Journal of Health and Social Behavior* 27: 90–105.

PATERNOSTER, RAYMOND, and LEEANN IOVANNI (1989). "The labeling perspective and delinquency: An elaboration of the theory and assessment of the evidence." *Justice Quarterly* 6: 359–394.

PAYNE, WILLIAM D. (1973). "Negative labels: Passageways and prisons." *Crime and Delinquency* 19: 33–40.

PETERS, HELGE (1996). "Worn out as a guerilla science but immortal as a theory: The labeling approach." *Kriminologisches Journal* 28(2): 107–115.

PETRUNIK, MICHAEL (1980). "The rise and fall of 'labelling theory': The construction and destruction of a sociological strawman." *Canadian Journal of Sociology* 6: 213–233.

PHILLIPS, CHARLES D., and SIMON DINITZ (1982). "Labelling and juvenile court dispositions: Official responses to a cohort of violent juveniles." *Sociological Quarterly* 23: 267–279.

RAFKY, DAVID M. (1973). "Police race attitudes and labeling." *Journal of Police Science and Administration* 1: 65–86.

RAINS, PRUDENCE (1975). "Imputations of deviance: A retrospective essay on the labeling perspective." *Social Problems* 23: 1–11.

RAY, MARSH (1961). "The cycle of abstinence and relapse among heroin addicts." *Social Problems* 9: 132–140.

RAY, MELVIN C., and WILLIAM R. DOWNS (1986). "An empirical test of labeling theory using longitudinal data." *Journal of Research in Crime and Delinquency* 23: 169–194.

REGOLI, ROBERT M., ERIC D. POOLE, and FINN-AAGE ESBENSEN (1985). "Labeling deviance: Another look." *Sociological Focus* 18: 19–28.

RICHARD, WAYNE C., CATHERINE G. MATES, and LAURA WHITTEN (1969). "Personality traits and attitudes of adolescent girls with behavior disorders." *Corrective Psychiatry and Journal of Social Therapy* 15: 34–44.

ROCK, PAUL (1974). "The sociology of deviancy and conceptions of moral order." *British Journal of Criminology* 14: 139–149.

ROGERS, JOSEPH W., and M. D. BUFFALO (1974). "Fighting back: Nine modes of adaptation to a deviant label." *Social Problems* 22: 101–118.

ROSENHAN, D. L. (1973). "On being sane in insane places." *Science* 179: 250–258.

SAMPSON, ROBERT J. (1986). "Effects of socioeconomic context on official reactions to juvenile delinquency." *American Sociological Review* 51: 876–885.

SCHEFF, THOMAS J. (1974). "The labeling theory of mental illness." *American Sociological Review* 39: 224–237.

——— (1988). "Shame and conformity: The deference-emotion system." *American Sociological Review* 53: 395–406.

SCHEFF, THOMAS J., and SUZANNE M. RETZINGER (1991). *Emotion and Violence: Shame and Rage in Destructive Conflicts.* Lexington, MA: Lexington.

SCHNELLER, DONALD, MARIO PEREZ-REILLY, RALPH BLANKENSHIP, and JAY SADLER (1981). "The police officer as a determining factor in the disposition of juvenile-police contacts." *California Sociologist* 4: 170–183.
SCHUR, EDWIN M. (1965). *Crimes without Victims.* Englewood Cliffs, NJ: Prentice Hall.
——— (1969). "Reactions to deviance: A critical assessment." *American Journal of Sociology* 75: 309–322.
——— (1971). *Labeling Deviant Behavior: Its Sociological Implications.* New York: Harper and Row.
——— (1973). *Radical Non-intervention: Rethinking the Delinquency Problem.* Englewood Cliffs, NJ: Prentice Hall.
——— (1984). *Labeling Women Deviant: Gender, Stigma, and Social Control.* New York: Random House.
SCHUR, EDWIN M., and HUGO ADAM BEDAU (1974). *Victimless Crimes: Two Sides of a Controversy.* Englewood Cliffs, NJ: Prentice Hall.
SCHWARTZ, RICHARD D., and JEROME H. SKOLNICK (1962). "Two studies of legal stigma." *Social Problems* 10: 133–138.
SCULL, ANDREW T. (1977). *Decarceration: Community Treatment and the Deviant: A Radical View.* Englewood Cliffs, NJ: Prentice Hall.
SHERMAN, LAWRENCE W., and DOUGLAS A. SMITH (1992). "Crime, punishment, and stake in conformity: Legal and informal control of domestic violence." *American Sociological Review* 57: 680–690.
SHERWOOD, NORMAN (1969). *Causes and Control of Deviant Behavior in Youth.* New York: National Council on Crime and Delinquency.
SHOHAM, SHLOMO (1970). *The Mark of Cain: The Stigma Theory of Crime and Social Deviation.* Dobbs Ferry, NY: Oceana Press.
SHOHAM, SHLOMO, and GIORA RAHAV (1968). "Social stigma and prostitution." *British Journal of Criminology* 8: 402–412.
SHORT, JAMES F., JR., and F. IVAN NYE (1958). "Extent of unrecorded juvenile delinquency: Tentative conclusions." *Journal of Criminal Law, Criminology, and Police Science* 49: 296–302.
SIMMONS, J. L. (1969). *Deviants.* Berkeley, CA: Glendessary Press.
SMITH, DOUGLAS A., and ROBERT BRAME (1994). "On the initiation and continuation of delinquency." *Criminology* 32: 607–629.
SMITH, DOUGLAS A., and RAYMOND PATERNOSTER (1990). "Formal processing and future delinquency: Deviance amplification as selection artifact." *Law and Society Review* 24: 1109–1132.
SOMMERS, IRA, and DEBORAH BASKIN (1990). "The prescription of psychiatric medications in prison: Psychiatric versus labeling perspectives." *Justice Quarterly* 7: 739–755.
STEFFENSMEIER, DARRELL J., and ROBERT M. TERRY (1973). "Deviance and respectability: An observational study of reactions to shoplifting." *Social Forces* 51: 417–426.
STILES, BEVERLY L., and HOWARD B. KAPLAN (1996). "Stigma, deviance and negative social sanctions." *Social Science Quarterly* 77: 685–696.
SZASZ, THOMAS S. (1970). *The Manufacture of Madness.* New York: Harper and Row.
TANNENBAUM, FRANK (1938). *Crime and the Community.* Boston: Ginn.
TERRELL, FRANCIS, and JEROME TAYLOR (1980). "Self concept of juveniles who commit black on black crimes." *Corrective and Social Psychiatry and Journal of Behavior Technology Methods and Therapy* 26: 107–109.
THOMAS, CHARLES W., and DONNA BISHOP (1985). "The effect of formal and informal sanctions on delinquency: A longitudinal comparison of labeling and deterrence theories." *Journal of Criminal Law and Criminology* 75: 1222–1245.
THORSELL, BERNARD, and LLOYD KLEMKE (1972). "The labeling process: Reinforcement or deterrent?" *Law and Society Review* 6: 393–403.

Tittle, Charles R. (1980). "Labelling and crime: An empirical evaluation." In W. R. Gove, ed., *The Labelling of Deviance: Evaluating a Perspective*, 157–179. Beverly Hills, CA: Sage.

Traver, Harold (1978). "Offender reaction, professional opinion, and sentencing." *Criminology* 16: 403–419.

Triplett, Ruth A. (1993)." The conflict perspective, symbolic interactionism, and the status characteristics hypothesis." *Justice Quarterly* 10: 541–558.

Triplett, Ruth A. and G. Roger Jarjoura (1994). "Theoretical and empirical specification of a model of informal labeling." *Journal of Quantitative Criminology* 10: 241–276.

Vanderwood, Paul J. (1993). "'Indios, fanaticos, bandidos': Labeling the millenarium movement at Tomochic, Mexico." *Criminal Justice History: An International Annual* 13: 161–189.

von Trotha, Trutz (1985). "Recent developments in the explanation of crime." In U. Gerhardt and M. Wadsworth, eds., *Stress and Stigma: Explanation and Evidence in the Sociology of Crime and Illness*, 65–84. New York: St. Martin's Press.

Walsh, Anthony (1990). "Twice labeled: The effect of psychiatric labeling on the sentencing of sex offenders." *Social Problems* 37: 375–389.

Ward, Richard H. (1971). "The labeling theory: A critical analysis." *Criminology* 9: 268–290.

Warren, Carol A. (1974). "The use of stigmatizing social labels in conventionalizing deviant behavior." *Sociology and Social Research* 58: 303–311.

Warren, Carol A., and John Johnson (1973). "A critique of labeling theory from the phenomenological perspective." In J. D. Douglas and R. Scott, eds., *Theoretical Perspectives on Deviance*, 69–92. New York: Basic Books.

Wellford, Charles F. (1975). "Labelling theory and criminology: An assessment." *Social Problems* 22: 332–345.

——— (1987). "Delinquency prevention and labeling." In J. Q. Wilson and G. C. Loury, eds., *From Children to Citizens*. Vol. 3: *Families, Schools, and Delinquency Prevention*, 257–267. New York: Springer–Verlag.

——— (1997). "Controlling crime and achieving justice: The American Society of Criminology 1996 presidential address." *Criminology* 35: 1–11.

Wellford, Charles F., and Ruth A. Triplett (1993). "The future of labeling theory: Foundations and promises." In F. Adler and W. S. Laufer, eds., *New Directions in Criminological Theory*, 1–22. New Brunswick, NJ: Transaction.

Wells, L. Edward, and Joseph Rankin (1983). "Self-concept as a mediating factor in delinquency." *Social Psychology Quarterly* 64: 11–22.

Werkentin, Falco, Michael Hofferbert, and Michael Baurmann (1974). "Criminology as police science; or, 'how old is the new criminology?'" *Crime and Social Justice* 2: 24–41.

Wilkins, Leslie T. (1965). *Social Deviance: Social Policy, Action, and Research*. Englewood Cliffs, NJ: Prentice Hall.

Wodarski, John, Ronald Feldman, and Stephen J. Pedi (1975). "Labeling by self and others: The comparison of behavior among 'anti-social' and 'pro-social' children in an open community agency." *Criminal Justice and Behavior* 2: 258–275.

Zhang, Lening (1997). "Informal reactions and delinquency." *Criminal Justice and Behavior* 24: 129–150.

——— (1994). "Peers' rejection as a possible consequence of official reaction to delinquency in Chinese society." *Criminal Justice and Behavior* 21: 387–402.

Zhang, Lening, and Steven F. Messner (1994). "The severity of official punishment for delinquency and change in interpersonal relations in Chinese society." *Journal of Research in Crime and Delinquency* 31: 416–433.

9

CONFLICT THEORY

INTRODUCTION

Criminological conflict theories emerged on the heels of labeling theory. Similar in some ways to labeling, conflict theories focus on the political nature of crime and examine the creation and application of criminal law. Although modern conflict theorist George Vold (1958) was writing at the same time as the early labeling theorists, his work attracted only mild interest. Perhaps because labeling was less politically oriented and therefore more acceptable to conservative criminologists, it was more popular than conflict theory until the 1970s.

Conflict theories share one fundamental assumption: societies are more appropriately characterized by conflict rather than by consensus. This assumption allows for several varieties of conflict theory that can be viewed as if they were on a continuum. At one end, pluralist versions suggest society is composed of a myriad of groups, varying in size, and often temporary, all of which are struggling to see their interests are maintained in any of a number of issues. At the other end, class-conflict versions argue two classes are present in a society, both of which are attempting to dominate that society.

Regardless of their position on this continuum of the number of groups and amount of power sought, conflict theorists view consensus as an aberration. That is, they see consensus as a temporary state of affairs that will either return to conflict or will have to be maintained at great expense. It is the use of power to create and maintain an image of consensus, then, that represents the problem to be studied. Conflict theorists are less concerned with individual behavior than with the making and enforcement of law. Further, they are rarely concerned with the behavior of the offender.

THE HERITAGE OF THE THEORY

The Social Heritage

The decade from 1965 to 1975 was a time of unrest in American society. After a period of optimism in the late 1950s and early 1960s, many people in the United States became disenchanted with their society. The success of the civil rights movement gave incentive to other "powerless" groups, such as women and homosexuals, who marched for recognition and for equality in social opportunities. Even students protested their treatment at the hands of college administrators.

The number of demonstrations against the Vietnam War grew in the years between 1965 and 1968. Though protest had been viewed as a political tool for students and African Americans, it was soon adopted by others, including teachers, physicians, and members of the clergy. Despite its growing popularity as a means of expression, demonstration was still not seen as acceptable behavior; polls at the time showed some 40 percent of the public believed citizens have no right to demonstrate even peacefully (National Commission on the Causes and Prevention of Violence, 1969:23). The shooting of protestors at Kent State University epitomized the ambivalent attitudes held by many people toward protest.

All these events were part of a mood among younger people that questioned the middle-class values of the United States. They often rejected the conventional lifestyles of their parents as being hypocritical and morally corrupt. As David Greenberg (1981:4) points out, even criminal law was seen as a product of "the relative power of groups determined to use the criminal law to advance their own special interests or to impose their moral preferences on others." People were discussing decriminalization of "victimless" crimes at the same time police were arresting civil rights workers. Finally, the political scandal of Watergate cast a shadow of doubt and cynicism on the morality and integrity of all aspects of American government. No longer did it seem there were merely a few corrupt individuals running a fundamentally sound government structure; instead, it appeared the structure of government itself might be flawed. With a U.S. president implicated in governmental crimes, conflict theories seemed to be an obvious candidate for serious criminological consideration.

The Intellectual Heritage

Conflict theories developed, in a sense, as an offshoot of labeling. While they had their own intellectual roots in a variety of German social theories (those of Hegel, Marx, Simmel, and Weber, for example), it took labeling to prepare the way. Reacting to the events of the time, social scientists began asking questions about social and legal structures that labeling had largely ignored. The early statements of both Austin Turk (1964) and

Richard Quinney (1965), for example, were directed to the notion of societal reaction.

Even though conflict had not been popular, a smattering of conflict-oriented writing had appeared in sociology proper, and there had even been an early twentieth-century attempt to create a theory of criminality by combining Marxist and psychoanalytic approaches (Bonger, 1916). The most important impetus for the development of pluralist (i.e., more conservative) forms of conflict theory was the work of two sociologists, Lewis Coser (1956) and Ralf Dahrendorf (1958, 1959). Their writings spurred sociological interest in conflict and enlarged the perspective in the 1960s. Meanwhile, the rising radicalization of academia in general revived interest in the earlier work of Marx, and some scholars began to apply Marxist theory to crime and legal structures.

THE THEORETICAL PERSPECTIVE

There are many forms of conflict theory bound together only by the assumption that conflict is natural to society. Just as the theories of anomie, subculture, and differential opportunity could be grouped under consensus theory even though there are obvious differences among them, conflict theory contains at least as many different approaches. Here, however, they are treated as one of two general forms: conservative (pluralist) or critical-radical. This would seem to be a common approach since others have made a similar distinction (Sykes, 1974; Gibbons, 1979; Farrell and Swigert, 1982; Vold and Bernard, 1986).

The Conservative (Pluralist) Conflict Perspective

The central concept of conservative conflict theories is that of **power** and its use. These theories assume conflict emerges between groups attempting to exercise control over particular situations or events. Thus, the conflict approach views social issues almost as though they were fields of combat with opposing armies fighting to see who will prevail and rule the land. As with armies, the matter of resources is a crucial one. It is the control of resources (money, land, political power) that provides the ability to successfully "fight" and to emerge victorious on a particular issue.

These social issues may arise out of problems of everyday life, because of lobbying by some group, or through the regular business and political process. In each, decisions are made to take one course of action or another. Since several groups may have **vested interests** in the outcome of a decision, each will attempt to exert influence on its own behalf. Further, the amount of influence each group will have is a product of the resources the group has available. Power to affect decisions is, therefore, synonymous with having resources.

An excellent example of power and vested interests can be seen whenever a state or federal legislative session opens. Different groups who would like laws passed, or who oppose the passage of certain laws, hire people to lobby the lawmakers. These lobbyists attempt by persuasion, and sometimes bribery, to influence legislation. When decisions are made on the floor of the legislature, the vested-interest groups usually have had much more say in the making of a law than the citizens each legislator represents.

Because power can be equated with **resources,** it seems evident that those who are higher up in the social class structure will be the more powerful members of society. Their influence in the making of social decisions, and their ability to impose values, will also be greater than those of the lower social classes. For conflict theorists, this explains the presence of a dominant middle-class value system in society. Similarly, the important statements of a society—its laws, for example—are bound up in middle-class values. This is so because, historically, the merchant class helped create the form of society we have today. We may now begin to ask whether the middle class has reached its peak of influence and some higher class is beginning to exert more control in society.

Law itself represents a resource. If a groups's values are embodied in law, it can use that law, and its enforcement, to its benefit. The agents of law, in their enforcement efforts, perpetuate the values embodied in law and thus help keep in power those who already have power. Further, those who have values, or interests, opposing those of the "winners" find themselves in the position of being the most likely targets of enforcement agents. At this point, labeling theory dovetails with conflict theory to produce an explanation of the reaction process by which the less powerful come to the attention of law enforcement agents. For example, the less powerful (or the "losers") are stigmatized by the more powerful because of their opposition. Laws are then created or modified to enhance official reaction to the less powerful.

A final point is implied in the relationship between the use of power and the creation of law. Since law embodies the values of those who create it, law is also more likely to criminalize the actions of those outside the power group. Put another way, people rarely object to their own way of doing things; thus, any objections are going to be to the behavior of others. Why should a group expend resources to have its values upheld if the results will be detrimental to the group? Obviously, then, power not only helps a group to create law in its own interest, it also serves to reduce the chances members of the group will be criminalized. When power is essentially equal between two groups, a give-and-take relationship can develop. The abortion issue provides an excellent illustration of this phenomenon. As the groups involved have gained or lost power, laws have been passed to restrict the activities of the other side. Thus, we have seen laws that prohibit blocking the entrance of an abortion clinic, and a Florida law made it unlawful for a pregnant woman to take drugs and thereby addict an unborn child. Three illustrative theories, characteristic of this form of conflict, are covered here.

George Vold (1958) produced a theory emphasizing the group nature of society and the various competing interests of those groups. He saw that "groups come into conflict with one another as the interests and purposes they serve tend to overlap, encroach on one another, and become competitive" (Vold and Bernard, 1986:272). Moreover, group members become more loyal and tightly knit as conflict escalates. Vold argued groups had to be watchful of their interests and ever-ready to defend them. Thus, a group is always engaged in a continuous struggle to maintain and improve its standing vis-à-vis other groups. The election struggles between the Republican and Democratic parties characterize this process. Another good example is each presidential administration's attempt to control the interpretation of law by appointing members to the Supreme Court who share the president's ideology.

From this viewpoint, Vold went on to discuss the presence of conflict in criminal law, writing that "the whole process of lawmaking, lawbreaking, and law enforcement directly reflects deep-seated and fundamental conflicts between group interests and the more general struggles among groups for control of the police power of the state" (Vold and Bernard, 1986:274). Finally, Vold observed that since minority groups lack the ability to strongly influence the legislative process, their behavior would most often be legislated as criminal. This criminalization then legitimates the use of the authorities on behalf of the more powerful group. In the 1920s and 1930s, for example, the Federal Bureau of Investigation was used on behalf of large companies to help control labor unions.

Austin Turk is another conflict theorist who saw social order as a product of powerful groups attempting to control society.[1] This control is exerted by putting values into law and then by having the authorities enforce that law. Turk began his conflict work with an article in which he called for the study of criminality as opposed to criminal behavior (1964). Suggesting the only explanation for criminality would be found in the criminal law, he proposed the examination of criminal law and its relationship to a definition of criminal status. His original concerns were to specify the conditions under which an individual would be defined as a criminal in an **authority-subject relationship.** He said crime is a status given to norm resisters whose perception of social norms and reality is inadequate to anticipate the result of their actions (1966). In other words, the less sophisticated the subjects are, the more likely their interaction with authorities will be characterized by conflict. Juveniles, for instance, have a higher probability of running afoul of authorities than adults do.

This concept of authority-subject relationships remains important in Turk's writings (1969, 1976). He sees as a fact of life that authorities must be

---

1. We would like to express appreciation to Austin Turk for his comments on this summary of his work.

dealt with, usually requiring a permanent adjustment of the subordinate to the powerful. There are, according to Turk, two major ways in which control can be exerted over a society. The first is coercion, or **physical force.** The more a population must be forced by the authorities to obey the law, the more difficult it will be to control that society. Thus, a delicate consensus-coercion balance has to be maintained by the powerful members of society.

The second form of control is much more subtle. This type is represented by the control of legal images and living time. The law itself can come to be seen as something that is more important than people. Further, there are two forms of law: the official list of undesirable forms of behavior and their associated punishments, and the established rules for processing people through the law-enforcement system. A legal process that is fashioned in favor of the powerful provides a degree of subtle control. Control of living time, on the other hand, is a later concept developed by Turk (1976, 1982). He notes that after a period of coercion, a society will adjust itself to new rules. As time goes on, the generation of people who were part of the old society will die out. The remaining people have experience only with the new society and thus are less likely to compare the new social order with the old one. When this happens, there will be little questioning of the rules of the new social order or, as Turk would put it, the relationship between authorities and the population (subjects).

These comments lead to a variety of propositions about criminality. Higher crime rates can be expected when physical coercion is more common than subtle forms of control. Similarly, the greater the power of the controlling groups, the higher will be the rate of criminalization for the less powerful. Finally, if the less powerful are organized, then likelihood of conflict with the authorities will be greater, with commensurately higher crime rates.

Richard Quinney, another of the major conflict theorists of the late 1960s and early 1970s, began to question the definitions of crime and the legal process being offered by authorities. In a widely quoted book, Quinney presented his theory of the **social reality of crime** in six propositions. While he was later to become a Marxist criminologist, his first conflict approach was of the pluralist variety and reflected on Vold's conflict theory as well as social interactionist theories. In truth, the theory was an integrative one which also incorporated concepts from differential association, social learning, and labeling. At the same time, Quinney was rejecting traditional ideas of science, by which researchers believed themselves to be working with the real world. He began to argue reality is merely what we perceive it to be (philosophical idealism).

He viewed crime, as did labeling theorists, as the product of reaction. The reaction of most importance, though, is that of the legitimate authorities. These authorities not only react to behavior but also impose definitions of the types of behavior that can be defined as criminal. They do so by using political power to create and place into criminal law those behaviors to which they object. Those in lower-class positions are more likely to engage

---

QUINNEY'S SOCIAL REALITY OF CRIME

PROPOSITION 1 (Definition of Crime): Crime is a definition of human conduct that is created by authorized agents in a politically organized society.

PROPOSITION 2 (Formulation of Criminal Definitions): Criminal definitions describe behaviors that conflict with the interests of the segments of society that have the power to shape political policy.

PROPOSITION 3 (Application of Criminal Definitions): Criminal definitions are applied by the segments of society that have the power to shape the enforcement and administration of criminal law.

PROPOSITION 4 (Development of Behavior Patterns in Relation to Criminal Definitions): Behavior patterns are structured in segmentally organized society in relation to criminal definitions, and within this context persons engage in actions that have relative probabilities of being defined as criminal.

PROPOSITION 5 (Construction of Criminal Conceptions): Conceptions of crime are constructed and diffused in the segments of society by various means of communication.

PROPOSITION 6 (The Social Reality of Crime): The social reality of crime is constructed by the formulation and application of criminal definitions, the development of behavior patterns related to criminal definitions, and the construction of criminal conceptions.

Source: Richard Quinney, *The Social Reality of Crime* (Boston: Little, Brown, 1970), 15–23.

---

in objectionable behavior and, indeed, learn such behaviors from those around them.

Crime, then, is the product of legal definitions constructed through the exercise of political power. But crime alone is not the entire picture. Just as crime is socially constructed, so is noncrime. That is, actions that are strikingly similar to illegal behavior are allowed through political definitions as desirable behavior. Both crime and noncrime definitions are spread through the media. With their pervasive effect, the media construct a social reality that certain actions are naturally crime and certain actions are naturally noncrime. Therefore, citizens tend not to think about the fact that definitions have been constructed for them.

As an example of socially constructed reality, Quinney used the example of the Lone Ranger radio program (1973b). The ingredients of an outnumbered "hero" who always prevails, the pure silver bullets with which he brings down evil, and the moralistic tone of the broadcast are all illustrations of a media construction of good guys and bad guys. Similarly, we go from televised athletic events sponsored by beer (alcohol) companies to news programs decrying drunken drivers and drug-related crime. Quinney was attempting to paint these kind of images with the brush of a socially constructed reality to demonstrate crime is part of a society controlled by the powerful and, in turn, is used by the powerful as a method of controlling people in that society. In a recent article, Williams (1997) used the Lone Ranger example to point out the controlled social reality of criminological research as well.

The Radical Conflict Perspective

Even more difficult than capturing conservative conflict positions with a broad stroke of the pen is a summary of radical conflict theorists. Their positions range from political anarchism (Tifft, 1979; Ferrell, 1993) through Marxism (Chambliss, 1975; Platt, 1982; Spitzer, 1975; Quinney, 1977) and economic materialism (Gordon, 1973) to value diversity (Pepinsky and Jesilow, 1985) and the new left realism (Young and Matthews, 1992). It is even difficult to determine exactly what to call these different approaches (Bohm, 1982). Regardless of this variety, though, most of the current radical versions of conflict theory can be traced to the writings of Karl Marx (Greenberg, 1981).

A preliminary version of radical conflict theories is characterized by the work of William Chambliss in the late 1960s and early 1970s. Chambliss became interested in the making of law and the process by which it was applied. His examination of the vagrancy laws in England (1964) exemplified the historical form of research the Marxist theories would use as evidence for their position. Documenting that the creation and changes in the vagrancy laws served to benefit the ruling classes, Chambliss focused on the importance of labor, resources, and control for the existing social order. Indeed, these were all themes he touched on in a 1969 statement of an interest-group, rather than a Marxist-oriented, theory.

In a 1971 publication entitled *Law, Order and Power*, with Robert Seidman, Chambliss began a Marxist analysis of the American criminal justice system. Chambliss and Seidman argued the ruling class controls the resources of society and uses law as a means of control. This class exercises control in two ways: by creating laws emphasizing the behaviors of the lower classes, the lower classes are criminalized, and by encouraging a myth that law serves the interests of everyone, the lower classes join in their own control. Chambliss and Seidman present their theory in a series of propositions that ultimately discuss the fact that each point of the criminal justice process favors the more powerful at the expense of the powerless. This statement served as a springboard for many analyses and conflict perspectives that followed. By 1975, Chambliss had turned his own theoretical commentary and analysis in a deeply Marxist direction.

Marxist Criminology

While Marx said very little about crime and criminals, many radical criminologists have adapted his general model of society to their explanations of crime. Marx saw conflict in society as being due to a scarcity of resources and a historical inequality in the distribution of those resources, notably power. This inequality creates a conflict of interest between those with and those without power. By the dawn of the Industrial Age, conflict had developed between two economic classes of society, the **proletariat** (the working class) and the dominant **bourgeoisie** (the nonworking owners of wealth).

The main theme in this conflict of classes was that of control of the **mode of production** (the owning and controlling of productive private property). As the controlling class exploited the labor of the working class, a struggle developed. Since Marx felt a group's position in society shaped its consciousness of that society, the working class was led to believe the capitalist structure of society was in their interest (**false consciousness**). As members of the exploited class became aware of their true position and common interests, they would gradually join forces and initiate overt conflict against the dominant class. This conflict would take the form of a revolution that would overthrow the ruling class and allow a classless society to exist in a socialist world without economic exploitation.

Marxist criminologists have assumed that **class struggle** affects crime on three fronts. First, they have argued that the *law itself is a tool of the ruling class*. The definitions of crime found in the law are a reflection of the interests of the ruling class and serve to perpetuate existing concepts of property, which is the foundation of capitalism. At the same time, the behavior of the ruling class is generally *not* placed under the rule of criminal law (Michalowski and Bohlander, 1976) and, instead, if placed into law at all, is found under administrative and regulatory laws. A belief in the validity of law deflects questions about its purpose and application and results in members of the working class policing themselves. Marxist criminologists prefer to speak of law as a violation of more general human rights (Schwendinger and Schwendinger, 1970, 1972, 1977; Platt, 1974).

The second major position of Marxist criminologists is they *view all crime (in capitalist nations) as the product of a class struggle* producing individualism and competition. The emphasis on accumulation of wealth and property leads to conflict between classes and even within classes. Thus, the chase to get ahead "manifests itself in the pursuit, criminal or otherwise, of property wealth and economic self-aggrandizement" (Bohm, 1982:570). Even violent crime is pictured as the result of the "brutal" conditions under which the working class must live (Quinney, 1977:53–54). For the working classes, then, it is their exclusion from the mode of production that creates a social structure conducive to criminal behavior. Not all Marxist criminologists have been comfortable with this position, however. Greenberg (1975) and others have declared that explaining all crime as a product of the capitalist system is too unidimensional.

Third, Marxist criminologists must deal with *relationships to the mode of production as an explanation for crime.* Richard Quinney (1977) and Steven Spitzer (1975) have discussed the problem of surplus labor in capitalist societies. Surplus labor guarantees wages will be low, but too large a surplus of labor may also cause problems. Spitzer (1975) lists five types of "problem populations": (1) the poor stealing from the rich, (2) those who refuse to work, (3) those who retreat to drugs, (4) those who refuse schooling or do not believe in the benefits of family life, and (5) those who actively propose a noncapitalist society. As long as the problem group is relatively quiet and poses no immediate threat to the ruling class, there is little need to expend scarce resources on their control. Skid-Row alcoholics are a typical group of this type, and Spitzer calls them "social junk." If, however, the group is active, then it poses a threat to the ruling class, and controlling its members becomes important. These groups (political activists, criminals, and revolutionaries) are called "social dynamite" by Spitzer and they draw a disproportionate share of the control agents' resources.

Major Concepts in Radical Explanations of Crime

Other than the elements already noted, radical and Marxist forms of criminological theory focus on five major concepts: social class and stratification, political economy, family disorganization, economic conditions, and surplus value. **Social class** is perhaps the most widespread concept, and it is found or implied in every other criminological theory as well. For radicals, social class is not simply one's position in the social order but a part of the internal working of capitalism. The two classes (proletariat and bourgeoisie) are created by capitalism largely because they are critical to a capitalist economy. The primary ingredients of class are wealth, power, and prestige, and are important because they affect the life chances and socialization of individuals in society. **Political economy** uses the concept of class but widens the meaning to take in the entire economic structure. This includes economic institutions and economic structures, or the ways in which corporations, monetary systems, and Wall Street are set up and arranged for the benefit of the bourgeoisie. By creating economic inequalities, these structures contribute to social inequalities that, in turn, affect the relationships between individuals. For instance, Ray Michalowski says "inequality tends to increase crime by weakening the social bond" (1985:410).

Family disorganization is one of the products of inequality. Mark Colvin and John Pauly (1983) propose that inequality and social relations in the workplace produce varying attitudes toward authority. When workplace control is authoritarian, hostility and alienation develop. These workplace experiences are reproduced in other social relations, such as the family, the school, and the peer group. Negative workplace experiences generate disorganized families and undesirable environments for children. This happens because lower-class workers tend to be employed in organizations depending on control techniques that are utilitarian (use material rewards), inconsistent, and coercive (erratic and stressful). As parents, such workers learn the same patterns of control and pass them on to their children. In such surroundings, children are more likely to engage in delinquency, particularly serious and sustained delinquency.

Economic conditions are also critical to many radical theories. Unemployment is among the most common of the factors assumed to be associated with crime. Quinney (1977:149) expresses the relationship nicely: "Unemployment simultaneously makes necessary various actions of survival by the unemployed surplus population and requires the state to control that population in some way." During periods of economic depression and recession, industry must reconcile a threat to its survival with downsizing its labor force. Such a move creates more control over those workers who are retained but also creates a surplus group of unemployed workers. To keep these workers from becoming a problem for the capitalist economy, control is given over to the criminal justice system and prisons are used to warehouse those most threatening to the social order. In Spitzer's terms, the problem is some of those unemployed will become social dynamite. The same problem holds true for workers displaced by technological innovation. Bob Bohm (1985) views the situation not as one of economic crises causing crime but of the capitalist system creating competition over scarce resources and promoting self-interest. The irony is that the saving of labor costs by using the criminal justice system to control surplus labor also results in the expenditure of scarce resources. Certainly, the corporate world is concerned about the high cost and amount of crime. Less costly approaches to the problem are continually being sought.

Finally, **surplus value** is the capitalist exploitation of the difference between the cost of production and the value of the product. If workers can be made to work longer for the same amount of money, or if they can be replaced by more cost-effective machines, the amount of surplus value increases. Not only does such a condition create unemployment, but it also creates underemployment, and many people barely manage to earn a living. Meanwhile, the value of the product increases. The combination of increasing marginal populations and increasing product value makes conditions particularly conducive to property crime.

Left Realism

After criticisms that much of the Marxist and radical theories were too simplistic, a new form of radical criminology emerged in the 1980s, characterized by the writings of Jock Young in Britain and Walter Dekeseredy in the United States. The British version seems to have been the product of radicals' disenchantment with their ability to change and reform society and the exceedingly conservative direction of the ruling British Labour Party (see Young, 1992). This version takes to heart the problem of translating radical ideas into **realistic social policy** (thus the term "realism") and is similar to the grounded labeling theory proposed by Dario Melossi, briefly reviewed in the previous chapter. As the British version of left realism was coming together, Tony Platt (1985) was echoing similar thoughts in the United States. The central task of a realist criminology is to make the perspective of practical use to policymakers without losing a critical perspective. Indeed, realists feel the best contribution criminology can make is to concern itself with specific analyses of crime and crime policies. In so doing they must take crime as a social problem seriously in a way that most radical criminology has failed to do.

The basic notion represents a deviation from the Marxist view that all crime is a product of the capitalist system. Realists also recognize the presence of crime in socialist countries and posit crime is a real problem for all. Indeed, crime constitutes a net loss in the quality of life for all classes, and the most common victims of crime are the working class. Rather than maintain the radical argument that the causes of crime are unemployment and poverty, a new and more complex explanation is offered. Trevor Jones, Brian MacLean, and Jock Young (1986) take pieces from both radical and traditional criminological theories and present four variables in their explanation of crime: **the victim, the offender, the state,** and **the community.** Further, the explanation combines both macrotheory and microtheory in an effort to demonstrate the effect of structural variables on processes that affect individuals.

Realists also believe crime control should be taken seriously, and they have embraced some traditional forms of research and policy. They have begun to use local surveys on victimization and fear of crime and have even examined local perceptions of the police. Proposals for policy initiatives have included democratic forms of control over the police and community participation in the formulation of crime prevention schemes. Finally, left realists have one major goal: to emphasize "social justice as a way of achieving a fair and orderly society" (Matthews and Young, 1991:6).

Anarchist Criminology

As a radical theory, anarchism is different from Marxist thought. Anarchists are opposed to hierarchies in all their forms. That is, anarchist criminology views authorities as agents of domination, serving one or several groups at the expense of others. Anarchists, then, defy all forms of domination, whether political, patriarchal, religious, or other. While the history of anarchy is much older, Larry Tifft (1979) created the first modern anarchist viewpoint within criminology and argued for a face-to-face form of justice. Few others wrote in this area until the recent publication of Jeff Ferrell's *Crimes of Style* (1993).

Ferrell argues domination is not merely accomplished through coercion but also through structures of knowledge, perception, and understanding. By this he means domination is the ability to control the way in which we define something, come to view that thing, and understand how it exists. To the extent our reality is defined for us by others, anarchists believe we should oppose those others. As Ferrell says (1993:161):

> Anarchism attacks these hierarchies of credibility, and seeks to dismantle the mythologies of certainty and truth on which they are built. It undercuts the taken-for-grantedness of the world, the reality which systems of authoritarian knowledge construct.

An anarchist criminology, then, seeks to "demythologize" the concepts behind the criminal justice system and the legal order on which it is based. In its place, anarchists prefer a pluralist set of ideas and rationales. Indeed, they prefer *ambiguity*, a world in which things are somewhat uncertain and without concrete meanings and purposes. How then does society exist under anarchy? The answer lies in the reconstruction of a society that appreciates diversity and tolerance. Such a society is decentralized and based on collective negotiations of the way people relate to and live with each other. Problems are solved and control is exercised by agreements between people and the groups of which they are a part. Finally, anarchism itself must avoid becoming an accepted formula for social order. To do this, thought and action are deemed of equal priority, and humor is used to overcome seriousness and emerging authority. An anarchist criminology is a criminology in which people are responsible for living with other people, negotiating flexible agreements about how they are to behave, and collectively administering control measures. Existing social structure, and authority, are deemed too rigid and harmful to the quality of human life.

CLASSIFICATION OF THE THEORY

First of all, conflict theories obviously assume that society is *conflict-oriented*, rather than consensus-oriented. They also tend to focus on the political structure of society, especially the making and enforcement of law. Therefore, conflict theories represent a break with a positivist tradition of explaining criminality and, instead, return to many of the concerns of the original Classical School. Conflict theories are more *classical* and emphasize crime rather than criminals. Yet at the same time, most criminological conflict theories share the positivist concern with explaining crime. They simply prefer that explanation be focused on the political and economic conditions of life.

Because of their emphasis on political and economic *structure*, conflict theories rarely engage in discussions of the process by which criminal behavior is produced. This leads to a classification of the conflict approach to crime as a *macrotheory*. Clearly, it is the nature of society and its subsequent effect on social institutions rather than behavior that is to be explained. Where conflict theories approach processual issues, their concerns are similar to those of strain theories—how to shift the macro-level effects of social structural to the individual level.

SUMMARY

The conflict perspective, whether pluralist or radical, has changed the nature of criminological theorizing over the last two decades. Most criminologists now acknowledge the presence of conflict in American society, although they reserve judgment about the extent to which it affects crime.

While it is difficult to characterize conflict theories because of their diversity (doing so is similar to discussing all consensus theories as if they were one theory), there are certain commonalities. First, of course, is the assumption that conflict is natural to society (Marxists actually argue conflict is unnatural but that it has almost always been with us). Second, resources are assumed to be scarce, or otherwise limited, and possession of these resources conveys power over others. Third, competition for resources always exists. Fourth, it is in this competition and use of power that law and law enforcement become tools to gain and maintain position in society. If a particular group gains control over enough resources and is able to maintain its position long enough, the conflict may result in a class system, with a ruling class and a subjugated class.

Marxist theorists assume these basic points but add that modern capitalist society creates conditions of life conducive to crime. Indeed, it is this divergence from conflict theories in general that characterizes the Marxist position. Richard Quinney and John Wildeman, in the third edition of their work *The Problem of Crime* (1991:78), provide an excellent summary of the Marxist conflict perspective. They locate four propositions as the essence of Marxist criminology: (1) crime is best understood under the Marxist perspective, (2) crime constitutes more than the state definition of crime, (3) the state version of crime and other social harms are a product of the class struggle, and (4) crime represents the alienation of individuals by capitalist social structures and institutions.

Major Points of the Theory

1. Conflict is a fact of life; society is most appropriately characterized by conflict.
2. Resources, both physical and social, are scarce and therefore in demand. It is the attempt to control these resources that generates the major portion of conflict in society.
3. Control of resources creates power, and that power is used to maintain and expand the resource base of one group at the expense of others.
4. Once a group achieves dominance over others, it seeks to use available societal mechanisms for its benefit to assure it remains dominant.
5. Law is a societal mechanism that provides the group in power with strong means of control over other, less powerful groups.

6. Laws are formulated so that they express the values and interests of the dominant group, and to restrict behavior common to less powerful groups.
7. The application and enforcement of law leads to a focus on the behavior of less-powerful groups, thus disproportionately "criminalizing" the members of those groups.
8. And for Marxist versions of conflict theory, the conditions generated under the capitalist political economy are the primary cause of political and economic actions that generate crime.

EPILOGUE: CURRENT DIRECTIONS AND POLICY IMPLICATIONS

Current Directions

Contemporary conflict theory is pursuing two generic avenues. First, the *basic conflict propositions dealing with power differential between groups and discriminatory processing* have been the target of much research. Discrimination research has produced such a large number of studies that we have listed only a few in the chapter bibliography (for reviews and bibliographies of this research, see Hagan, 1974, 1980, 1989, and Williams, 1980). At this point, the evidence is somewhat questionable. Some studies have found support for class, race, or gender discrimination and others have not. Most notable is the argument recently waged between William Wilbanks and Coramae Richey Mann. Wilbanks has published a book *(The Myth of a Racist Criminal Justice System,* 1987) analyzing the discrimination research and coming to the conclusion no systematic discrimination exists. Mann has examined the issue in her *Unequal Justic: A Question of Color (1993)* and come to the opposite conclusion. Indeed, depending on which studies one examines and the critical way in which they are assessed, a case can be made for either side of the issue.

Actually, two considerations are relevant to the argument and may help resolve some of the problems. First, the form of research design and mode of analysis are inextricably tied to the results and conclusions drawn from the various studies. If researchers use data gathered by the criminal justice system, there may be some question that the data represent actual processing behaviors. Also, if the important variables are poorly measured, potential discrimination may be difficult to find regardless of the sophistication of the analysis. Second, many conflict theorists might even argue the issue of discrimination is spurious, that the making of laws is the important issue. If laws are made that have a discriminatory focus on certain groups in society, then those individuals can be arrested in large numbers and processed nondiscriminatorily. Under this scenario, discrimination is still taking place, but not on the processing level. Regardless of these concerns, though, there is no evidence that the issue is about to be resolved.

The second general avenue being pursued is a group of related theoretical concerns that Jim Thomas and Aogan O'Maolchatha (1989) characterize as a *transcending of dominant social control ideas.* They list four contemporary areas in which radical and Marxist criminologists are making contributions. First, there is the newly emerging realist criminology. Second, a new peacemaking criminology is developing (see Chapter 14). Third, feminist scholars have begun developing a new form of radical criminology based on gender (see Chapter 13). Fourth, a postmodernist (or deconstructionist) criminology has emerged from European philosophical and linguistic positions (see Chapter 14). Ray Michalowski (1996) echoes these sentiments while categorizing the various critical efforts differently. He sees critical criminology as working within broad social theories (feminism, political economy, post-structuralism, and post-modernism) and within "hybrid" theories such as anarchist criminology, constitutive criminology, cultural criminology, news-making criminology, peacemaking criminology, and left realist criminology. In short, all these areas are exploring different ways of examining the problem of crime, but at the same time all are attempting to develop conceptions that do not rely on traditional analyses of crime.

Policy Implications

While radical theories have had little effect on policy, conflict theories in general have at least contributed to a greater concern with equality in the criminal justice system. Earlier proposals for policy changes generally followed a scheme for a major restructuring of society along socialist lines. Today, however, radical criminologists are much more sensitive to the practical nature of policy. Michael Lynch and Byron Groves (1989:128–129) note several policy changes have been suggested, or might be suggested, by radicals. These include reforming the bail system to provide equal justice to arrested individuals, abolishing mandatory sentences, prosecuting corporate crimes, and promoting community alternatives to imprisonment. Other policies endorsed by conflict criminologists are schemes to reduce prison overcrowding, informal arbitration and mediation "courts" to keep people out of the criminal justice system, a de-emphasis on repressive sanctions, and community-based strategies for controlling crime and delinquency.

Two research examples from Texas serve to demonstrate the practical policy uses of a realist conflict-oriented criminology. Marilyn McShane (1987) conducted a study of one of the least-powerful groups in the Texas Department of Corrections: immigrant inmates. Her conflict argument was that not only are things done to those with little power, but there are also times when nothing is done *for* them either. After committing a felony, these inmates were no longer eligible to remain in the United States. She found alien inmates, on average, were serving more prison time than their resident counterparts, largely because the Immigration and Naturalization Service (INS) had placed a detainer on them. After demonstrating the cost to the Department of Corrections, and the bed space occupied, a policy was put into place to release the aliens to the INS as soon as possible. This reduced the undeserved time these inmates served. Charles Fields (1984) examined the Texas Intensive Supervised Probation Program (ISP), finding it a less oppressive sanction than prison. By statistically demonstrating about half of the ISP population would have gone to prison if the program had not been available, the Texas legislature extended the program as a method of diversion from prison. By a conservative estimate, Fields's research resulted in the state saving the cost of placing several thousand felony offenders in prison by placing them in the less restrictive ISP.

Concerning white-collar crime, policies supported by conflict theorists would include allocation of more resources to regulatory agencies fighting corporate and occupational crime, requirements for codes of ethics in corporations, and the teaching of ethics courses in business schools. A redefinition of crime to include most cases of harm inflicted on society would also be encouraged. On a broader scale, radical criminologists propose programs to eliminate racism and sexism in the criminal justice system and in society at large, increased employment opportunities and enhanced skills training for large sectors of the population, and reductions in social stratification and inequality.

Elliot Currie (1989), in a policy-conscious article, goes on to sketch larger policy directions that might be undertaken. He suggests programs such as Head Start be made available to all children who are at risk of growing up uneducated. Health services (and mental health services as well) should be provided to all children at risk of disease and emotional trauma. Family support programs should have a greater governmental commitment—particularly in the areas of domestic violence and child abuse. Programs to fight drug use should be reevaluated, and a greater share of resources given to treatment-oriented, nonpunitive models. Finally, Currie suggests all forms of services needed by young children should be enhanced and greater efforts made to provide them. Austin Turk (1995), in another policy article, also argues that the conflict perspective has many practical suggestions to offer.

Policy directions, then, are available under conflict and radical theories. With the emergence of the left realist movement, we anticipate many, very practical, proposals will be made.

BIBLIOGRAPHY

ADAMSON, C. R. (1984). "Toward a Marxian penology: Captive criminal populations as economic threats and resources." *Social Problems* 31: 435–458.

AKERS, RONALD L. (1979). "Theory and ideology in Marxist criminology: Comments on Turk, Quinney, Toby, and Klockars." *Criminology* 16: 527–544.

ANDERSON, KEVIN (1991). "Radical criminology and the overcoming of alienation: Perspectives from Marxian and Gandhian humanism." In H. E. Pepinsky and R. Quinney, eds., *Criminology as Peacemaking*, 14–29. Bloomington: Indiana University Press.

BAILEY, WILLIAM C. (1981). "Inequality in the legal order: Some further analysis and commentary." *Social Problems* 29: 51–60.

BALKWELL, JAMES (1990). "Ethnic inequality and the rate of homicide." *Social Forces* 69: 53–70.

BALL-ROKEACH, SANDRA J. (1980). "Normative and deviant violence from a conflict perspective." *Social Problems* 28: 45–59.

BARAK, GREGG L. (1982). "Punishment and corrections." *Crime and Social Justice* 18: 108–117.

—— (1980). *In Defense of Whom? A Critique of Criminal Justice Reform*. Cincinnati, OH: Anderson.

——, ed. (1991). *Crimes by the Capitalist State: An Introduction to State Criminality.* SUNY Series in Radical Social and Political Theory. Albany: State University of New York Press.

BARAK, GREGG L., and ROBERT M. BOHM (1989). "The crimes of the homeless or the crime of homelessness? On the dialectics of criminalization, decriminalization, and victimization." *Contemporary Crises* 13: 275–288.

BARLOW, DAVID E., MELISSA H. BARLOW, and THEODORE G. CHIRICOS (1993). "Long economic cycles and the criminal justice system in the U.S." *Crime Law and Social Change* 19: 143–169.

BELKNAP, MICHAEL R. (1995). *Federal Law and Southern Order: Racial Violence and Constitutional Conflict in the Post-Brown South.* Athens: University of Georgia Press.

BERK, RICHARD A., and PETER H. ROSSI (1977). *Prison Reform and State Elites.* Cambridge, MA: Ballinger.

BERNARD, THOMAS J. (1981). "The distinction between conflict and radical criminology." *Journal of Criminal Law and Criminology* 72: 362–379.

—— (1986). "Punishment and social structure: What does the future hold?" In W. B. Groves and G. Newman, eds., *Punishment and Privilege*, 131–143. Albany, NY: Harrow and Heston.

BLOOM, DIANA M., and CHARLES E. REASONS (1978). "Ideology and crime: A study in the sociology of knowledge." *International Journal of Criminology and Penology* 6: 19–30.

BOHM, ROBERT M. (1982). "Radical criminology: An explication." *Criminology* 19: 565–589.

—— (1985). "Beyond unemployment: Toward a radical solution to the crime problem." *Crime and Social Justice* 21–22: 213–222.

BOND-MAUPIN, LISA, CAROL C. LUJAN, and M. A. BORTNER (1995). "Jailing of American Indian adolescents: The legacy of cultural domination and imposed law." *Crime Law and Social Change* 23: 1–16.

BONGER, WILLEM A. (1916). *Criminality and Economic Conditions.* Trans. H. P. Horton. Boston: Little, Brown.

BOSWORTH, MARY (1996). "Resistance and compliance in women's prisons: Towards a critique of legitimacy." *Critical Criminology* 7: 5–19.

BOX, STEVEN (1987). *Recession, Crime and Punishment.* Totowa, NJ: Barnes and Noble.

BOX, STEVEN, and C. HALE. (1982). "Economic crisis and the rising prisoner population in England and Wales." *Crime and Social Justice* 17: 20–35.

—— (1985). "Unemployment, imprisonment and prison overcrowding." *Contemporary Crises* 9: 209–228.

BRASS, PAUL, ed. (1996). *Riots and Pogroms.* New York: New York University Press.

BROWN, DAVID, and RUSSELL HOGG (1992). "Essentialism, radical criminology and left realism." *Australian and New Zealand Journal of Criminology* 25: 195–230.

BROWN, M. CRAIG, and BARBARA WARNER (1992). "Immigrants, urban politics, and policing in 1990." *American Sociological Review* 57: 293–305.

BUCHANAN, ALLEN E. (1996). *Marx and Justice: The Radical Critique of Liberalism.* Totowa, NJ: Rowman and Littlefield.

BURGER, WILLIAM (1993). *American Crime and Punishment: The Religious Origins of American Criminology.* Buchanan, MI: Vande Vere Publishing.

CARDARELLI, ALBERT P., and STEPHEN C. HICKS (1993). "Radicalism in law and criminology: A retrospective view of critical legal studies and radical criminology." *Journal of Criminal Law and Criminology* 84: 502–553.

CARLEN, PAT (1990). "Women, crime, feminism, and realism." *Social Justice* 17: 106–123.

CHAMBLISS, WILLIAM B. (1964). "A sociological analysis of the law of vagrancy." *Social Problems* 12: 67–77.

——— (1974). "The state, the law and the definition of behavior as criminal or delinquent." In D. Glaser, ed., *Handbook of Criminology*, 7–44. Chicago: Rand McNally.

——— (1975). "Toward a political economy of crime." *Theory and Society* 2: 152–153.

——— (1989). "State-organized crime: The American Society of Criminology, 1988 presidential address." *Criminology* 27: 185–186.

——— (1994). "Policing the ghetto underclass: The politics of law and law enforcement." *Social Problems* 41: 177–194.

CHAMBLISS, WILLIAM B., and MILTON MANKOFF (1976). *Whose Law? What Order? A Conflict Approach to Criminology.* New York: Wiley.

CHAMBLISS, WILLIAM B., and ROBERT B. SEIDMAN (1971). *Law, Order and Power.* Reading, MA: Addison-Wesley.

CHAMLIN, MITCHELL (1989). "Conflict theory and police killings." *Deviant Behavior* 10: 353–368.

——— (1990). "Determinants of police expenditures in Chicago, 1904–1958." *Sociological Quarterly* 31: 485–494.

CHIRICOS, THEODORE G. (1987). "Rates of crime and unemployment: An analysis of aggregate research evidence." *Social Problems* 34: 187–212.

CHIRICOS, THEODORE G., and MIRIAM DELONE (1992). "Labor surplus and punishment: A review and assessment of theory and evidence." *Social Problems* 39: 421–446.

CHIRICOS, THEODORE G., and GORDON P. WALDO (1975). "Socioeconomic status and criminal sentencing: An empirical assessment of a conflict perspective." *American Sociological Review* 40: 753–772.

CHURCHILL, WARD, and JIM VANDER WALL (1988). *Agents of Repression: The FBI's Secret Wars against the Black Panther Party and the American Indian Movement.* Boston: South End Press.

COLVIN, MARK, and JOHN PAULY (1983). "A critique of criminology: Toward an integrated structural-Marxist theory of delinquency production." *American Journal of Sociology* 89: 513–551.

COOK, LEE, and BARBARA HUDSON, eds. (1993). *Racism and Criminology.* London, UK: Sage.

COOK, P. J., and G. A. ZARKIN (1986). "Homicide and economic conditions: A replication and critique of M. Harvey Brenner's *New Report to the U.S. Congress.*" *Journal of Quantitative Criminology* 2: 69–80.

COONEY, MARK (1997). "From warre to tyranny: Lethal conflict and the state." *American Sociological Review* 62: 316–338.

CORZINE, JAY, J. L. CORZINE, and C. CREECH (1988). "The tenant labor market and lynching in the South: A test of split labor market theory." *Sociological Inquiry* 58: 261–278.

COSER, LEWIS (1956). *The Functions of Social Conflict.* New York: Macmillan.

CURRIE, ELLIOTT (1989). "Confronting crime: Looking toward the twenty-first century." *Justice Quarterly* 6: 5–25.

DAHRENDORF, RALF (1958). "Out of utopia: Toward a reconstruction of sociological analysis." *American Journal of Sociology* 67: 115–127.

——— (1959). *Class and Class Conflict in an Industrial Society.* London: Routledge and Kegan Paul.

DAS, DILIP (1983). "Conflict views on policing: An evaluation." *American Journal of Police* 3: 51–81.

DEKESEREDY, WALTER S., and BRIAN MacLEAN (1991). "Exploring the gender, race and class dimensions of victimization: A left realist critique of the Canadian Urban Victimization Survey." *International Journal of Offender Therapy and Comparative Criminology* 35: 143–161.

DEKESEREDY, WALTER S., and MARTIN D. SCHWARTZ (1991). "British and U.S. left realism: A critical comparison." *International Journal of Offender Therapy and Comparative Criminology* 35: 248–262.

DENQ, FURJEN, LOU JOU LEE, and MICHAEL S. VAUGHN (1996). "Drug crime in Taiwan: A time-series analysis from 1965 to 1994." *Deviant Behavior* 17: 347–368.

DICRISTINA, BRUCE (1995). *Method in Criminology: A Philosophical Primer*. Albany, NY: Harrow and Heston.

FARRELL, RONALD A., and VICTORIA L. SWIGERT (1982). *Deviance and Social Control*. Glenview, IL: Scott, Foresman.

FERRELL, JEFF (1993). *Crimes of Style: Urban Graffiti and the Politics of Criminality*. New York: Garland.

FERRELL, JEFF, and CLINTON R. SANDERS, eds. (1995). *Cultural Criminology*. Boston: Northeastern University Press.

FIELDS, CHARLES B. (1984). *The Intensive Supervision Probation Program in Texas: A Two-Year Assessment*. Unpublished doctoral diss.: Sam Houston State University, Huntsville, TX.

FLEMING, THOMAS, ed. (1985). *The New Criminologies in Canada: State, Crime, and Control*. Toronto, Canada: Oxford University Press.

FLYNN, EDITH (1980). "From conflict theory to conflict resolution: Controlling collective violence in prisons." *American Behavioral Scientist* 23: 745–776.

FOX, JAMES G. (1984). "The new right and social justice: Implications for the prisoners' movement." *Crime and Social Justice* 20: 63–76.

FRENCH, LAURENCE (1994). *The Winds of Injustice*. New York: Garland.

FRIEDRICHS, DAVID O. (1982). "Crime, deviance and criminal justice: In search of a radical humanistic perspective." *Humanity and Society* 6: 200–226.

GALSTER, G. C., and L. A. SCATURO (1985). "The U.S. criminal justice system: Unemployment and the severity of punishment." *Journal of Research in Crime and Delinquency* 22: 163–189.

GARLAND, DAVID (1990). *Punishment and Modern Society: A Study in Social Theory*. Chicago: University of Chicago Press.

GAROFALO, JAMES (1978). "Radical criminology and criminal justice: Points of divergence and contact." *Crime and Social Justice* 10: 17–27.

GIBBONS, DON C. (1979). *The Criminological Enterprise: Theories and Perspectives*. Englewood Cliffs, NJ: Prentice Hall.

GORDON, DAVID M. (1973). "Capitalism, class and crime in America." *Crime and Delinquency* 19: 163–186.

GRABOSKY, PETER (1978). "Theory and research on variations in penal severity." *British Journal of Law and Society* 5: 103–114.

GREENBERG, DAVID F. (1975). "On one-dimensional Marxist criminology." *Theory and Society* 3: 610–621.

———, ed. (1981). *Crime and Capitalism: Readings in Marxist Criminology*. Palo Alto, CA: Mayfield.

———, ed. (1993). *Crime and Capitalism: Readings in Marxist Criminology*. Expanded and updated ed. Philadelphia: Temple University Press.

GREENBERG, DAVID F., RONALD KESSLER, and COLIN LOFTIN (1985). "Social inequality and crime control." *Journal of Criminal Law and Criminology* 76: 684–704.

GREENLEAF, RICHARD G., and LONN LANZA-KADUCE (1995). "Sophistication, organization, and authority-suspect conflict: Rediscovering and unraveling Turk's theory of norm resistance." *Criminology* 33: 565–586.

GROSE, GREGORY, and W. BYRON GROVES (1988). "Crime and human nature: A Marxist perspective." *Contemporary Crises* 12: 145–171.

GROVES, W. BYRON (1985). "Marxism and positivism." *Crime and Social Justice* 23: 129–150.

GROVES, W. BYRON, and ROBERT J. SAMPSON (1986). "Critical theory and criminology." *Social Problems* 33: 58–80.

—— (1987). "Traditional contributions to radical criminology." *Journal of Research in Crime and Delinquency* 24: 181–214.

HABERMAS, JURGEN (1971). *Toward a Rational Society.* Boston: Beacon Press.

HAGAN, JOHN (1974). "Extra-legal attributes and criminal sentencing: An assessment of a sociological viewpoint." *Law and Society Review* 8: 357–383.

—— (1980). "The legislation of crime and delinquency: A review of theory, research and method." *Law and Society Review* 14. 603–628.

—— (1989). *Structural Criminology.* New Brunswick, NJ: Rutgers University Press.

HAGAN, JOHN, A. R. GILLIS, and J. CHAN (1978). "Explaining official delinquency: A spatial study of class, conflict and control." *Sociological Quarterly* 19: 386–398.

HAGAN, JOHN, A. R. GILLIS, and JOHN SIMPSON (1985). "The class structure of gender and delinquency: Toward a power control theory of common delinquent behavior." *American Journal of Sociology* 90: 1151–1178.

—— (1987). "Class in the household: A power-control theory of gender and delinquency." *American Journal of Sociology* 92: 788–816.

HAGAN, JOHN, and RUTH D. PETERSON, eds. (1995). *Crime and Inequality.* Stanford, CA: Stanford University Press.

HALE, C. (1989a). "Economy, punishment and imprisonment." *Contemporary Crises* 13: 327–349.

—— (1989b). "Unemployment, imprisonment, and the stability of punishment hypothesis: Some results using cointegration and error correction models." *Journal of Quantitative Criminology* 5: 169–191.

HALL, STUART (1978). *Policing the Crisis: Mugging, the State, and Law and Order.* New York: Holmes and Meier.

HARRING, SIDNEY L. (1983). *Policing a Class Society: The Experience of American Cities, 1865–1915.* New Brunswick, NJ: Rutgers University Press.

HENRY, STUART, and DRAGAN MILOVANOVIC (1991). "Constitutive criminology: The maturation of critical theory." *Criminology* 29: 293–315.

—— (1996). *Constitutive Criminology.* Thousand Oaks, CA: Sage.

HEPBURN, JOHN (1977). "Social control and the legal order: Legitimated repression in a capitalist state." *Contemporary Crises* 1: 77–90.

HEWITT, JOHN D., and DWIGHT W. HOOVER (1982). "Local modernization and crime: The effects of modernization on crime in Middletown, 1845–1910." *Law and Human Behavior* 6: 313–326.

HOGG, RUSSELL (1988). "Taking crime seriously: Left realism and Australian criminology." In M. Findlay and R. Hogg, eds., *Understanding Crime and Criminal Justice,* 24–51. North Ryde, Australia: Law Book Company.

HOLMES, MALCOLM D., HARMON M. HOSCH, HOWARD C. DAUDISTEL, DOLORES A. PEREZ, and JOSEPH B. GRAVES. (1996). "Ethnicity, legal resources, and felony dispositions in two Southwestern jurisdictions." *Justice Quarterly* 13: 11–30.

HORTON, JOHN, and TONY PLATT (1986). "Crime and criminal justice under capitalism and socialism: Towards a Marxist perspective." *Crime and Social Justice* 25: 115–135.

HUMPHRIES, DREW (1984). "Reconsidering the justice model." *Contemporary Crises* 8: 167–173.

HUNT, ALAN (1980). "The radical critique of law: An assessment." *International Journal of the Sociology of Law* 8: 33–46.

INCIARDI, JAMES A., ed. (1980). *Radical Criminology: The Coming Crises*. Beverly Hills, CA: Sage.

JACOBS, DAVID (1978). "Inequality and the legal order: An ecological test of the conflict model." *Social Problems* 25: 515–525.

——— (1979). "Inequality and police strength: Conflict theory and coercive control in metropolitan areas." *American Sociological Review* 44: 913–925.

JACOBS, DAVID, and DAVID BRITT (1979). "Inequality and police use of deadly force: An empirical assessment of a conflict hypothesis." *Social Problems* 26: 403–412.

JANKOVIC, I. (1977). "Labor market and imprisonment." *Crime and Social Justice* 8: 17–31.

JENKINS, PHILIP (1982). "The radicals and the rehabilitative ideal, 1890–1930." *Criminology* 20: 347–372.

——— (1989). "The assassination of Olof Palme: Evidence and ideology." *Contemporary Crises* 13: 15–33.

JESILOW, PAUL (1982). "Adam Smith and white-collar crime." *Criminology* 20: 319–328.

JOE, TOM (1987). "Economic inequality: The picture in black and white." *Crime and Delinquency* 33: 287–299.

JONES, TREVOR, BRIAN MACLEAN, and JOCK YOUNG (1986). *The Islington Crime Survey*. Aldershot, England: Gower.

KAMENKA, EUGENE, and ALICE EHR-SOON TAY (1987). "Marxist ideology, communist reality, and the concept of criminal justice." *Criminal Justice Ethics* 6: 3–29.

KLOCKARS, CARL B. (1979). "The contemporary crises of Marxist criminology." *Criminology* 16: 477–515.

KRAHN, HARVEY, TIMOTHY HARTNAGEL, and JOHN W. GARTRELL (1986). "Income inequality and homicide rates: Cross-national data and criminological theories." *Criminology* 24: 269–295.

KRISBERG, BARRY (1975). *Power and Privilege: Toward a New Criminology*. Englewood Cliffs, NJ: Prentice Hall.

LAFFARGUE, B., and T. GODEFROY (1989). "Economic cycles and punishment: Unemployment and imprisonment." *Contemporary Crises* 13: 371–404.

LANZA-KADUCE, LONN, and RICHARD G. GREENLEAF (1994). "Police-citizen encounters: Turk on norm resistance." *Justice Quarterly* 11: 605–623.

LAWRENCE, REGINA G. (1996). "Accidents, icons, and indexing: The dynamics of news coverage of police use of force." *Political Communication* 13: 437–454.

LEA, J. (1987). "Left realism: A defense." *Contemporary Crises* 11: 357–370.

LEE, NELLA (1995). "Culture conflict and crime in Alaskan native villages." *Journal of Criminal Justice* 23: 177–189.

LEIBER, MICHAEL J. (1995). "Toward clarification of the concept of 'minority' status and decision-making in juvenile court proceedings." *Journal of Crime and Justice* 18: 79–108.

LEIBER, MICHAEL J., and KATHERINE M. JAMIESON (1995). "Race and decision making within juvenile justice: The importance of context." *Journal of Quantitative Criminology* 11: 363–388.

LIZOTTE, ALAN (1978). "Extra-legal factors in Chicago's criminal courts: Test of the conflict model of criminal justice." *Social Problems* 25: 564–580.

LOPEZ, ANTOINETTE SEDILLO, ed. (1995). *Latinos in the United States: History, Law and Perspective*. New York: Garland.

LOWMAN, JOHN, and BRIAN D. MACLEAN, eds. (1992). *Realist Criminology: Crime Control and Policing in the 1990s*. Ontario: University of Toronto Press

LYNCH, MICHAEL J. (1987). "Quantitative analysis and Marxist criminology: Some old answers to a dilemma in Marxist criminology." *Crime and Social Justice* 29: 110–129.

——— (1988). "The extraction of surplus value, crime and punishment: A preliminary examination." *Contemporary Crises* 12: 329–344.

LYNCH, MICHAEL J., and BYRON W. GROVES (1986). *A Primer in Radical Criminology.* New York: Harrow and Heston.

——— (1989). *A Primer in Radical Criminology,* 2nd ed. New York: Harrow and Heston.

LYNCH, MICHAEL J., W. BYRON GROVES, and ALAN LIZOTTE (1994). "The rate of surplus value and crime. A theoretical and empirical examination of Marxian economic theory and criminology." *Crime, Law, and Social Change* 21: 15–48.

LYNCH, MICHAEL J., and E. BRITT PATTERSON, eds. (1996). *Justice with Prejudice: Race and Criminal Justice in America.* Albany, NY: Harrow and Heston.

MACLEAN, BRIAN D. (1991). "In partial defense of socialist realism: Some theoretical and methodological concerns of the local crime survey." *Crime, Law and Social Change* 15: 213–254.

——— (1993). "Left realism, local crime surveys and policing of racial minorities: A further analysis of data from the first sweep of the Islington Crime Survey." *Crime, Law, and Social Change* 19: 51–86.

MACLEAN, BRIAN D., and DRAGAN MILOVANOVIC, eds. (1990). *Racism, Empiricism, and Criminal Justice.* Vancouver, Canada: Collective Press.

MAGUIRE, BRENDAN (1988). "The applied dimension of radical criminology: A survey of prominent radical criminologists." *Sociological Spectrum* 8: 133–151.

——— (1990). "The police in the 1800s: A three city analysis." *Journal of Crime and Justice* 13: 103–132.

MANKOFF, MILTON (1978). "On the responsibility of Marxist criminologists: A reply to Quinney." *Contemporary Crises* 2: 293–301.

MANN, CORAMAE RICHEY (1993). *Unequal Justice: A Question of Color.* Bloomington: Indiana University Press.

Marcuse, Herbert (1960). *Reason and Revolution.* Boston: Beacon Press.

——— (1972). *Counter-revolution and Revolt.* Boston: Beacon Press.

MARENIN, OTWIN., A. W. PISCIOTTA, and T. J. JULIANI (1983). "Economic conditions and social control: An empirical assessment of the relationship between unemployment and incarceration in the U.S.A., 1958 to 1978." *Criminal Justice Review* 8: 43–53.

MATTHEWS, ROGER (1987). "Taking realist criminology seriously." *Contemporary Crises* 11: 371–401.

MATTHEWS, ROGER, and JOCK YOUNG (1986). *Confronting Crime.* Beverly Hills, CA: Sage.

——— (1992). "Reflections on realism." In J. Young and R. Matthews, eds., *Rethinking Criminology: The Realist Debate,* 1–23. Newbury Park, CA: Sage.

———, eds. (1992). *Issues in Realist Criminology.* Newbury Park, CA: Sage.

MCSHANE, MARILYN D. (1987). "Immigration processing and the alien inmate: Constructing a conflict perspective." *Journal of Crime and Justice* 10: 171–194.

MEIER, ROBERT F. (1976). "The new criminology: Continuity in criminological theory." *Journal of Criminal Law and Criminology* 67: 461–469.

MESSNER, STEVEN F., and MARVIN D. KROHN (1990). "Class, compliance structures, and delinquency: Assessing integrated structural Marxist theory." *American Journal of Sociology* 96: 300–328.

MICHALOWSKI, RAYMOND J. (1983). "Crime control in the 1980s: A progressive agenda." *Crime and Social Justice* 19: 13–23.

——— (1985). *Order, Law and Crime: An Introduction to Criminology.* New York: Random House.

——— (1996). "Critical criminology and the critique of domination: The story of an intellectual movement." *Critical Criminology* 7: 9–16.

MICHALOWSKI, RAYMOND J., and EDWARD W. BOHLANDER (1976). "Repression and criminal justice in capitalist America." *Sociological Inquiry* 46: 95–106.

MICHALOWSKI, RAYMOND J., and RONALD KRAMER (1995). "Justice under Clinton." *Social Justice* 22: 1–138.

MILOVANOVIC, DRAGAN (1981). "The commodity exchange theory of law." *Crime and Social Justice* 16: 41–49.

—— (1987). "The political economy of 'liberty' and 'property' interests." *Legal Studies Forum* 11: 147–172.

—— (1988). *A Primer in the Sociology of Law.* New York: Harrow and Heston.

MINTZ, ROBERT (1974). "Interview with Ian Taylor, Paul Walton, and Jock Young." *Issues in Criminology* 9: 33–53.

MUGFORD, STEPHEN, and PAT O'MALLEY (1991). "Heroin policy and deficit models: The limits of left realism." *Crime, Law, and Social Change* 15: 19–36.

MYERS, HOWARD P. (1985). "The effect of sexual stratification by race on arrest in sexual battery cases." *American Journal of Criminal Justice* 9: 172–184.

MYERS, MARTHA (1990a). "Black threat and incarceration in postbellum Georgia." *Social Forces* 69: 373–393.

—— (1990b). "Economic threat and racial disparities in incarceration: The case of postbellum Georgia." *Criminology* 28: 627–656.

—— (1991). "Economic conditions and punishment in postbellum Georgia." *Journal of Quantitative Criminology* 7: 99–121.

MYERS, S. L., and W. J. SABOL (1987). "Unemployment and racial differences in imprisonment." *Review of Black Political Economy* 16: 189–209.

NATIONAL COMMISSION ON THE CAUSES and PREVENTION OF VIOLENCE (1969). *The Politics of Protest: Task Force Report on Violent Aspects of Protest and Confrontation.* New York: Simon and Schuster.

O'MALLEY, PAT (1987). "Marxist theory and Marxist criminology." *Crime and Social Justice* 29: 70–87.

—— (1988). "The purpose of knowledge: Pragmatism and the praxis of Marxist criminology." *Contemporary Crises* 12: 65–79.

PARKER, ROBERT N., and ALLEN V. HOROWITZ (1986). "Unemployment, crime, and imprisonment: A panel approach." *Criminology* 24: 751–773.

PEARCE, FRANK (1976). *Crimes of the Powerful: Marxism, Crime and Deviance.* London: Pluto Press.

PEPINSKY, HAROLD E. (1976). *Crime and Conflict: A Study of Law and Society.* New York: Academic Press.

—— (1978). "Communist anarchism as an alternative to the rule of criminal law." *Contemporary Crises* 2: 315–327.

—— (1980). "A radical alternative to 'radical' criminology." In J. A. Inciardi, ed., *Radical Criminology: The Coming Crises,* 299–315. Beverly Hills, CA: Sage.

PEPINSKY, HAROLD E., and PAUL JESILOW (1985). *Myths That Cause Crime,* 2nd ed., annotated. Cabin John, MD: Seven Locks Press.

PETCHESKY, R. P. (1981). "At hard labor: Penal confinement and production in nineteenth-century America." In D. F. Greenberg, ed., *Crime and Capitalism: Readings in Marxist Criminology,* 341–357. Palo Alto, CA: Mayfield.

PLATT, TONY (1974). "Prospects for a radical criminology in the United States." *Crime and Social Justice* 1: 2–6.

—— (1978). "Street crime: A view from the left." *Crime and Social Justice* 9: 26–34.

—— (1982). "Crime and punishment in the United States: Immediate and long-term reforms from a Marxist perspective." *Crime and Social Justice* 18: 38–45.

—— (1985). "Criminology in the 1980s: Progressive alternatives to law and order." *Crime and Social Justice* 21–22: 191–199.

—— (1987). "U.S. criminal justice in the Reagan era: An assessment." *Crime and Social Justice* 29: 58–69.

POMERSHEIM, FRANK, and STEVE WISE (1989). "Going to the penitentiary: A study of disparate sentencing in South Dakota." *Criminal Justice and Behavior* 16: 155–165.

QUINNEY, RICHARD (1965). "Is criminal behaviour deviant behaviour?" *British Journal of Criminology* 5: 132–142.

——— (1970). *The Social Reality of Crime.* Boston: Little, Brown.

——— (1972). "The ideology of law: Notes for a radical alternative to legal oppression." *Issues in Criminology* 7: 1–35.

——— (1973a). "Crime control in capitalist society: A critical philosophy of legal order." *Issues in Criminology* 8: 75–95.

——— (1973b). "There's a lot of folks grateful to the Lone Ranger: Some notes on the rise and fall of American criminology." *Insurgent Sociologist* 4: 56–64.

——— (1974a). *Criminal Justice in America.* Boston: Little, Brown.

——— (1974b). *Critique of Legal Order.* Boston: Little, Brown.

——— (1977). *Class, State and Crime: On the Theory and Practice of Criminal Justice.* New York: McKay.

——— (1978). "The production of a Marxist criminology." *Contemporary Crises* 2: 277–292.

——— (1979). "The production of criminology." *Criminology* 16: 445–457.

——— (1980). *Class, State and Crime,* 2nd ed. New York: Longman.

——— (1982). *Social Existence: Metaphysics, Marxism and the Social Sciences.* Beverly Hills, CA: Sage.

QUINNEY, RICHARD, and JOHN WILDEMAN (1991). *The Problem of Crime: A Peace and Social Justice Perspective,* 3rd ed. Mountain View, CA: Mayfield.

REIMAN, JEFFREY (1984). *The Rich Get Richer and the Poor Get Prison.* New York: Wiley.

——— (1987). "The Marxian critique of criminal justice." *Criminal Justice Ethics* 6: 30–50.

RUSCHE, GEORGE, and OTTO KIRCHHEIMER (1939). *Punishment and Social Structure.* New York: Columbia University Press. (Reprinted 1968.)

SCHUMANN, KARL F. (1976). "Theoretical presuppositions for criminology as a critical enterprise." *International Journal of Criminology and Penology* 4: 285–294.

SCHWARTZ, MARTIN D., and WALTER DEKESEREDY (1991). "Left realist criminology: Strengths, weaknesses and the feminist critique." *Crime, Law, and Social Change* 15: 51–72.

SCHWARTZ, MARTIN D., and DRAGAN MILOVANOVIC, eds. (1996). *Race, Gender, and Class in Criminology.* New York: Garland.

SCHWENDINGER, HERMAN, and JULIA SCHWENDINGER (1970). "Defenders of order or guardians of human rights?" *Issues in Criminology* 5: 113–146.

——— (1972). "The continuing debate on the legalistic approach to the definition of crime." *Issues in Criminology* 7: 71–81.

——— (1977). "Social class and the definition of crime." *Crime and Social Justice* 7: 4–13.

SCRATON, PHIL, ed. (1987). *Law, Order and the Authoritarian State: Readings in Critical Criminology.* Milton Keynes, UK: Open University Press.

SELVA, LANCE H., and ROBERT M. BOHM (1987). "A critical examination of the informalism experiment in the administration of justice." *Crime and Social Justice* 29: 43–57.

SHELLEY, LOUISE I. (1996). *Policing Soviet Society: The Evolution of State Control.* London, UK: Routledge

SIMS, BARBARA A. (1997). "Crime, punishment, and the American dream: Toward a Marxist integration." *Journal of Research in Crime and Delinquency* 34: 5–24.

SMITH, BRENT L., and KELLY R. DAMPHOUSE (1996). "Punishing political offenders: The effect of political motive on federal sentencing decisions." *Criminology* 34: 289–321.

SPITZER, STEVEN (1975). "Towards a Marxian theory of deviance." *Social Problems* 22: 638–651.

STERN, L. T. (1940). "The effect of the Depression on prison commitments and sentences." *Journal of Criminal Law and Criminology* 31: 696–711.

SYKES, GRESHAM M. (1974). "The rise of critical criminology." *Journal of Criminal Law and Criminology* 65: 206–213.

TAYLOR, IAN, PAUL WALTON, and JOCK YOUNG (1973). *The New Criminology: For a Social Theory of Deviance.* London: Routledge and Kegan Paul.

———, eds. (1975). *Critical Criminology.* Boston: Routledge and Kegan Paul.

THOMAS, JIM, and AOGAN O'MAOLCHATHA (1989). "Reassessing the critical metaphor: An optimistic revisionist view." *Justice Quarterly* 6: 143–171.

TIFFT, LARRY L. (1979). "The coming redefinitions of crime: An anarchist perspective." *Social Problems* 26: 392–402.

TOBY, JACKSON (1979). "The new criminology is the old sentimentality." *Criminology* 16: 516–526.

TOLNAY, STEWART E., GLENN DEANE, and E. M. BECK (1996). "Vicarious violence: Spatial effects on Southern lynchings, 1890–1919." *American Journal of Sociology* 102: 788–815.

TURK, AUSTIN T. (1964). "Prospects for theories of criminal behavior." *Journal of Criminal Law, Criminology and Police Science* 55: 454–461.

——— (1966). "Conflict and criminality." *American Sociological Review* 31: 338–352.

——— (1969). *Criminality and Legal Order.* Chicago: Rand McNally.

——— (1976). "Law as a weapon in social conflict." *Social Problems* 23: 276–291.

——— (1982). *Political Criminality: The Defiance and Defense of Authority.* Beverly Hills, CA: Sage.

——— (1995). "Transformation versus Revolutionism and Reformism: Policy Implications of Conflict Theory." In Hugh D. Barlow, ed. *Crime and Public Policy: Putting Theory to Work*, xxx–xxx. Boulder, CO: Westview Press.

UNNEVER, JAMES D., CHARLES E. FRAZIER, and JOHN C. HENRETTA (1980). "Race differences in criminal sentencing." *Sociological Quarterly* 21: 197–206.

VENBRUX, ERIC (1995). *A Death in the Tiwi Islands: Conflict, Ritual and Social Life in an Australian Aboriginal Community.* Cambridge, UK: Cambridge University Press.

VOLD, GEORGE B. (1958). *Theoretical Criminology.* New York: Oxford University Press.

VOLD, GEORGE B., and THOMAS J. BERNARD (1986). *Theoretical Criminology*, 3rd ed. New York: Oxford University Press.

WALKLATE, SANDRA (1990). "Researching victims of crime: Critical victimology." *Social Justice* 17: 25–42.

WALLACE, D. (1981). "The political economy of incarceration trends in late U.S. capitalism: 1971–1977." *Insurgent Sociologist* 10: 59–67.

WEBSDALE, NEIL S. (1994). "Nonpolicing, policing and progressivism in Eugene, Oregon." *Policing and Society* 4: 131–173.

WEITZER, RONALD (1996). "Racial discrimination in the criminal justice system: Findings and problems in the literature." *Journal of Criminal Justice* 24: 309–322.

WILBANKS, WILLIAM (1987). *The Myth of a Racist Criminal Justice System.* Monterey, CA: Brooks-Cole.

WILLIAMS, FRANK P. III (1980). "Conflict theory and differential processing: An analysis of the research literature." In J. A. Inciardi, ed., *Radical Criminology: The Coming Crises*, 213–232. Beverly Hills, CA: Sage.

——— (1981a). "The impact of discretion on station-house release." *American Journal of Police* 1: 1–22.

——— (1981b). "Keeping defendants out of jail: An analysis of a release on recognizance project." *California Sociologist* 4: 206–218.

——— (1996). "There's still a lot of folks grateful to the Lone Ranger." *Social Pathology* 3: 16–23.

WILLIAMS, FRANK, P. III, and MARILYN D. MCSHANE (1990). "Inclinations of prospective jurors in capital cases." *Sociology and Social Research: An International Journal* 74(2): 85–94.

——— (1992). "Radical victimology: A critique of the concept of victim in traditional victimology." *Crime and Delinquency* 38: 258–271.

WILLIAMS, JIMMY J. (1991). "Predicting decisions rendered in criminal appeals." *Journal of Criminal Justice* 19: 463–469.

WITT, DAVID (1987). "A conflict theory of family violence." *Journal of Family Violence* 2: 291–301.

YEAGER, MATTHEW G. (1979). "Unemployment and imprisonment." *Journal of Criminal Law and Criminology* 70: 586–588.

YOUNG, JOCK (1986). "The failure of criminology: The need for a radical realism." In R. Matthews and J. Young, eds., *Confronting Crime*, 4–30. Beverly Hills, CA: Sage.

——— (1987). "The tasks of a realist criminology." *Contemporary Crises* 12: 337–356.

——— (1988). "Radical criminology in Britain: The emergence of a competing paradigm." *British Journal of Criminology* 28: 159–183.

——— (1992). "Ten points of realism." In R. Matthews and J. Young, eds., *Rethinking Criminology: The Realist Debate,* 24–68. Newbury Park, CA: Sage.

YOUNG, JOCK, and ROGER MATTHEWS, eds. (1992). *Rethinking Criminology: The Realist Debate.* Newbury Park, CA: Sage.

10

SOCIAL CONTROL THEORY

INTRODUCTION

As the popularity of labeling theory began to wane and conflict theory moved toward more radical perspectives, control theory began to appeal to conservative criminologists. Although certainly not new, the term "control theory" refers to any perspective that discusses the control of human behavior (Empey, 1978). Among their various forms, such theories include explanations based on genetics, neurochemistry, sociobiology, personality, and environmental design. *Social* control theories attribute crime and delinquency to the usual sociological variables (family structures, education, peer groups, for example), thus their approach is different from other control theories.

Despite differences in the way social control theorists explain criminal behavior, they all share one basic thought. Rather than asking the typical criminological question, "What makes people criminal?" these theorists share a conviction that deviant behavior is to be expected. What must be explained, they say, is "why people obey rules" (Hirschi, 1969:10). As a result, some social control theories demonstrate a view of human nature that reflects the beliefs of Thomas Hobbes, a seventeenth-century English philosopher who was convinced humans are basically evil. This view is not particularly crucial for the creation of social control theories, but they must at least assume a neutral human nature. The critical component of all social control theories, then, is their attempt to explain factors keeping people from committing criminal or delinquent behavior.

Another way to look at social control theory is to call it socialization theory. Since unsocialized humans—babies, for example—will simply act out their desires, it is the presence of other people that necessitates those behaviors be controlled. The most important way we exercise control is through the process of socialization. We teach the "right" way to do things (rules, norms), both informally, as in the family, and formally, as in school. In fact, much of our early upbringing is designed to socialize us so we can function in society. Social control theories emphasize the quality of this process.

THE HERITAGE OF THE THEORY

The Social Heritage

Because control theory has wide-ranging perspectives and spans a number of years, a discussion of the heritage of this approach has more to do with an explanation of its recent popularity than with its origins. Therefore, the discussion here focuses on explaining the theory's current acceptance.

While the 1960s brought about a questioning of social values and traditional institutions, there were also those who defended the status quo. Our previous characterizations of the decade should not be taken to mean all, or even a majority, were protesting and voicing their opinions about change in America. Within any period, the dominant group is a relatively conservative one. Thus, life for most people continued with relatively little change.

Some of the subtle changes taking place in society, however, would affect those who were more conservative. Religion became more important for many, and the "born-again" movement grew throughout the 1970s. A cynicism about government, fostered by Watergate, further disillusioned those who had thought the United States could become a "Great Society." Even the skyrocketing prices of gasoline in the mid-1970s heightened economic concerns. Finally, the taking of American hostages in Iran seemed to act as a catalyst for a politically conservative movement. As opposed to the liberal climate of the mid- to late 1960s, the mood of the following decade could be more accurately characterized as increasingly conservative. While conservatism enhanced the popularity of control theories, however, the theories themselves are not inherently conservative. The neutralization theory of Gresham Sykes and David Matza was not particularly conservative, nor was the drift theory subsequently proposed by Matza.

The Intellectual Heritage

The intellectual heritage of social control theories is difficult to ascertain. It may, however, be accurate to say the modern versions were originally developed as alternatives to strain theories. Clearly, this is the case for the 1950s theories of Albert Reiss (1951), Walter Reckless (1955), Sykes and Matza (1957), and F. Ivan Nye (1958). For later theories, especially those of Matza (1964) and Travis Hirschi (1969), the same may be inferred from their critical discussions of anomie and subculture theories. Even the usual identification of Emile Durkheim as the father of social control theory suggests there is a connection with strain theories.

Chicago School ideas were also critical to the development of social control theories. Arguably, many of the Chicago School's ideas may be viewed as emergent social control theory. This is particularly true of the social disorganization concept, which posits that a socially disorganized area frees juveniles to engage in delinquent acts. Solomon Kobrin's notions of nonintegrated neighborhoods lacking control over their youths is a direct product of the Chicago School. Among the first of the modern social control theorists, Reiss and Reckless were students at Chicago, and Nye was closely affiliated with the school.

The rise in popularity of social control theory did not occur until the mid-1970s, suggesting the blossoming of the theory may have been a result of three distinct trends within criminology. The first was a reaction to the labeling and conflict orientation and a return to the examination of criminal behavior. Conservative criminologists had little interest in the "new" criminology and wanted to return to the field's traditional subject matter, the criminal. Second, the rise of the study of criminal justice as a discipline helped move criminology in a more pragmatic and system-oriented direction. The increase in the government's interest and funding for criminal justice projects and crime fighting served to enhance the pragmatic nature of the movement. As a result, criminology was relatively free of theoretical work and left with its final theoretical inventions from the 1960s (Williams, 1984). The theory meeting nearly everyone's personal explanation for criminal behavior was Hirschi's version of social control theory.

Finally, social control theories have been linked with a new research technique for locating delinquent behavior, the self-report survey (Vold and Bernard, 1986:247). By the time 1960s versions of social control theory were proposed, self-report studies had become the dominant form of criminological evidence. Surveys of juveniles, asking about their behaviors, were so in vogue they became a new paradigm for criminology. The theory proposed by Hirschi was the first one to be expressly rooted in the self-report tradition. As a result, social control theories gave criminologists theoretical puzzles to solve with the new methodology.

THE THEORETICAL PERSPECTIVE

Durkheim's Social Control Theory

Theories of social control all rely on social factors to explain how people are restrained from acting in ways harmful to others. The earliest explanation of this approach was that of Durkheim (1895). He said a society will always have a certain number of deviants and deviance is really a *normal* phenomenon. By examining various societies around the world, Durkheim concluded every society has crime. If that is so, then crime must serve a function in society. Any society without crime and deviance is, by definition, abnormal. Further, deviance assists in maintaining social order, because there are vague moral "boundaries" that define which acts are allowed and which are disapproved. These boundaries specify the various degrees of disapproval for various acts, ranging from mild displeasure to legal sanctions and imprisonment. Since the actual boundary lines are not clear, it is the social reaction to someone else's deviant act that helps people determine what they should not do. Thus, Durkheim argued behavior is controlled by social reaction (displeasure, punishment).

To illustrate the issue that crime serves a boundary maintenance function, Durkheim gave an example of a "society of saints." In this society, there would be no crime as we know it. Indeed, most behavior we believe to be harmful would not occur. Yet crime would still be present. Crimes in such a society would represent behavior we do not think twice about but for the saints would be repulsive and harmful. Imagine a new crime of failing to say a blessing before a meal, or of using the Lord's name in vain. If crime represents harm to society, such behavior for the saints could threaten their social order. Controls, then, are necessary for order to exist and for people to understand the boundaries of accepted behavior.

Durkheim also related anomie to the existence of controls. A normal (non-anomic) society is one in which social relationships are working well and social norms (regulations) are clearly specified. When relationships and norms begin to break down, the controls they create begin to deteriorate. Durkheim noted a breakdown of those controls leads to crime and suicide. He was particularly concerned with situations in which uncontrolled rising aspirations lead to suicide. Whenever anomie exists in society, controls begin to disappear.

Personality-oriented Social Control Theories

In the 1950s several theorists presented social control explanations of delinquency. These theories set the stage for the contemporary approach to explaining crime and delinquency. Since Durkheim's time, the notion of social control had gone through several adaptations. The concepts of personality and socialization had become commonplace, and one or the other was being used in most of the sociological work on deviance. In addition, there had been several decades of research and writing on the ability of the family environment, religious institutions, schools, proper friends and associates, and community organizations to control delinquency.

Albert J. Reiss, Jr. (1951) combined concepts of **personality** and **socialization** with the work of the Chicago School to produce a social control theory that anticipated most of the later work. Although Reiss used psychoanalytic theory and wrote at length on the importance of personality, his theory suggested that three components of social control explained delinquency

(1951:196). He said delinquency would result from any or all of (1) a lack of proper internal controls developed during childhood; (2) a breakdown of those internal controls; (3) an absence of, or conflict in, social rules provided by important social groups (the family, close others, the school). These three factors have been used, in whole or in part, by almost every social control theorist writing since then. In fact, Reiss's statement may well represent the best summary of social control theory.

Containment Theory

The next approach was developed by Walter Reckless, with subsequent work in collaboration with a colleague, Simon Dinitz. This theory, referred to as **containment theory,** explains delinquency as the interplay between two forms of control: internal (inner) and external (outer). Reckless expressly saw his theory as an explanation of both conformity and deviance (1961: 42). At the same time, he did not claim containment theory explained all forms of deviance; indeed, he referred to it as a "middle-range" theory. He excluded behavior resulting from inner pushes (psychoses, personality disorders, compulsions, organic brain disorders, and neuroses) and from the playing of expected roles (subcultural dictates, certain forms of culture conflict, and organized crime). However, this middle range of behavior is very large.

Inner containment, while never clearly specified by Reckless, was presented as components of the "self." A laundry list of these components (Reckless, 1961:44) includes self-control, good self-concept, ego strength, well-developed superego, high frustration tolerance, high resistance to diversions, high sense of responsibility, goal orientation, and ability to find substitute satisfactions. Outer containment was viewed as the social environment. Examples of outer containment are family and school reinforcement of social norms and values, effective supervision and discipline, reasonable opportunities for social activity, availability of alternatives to deviance, and "opportunities for acceptance, identity, and belongingness."

Emphasizing inner containment, Reckless said a **self-concept** exists in people and is formed when they are quite young. This self-concept provides either a "good" or a "bad" image of the self and acts as a buffer to outside influences. He also stressed that there are a variety of "pushes and pulls" toward deviant behavior that all individuals experience. The effect of these inducements to commit delinquent acts depends on the strength of an individual's inner and outer containments. If the self-concept were bad, outer social controls would have little effect on the individual and delinquency would be more likely to result. On the other hand, an individual with a good self-concept could withstand weak external social control and resist committing delinquent acts. While Reckless discussed both external and internal forms of containment, it is clear he perceived the internal to be the more important of the two.

Social Bonding Theories

The concept of external social controls came into prominence with the work of David Matza. His first writing on the subject, coauthored with Gresham Sykes (1957), was a critique of Albert Cohen's subculture theory. In that critique, however, was the notion that everyone, even the lower-class gang delinquent, is bound to the dominant value system of society. Sykes and Matza proposed that one becomes "free" for delinquent acts through the use of **techniques of neutralization.** These techniques allow individuals to neutralize and temporarily suspend their commitment to societal values, thus providing the freedom to commit delinquent acts. Sykes and Matza listed five forms of neutralization, which they called *denial of responsibility, denial of injury, denial of the victim, condemnation of the condemners,* and *appeal to higher loyalties.* Further, they argued that these neutralizations are available not just to lower-class youth but are generally available throughout society.

Matza's later work (1964) included an explicit use of the term **bond to the moral order,** by which he meant the tie that exists between individuals and the dominant values of society. The problem for criminology is to explain how this bond could be either strengthened or weakened. Matza used neutralizations to explain how a person might be available for deviant behavior. Once neutralizations were used, he said, the individual was in a

---

SYKES AND MATZA'S TECHNIQUES OF NEUTRALIZATION

Denial of Responsibility   Acts are the product of forces beyond the control of the delinquent. A "billiard ball" conception of self where the delinquent is continually pulled/pushed into situations beyond his or her control. "I didn't mean it."

Denial of Injury   Acts do not really cause any harm. The victim can easily afford the damage or loss. "I didn't really hurt anybody."

Denial of the Victim   Acts, given the circumstances, were not really wrong. The offender is actually retaliating for a previous act of the victim. The victim deserves the injury. Or, there is no real victim. "They had it coming to them."

Condemnation of the Condemners   The motives and behaviors of those who disapprove of the act are suspect. The condemners are hypocrites or are reacting out of personal spite. "Everybody's picking on me."

Appeal to Higher Loyalties   Societal rules have to take a "back seat" to the demands of loyalty to important others or groups. You always help a buddy and never squeal on a friend. "I didn't do it for myself."

state of limbo or **drift** that made deviant acts permissible. From this point it was possible either to reenter conformity or to commit a deviant act.

The thrust or impetus for action is centered around the *will* to do something. The will has two activating conditions: preparation, which provides for the repetition of old behavior, and desperation, which precipitates new behavior. These two theoretical components pull an individual out of drift and allow behavior to take place. Whether the behavior is conforming or deviant, however, depends on the situation and on the form of the neutralizations.

Other theorizing by James Short and Fred Strodtbeck (1965), while not directed to Matza's theory, emphasized the importance of **attachment** to peers and the rewards provided by those peers in strengthening or weakening bonds to society. Finally, Scott Briar and Irving Piliavin (1965), elaborating on an earlier work by Jackson Toby (1957), introduced the concept of **commitments to conformity.** By this they referred to the investment one makes in conventional images and appearances (student government president, for example). Those with the greater investments have correspondingly greater potential losses from being discovered to be deviant. Great potential losses mean not only material deprivation and punishment but also social deprivation. If one extends the idea of investments to material things, such as property, business, and wealth, then Briar and Piliavin's theory can be viewed as a direct precursor to contemporary social control theory.

Hirschi's Social Control Theory

The most popular version of social control theory during the 1970s and 1980s was the one presented by Travis Hirschi (1969). Synthesizing and elaborating on the work of other social control theorists, Hirschi provided a clearer picture of what was meant by a social bond. Indeed, some criminologists refer to the theory as "social bonding" theory. Rather than seeing individuals as deviant or conforming, Hirschi, like Durkheim, believed behavior reflects varying degrees of morality. He argued that the power of internalized norms, conscience, and the desire for approval encourage conventional behavior. As did Sykes and Matza, Hirschi saw that a person becomes "free" to engage in delinquency. Instead of using neutralizing techniques, however, he blamed broken or weakened bonds to society. While not all social control theorists have done so, Hirschi expressly rejected the idea that any motivation is necessary for deviant behavior to occur. Actually, he viewed individuals as self-interested and therefore ready to act in a fashion that provides the greatest benefits. Society serves as a restraint on that behavior, and, if the restraints are loosened, self-interested behavior will emerge.

Hirschi has acknowledged some of the hidden theoretical threads from which his theory was woven. In an interview with Clemens Bartollas

(1985:190), he noted that the Chicago School's social disorganization theory is at the root of his approach. At the time he proposed his social control theory, however, social disorganization was in disrepute, and he avoided making references to it. The entire issue of weakened controls (disorganization) was at the heart of the Chicago School's treatment of deviance. In a major divergence with the Chicago School, however, Hirschi refused to give credence to the possibility that deviant behavior is relative. Where the Chicago School saw a variety of situations with their own conforming definitions, Hirschi saw only one legitimate definition of behavior: the common value system of society at large (Bernard, 1987). As a result, no behavior can simultaneously both conform to the norms of a smaller group and be deviant according to larger society; it is simply deviant. In short, conventional society governs the perspective from which the behavior is to be viewed.

Hirschi characterized the social bond as having four elements or dimensions (1969:16–34): attachment, involvement, commitment, and belief. The most important element is **attachment.** The strength of the attachments, or ties, one has to significant others (parents, friends, role models) or to institutions (schools, clubs) can inhibit deviance. Attachment is important for creating conformity even when those others are deviant themselves. Second, **involvement** means the degree of activity (the time and energy) available

HIRSCHI'S ELEMENTS OF THE BOND	
Element	Examples
Attachment	Identification with peers or parents, emotional bond between child and parent, concern and respect for parents' or peers' opinions, engaging in activities with peers, supervision by parents, intimate communications with parents, attitudes toward school, concern for teachers' opinions, general sensitivity to the opinions of others
Involvement	Time-consuming activity (work, sports, recreation, hobbies), time spent on homework, lack of boredom, amount of nonactive leisure time, time spent talking with friends
Commitment	Investment in society (education, career, family), academic competence, educational aspirations and expectations, achievement orientation, expected occupation, importance of reputation
Belief	Respect for authorities, importance of and respect for law, absence of neutralizations

for conventional or unconventional behavior. Those most occupied by conventional activities simply have less time to be involved in deviance. Thus, participation in clubs, recreational activities, and other extracurricular activities serves to increase levels of conformity.

Commitment represents the investment one has already built up in conventional society. This investment may take such forms as the amount of education, a good reputation, or the establishment of a business. Those with these forms of commitment to conventional society also have more to lose if they are caught engaging in deviant behavior. College students, for instance, have already built up a strong degree of investment in education. Clearly, to engage in crime and get caught would represent a potential loss of that investment. The last element, **belief,** constitutes the acknowledgment of society's rules as being fair. That is, one has a respect for those rules and norms and feels a moral obligation to obey them. The critical component here is a respect for the common value system. In a sense, the more one believes in "behaving properly," the more likely one is to be conforming.

These four elements all affect the bond between an individual and society. Since all individuals exhibit some bonding to society, the question before criminologists is how much these bonds need to be weakened before deviance results. As any of the four elements are weakened, the freedom to engage in deviant behavior increases. What is less clear is the extent to which a weakening or absence of any one component of the bond affects the other elements. For instance, does the strong presence of three elements, and the absence of a fourth, mean deviance will result? The elements also, obviously, interact with each other to produce varying degrees of effect. While Hirschi did discuss some of the relationships among the elements, he saw this as an empirical question (an issue for research to answer) and preferred to keep the question open.

A final point should be made about Hirschi's and others' versions of social control theory: they all rely on a specialized methodology of discovering crime and criminality—self-report studies—for their evidence. Other methodologies, such as the use of official crime report statistics or victimization data, do not particularly lend themselves to the social control approach. When those other methodologies are used to produce evidence, social control theory suffers. In a real sense, then, social control theories are somewhat methodologically bound.

Gottfredson and Hirschi's General Theory of Crime (Self-Control Theory)

The most recent version of social control theory is Michael Gottfredson and Travis Hirschi's "general theory of crime" or, as it has been popularly called, **self-control theory** (an earlier version was entitled "propensity-event theory"). In three articles and one book (Hirschi and Gottfredson, 1983; Gottfredson and Hirschi, 1989; Hirschi and Gottfredson, 1989; Gottfredson and

Hirschi, 1990), Gottfredson and Hirschi present a theory of crime based on an examination of both crime and criminality. Its key ingredients are underlying propensities (crime-proneness) and the conditions under which these propensities translate into crime.

First, Gottfredson and Hirschi redefine the concept of crime to allow more latitude in capturing various forms of criminality. They did this primarily because white-collar crimes are not normally recognized by most existing theories. Their new definition of crime is *"acts of force or fraud undertaken in the pursuit of self-interest"* (1990:15, emphasis added). While apparently broader than some legal definitions of crime, this definition may not capture some forms of crime, such as crimes of accident or negligence. However, the definition does serve a broader theoretical interest and provides focus to what Gottfredson and Hirschi mean to explain. Further, the definition is compatible with Hirschi's social control assumption that people are, by nature, self-interested (see the discussion in Chapter 10).

Second, Gottfredson and Hirschi reject the traditional core concepts of other criminological theories, particularly class and race. Indeed, they maintain that these concepts are ambiguous enough to be relatively useless. The concepts are still with us, the authors claim, because they are at the very core of sociology. Better, however, is to view crime by its common characteristics: immediate gratification; easy or simple gratification; exciting, risky, or thrilling; few or meager long-term benefits; little skill or planning; and pain and discomfort for the victim (1990:89). These characteristics convinced Gottfredson and Hirschi that crime is basically a problem of low **self-control.** This new core concept, "self-control," is essentially derived from Hirschi's earlier social control theory but is more focused on the individual rather than on external sources of control. Self-control is defined as "the idea that people also differ in the extent to which they are vulnerable to the temptations of the moment" (1990:87) or, in other words, their ability to restrain themselves.

Commensurate with Hirschi's assumptions behind social control theory, the new theory also presumes criminals have no special motivations (or needs and desires). All individuals have access to the same motivations. The real problem is self-control. Low self-control yields a higher probability that an individual will engage in crime, whereas high self-control yields a low probability for criminal behavior (1990:89).

The general theory of crime declares individuals have certain **traits,** among them impulsivity, insensitivity, self-centeredness, and lower than average intelligence. These traits affect low social control mainly by affecting an individual's ability to accurately calculate the consequences of an action (1990:95). Gottfredson and Hirschi argue that these traits are established early and persist throughout life. They view **child-rearing practices** as the major influence on the formation of certain propensities (1990:97). Inadequate child-rearing practices affect traits in ways that are conducive to criminality. These traits are often associated with particular social settings and thus are difficult to separate from those settings. The relationship of these traits with crime is less than perfect because they are not necessary conditions for crime and, in fact, will reveal themselves in noncriminal activities as well. Those other activities, though, may share some of the characteristics of crime (e.g., alcohol or drug use). In short, Gottfredson and Hirschi assume criminality traits are naturally present and "in the absence of socialization the child will tend to be high on crime potential" (1989:61).

Crime, on the other hand, is viewed by Gottfredson and Hirschi as an event in time and space, and several factors may need to be present for a crime to occur. Crime has an attractiveness to those with propensities toward it, thus the crime-propensity affinity entices individuals and promises pleasure. The rationalist perspective of the theory proposes that the crime event must be capable of gratifying the offender, and the consequences (perceived or real) must not overcome the pleasure to be gained from the event. Of course, the event requires certain conditions, namely, that there be some potential target and that the situation suggest a lack of undesirable consequences. There may also be internal conditions (strength, speed, presence of alcohol) assisting in the evaluation of the event.

Finally, Gottfredson and Hirschi note that their theory does not require an individual with low self-control to commit a crime. In fact, low self-control results in a wide variety of behaviors, only one of which is crime. Because of this, they believe any action taken to raise self-control will not only affect crime but will also decrease other undesirable social behaviors (for instance, truancy, runaway, aggression, auto accidents, and alcohol abuse). Thus, there is no displacement effect to other forms of deviance when crime is lowered.

Major Points of Low Self-control Theory

1. Humans naturally act in a self-interested fashion.
2. Socialization and training are necessary to restrict human self-interest and create self-control.
3. Improper or inadequate child-rearing practices result in traits that lend themselves to low levels of self-control.
4. Low levels of self-control result in high frequencies of short-term, pleasure-seeking behaviors.
5. Crime is among the various self-interested behaviors.
6. Increasing self-control results in lower levels of crime as well as in other allied behaviors.

CLASSIFICATION OF THE THEORY

Social control theories are *positivist* theories in that they endeavor to explain behavior, albeit conforming behavior. Moreover, they imply (and in some cases overtly declare) criminal behavior should be treated by increasing the influence of the family, schools, churches, and law-abiding peers. They also concentrate on the *process* by which the social bond is weakened rather than on the structural reasons for the existence of that bond.

The issue of whether social control theories are consensus- or conflict-oriented is more difficult. They are based on the assumption human nature is either neutral or, in the Hobbesian view, evil; therefore, conflict seems inevitable. However, it is the assumption of the existence of a dominant moral order that orients social control theories toward a *consensus* view of society. Uniformly, social control theories posit the existence of a common value system in society. Finally, these theories are in the *microtheoretical* range. Clearly, they focus on etiological issues rather than on explaining social structure. In fact, other than assuming a moral order exists, they state little about social structure itself. Instead, they set forth at length how the weakening of the effect of various social institutions allows for an increase in deviant behavior among individuals.

The currently popular self-control theory is very much a form of social control theory, but with a few twists. Its focus tends to be on the *process* of committing a crime, with an assumption that a dominant *consensus-oriented* social order exists. It explains behavior, so it is a *positivistic* theory. The theory tends toward a *microtheoretical* approach because it maintains that individuals acquire different degrees of socialization through child rearing. There is, however, a macrotheoretical component corresponding to the structuring of child rearing in society. If various social institutions uniformly regulate child rearing, then one could argue low self-control has origins in, or is critically influenced by, the social structure.

SUMMARY

Social control theory, for all its recent popularity, is not new. Moreover, it is probably the one theoretical approach most closely matching the public's conception of why people become criminals. Whether one believes a person becomes criminal because of associating with the wrong friends, an improper family upbringing, a lack of religion, or a lack of education, social control theory can be seen to reflect that belief. Further, for criminologists themselves, this theory contains bits and pieces of the theories of social disorganization, differential association, and anomie, making it especially attractive to those criminologists who have been reluctant to embrace conflict theories.

In sum, social control theory takes a view of human nature that assumes deviance is natural (which makes this theory similar to labeling in this regard). Conformity, then, is the real question worthy of explanation. Positing a moral order, or a conventional framework in society, social control theory finds common social institutions that strengthen the bond. When these institutions are weakened, whatever the cause, the bond that ties individuals to the moral order is also weakened. This weakened bond automatically permits a greater degree of deviance to occur.

Major Points of the General Social Control Theory Approach

1. Self-preservation and gratification are characteristic of human nature; therefore, human behavior tends to be "self-interested."
2. Human behavior must be restrained and regulated for the benefit of all.
3. The rules and regulations for living in a society constitute a moral order.
4. Humans are bound to the moral order beginning with childhood socialization and later through the institutions of society.
5. The bond to the moral order is composed of elements that maintain and strengthen conformity.
6. The elements of the bond include attachment to important others and institutions, commitment to or investment in conventional society, involvement in conventional activities, and belief in societal values.
7. These elements are present in varying degrees. To the extent they may become weak, or are absent, individuals have more freedom to pursue self-interested and deviant behavior.

EPILOGUE: CURRENT DIRECTIONS AND POLICY IMPLICATIONS

Current Directions

Criminological researchers have spent many hours testing social control theories, primarily Hirschi's version. In fact, social control theory is probably the most tested theory in criminology, largely because Hirschi himself presented the theory in conjunction with his research results. The points of the theory are relatively straightforward and testable. While the research results are not totally clear, several issues have emerged.

Testing the Theory   Social control theory may be best for explaining less serious forms of delinquency. Because of its grounding in self-report studies, which traditionally have focused on less serious forms of behavior, it makes sense that social control theory works best for minor to moderate delinquency (Wiatrowski, Griswold, and Roberts, 1981). Another problem centers on the relationship of the attachment element to delinquency. The predicted relationship says any attachment to others should result in a reduction of delinquency. Hirschi's own research found a positive relationship for delinquents and friends; that is, delinquents were attached to delinquent peers. Others have noted this problem as well (Empey and Lubeck, 1971; Hindelang, 1973; Krohn and Massey, 1980).

Data-specific Results   The theory also does best when tested with cross-sectional data (Krohn, 1991). Causal order (what comes first) is difficult to determine in cross-sectional data because they are collected at only one point in time. As a result, we do not know whether attachment or commitment occurred before or after delinquency. When longitudinal data are used (data collected at more than one point in time), the theory does not fare as well (Agnew, 1985, 1991). Allen Liska and Mark Reed (1985), for instance, report that their longitudinal research indicates peer attachments affect delinquency and delinquency, in turn, affects school attachments. In other words, a weakening of the social bond may be a result of delinquency rather than a cause. Of course, the same problem applies to most of the other theories we have discussed.

Generic Explanation of Crime Social control theory appears to have promise as an explanation for a wide variety of behavior. Because it is not based on assumptions about the criminal propensities of different social classes, social control theory should be able to explain lower-, middle-, and upper-class crime and delinquency equally well. In fact, Travis Hirschi and Michael Gottfredson (1987) have already used it as an explanation of white-collar crime. Others have examined middle-class delinquency from the perspective of control theory (Hennessy, Richards, and Berk, 1978; Linden, 1978; Grinnell and Chambers, 1979).

Maturing out of Crime Another important use of social control theory is as an explanation of the long-observed fact that most delinquents grow out of delinquency. That is, they seem to quit engaging in delinquent acts without any intervention on the part of others. Indeed, this is the origin of the labeling theory suggestion that we simply leave delinquents alone (Edwin Schur's "radical nonintervention"). In an early commentary on the effect of commitment, Larry Karacki and Jackson Toby (1962) suggested an adolescent's "stakes in conformity" increase with age. Hirschi's version similarly posits commitment to conventional activity is an important piece of the social bond. If juveniles and youths continue to increase their levels of commitment as they grow older (go to work, increase their education, perhaps get married), then the result is a maturing out of delinquency and crime. Thomas Bernard (1987) has argued commitment is the primary element of the social bond, influencing all other elements. If he is correct, the maturation hypothesis is an important part of social control theory. In addition, adolescence in our culture has long been regarded as a period characterized by leisure time. As we get older, leisure time decreases in favor of the work world.

Integration with Other Theories Several criminologists have suggested integration of social control theory concepts with other theories. Rand Conger (1976) has, for instance, argued social control and social learning theories can be profitably merged. Ron Akers, the prime architect of social learning theory, has agreed his theory is most compatible with social control (1985:67). Actually, just about every attempt to integrate theories has incorporated social control theory (see, for example, Cernkovich, 1978a; Aultman and Wellford, 1979; Elliott, Ageton, and Canter, 1979; Johnson, 1979; Segrave and Hasted, 1983; Elliott, Huizinga, and Ageton, 1985; and Huizinga, Esbensen, and Elliott, 1988). However,

Hirschi (1979) rejects attempts at integration of his social control theory with other theoretical concepts or models. He believes the theory is substantially changed by these additions. A preferable approach, he believes, is to create a new theory with a logically coherent set of assumptions. One might argue that is exactly what he and Gottfredson did with self-control theory. Hirschi himself has made no comments on the connections between his earlier social control theory and the current one.

Self-control Theory The combination of propensity and event within one theory shows promise. It accepts psychological, and even biological, evidence about individual differences while highlighting the social setting that provides for patterns of both child-rearing practice and structured events. Thus, the theory tolerates variation from a variety of sources and even maintains that other, similarly pleasurable behavioral events may substitute for crime. This, however, may also be the theory's greatest problem: the prediction of crime requires the identification and prediction of other outcome events as well, such as drug use, aggression, and truancy.

Although the publication of this theory is relatively recent, some criminologists have already identified other problems. Kenneth Polk (1991), for example, finds fault with the evidence used by Gottfredson and Hirschi. He claims they have conveniently overlooked evidence that would be damaging to their theory and declared evidence on their side as "good" evidence. He and Ron Akers (1991) also feel the definition of crime is too restrictive and there are non-self-interested crimes that lie outside the purview of the theory. Akers believes Gottfredson and Hirschi have overstated the view that their theory opposes all other contemporary crime theories. In fact, Akers views much of the general theory as compatible with his own social learning theory.

There is also some research on self-control theory with mixed, though generally supportive results (Gibbs and Giever, 1995). Self-control is, according to the theory, a relatively stable characteristic over the life of the individual. This is the one point about which research seems uncertain (see Junger-Tas, 1992; Moffitt, 1993; Elliott, 1994; Cohen and Vila, 1996; Warr, 1996). Indeed, Robert Sampson and John Laub (1993, 1995) have produced a theory of developmental change over the life course based on contrary evidence to the self-control position. Another major point of the theory is that it is a "general" theory; thus, it explains any behavior falling within its range. Benson and Moore (1992) have examined white-collar offenders and present evidence they may be different from other offenders (particularly "typical" street-crime offenders) (see also Reed and Yeager, 1996).

Policy Implications

Social control theories suggest a group of commonsense policies for crime and delinquency control. Perhaps it is for this reason they have been popular; yet very few policies or programs seem to have been expressly created from social control concepts. Nonetheless, the theoretical perspective has allowed criminologists to approve of projects that in the popular mind "just make good sense."

Examples of such projects are school-based programs to keep children busy. The more conventional activities they engage in, the less time is available for delinquent activities. Thus, recreational programs, social groups, and athletic events are all designed from the viewpoint of involvement. Social clubs, 4-H clubs, Boy Scouts, Girl Scouts, and Little League baseball are classic examples of programs designed to assist children in learning conventional values (becoming committed) and being involved in conventional activities. Of course, schools are not the only source of these programs. Religious groups generate their share, especially those focusing on the values important to the group. YMCA and YWCA programs are commonplace in larger cities.

Over the past two decades, social policy to help juveniles in danger of becoming delinquent has consistently championed strategies like the Big Brother/Big Sister programs. These programs couple a role model with conventional activities for children. In addition, strategies to increase the stability of families have been developed, among them parenting programs. Finally, any approach that emphasizes social activities, keeping children in school, or improving scholastic skills, or one that stresses the values of the "American Way" is compatible with social control theories.

Self-control Theory and Policy   In contrast to many other theoretical presentations, Gottfredson and Hirschi (1990:255–275) expressly treat policy implications. First, they believe that from the perspective of the theory certain existing policies are useless. Short-term changes in arrest rates or length of sentences do not substantially affect estimates of consequences. Second, programs that attack assumed causes of delinquency, such as truancy, will not reduce crime because *both* truancy and delinquency are symptoms of low self-control. Third, attacking crime by reducing poverty or other social ills assumed to drive people into crime will have no effect because these things do not result in "overwhelming impulses to commit crime" (1990:256).

Policies that low self-control theory would advocate include programs to properly socialize children within the first six to eight years of life. Indeed, Gottfredson and Hirschi explicitly state "policies directed toward enhancement of the ability of familial institutions to socialize children are the only realistic long-term state policies with potential for substantial crime reduction" (1990:272–273). By familial institutions, however, they do not necessarily mean the traditional family itself. Potential program emphases include training in parenting, instilling discipline in children, and teaching responsibility. Another policy direction of reducing the attractiveness of criminal events would be more difficult to accomplish. Perhaps the best direction here can be found in environmental design concepts, with changes that make crime more difficult to commit.

BIBLIOGRAPHY

AGNEW, ROBERT (1984). "Appearance and delinquency." *Criminology* 22: 421–440.
——— (1985). "Social control theory and delinquency: A longitudinal test." *Criminology* 23: 47–61.
——— (1990). "Adolescent resources and delinquency." *Criminology* 28: 535–561.
——— (1991). "A longitudinal test of social control theory and delinquency." *Journal of Research in Crime and Delinquency* 28: 126–156.
——— (1993). "Why do they do it? An examination of the intervening mechanisms between 'social control' variables and delinquency." *Journal of Research in Crime and Delinquency* 30: 245–266.
AGNEW, ROBERT, and ARDITH A. R. PETERS (1986). "The techniques of neutralization: An analysis of predisposing and situational factors." *Criminal Justice and Behavior* 13: 81–97.
AKERS, RONALD L. (1985). *Deviant Behavior: A Social Learning Approach*, 3rd ed. Belmont, CA: Wadsworth.
——— (1991). "Self-control as a general theory of crime." *Journal of Quantitative Criminology* 7: 201–211.
AULTMAN, MADELINE G. (1979). "Delinquency causation: A typological comparison of path models." *Journal of Criminal Law and Criminology* 70: 152–163.
AULTMAN, MADELINE G., and CHARLES F. WELLFORD (1979). "Towards an integrated model of delinquency causation: An empirical analysis." *Sociology and Social Research* 63: 316–327.
BALL, RICHARD A. (1983). "Development of basic norm violation." *Criminology* 21: 75–94.
BARTOLLAS, CLEMENS (1985). *Juvenile Delinquency*. New York: Macmillan.
BARTON, WILLIAM, and JOSEFINA FIGUEIRA-MCDONOUGH (1985). "Attachments, gender, and delinquency." *Deviant Behavior* 6: 119–144.
BECKER, HOWARD S. (1960). "Notes on the concept of commitment." *American Journal of Sociology* 66: 32–40.
BENDA, BRENT B., and LEANNE WHITESIDE (1995). "Testing an integrated model of delinquency using LISREL." *Journal of Social Science Research* 21: 1–32.
BENSON, MICHAEL L., and ELIZABETH MOORE (1992). "Are white-collar and common offenders the same?: An empirical and theoretical critique of a recently proposed general theory of crime." *Journal of Research in Crime and Delinquency* 29: 251–272.
BERNARD, THOMAS J. (1987). "Structure and control: Reconsidering Hirschi's concept of commitment." *Justice Quarterly* 4: 409–424.
BLASKE, DAVID M. (1989). "Individual, family, and peer characteristics of adolescent sex offenders and assaultive offenders." *Developmental Psychology* 25: 846–855.
BLUMSTEIN, ALFRED, JACQUELINE COHEN, and DAVID P. FARRINGTON (1988). "Criminal career research: Its value for criminology." *Criminology* 26: 1–36.
BRAITHWAITE, JOHN (1991). "Poverty, power, white-collar crime and the paradoxes of criminological theory." *Australian and New Zealand Journal of Criminology* 24: 40–48.
BREZITZ, T. (1975). "Juvenile delinquents' perceptions of own and other's commitment to delinquency." *Journal of Research in Crime and Delinquency* 12: 124–132.
BRIAR, SCOTT, and IRVING PILIAVIN (1965). "Delinquency, situational inducements, and commitment to conformity." *Social Problems* 13: 35–45.
BRITT, CHESTER, L., III (1992). "Constancy and change in the U.S. age distribution of crime: A test of the 'invariance hypothesis'" *Journal of Quantitative Criminology* 8: 175–187.
BROWNFIELD, DAVID (1987). "Father-son relationships and violent behavior." *Deviant Behavior* 8: 65–78.

BROWNFIELD, DAVID, and ANN MARIE SORENSON (1993). "Self-control and juvenile delinquency: Theoretical issues and an empirical assessment of selected elements of a general theory of crime." *Deviant Behavior* 14: 243–264.

BURKETT, STEVEN R., and BRUCE WARREN (1987). "Religiosity, peer associations, and adolescent marijuana use: A panel study of underlying causal structures." *Criminology* 25: 109–131.

CAMPBELL, ANNE (1987). "Self-reported delinquency and home life: Evidence from a sample of British girls." *Journal of Youth and Adolescence* 16: 167–177.

——— (1988). "Intrapersonal and interpersonal discrepancy among delinquent and non-delinquent girls: A research note." *Journal of Child Psychology and Psychiatry* 29: 73–78.

CANTER, RACHELLE (1982). "Family correlates of male and female delinquency." *Criminology* 20: 149–167.

CATALANO, RICHARD F., RICK KOSTERMAN, and J. DAVID HAWKINS (1996). "Modeling the etiology of adolescent substance use: A test of the social development model." *Journal of Drug Issues* 26: 429–455.

CERNKOVICH, STEPHEN A. (1978a). "Evaluating two models of delinquency causation: Structural theory and control theory." *Criminology* 16: 355–362.

——— (1978b). "Value orientations and delinquency involvement." *Criminology* 15: 443–448.

CERNKOVICH, STEPHEN A., and PEGGY GIORDANO (1987). "Family relationships and delinquency." *Criminology* 25: 295–321.

——— (1992). "School bonding, race, and delinquency." *Criminology* 30: 261–291.

COCHRAN, JOHN K., and RONALD L. AKERS (1989). "Beyond hellfire: An exploration of the variable effects of religiosity on adolescent marijuana and alcohol use." *Journal of Research in Crime and Delinquency* 26: 198–225.

COHEN, LAWRENCE E., and KENNETH C. LAND (1987). "Sociological positivism and the explanation of criminality." In M. R. Gottfredson and T. Hirschi, eds., *Positive Criminology*, 43–55. Newbury Park, CA: Sage.

COHEN, LAWRENCE E., and RICHARD MACHALEK (1988). "A general theory of expropriative crime: An evolutionary ecological approach." *American Journal of Sociology* 94: 465–501.

COHEN, LAWRENCE E., and BRYAN J. VILA (1996). "Self-control and social control: An exposition of the Gottfredson-Hirschi/Sampson-Laub debate." *Studies on Crime and Crime Prevention* 5: 125–150.

CONGER, RAND (1976). "Social control and social learning models of delinquent behavior: A synthesis." *Criminology* 17: 17–40.

DABNEY, DEAN (1995). "Neutralization and deviance in the workplace: Theft of supplies and medicines by hospital nurses." *Deviant Behavior* 16: 313–331.

DINITZ, SIMON, BARBARA KAY, and WALTER C. RECKLESS (1962). "Delinquency vulnerability: A cross group and longitudinal analysis." *American Sociological Review* 27: 515–517.

DINITZ, SIMON, and B. A. PFAU-VICENT (1982). "Self-concept and juvenile delinquency." *Youth and Society* 14: 133–158.

DODDER, RICHARD A., and J. R. LONG (1980). "Containment theory re-evaluated: An empirical explanation." *Criminal Justice Review* 5: 74–84.

DULL, R. THOMAS (1984). "An empirical examination of the social bond theory of drug use." *International Journal of the Addictions* 19: 265–286.

DURKHEIM, EMILE (1895). *The Rules of the Sociological Method.* Trans. Sarah A. Solovay and John H. Mueller. New York: Free Press. (Reprinted 1965.)

EDWARDS, WILLIE J. (1996). "A measurement of delinquency differences between a delinquent and nondelinquent sample: What are the implications?" *Adolescence* 31: 973–989.

ELLIOTT, DELBERT S., (1994). "Serious violent offenders: Onset, developmental course, and termination." *Criminology* 32: 1–22.

ELLIOTT, DELBERT S., SUZANNE S. AGETON, and RACHELLE J. CANTER (1979). "An integrated theoretical perspective on delinquent behavior." *Journal of Research in Crime and Delinquency* 16: 3–27.

ELLIOTT, DELBERT S., DAVID HUIZINGA, and SUZANNE S. AGETON (1985). *Explaining Delinquency and Drug Use.* Beverly Hills, CA: Sage.

ELLIS, DESMOND (1989). "Male abuse of a married or cohabiting female partner: The application of sociological theory to research findings." *Violence and Victims* 4: 235–255.

EMPEY, LAMAR T. (1978). *American Delinquency: Its Meaning and Construction.* Homewood, IL: Dorsey.

EMPEY, LAMAR T., and STEVEN G. LUBECK (1971). *Explaining Delinquency.* Lexington, MA: Heath.

EYO, I. E. (1981). "British delinquents and nondelinquents on seven domains of the self-concept." *Journal of Psychology* 109: 137–145.

FAGAN, JEFFREY (1990). "Social and legal policy dimensions of violent juvenile crime." *Criminal Justice and Behavior* 17: 93–133.

FAGAN, JEFFREY, and EDWARD PABON (1990). "Contributions of delinquency and substance use to school dropout among inner-city youths." *Youth and Society* 21: 306–354.

FAGAN, JEFFREY, JOSEPH WEIS, and YU-TEH CHENG (1990). "Delinquency and substance use among inner-city students." *Journal of Drug Issues* 20: 351–402.

FARNWORTH, MARGARET (1984). "Male-female differences in delinquency in a minority-group sample." *Journal of Research in Crime and Delinquency* 21: 191–212.

FERDINAND, THEODORE (1989). "Juvenile delinquency or juvenile justice? Which came first?" *Criminology* 27: 79–106.

FIGUIERA-McDONOUGH, JOSEFINA (1986). "School context, gender, and delinquency." *Journal of Youth and Adolescence* 15: 79–98.

FISHBEIN, M., and I. AJZEN (1975). *Belief, Attitude, Intention and Behavior.* Reading, MA: Addison-Wesley.

FISHER, GENE A., and MAYNARD ERICKSON (1973). "On assessing the effects of official reactions to juvenile delinquency." *Journal of Research in Crime and Delinquency* 10: 177–194.

FREASE, DEAN E. (1972). "The schools, self-concept and juvenile delinquency." *British Journal of Criminology* 12: 133–146.

FRIEDMAN, JENNIFER, and DENNIS ROSENBAUM (1988). "Social control theory: The salience of components by age, gender, and type of crime." *Journal of Quantitative Criminology* 4: 363–381.

GARDNER, LEGRANDE, and DONALD SHOEMAKER (1989). "Social bonding and delinquency: A comparative analysis." *Sociological Quarterly* 30: 481–500.

GELLES, RICHARD (1983). "An exchange/social control theory." In D. Finkelhor, G. Hoteling, R. Gelles, and M. Straus, eds., *The Dark Side of Families: Current Family Violence Research*, 151–165. Beverly Hills, CA: Sage.

GIBBS, JOHN J., and DENNIS GIEVER (1995). "Self-control and its manifestations among university students: An empirical test of Gottfredson and Hirschi's general theory." *Justice Quarterly* 12: 231–255.

GIORDANO, PEGGY C., STEPHEN A. CERNKOVICH, and M. D. PUGH (1986). "Friendships and delinquency." *American Journal of Sociology* 91: 1170–1202.

GOTTFREDSON, MICHAEL, and TRAVIS HIRSCHI (1986). "The true value of lambda would appear to be zero: An essay on career criminals, criminal careers, selective incapacitation, cohort studies, and related topics." *Criminology* 24: 213–234.

——— (1988). "Science, public policy, and the career paradigm." *Criminology* 26: 37–55.

——— (1989). "A propensity-event theory of crime." In W. S. Laufer and F. Adler, eds., *Advances in Criminological Theory*, vol. 1, 57–67. New Brunswick, NJ: Transaction.

——— (1990). *A General Theory of Crime*. Stanford, CA: Stanford University Press.

GRASMICK, HAROLD G., ROBERT J. BURSIK JR., and JOHN K. COCHRAN (1991). "'Render unto Caesar what is Caesar's': Religiosity and taxpayers' inclinations to cheat." *Sociological Quarterly* 32: 251–266.

GRASMICK, HAROLD G., and DONALD E. GREEN (1980). "Legal punishment, social disapproval and internalization as inhibitors of illegal behavior." *Journal of Criminal Law and Criminology* 71: 325–335.

GRASMICK, HAROLD G., and STEVEN D. MCLAUGHLIN (1978). "Deterrence and social control (comment on Silberman, ASR, June, 1976)." *American Sociological Review* 43: 272–278.

GRASMICK, HAROLD G., CHARLES R. TITTLE, and ROBERT J. BURSIK JR. (1993). "Testing the core empirical implications of Gottfredson and Hirschi's general theory of crime." *Journal of Research in Crime and Delinquency* 30: 5–29.

GREEN, DONALD E. (1990). "Measuring self-reported deviance: Cross-sectional or panel data?" *Social Science Research* 19: 301–321.

GREENBERG, DAVID (1991). "Modeling criminal careers." *Criminology* 29: 17–46.

GRINNELL, RICHARD M., and CHERYL A. CHAMBERS (1979). "Broken homes and middle-class delinquency: A comparison." *Criminology* 17: 395–400.

GROVES BYRON, and GRAEME NEWMAN (1989). "Against general theory in comparative research." *International Journal of Comparative and Applied Criminal Justice* 13: 23–29.

HAGAN, JOHN (1991). "Destiny and drift: Subcultural preferences, status attainments, and the risks and rewards of youth." *American Sociological Review* 56: 567–582.

HAGAN, JOHN, and ALBERT PALLONI (1988). "Crimes as social events in the life course: Reconceiving a criminological controversy." *Criminology* 26: 87–100.

HAMLIN, JOHN E. (1988). "The misplaced role of rational choice in neutralization theory." *Criminology* 26: 25–438.

HAMM, MARK S. (1987). "The Human Potential Seminar: A strategy for teaching socially adaptive behavior in a correctional classroom." *Journal of Correctional Education* 38: 4–7.

HAWKINS, J. DAVID, and TONY LAM (1987). "Teacher practices, social development, and delinquency." In J. D. Burchard and S. Burchard, eds., *Prevention of Delinquent Behavior*, 241–274. Newbury Park, CA: Sage.

HAWKINS, J. DAVID, and DENISE M. LISHNER (1987). "Schooling and delinquency." In E. H. Johnson, ed., *Handbook on Crime and Delinquency Prevention*, 179–221. Westport, CT: Greenwood Press.

HAYES, HENNESSEY D. (1997). "Using integrated theory to explain the movement into juvenile delinquency." *Deviant Behavior* 18: 161–184.

HAZANI, MOSHE (1991). "The universal applicability of the theory of neutralization: German youth coming to terms with the Holocaust." *Crime, Law and Social Change* 15: 135–149.

HEIMER, KAREN (1996). "Gender, interaction, and delinquency: Testing a theory of differential social control." *Social Psychology Quarterly* 59: 39–61.

HEIMER, KAREN, and ROSS L. MATSUEDA (1994). "Role-taking, role commitment, and delinquency: A theory of differential social control." *American Sociological Review* 59: 365–390.

HENNESSY, MICHAEL, PAMELA J. RICHARDS, and RICHARD A. BERK (1978). "Broken homes and middle-class delinquency: A reassessment." *Criminology* 15: 505–528.

HEPBURN, JOHN R. (1976). "Testing alternative models of delinquency causation." *Journal of Criminal Law and Criminology* 67: 450–460.

Hier, Sally J., Paula Korboot, and Robert D. Schweitzer (1990). "Social adjustment and symptomatology in two types of homeless adolescents: Runaways and throwaways." *Adolescence* 25: 761–771.

Hill, Gary D., and Maxine P. Atkinson (1988). "Gender, familial control, and delinquency." *Criminology* 26: 127–149.

Hindelang, Michael J. (1970). "The commitment of delinquents to their misdeeds: Do delinquents drift?" *Social Problems* 17: 502–509.

——— (1973). "Causes of delinquency: A partial replication and extension." *Social Problems* 20: 471–487.

Hirschi, Travis (1969). *Causes of Delinquency.* Berkeley: University of California Press.

——— (1979). "Separate and unequal is better." *Journal of Research in Crime and Delinquency* 16: 34–38.

——— (1983). "Crime and the Family." In J. Q. Wilson, ed., *Crime and Public Policy*, 53–68. San Francisco: Institute for Contemporary Studies.

Hirschi, Travis, and Michael Gottfredson (1983). "Age and the explanation of crime." *American Journal of Sociology* 89: 522–584.

——— (1987). "Causes of white-collar crime." *Criminology* 25: 949–974.

——— (1989). "The significance of white-collar crime for a general theory of crime." *Criminology* 27: 359–371.

———, eds. (1994). *The Generality of Deviance.* New Brunswick, NJ: Transaction.

——— (1995a). "Commentary: Testing the general theory of crime." *Journal of Research in Crime and Delinquency* 30: 47–54.

——— (1995b). "Control theory and life-course perspective." *Studies on Crime Prevention* 4: 131–142.

Hirschi, Travis, and Rodney Stark (1969). "Hellfire and delinquency." *Social Problems* 17: 202–212.

Huizinga, David, Finn-Aage Esbensen, and Delbert S. Elliott (1988). *The Denver Youth Survey: Project Overview, Project Report No. 1.* Boulder, CO: Institute of Behavioral Sciences.

Jang, Sung Joon, and Marvin D. Krohn (1995). "Developmental patterns of sex differences in delinquency among African American adolescents: A test of the sex-invariance hypothesis." *Journal of Quantitative Criminology* 11: 195–222.

Jarjoura, G. Roger (1996). "The conditional effect of social class on the dropout-delinquency relationship." *Journal of Research in Crime and Delinquency* 33: 232–255.

Jensen, Gary F. (1973). "Inner containment and delinquency." *Journal of Criminal Law and Criminology* 64: 464–470.

Jensen, Gary F., and David Brownfield (1983). "Parents and drugs: Specifying the consequences of attachment." *Criminology* 21: 543–554.

Johnson, Richard E. (1979). *Juvenile Delinquency and Its Origins: An Integrated Theoretical Approach.* New York: Cambridge University Press.

Junger-Tas, Josine (1992). "An empirical test of social control theory." *Journal of Quantitative Criminology* 8: 9–28.

Kandel, Denise, and Mark Davies (1991). "Friendship networks, intimacy, and illicit drug use in young adulthood: A comparison of two competing theories." *Criminology* 29: 441–469.

Kaplan, Howard B. (1976). "Self-attitudes and deviant response." *Social Forces* 54: 788–801.

——— (1985). "Testing a general theory of drug abuse and other deviant adaptations." *Journal of Drug Issues* 15: 477–492.

Kaplan, Howard B., S. Martin, and C. Robbins (1984). "Pathways to adolescent drug use: Self-derogation, peer influence, weakening of social controls and early substance use." *Journal of Health and Social Behavior* 25: 270–289.

KARACKI, LARRY, and JACKSON TOBY (1962). "The uncommitted adolescent: Candidate for gang socialization." *Sociological Inquiry* 32: 203–215.

KEANE, CARL, PAUL S. MAXIM, and JAMES J. TEEVAN (1993). "Drinking and driving, self-control, and gender: Testing a general theory of crime." *Journal of Research in Crime and Delinquency* 30: 30–46.

KELLEY, THOMAS M. (1996). "A critique of social bonding and control theory of delinquency using the principles of psychology of mind." *Adolescence* 31: 321–337.

KELLY, DELOS H. (1976). "Track position, school misconduct, and youth deviance." *Urban Education* 10: 379–388.

KELLY, DELOS H., and WILLIAM T. PINK (1971). "School commitment and student career flows." *Youth and Society* 3: 225–236.

KELLY, FRANCIS J., and DANIEL BAER (1968). *Outward Bound Schools as an Alternative to Institutionalization for Adolescent Delinquent Boys.* Boston: Fandel Press.

KEMPF, KIMBERLY L. (1993). "The empirical status of social control theory." In F. Adler and W. S. Laufer, eds., *New Directions in Criminological Theory*, 143–185. New Brunswick, NJ: Transaction.

KNIGHT, KAREN W., and TONY TRIPODI (1996). "Societal bonding and delinquency: An empirical test of Hirschi's theory of control." *Journal of Offender Rehabilitation* 23: 117–129.

KORNHAUSER, RUTH (1978). *Social Sources of Delinquency.* Chicago: University of Chicago Press.

KROHN, MARVIN (1991). "Control and deterrence theories." In J. F. Sheley, ed., *Criminology: A Contemporary Handbook*, 295–313. Belmont, CA: Wadsworth.

KROHN, MARVIN, and JAMES MASSEY (1980). "Social control and delinquent behavior: An examination of the elements of the social bond." *Sociological Quarterly* 21: 529–544.

LAGRANGE, RANDY L., and HELENE RASKIN WHITE (1985). "Age differences in delinquency: A test of theory." *Criminology* 23: 19–45.

LASLEY, JAMES R. (1988). "Toward a control theory of white-collar offending." *Journal of Quantitative Criminology* 4: 347–362.

LAUB, JOHN H., and ROBERT J. SAMPSON (1988). "Unraveling families and delinquency: A reanalysis of the Gluecks' data." *Criminology* 26: 355–380.

LE BLANC, MARC, and AARON CAPLAN (1993). "Theoretical formalization, a necessity: The example of Hirschi's bonding theory." In F. Adler and W. S. Laufer, eds., *New Directions in Criminological Theory*, 327–336. New Brunswick, NJ: Transaction.

LEUNG, KWOK, and SING LAU (1989). "Effects of self-concept and perceived disapproval of delinquent behavior in school children." *Journal of Youth and Adolescence* 18: 345–359.

LINDEN, RICK (1978). "Myths of middle-class delinquency: A test of the generalizability of social control theory." *Youth and Society* 9: 407–431.

LISKA, ALLEN E., and MARK D. REED (1985). "Ties to conventional institutions and delinquency: Estimating reciprocal effects." *American Sociological Review* 50: 547–560.

LYERLY, ROBERT R., and JAMES K. SKIPPER (1981). "Differential rates of rural-urban delinquency: A social control approach." *Criminology* 19: 385–399.

MACCOBY, ELEANOR E., JOSEPH P. JOHNSON, and RUSSELL M. CHURCH (1958). "Community integration and the social control of juvenile delinquency." *Journal of Social Issues* 14: 38–51.

MACMILLAN, ROSS (1995). "Changes in the structure of life courses and the decline of social capital in Canadian society: A time series analysis of property crime rates." *Canadian Journal of Sociology* 20: 51–79.

MAK, ANITA S. (1990). "Testing a psychosocial control theory of delinquency." *Criminal Justice and Behavior* 17: 215–230.

———— (1991). "Psychosocial control characteristics of delinquents and nondelinquents." *Criminal Justice and Behavior* 18: 287–303.

Makkai, Toni, and John Braithwaite (1991). "Criminological theories and regulatory compliance." *Criminology* 29: 191–217.

Marcos, Anastosios C., and Stephen J. Bahr (1988). "Control theory and adolescent drug use." *Youth and Society* 19: 395–425.

Marcos, Anastosios C., Stephen J. Bahr, and Richard E. Johnson (1987). "Test of a bonding/association theory of adolescent drug use." *Social Forces* 65: 135–161.

Marenin, Otwin, and Michael D. Reisig. (1995). "'A general theory of crime' and patterns of crime in Nigeria: An exploration of methodological assumptions." *Journal of Criminal Justice* 23: 501–518.

Marshall, T. F. (1973). "An investigation of the delinquency self-concept theory of Reckless and Dinitz." *British Journal of Criminology* 13: 227–236.

Martin, Randy, Robert J. Mutchnick, and W. Timothy Austin (1990a). "Walter Cade Reckless." In R. Martin, R. Mutchnick, and T. Austin *Criminological Thought: Pioneers Past and Present*, 179–206. New York: Macmillan.

———— (1990b). "Gresham McCready Sykes." In R. Martin, R. Mutchnick, and T. Austin, *Criminological Thought: Pioneers Past and Present*, 299–320. New York: Macmillan.

Massey, James L., and Marvin D. Krohn (1986). "A longitudinal examination of an integrated social process model of deviant behavior." *Social Forces* 65: 106–134.

Mathur, M., and Richard A. Dodder (1985). "Delinquency and the attachment bond in Hirschi's control theory." *Free Inquiry in Creative Sociology* 113: 99–103.

Matsueda, Ross L. (1989). "The dynamics of moral beliefs and minor deviance." *Social Forces* 68: 428–457.

Matsuedo, Ross L., and Karen Heimer (1987). "Race, family structure and delinquency: A test of differential association and social control theories." *American Sociological Review* 52: 826–840.

Matza, David (1964). *Delinquency and Drift*. New York: Wiley.

McCarthy, Belinda R. (1991). "Social structure, crime and social control: An examination of factors influencing rates and probabilities of arrest." *Journal of Criminal Justice* 19: 19–29.

McCarthy, John D., and Dean R. Hoge (1984). "The dynamics of self-esteem and delinquency." *American Journal of Sociology* 90: 396–410.

McKinney, Fred, David J. Miller, Leo Beier, and Stephen R. Bohannon (1978). "Self-concept, delinquency and positive peer culture." *Criminology* 15: 529–537.

Mednick, Birgitte R., Robert L. Baker, and Linn E. Carothers (1990). "Patterns of family instability and crime: The association of timing of the family's disruption with subsequent adolescent and young adult criminality." *Journal of Youth and Adolescence* 19: 201–220.

Meier, Robert F., Steven Burkett, and Carol A. Hickman (1984). "Sanctions, peers, and deviance: Preliminary models of a social control process." *Sociological Quarterly* 25: 67–82.

Meisenhelder, Thomas (1977). "An exploratory study of exiting from criminal careers." *Criminology* 15: 319–334.

Messner, Steven F., and Marvin Krohn (1990). "Class, compliance structures, and delinquency: Assessing integrated structural-Marxist theory." *American Journal of Sociology* 96: 300–328.

Miller, Susan L., and Cynthia Burack (1993). "A critique of Gottfredson and Hirschi's general theory of crime: Selective (in)attention to gender and power positions." *Women and Criminal Justice* 4: 115–134.

Minor, William M. (1980). "The neutralization of criminal offense." *Criminology* 18: 103–120.

———— (1981). "Techniques of neutralization: A reconceptualization and empirical examination." *Journal of Research in Crime and Delinquency* 18: 295–318.

MOFFITT, TERRI E. (1993). "Adolescence-limited and life-course-persistent antisocial behavioral: A developmental taxonomy." *Psychological Review* 100: 674–701.

NAGIN, DANIEL S., and RAYMOND PATERNOSTER (1994). "Personal capital and social control: The deterrence implications of a theory of individual differences in criminal offending." *Criminology* 32: 581–606.

NISBET, ROBERT (1970). *The Social Bond.* New York: Knopf.

NYE, F. IVAN (1958). *Family Relationships and Delinquent Behavior.* New York: Wiley.

ORCUTT, JAMES D. (1970). "Self-concept and insulation against delinquency: Some critical notes." *Sociological Quarterly* 2: 381–390.

OTTO, LUTHER, and DUANE ALWIN (1977). "Athletics, aspirations and attainments." *Sociology of Education* 42: 102–113.

PATERNOSTER, RAYMOND, and DANIEL S. NAGIN (1994). "Personal capital and social control: The deterrence implications of a theory of individual differences in criminal offending." *Criminology* 32: 581–606.

PATTERSON, GERALD R., and DISHION, THOMAS J. (1985). "Contributions of families and peers to delinquency." *Criminology* 23: 63–80.

PHILLIPS, JOHN C., and DELOS H. KELLY (1979). "School failure and delinquency: Which causes which?" *Criminology* 17: 194–207.

POLAKOWSKI, MICHAEL (1994). "Linking self and social control with deviance: Illuminating the structure underlying a general theory of crime and its relation to deviant activities." *Journal of Quantitative Criminology* 10: 41–78.

POLK, KENNETH (1975). "Schools and the delinquency experience." *Criminal Justice and Behavior* 2: 315–337.

———— (1991). "Book review of *A General Theory of Crime.*" *Crime and Delinquency* 37: 275–279.

POLK, KENNETH, DEAN FREASE, and F. LYNN RICHMOND (1974). "Social class, school experience, and delinquency." *Criminology* 12: 84–96.

POLK, KENNETH, and DAVID HALFERTY (1966). "School cultures, adolescent commitments, and delinquency." *Journal of Research in Crime and Delinquency* 4: 82–96.

POOLE, ERIC, and ROBERT REGOLI (1979). "Parental support, delinquent friends, and delinquency: A test of interaction effects." *Journal of Criminal Law and Criminology* 70: 188–193.

PORTER, SHEILA (1990). "Adolescent sex offenders: A study of the relationship between self-concept and sexual behavior in adolescent males." *American Journal of Forensic Psychology* 8: 61–73.

RANKIN, JOSEPH H. (1976). "Investigating the interrelations among social control variables and conformity." *Journal of Criminal Law and Criminology* 67: 470–480.

RANKIN, JOSEPH H., and L. EDWARD WELLS (1990). "The effect of parental attachments and direct controls on delinquency." *Journal of Research in Crime and Delinquency* 27: 140–165.

RECKLESS, WALTER C. (1955). *The Crime Problem.* New York: Appleton- Century-Crofts.

———— (1961). "A new theory of delinquency and crime." *Federal Probation* 25: 42–46.

RECKLESS, WALTER C., and SIMON DINITZ (1967). "Pioneering with self-concept as a vulnerability factor in delinquency." *Journal of Criminal Law, Criminology and Police Science* 58: 515–523.

RECKLESS, WALTER C., SIMON DINITZ, and BARBARA KAY (1957). "The self-component in potential delinquency and potential nondelinquency." *American Sociological Review* 22: 566–570.

RECKLESS, WALTER C., SIMON DINITZ, and ELLEN MURRAY (1956). "Self-concept as an insulator against delinquency." *American Sociological Review* 21: 744–756.

———— (1957). "The 'good boy' in a high delinquency area." *Journal of Criminal Law, Criminology and Police Science* 68: 18–25.

Reed, Gary E., and Peter C. Yeager (1996). "Organizational offending and neoclassical criminology: Challenging the reach of a general theory of crime." *Criminology* 34: 357–382.

Reed-Sanders, D., and Richard A. Dodder (1979). "Labeling versus containment theory: An empirical test with delinquency." *Free Inquiry in Creative Sociology* 7: 18–22.

Regoli, Robert, and Eric Poole (1978). "The commitment of delinquents to their misdeeds: A re-examination." *Journal of Criminal Justice* 6: 261–268.

Reiss, Albert J., Jr. (1951). "Delinquency as the failure of personal and social controls." *American Sociological Review* 16: 196–207.

Rhodes, Albert L., and Albert J. Reiss, Jr. (1969). "Apathy, truancy and delinquency as an adaptation to school failure." *Social Forces* 48: 12–22.

Rogers, Joseph W., and M. D. Buffalo (1974). "Neutralization techniques: Toward a simplified measurement scale." *Pacific Sociological Review* 17: 313–331.

Rosenbaum, Jill Leslie, and James R. Lasley (1990). "School, community context, and delinquency: Rethinking the gender gap." *Justice Quarterly* 7: 493–513.

Rowe, David C. (1986). "Sibling interaction and self-reported delinquent behavior: A study of 265 twin pairs." *Criminology* 23: 223–240.

Sampson, Robert J. (1986). "Crime in cities: The effects of formal and informal social control." In A. J. Reiss and M. Tonry, eds., *Communities and Crime. Crime and Justice: A Review of Research,* vol. 8, 271–311. Chicago: University of Chicago Press.

Sampson, Robert J., and John Laub (1990). "Crime and deviance over the life course: The salience of adult social bonds." *American Sociological Review* 55: 609–627.

―――― (1993). *Crime in the Making: Pathways and Turning Points Through Life.* Cambridge, MA: Harvard University Press.

―――― (1994). "Urban poverty and the family context of delinquency: A new look at structure and process in a classic study." *Child Development* 65: 523–540.

―――― (1995). "Understanding variability in lives through time: Contributions of life-course criminology." *Studies on Crime and Crime Prevention* 4: 143–158.

Scarpitti, Frank R., Ellen Murray, Simon Dinitz, and Walter C. Reckless (1960). "The 'good boy' in a high delinquency area: Four years later." *American Sociological Review* 25: 555–558.

Schwartz, Michael, and Sandra S. Tangri (1965). "A note on self-concept as an insulator against delinquency." *American Sociological Review* 30: 922–926.

Segrave, Jeffrey O., and Douglas N. Hasted (1983). "Evaluating structural and control models of delinquency causation: A replication and extension." *Youth and Society* 14: 437–456.

Seydlitz, Ruth (1990). "The effects of gender, age, and parental attachment on delinquency: A test for interactions." *Sociological Spectrum* 10: 209–225.

―――― (1993). "Complexity in the relationships among direct and indirect parental controls and delinquency." *Youth and Society* 24: 243–275.

Shavit, Yossi, and Arye Rattner (1988). "Age, crime, and the early life course." *American Journal of Sociology* 93: 1457–1470.

Sheley, Joseph F. (1980). "Is neutralization necessary for criminal behavior?" *Deviant Behavior* 2: 49–71.

Short, James F., Jr., and Fred L. Strodtbeck (1965). *Group Process and Gang Delinquency.* Chicago: University of Chicago Press.

Silverberg, Norman E., and Margaret C. Silverberg (1971). "School achievement and delinquency." *Review of Educational Research* 41: 17–33.

Simcha-Fagan, Ora, Joanne Gersten, and Thomas Langner (1986). "Early precursors and concurrent correlates of patterns of illicit drug use in adolescence." *Journal of Drug Issues* 16: 7–28.

SIMPSON, JON, SIMON DINITZ, BARBARA KAY, and WALTER C. RECKLESS (1960). "Delinquency potential of preadolescents in a high delinquency area." *British Journal of Delinquency* 10: 211–215.

SMITH, DOUGLAS A. (1979). "Sex and deviance: An assessment of major sociological variables." *Sociological Quarterly* 20: 183–195.

SMITH, DOUGLAS A., and ROBERT BRAME (1994). "On the initiation and continuation of delinquency." *Criminology* 32: 607–629.

SMITH, DOUGLAS A., CHRISTY VISHER, and ROGER JARJOURA (1990). "Dimensions of delinquency: Exploring the correlates of participation, frequency, and persistence of delinquent behavior." *Journal of Research in Crime and Delinquency* 28: 6–32.

SNORTUM, JOHN, THOMAS HANNUM, and DAVID MILLS (1970). "The relationship of self-concept and parent image to rule violations in a women's prison." *Journal of Clinical Psychology* 26: 284–287.

SOKOL-KATZ, JAN, ROGER DUNHAM, and RICK ZIMMERMAN (1997). "Family structure versus parental attachment in controlling adolescent deviant behavior: A social control model." *Adolescence* 32: 199–215.

STARK, RODNEY, LORI KENT, and ROGER FINKE (1987). "Sports and delinquency." In M. R. Gottfredson and T. Hirschi, eds., *Positive Criminology*, 115–124. Newbury Park, CA: Sage

SYKES, GRESHAM M., and DAVID MATZA (1957). "Techniques of neutralization: A theory of delinquency." *American Sociological Review* 22: 664–670.

TANGRI, SANDRA S., and MICHAEL SCHWARTZ (1967). "Delinquency research and the self-concept variable." *Journal of Criminal Law, Criminology and Police Science* 58: 182–190.

TANIOKA, ICHIRO, and DANIEL GLASER (1991). "School uniforms, routine activities, and the social control of delinquency in Japan." *Youth and Society* 23: 50–75.

THOMPSON, WILLIAM E., ELAINE ADAMS, KATHLEEN SMITH-DIJUILIO, and TOM MATTHEWS (1982). "Social control theory: Evaluating a model for the study of adolescent alcohol and drug use." *Youth and Society* 13: 303–326.

THOMPSON, WILLIAM E., and RICHARD A. DODDER (1983). "Juvenile delinquency explained? A test of containment theory." *Youth and Society* 15: 171–194.

——— (1986). "Containment theory and juvenile delinquency: A reevaluation through factor analysis." *Adolescence* 21: 365–376.

THOMPSON, WILLIAM E., JIM MITCHELL, and RICHARD A. DODDER (1984). "An empirical test of Hirschi's control theory of delinquency." *Deviant Behavior* 5: 11–22.

THORNBERRY, TERENCE P. (1987). "Toward an interactional theory of delinquency." *Criminology* 25: 863–891.

THORNBERRY, TERENCE P., ALAN J. LIZOTTE, MARVIN D. KROHN, MARGARET FARNWORTH, and SUNG JOON JANG (1991). "Testing interactional theory: An examination of reciprocal causal relationships among family, school, and delinquency." *Journal of Criminal Law and Criminology* 82: 3–35.

THORNBERRY, TERENCE P., ROLF LOEBER, and DAVID HUIZINGA (1991). "Symposium on the causes and correlates of juvenile delinquency." *Journal of Criminal Law and Criminology* 82: 1–155.

THORNBERRY, TERENCE P., MELANIE MOORE, and R. L. CHRISTENSON (1985). "The effect of dropping out of high school on subsequent criminal behavior." *Criminology* 23: 3–18.

TIBBETTS, STEPHEN G., and DENISE C. HERZ (1996). "Gender differences in factors of social control and rational choice." *Deviant Behavior* 17: 183–208.

TITTLE, CHARLES (1988). "Two empirical regularities (maybe) in search of an explanation: Commentary on the age/crime debate." *Criminology* 26: 75–85.

TITTLE, CHARLES R., and DAVID A. WARD (1993). "The interaction of age with the correlates and causes of crime." *Journal of Quantitative Criminology* 9: 3–53.

Toby, Jackson (1957). "Social disorganization and stake in conformity: Complimentary factors in the predatory behavior of hoodlums." *Journal of Criminal Law, Criminology and Police Science* 48: 12–17.

Tomita, Susan (1990). "The denial of elder mistreatment by victims and abusers: The application of neutralization theory." *Violence and Victims* 5: 171–184.

Verlade, A. J. (1978). "Do delinquents really drift?" *British Journal of Criminology* 18: 23–39.

Vold, George B., and Thomas J. Bernard (1986). *Theoretical Criminology*, 3rd ed. New York: Oxford University Press.

Voss, Harwin L. (1969). "Differential association and containment theory: A theoretical convergence." *Social Forces* 47: 381–390.

Walters, Glenn, and Thomas White (1991). "Attachment and social bonding in maximum and minimum security prisons." *American Journal of Criminal Justice* 16: 1–15.

Warr, Mark (1993a). "Parents, peers, and delinquency." *Social Forces* 72: 247–264.

—— (1993b). "Age, peers, and delinquency." *Criminology* 31: 17–40.

—— (1996). "Organization and instigation in delinquent groups." *Criminology* 34: 11–38.

Wiatrowski, Michael, and Kristine Anderson (1987). "The dimensionality of the social bond." *Journal of Quantitative Criminology* 3: 65–81.

Wiatrowski, Michael, David B. Griswold, and Mary K. Roberts (1981). "Social control and delinquency." *American Sociological Review* 46: 525–541.

Wiatrowski, Michael, Stephen Hansell, Charles R. Massey, and David L. Wilson (1982). "Curriculum tracking and delinquency." *American Sociological Review* 47: 151–160.

Williams, Frank, P. III (1984). "The demise of the criminological imagination: A critique of recent criminology." *Justice Quarterly* 1: 91–106.

—— (1985). "Deterrence and social control: Rethinking the relationship." *Journal of Criminal Justice* 12: 141–151.

Williams, Kirk, and Richard Hawkins (1989). "Controlling male aggression in intimate relationships." *Law and Society Review* 23: 591–612.

Wood, Peter B., Betty Pfefferbaum, and Bruce J. Arneklev (1993). "Risk-taking and self-control: Social psychological correlates of delinquency." *Journal of Crime and Justice* 16: 111–130.

11

SOCIAL LEARNING THEORY

INTRODUCTION

Even though social learning theory was developed a short time (1965–1966) before Hirschi's social control theory, it is newer than the other versions of social control theory and has become popular since 1975. There are really two theories under this generic name. The first was developed by C. Ray Jeffery as a direct application of popular operant-based learning theories from psychology. The other, which has received greater acceptance by criminologists, is Ronald Akers's *social* learning theory. Akers's theory evolved from its 1966 origins, and the version popular today was developed mostly in the 1970s. In addition, social learning theory is primarily an extension of Edwin Sutherland's differential association theory. Had we not been attempting in this book to keep the theories in chronological order, social learning theory would best have been placed after the chapter on differential association.

Both these theories rely on behavioral psychology. There are two general types of psychological approaches: Skinnerian, or operant theory, and social learning theory. B. F. Skinner's original version of operant theory allows only for direct material sources of reinforcement and punishment. Social versions of learning, on the other hand, begin with Skinner's theory and add the concept of indirect social stimuli and cognitive processes. Jeffery uses the more straightforward Skinnerian approach, whereas Akers relies on the social learning variety.

THE HERITAGE OF THE THEORY

The Social Heritage

Behavioral theories in psychology rose to the peak of their popularity in the 1960s. The optimistic spirit of the early part of the decade led psychologists to believe otherwise untreatable behavior problems could be successfully treated by using the newly developed behavioral therapies. The civil rights campaign had also spilled over into mental health issues. A recognition of the rights of mental patients gave them a right to treatment, rather than just being warehoused. Further, behavior modification, a branch of applied behavioral psychology, was especially suitable for training in life skills so that the patient could eventually be released from the institution.

As part of the Great Society concept, schools were experimenting with new and better ways of learning. Education began championing behavior modification and adapting it to the classroom setting. By the 1970s, people felt so convinced that behavioral psychologies were the answer to behavior problems that Skinner made the bestseller list with two popular books, *Beyond Freedom and Dignity* and *Walden II*. A futuristic movie, *A Clockwork Orange*, even featured the use of a punishment-oriented version of behavior modification.

An optimistic philosophy had also developed in corrections and the juvenile justice system, with state and federal governments funding several experimental programs. Among those programs, behavior modification appeared to have the most promise, largely because it seemed to work within institutions, if not outside them. Even at the end of the decade, when people had become cynical about treatment programs, behavior modification programs were still in use (those versions based on punishment were, however, beginning to come under fire). *A Clockwork Orange* ultimately influenced the public's conception of behavioral psychology and created a strong reaction against the behavior modification movement. Radicals, in particular, objected to the use of behavior modification, claiming it was an elite plan to brainwash those who threatened the state.

The Intellectual Heritage

The most obvious intellectual source of social learning theory is behavioristic psychology. Ray Jeffery adopted the approach as a faculty member at Arizona State University, where two prominent psychologists, Arthur and Carolyn Staats, were making strides in the new field of behavior modification. In addition, Jeffery was involved in the Washington, DC, Dropout Project, a program that attempted to apply the principles of behavior modification to delinquent youth. Ron Akers, on the other hand, developed his theory as the result of interaction with another young faculty member, Robert Burgess, in the sociology department at the University of Washington (Akers, 1985). Burgess had studied behavioral psychology and convinced Akers it could profitably be applied to criminology. Burgess was later to employ learning theory in several environmental programs, including an anti-littering program for a park system.

Perhaps as important as psychology is the heritage gained from differential association. Both Jeffery and Akers published their original learning theory articles as an explanation of Sutherland's statement, "Criminal behavior is learned." Jeffery was, in fact, one of the last of Sutherland's students. Akers, who earned his doctoral degree under Richard Quinney, was intimately familiar with Sutherland's work, especially since Quinney was working on a reformulation of differential association theory (DeFleur and Quinney, 1966). Indeed, many criminologists today see social learning theory as an extension and modernization of differential association theory.

THE THEORETICAL PERSPECTIVE

Operant and General Social Learning Theories

Before one can appreciate criminological learning theories, a basic understanding of operant-based learning theory is necessary. Operant learning theory is concerned with the effect an individual's behavior has on the environment and, subsequently, the consequences of that effect on the individual. As Skinner (1971:16) relates, behavior is shaped and maintained by its consequences. Therefore, behavior is a product of present and past events in the life of the individual. The contingencies of reinforcement and punishment (aversive stimuli) determine whether the frequency of any particular behavior is increased or diminished.

We discuss here six basic principles: positive reinforcement, negative reinforcement, positive punishment, negative punishment, discriminative stimuli, and schedules. **Reinforcement** may be described as any event that follows the occurrence of behavior and that alters and increases the frequency of the behavior. Some events directly increase the frequency of behavior they follow. These are *positive* reinforcers, or rewards. A mother who gives her child a cookie for doing something good is providing positive reinforcement. Other events increase the frequency of behavior if they remove something undesirable following the behavior. These are called *negative* reinforcers. If a child does something bad and then says he is sorry, the mother may not punish the child. Perhaps the easiest way to distinguish between the two is positive reinforcement provides a reward and negative reinforcement removes some form of punishment.

Punishment, or aversive stimuli, is the opposite of reinforcement. That is, it reduces the frequency of any behavior it follows. The process of decreasing the emission of behavior through the presence of an aversive stimulus is called *positive* punishment. This is the typical reason for spanking a child. *Negative* punishment results in the removal of rewards that would ordinarily have been present after a behavior. In this case, the child does not get the cookie.

Discriminative stimuli, on the other hand, do not occur after behavior but are present either before or as the behavior occurs. Further, they can be used to control behavior because they indicate whether reinforcement or punishment is forthcoming. Thus, they function as *cues*, or signals, that help the individual determine those situations in which a particular behavior may be appropriate (likely to be reinforced). It is this form of stimulus that is crucial in social settings; almost all our social world is composed of discriminative stimuli. Advertising, for example, is primarily based on the use of discriminative stimuli to get us to associate a product with something we find rewarding.

A final concept is that of the **schedule** of consequences. This refers to the frequency with which and probability a particular consequence will occur, as well as to the length of time it occurs after the behavior. Those consequences immediately following behavior and having a high probability of occurrence are the ones that have the strongest effect on the individual. This means some forms of behavior will be preferred over others because of their reinforcement schedule. Conversely, it means if we wait too long to punish someone for a crime, for example, the punishment will lose much of its effect.

Learning, then, takes place because of the consequences associated with behavior. If an individual is reinforced after doing something, that behavior will occur again: the behavior has been learned. On the other hand, if punishment occurs after certain behavior, the individual learns to avoid that kind of behavior. Since people do not all have the same reward and punishment experiences in their past, some people will have learned some behavior while others will not have. Finally, any social environment contains several possible situations, each of which might provide different cues and consequences for a behavior. It is relatively easy to misinterpret a situation and assume previous learning will apply when in fact it will not.

Social learning theory also considers the concept of imitation, or **modeling,** to be central to the learning process (Bandura, 1969:118–203). This involves the process of learning by observing the behavior of others. If, for instance, some other person is rewarded for certain behavior, an individual watching that situation can also learn the behavior. In this way, the observer is "vicariously reinforced." Strict operant learning theory insists learning must be based on behavior and consequences applied to the individual, not some other person. Therefore, social learning theory is different in that it adds the social environment to the learning process. Under this approach, it is possible to learn not only from other people around us but also from television and movies.

Jeffery's Differential Reinforcement Theory[1]

In 1965, Jeffery published the first article linking criminal behavior and operant learning theory. His thesis was differential association is "not valid in its present form, though it is basically sound in asserting that criminal behavior is learned" (1965:294). Sutherland's theory needed reformulation into modern learning theory, but Jeffery maintained that once that was done the theory no longer would be a theory of *social* reinforcement. It would be, he said, a more complete theory that could explain how "criminal behavior can be maintained without social approval" (1965:296).

Jeffery began his theory of differential reinforcement with a brief description of the six basic operant principles. He added one more set of concepts to his discussion: *satiation* and *deprivation*. It suggests a stimulus will be more or less reinforcing depending on the individual's current condition. For example, a person who already has wealth (satiated) will be less likely to find robbing someone of their money to be reinforcing, while the impoverished individual (deprived) will more likely see the money as a reinforcer. Such a concept of the condition of the individual allows for similar interpretations of the effect of social class and poverty as those we saw in the strain theories of Robert Merton, Albert Cohen, and Richard Cloward and Lloyd Ohlin.

A brief summary of the elements of differential reinforcement is as follows (Jeffery, 1965:295). People do not have the same past experiences; therefore, their conditioning histories are different. The stimuli people experience daily also have distinct meanings that produce differing qualities of reinforcement. Among these stimuli are some that have previously affected criminal behavior. Thus, some people have been reinforced for criminal behavior and some have been punished. Since most consequences are relatively intermittent (rarely is anything rewarded or punished every time), criminal behavior is not reinforced or punished each time it occurs. Instead, past experience is sufficient to maintain the current criminal behavior.

Finally, Jeffery also insisted that the most important forms of reinforcers are material, such as money and cars. As a result, differential reinforcement maintains that one does not need associates to provide reinforcing consequences for criminal behavior, for the product of the crime itself can be the reinforcer. Other people are said to be important for their discriminative value; that is, they provide cues about the probability of being rewarded for a criminal act. This decreased emphasis on social reinforcement has continued to characterize Jeffery's work. His book, *Crime Prevention through Environmental Design* (1977), incorporates his work in sociobiol-

---

1. We would like to express our appreciation to C. Ray Jeffery for his review and comments on an earlier version of this summary.

ogy and states the reinforcing quality of all behavior lies in the brain. By this Jeffery means that the brain contains pleasure and pain centers that mediate and interpret all stimuli. Thus, he now says social reinforcement is really a secondary form of reinforcement and is maintained only by a relationship with the more primary form of biological reinforcement (1977:312).

Jeffery is continuing his work on brain-mediated behavior and proposes interdisciplinary work on the problem. He now believes a general theory of crime should have three components: genetics, brain structure and function, and learning theory (1989b:73). His perspective is that sociological, psychological, and biological characteristics should be seen as interacting together in a total system to produce criminal behavior. He posits individuals are born with particular biological (genetic) and psychological characteristics that not only may predispose, but may actually cause, certain forms of behavior. This "nature" is independent of the socialization process present in the social environment. There is, however, a good deal of interplay between nature and socialization through physical environments and the feedback mechanisms existing in biochemical systems. For example, Jeffery notes poverty translates to a certain type of diet and exposure to pollutants. Both of these are transformed by the biochemical system into neurochemical compounds within the brain. Thus, poverty indirectly leads to behavioral differences (and, potentially, criminal behavior) through the interaction of individual and environment.

Jeffery clearly suggests that any theory of criminal behavior is incomplete without a consideration of all elements making up the human organism. In addition, he notes that the study of criminal behavior is not possible without an understanding and theory of criminal law. A summary of his overall approach combining both behavior and law is as follows: humans are born with biological and psychological differences. These differences lead to direct conflict with other humans. To reduce this conflict, humans must be socialized into conformity, and, lacking this, control systems (the state and criminal law) must be created to restrict behavior. Criminal behavior is behavior restricted by these control systems.

Akers's Social Learning Theory[2]

Akers and Burgess provided criminology with the second connection between psychological learning theory and differential association (Burgess and Akers, 1966b). After reading Jeffery's 1965 article, they decided a more detailed statement of learning theory would be beneficial and began the process of fully reformulating the propositions of differential association theory. The final version of seven propositions, which they labeled "differential association-reinforcement theory," was not originally intended as an

2. We would like to express our appreciation to Ron Akers for his review and comments on an earlier version of this summary.

alternative to Sutherland's theory. Of necessity, however, it became a "new, broader theory" (Akers, 1985:41).

In contrast to Jeffery's approach, it is obvious Akers views the social environment as the most important source of reinforcement. He even suggests that most of the learning of deviant behavior is the result of social interaction (1985:45). In fact, it is the presence of various subcultures in society that allows us to predict which stimuli are likely to be effective reinforcers for people. This approach leads to the presence of *definitions* as one of the crucial aspects of the theory.

Definitions of behavior, both for Sutherland and Akers, are the moral components of social interaction expressing whether something is right or wrong. Akers refers to these definitions as verbal behavior and notes they are learned just as any other behavior is learned. Once learned, however, definitions become a form of discriminative stimuli or cues about the consequences to be expected from other behavior. They can be general beliefs, applying to a range of behavior, or specifically focused on a single form of behavior. Those indicating approval of certain behavior are clearly positive in their action; that is, they denote the behavior is morally correct and will be rewarded (positive reinforcement). Others are neutralizing definitions, providing a way to avoid some (or all) of an expected punishment and justifying or excusing the behavior (negative reinforcement).

Akers has continued the development of the theory, most notably in his book *Deviant Behavior: A Social Learning Approach* (1985). The most recent version of social learning theory retains the seven-proposition format of the original.

1. Deviant behavior is learned according to the principles of operant conditioning.
2. Deviant behavior is learned both in nonsocial situations that are reinforcing or discriminating and through that social interaction in which the behavior of other persons is reinforcing or discriminating for such behavior.
3. The principal part of the learning of deviant behavior occurs in those groups which comprise or control the individual's major source of reinforcements.
4. The learning of deviant behavior, including specific techniques, attitudes, and avoidance procedures, is a function of the effective and available reinforcers and the existing reinforcement contingencies.
5. The specific class of behavior learned and its frequency of occurrence are a function of the effective and available reinforcers, and the deviant or nondeviant direction of the norms, rules, and definitions which in the past have accompanied the reinforcement.
6. The probability that a person will commit deviant behavior is increased in the presence of normative statements, definitions, and verbalizations which, in the process of differential reinforcement of such behavior over conforming behavior, have acquired discriminative value.
7. The strength of deviant behavior is a direct function of the amount, frequency, and probability of its reinforcement. The modalities of association with deviant patterns are important insofar as they affect the source, amount, and scheduling of reinforcement. (*Source*: Ronald L. Akers, *Deviant Behavior: A Social Learning Approach*, 3rd ed. Belmont, CA: Wadsworth, 1985. Used by permission of the author.)

Social learning theory, then, states people learn both deviant behavior and the definitions that go along with it. The learning can be direct, as through conditioning, or indirect, as through imitation and modeling. The learned deviance can then be strengthened by reinforcement or weakened by punishment. Its continued maintenance depends not only on its own reinforcement but also on the quality of the reinforcement available for alternative behavior. If the definitions of deviant behavior are reinforcing and if alternative behaviors are not reinforced as strongly, an individual is likely to engage in deviant behavior. In the further development and empirical testing of the theory, Akers has focused on the principal processes of differential association, definitions, differential reinforcement, and imitation.

CLASSIFICATION OF THE THEORY

Social learning qualifies as a *positivist* theory. Compared with other theories, it focuses more directly on behavior and presents an obvious treatment or remedy for deviance. Similarly, because learning theory is focused on the individual, it is not easily classified as a *microtheory*. Even though the theoretical principles are general enough to apply to all behavior, it is a direct attempt to explain how individuals come to engage in criminal behavior.

Social learning is also a *processual* theory. It explains the process by which criminal behavior takes place and tells us why that behavior occurs. The more difficult point of classification is that of consensus-conflict. The theory itself does not require either orientation, so we must look to the theorists to determine which it is. We would infer Jeffery takes a consensus orientation to society. This appears to be the case because his work provides many applications to "treat" criminal behavior, yet he does not question the origin of those laws requiring that treatment. In fairness to Jeffery, however, he does state a theory of the creation of law is necessary before one can discuss criminal behavior. Akers, on the other hand, believes there is a "core of consensual values" while "admitting the importance of power and conflict" (1985:19). This, he says, is a pluralist conflict approach (what we have earlier called conservative conflict theory). Since both these theorists seem to assume a core set of common social values, however, we will classify social learning theory as a *consensus* theory.

SUMMARY

Social learning theory developed from the combination of differential association theory with psychological learning theories. Though Jeffery's current version de-emphasizes the social aspects of learning, Akers's theory is still directly associated with Sutherland's perspective. They both, however, explain deviant behavior by emphasizing reinforcement and discriminative stimuli.

Behavior, whether deviant or not, can be expected to be maintained if it is reinforced in the social environment. Thus, the problem for behavioral criminologists is to determine where these reinforcements originate. Jeffery now suggests reinforcement is biologically based in the pleasure-pain center of the brain. Preferring to keep his theory on a social level, Akers finds the origin of deviance reinforcement in common rationalizations and in the various groups and subcultures of society.

As has been the case for social control theory, the popularity of social learning theory has increased during the past two decades. However, some sociologically oriented criminologists remain skeptical of the approach because it is directly derived from psychology. Nonetheless, as one of the two major theories not requiring an acceptance of the conflict position (though Akers says that he views social learning as compatible with a pluralist conflict position), social learning theory has been steadily gaining in acceptance. It is now quite common to see commentary or research on the theory in the various criminological journals. Some theorists have even attempted to integrate social control and social learning theories (Conger, 1976), an effort Akers would seem to encourage (1985:67; 1989). Actually, Akers has stated he views social learning theory as a major approach to integrating other deviance-oriented theories (1985:70).

Major Points of the Theory

1. Human behavior is organized around the seeking of pleasure and the avoidance of pain.
2. The two concepts involved in the learning of behavior are reinforcement and punishment. Reinforcement increases the frequency of a behavior, whereas punishment decreases the frequency.
3. Criminal behavior is learned through both material and social reinforcements in the same way as is any other behavior. This learning process is a product of past and present experiences; therefore, all individuals have a different set of learned behaviors and expected consequences.
4. Social reinforcements serve both as factors in learning deviant behavior and in setting the values (definitions) that define behavior as good or bad, desirable or undesirable. The social environment also provides various behavior models that can be imitated.
5. Social definitions, which are originally learned in the same way as any other behavior, act as cues signaling whether a particular behavior will or will not be reinforced.
6. Definitions assist in the learning of crime as direct signals that a reward is forthcoming or as rationalizations used to avoid punishment for criminal behavior.
7. Criminal behavior is behavior that has been differentially reinforced through social definitions and material rewards in the individual's subcultural environment.
8. Material reinforcements are often provided by crime itself. Therefore, when individuals are deprived, criminal behavior may be maintained by its own rewards.

EPILOGUE: CURRENT DIRECTIONS AND POLICY IMPLICATIONS

Current Directions

Social learning theories continue to be relatively popular. Several criminologists have attempted to test the approach, particularly Akers's version of the theory. Indeed, Akers himself has led the way with several research projects, most of which have focused on drug use (Akers et al., 1979, 1989; Krohn, Lanza-Kaduce, and Akers, 1984; Akers and Cochran, 1985; Akers and LaGreca, 1991; Akers and Lee, 1996;). Other tests of theories, such as Delbert Elliott, David Huizinga, and Suzanne Ageton's (1985) major work in delinquency, have commonly found that social learning variables explain at least as much of deviant behavior as other theories do. Actually, the findings usually are that social learning explains delinquency and deviance *better* than most other theories (Winfree, Griffiths, and Sellers, 1989).

Other approaches to learning theory have also been developed, particularly with reference to personality traits (see Eysenck, 1989, 1996; Eysenck and Gudjonnson, 1989). One of the more popular versions in criminology is an adaptation of differential association theory by Daniel Glaser. In his 1978 book, *Crime in Our Changing Society,* Glaser proposed a theory of **differential anticipation.** Drawing on his previous idea that identification with criminal roles is more important than one's associates, he incorporated social learning concepts and said expectations determine conduct. Indeed, he saw three sources of expectations: pro- and anticriminal social bonds, differential learning, and perceived opportunities. Individuals have different groups of people around them who may reward behavior according to different values. Therefore, people have different sources of behavior and values and thus learn differently. The process involves learning discriminative stimuli as a way of knowing what behavior will be rewarded and punished. Finally, opportunities for crime involve an assessment of risks and gains individuals expect to receive from committing a crime. Glaser's basic idea is that an individual will commit a crime when the expected (anticipated) gains outweigh the expected punishments. These expectations, of course, are all learned from one's social environment.

Finally, social learning theory has been a mainstay of attempts to integrate criminological theories. Elliott and colleagues (1979, 1985) have used the theory as an integral part of explaining delinquency and drug use. Most common is an attempt to combine it with social control (Conger, 1976; Benda and Whiteside, 1995), to which others have added labeling (Hayes, 1997; Edwards, 1992) and/or strain (Edwards, 1992; Menard, 1992). Akers has proposed relationships with each of the other major theories, explaining that social learning acts to explain the general process in which those theories translate to the behavior of individuals. Moreover, Akers has argued social learning concepts are compatible with, and even part of, rational choice models and deterrence (1990). His integrative approach is one of "conceptual absorption" which he defines as "subsuming concepts from one theory as special cases of the phenomena defined by the concepts of another" (Akers, 1997:209). In other words, integration can be accomplished by joining theories together or by incorporating concepts from other theories into an existing theory. Akers has clearly identified concepts of social control theory as adaptable to integration, and the structural components of anomie and subculture theories can be used to demonstrate how groups produce differential learning experiences.

Policy Implications

While crime policies have not been directly proposed from social learning theories, there are several examples of behavior modification projects involving inmates and delinquents. In most of these instances, the program has been set up to reward inmates or delinquents for correct behavior and punish incorrect behavior. Often referred to as an "M&M" economy, after the popular candy, the treatment scheme is designed to move the individual through successive stages of behavior. Beginning with a simple behavioral change (e.g., doing nothing wrong for ten minutes), the individual progresses through longer and more complex steps. At each stage, the individual is rewarded for doing something correctly and thereby "learns" the new behavior. The results of such programs, whether carried out in prison or some other controlled environment, have been uniformly positive. People can indeed learn to behave in more "correct" ways and to keep those behaviors in place. After they leave the controlled environment, the learned behaviors tend to disappear, however. In other words, they learn or relearn behaviors appropriate for the regular social environment. The problem for these treatment programs is to find ways of making the learned behaviors carry over to the outside environment.

Another policy implication of social learning theories involves environmental design. As Jeffery would put it, the more difficult it is to commit a behavior, the less likely an individual will be to do that act. From the perspective of learning theory then, the behavior has little probability of being rewarded and thus will be extinguished. With this in mind, Jeffery has helped to design neighborhood convenience stores so that committing a crime is more difficult, the rewards from crime are diminished, and the probability of being caught is greater. For instance, raising the clerk's counter and positioning it where it can be seen from outside the store (surveillance), and placing all large bills in a locked floor safe are part of the design. The federal government and many business corporations have embraced environmental design ideas.

Other potential policy ideas include teaching prosocial definitions in schools, encouraging religious training (morality), and emphasizing the important values present in law. Another central idea is providing school-based instruction that emphasizes the importance of current behavior for future life opportunities. Learning theories tell us behavior will be based on immediate rewards and punishment unless discriminative stimuli are developed to reinforce the presence of future rewards. In short, without a learning process (socialization, perhaps), teenage behavior will tend to be hedonistic and based on short-term rewards. The problems are how to teach juveniles the implications of those behaviors for long-term rewards and how to assess the long-term effects of their behavior. Clearly, such goals are difficult to achieve, yet the work of behavior modification specialists in such areas as mental illness has demonstrated a high degree of effectiveness. Social learning theories are quite useful at the policy level; we simply need to develop ideas for their use.

BIBLIOGRAPHY

ADAMS, REED, L. (1973). "Differential association and learning principles revisited." *Social Problems* 20: 458–470.

AGNEW, ROBERT (1993). "Why do they do it? An examination of the intervening mechanisms between 'social control' variables and delinquency." *Journal of Research in Crime and Delinquency* 30: 245–266.

AKERS, RONALD L. (1977). *Deviant Behavior: A Social Learning Approach*, 2nd ed. Belmont, CA: Wadsworth.

——— (1981). "Reflections of a social behaviorist on behavioral sociology." *American Sociologist* 16: 177–180.

——— (1985). *Deviant Behavior: A Social Learning Approach*, 3rd ed. Belmont, CA: Wadsworth.

——— (1989). "A social behaviorist's perspective on integration of theories of crime and deviance." In S. F. Messner, M. D. Krohn, and A. E. Liska, eds., *Theoretical Integration in the Study of Deviance and Crime: Problems and Prospects*, 23–36. Albany: State University of New York Press.

——— (1990). "Rational choice, deterrence, and social learning theory in criminology: The path not taken." *Journal of Criminal Law and Criminology* 81: 653–676.

——— (1996). "Is differential association/social learning cultural deviance theory?" *Criminology* 34: 229–247.

——— (1997). *Criminological Theories: Introduction and Evaluation*. Los Angeles: Roxbury.

AKERS, RONALD L., and JOHN K. COCHRAN (1985). "Adolescent marijuana use: A test of three theories of deviant behavior." *Deviant Behavior* 6: 323–346.

AKERS, RONALD L., and MARVIN D. KROHN (1981). "Social characteristics and self-reported delinquency: Differences in extreme types." In G. Jensen, ed., *Sociology of Delinquency: Current Issues*, 48–62. Beverly Hills, CA: Sage.

AKERS, RONALD L., MARVIN D. KROHN, LONN LANZA-KADUCE, and MARCIA J. RADOSEVICH (1979). "Social learning and deviant behavior: A specific test of a general theory." *American Sociological Review* 44: 636–655.

AKERS, RONALD L., and ANTHONY J. LA GRECA (1991). "Alcohol use among the elderly: Social learning, community context, and life events." In D. J. Pittman and H. R. White, eds., *Society, Culture, and Drinking Patterns Re-examined*, 242–262. New Brunswick, NJ: Rutgers Center of Alcohol Studies.

AKERS, RONALD L., ANTHONY J. LA GRECA, JOHN COCHRAN, and CHRISTINE SELLERS (1989). "Social learning theory and alcohol behavior among the elderly." *Sociological Quarterly* 30: 625–638.

AKERS, RONALD L., ANTHONY J. LA GRECA, and CHRISTINE SELLERS (1988). "Theoretical perspectives on deviant behavior among the elderly." In B. McCarthy and R. Langworthy, eds., *Older Offenders*, 35–50. New York: Praeger.

AKERS, RONALD L., and GANG LEE (1996). "A longitudinal test of social learning theory: Adolescent smoking." *Journal of Drug Issues* 26: 317–343.

ANDREWS, KENNETH H., and DENISE B. KANDEL (1979). "Attitude and behavior: A specification of the contingent consistency hypothesis." *American Sociological Review* 44: 298–310.

BACH, PAUL J., and PHILIP H. BORNSTEIN (1981). "A social learning rationale and suggestions for behavioral treatment of American Indian alcohol abusers." *Addictive Behavior* 6: 75–81.

BALDWIN, JOHN D. (1981a). *Behavior Principles in Everyday Life*. Englewood Cliffs, NJ: Prentice Hall.

—— (1981b). "George Herbert Mead and modern behaviorism." *Pacific Sociological Review* 24: 411–440.

—— (1985). "Thrill and adventure seeking and the age distribution of crime: Comment on Hirschi and Gottfredson." *American Journal of Sociology* 90: 1326–1330.

BALDWIN, JOHN D., and JANICE I. BALDWIN (1978). "Behaviorism on verstehen and eklaren." *American Sociological Review* 43: 335–347.

BANDURA, ALBERT (1969). *Principles of Behavior Modification*. New York: Holt, Rinehart and Winston.

—— (1973). *Aggression: A Social Learning Analysis*. Englewood Cliffs, NJ: Prentice Hall.

—— (1977). *Social Learning Theory*. Englewood Cliffs, NJ: Prentice Hall.

BANKSTON, CARL L., III, and STEPHEN J. CALDAS (1996). "Adolescents and deviance in a Vietnamese American community: A theoretical synthesis." *Deviant Behavior* 17: 159–181.

BELLE, O. S., and A. M. AKRAM (1969). "A pilot study of antisocial and prosocial offenders." *Canadian Journal of Corrections* 11: 255–261.

BENDA, BRENT B. (1997). "An examination of a reciprocal relationship between religiosity and different forms of delinquency within a theoretical model." *Journal of Research in Crime and Delinquency* 34: 163–186.

BENDA, BRENT B., and FREDERICK A. DIBLASIO (1991). "Comparison of four theories of adolescent sexual exploration." *Deviant Behavior* 12: 235–257.

BENDA, BRENT B., and LEANNE WHITESIDE (1995). "Testing and integrated model of delinquency using LISREL." *Journal of Social Service Research* 21: 1–32.

BROWNFIELD, DAVID, and ANN MARIE SORENSON (1994). "Sibship size and sibling delinquency." *Deviant Behavior* 15: 45–61.

BROWNFIELD, DAVID, and KEVIN THOMPSON (1991). "Attachment to peers and delinquent behaviour." *Canadian Journal of Criminology* 33: 45–60.

BURGESS, ROBERT L., and RONALD L. AKERS (1966a). "Are operant principles tautological?" *Psychological Record* 16: 305–312.

—— (1966b). "A differential association-reinforcement theory of criminal behavior." *Social Problems* 14: 128–147.

BURGESS, ROBERT L., and DON BUSHELL, JR. (1969). *Behavioral Sociology: The Experimental Analysis of Social Process*. New York: Columbia University Press.

BURGESS, ROBERT L., and JOYCE M. NIELSEN (1974). "An experimental analysis of some structural determinants of equitable and inequitable exchange relations." *American Sociological Review* 39: 427–443.

BURKETT, STEVEN R., and ERIC L. JENSEN (1975). "Conventional ties, peer influence, and the fear of apprehension: A study of adolescent marijuana use." *Sociological Quarterly* 16: 522–533.

BURKETT, STEVEN R., and BRUCE O. WARREN (1987). "Religiosity, peer associations, and adolescent marijuana use: A panel study of underlying causal structures." *Criminology* 25: 109–131.

CATALANO, RICHARD F., RICK KOSTERMAN, and J. DAVID HAWKINS (1996). "Modeling the etiology of adolescent substance use: A test of the social development model." *Journal of Drug Issues* 26: 429–455.

CHANCE, PAUL (1979). *Learning and Behavior.* Belmont, CA: Wadsworth.

CONGER, RAND (1976). "Social control and social learning models of delinquency: A synthesis." *Criminology* 14: 17–40.

CORNISH, DEREK (1993). "Theories of action in criminology: Learning theory and rational choice approaches." *Advances in Criminological Theory* 5: 351–382.

DABNEY, DEAN (1995). "Neutralization and deviance in the workplace: Theft of supplies and medicines by hospital nurses." *Deviant Behavior* 16: 313–331.

DEFLEUR, MELVIN L., and RICHARD QUINNEY (1966). "A reformulation of Sutherland's differential association theory and a strategy for empirical verification." *Journal of Research in Crime and Delinquency* 3: 1–22.

DEMBO, RICHARD, GARY GRANDON, LAWRENCE LA VOIE, JAMES SCHMEIDLER, and WILLIAM BURGOS (1986). "Parents and drugs revisited: Some further evidence in support of social learning theory." *Criminology* 24: 85–104.

DIBLASIO, FREDERICK A. (1986). "Drinking adolescents on the roads." *Journal of Youth and Adolescence* 15: 173–189.

EDWARDS, WILLIE, J. (1992). "Predicting juvenile delinquency: A review of correlates and a confirmation by recent research based on an integrated theoretical model." *Justice Quarterly* 9: 553–583.

ELLIOTT, DELBERT S., SUZANNE S. AGETON, and RACHELLE J. CANTER (1979). "An integrated theoretical perspective on delinquent behavior." *Journal of Research in Crime and Delinquency* 16: 3–27.

ELLIOTT, DELBERT S., DAVID HUIZINGA, and SUZANNE S. AGETON (1985). *Explaining Delinquency and Drug Use.* Beverly Hills, CA: Sage.

EMERSON, RICHARD N. (1981). "Social exchange theory." In M. Rosenberg and R. Turner, eds., *Social Psychology,* 30–65. New York: Basic Books.

EYSENCK, HANS J. (1989). "Personality and criminality: A dispositional analysis." In W. S. Laufer and F. Adler, eds., *Advances in Criminological Theory,* vol. 1, 89–110. New Brunswick, NJ: Transaction.

—— (1996). "Personality and crime: Where do we stand?" *Psychology, Crime and Law* 2: 143–152.

EYSENCK, HANS J., and ISLI H. GUDJONNSON (1989). *The Causes and Cures of Criminality.* New York: Plenum Press.

FAGAN, JEFFREY, and EDWARD PABON (1990). "Contributions of delinquency and substance use to school dropout among inner-city youths." *Youth and Society* 21: 306–354.

FAGAN, JEFFREY, and SANDRA WEXLER (1987). "Crime at home and in the streets: The relationship between family and stranger violence." *Violence and Victims* 2: 5–23.

GLASER, DANIEL (1978). *Crime in Our Changing Society.* New York: Holt, Rinehart and Winston.

GOLDIAMOND, ISRAEL (1976). "Self-reinforcement." *Journal of Applied Behavior Analysis* 9: 509–514.

GOLDSTEIN, ARNOLD (1990). *Delinquents on Delinquency.* Champaign, IL: Research Press.

GRASMICK, HAROLD G., and DONALD E. GREEN (1980). "Legal punishment, social disapproval, and internalization as inhibitors of illegal behavior." *Journal of Criminal Law and Criminology* 71: 325–335.

GRAY, L. N., and I. TALLMAN (1987). "Theories of choice: Contingent reward and punishment application." *Social Psychology Quarterly* 50: 16–23.

GREEN, GARY S. (1990). "Resurrecting polygraph validation of self-reported crime data: A note on research method and ethics using the deer poacher." *Deviant Behavior* 11: 131–137.

GREENWOOD, PETER (1986). "Predictors of chronic behavior." In P. W. Greenwood, ed., *Intervention Strategies for Chronic Juvenile Offenders: Some New Perspectives*, 75–89. New York: Greenwood Press.

GWARINEY-GIBBS, P. A., J. STOCKARD, and S. BOHMER (1987). "Learning courtship aggression: The influence of parents, peers, and personal experiences." *Family Relations* 36: 276–282.

HALBASCH, KEITH (1979). "Differential reinforcement theory examined." *Criminology* 17: 217–229.

HAMBLIN, ROBERT L. (1979). "Behavioral choice and social reinforcement: Step function versus matching." *Social Forces* 57: 1141–1156.

HAMBLIN, ROBERT L., and JOHN H. KUNKEL, eds. (1977). *Behavioral Theory in Sociology: Essays in Honor of George C. Homans*. New Brunswick, NJ: Transaction.

HAMBLIN, ROBERT L., and JERRY L. MILLER (1976). "Reinforcement and the origin, rate and extent of cultural diffusion." *Social Forces* 54: 743–749.

HARDING, RICHARD W. (1993). "Gun use in crime, rational choice, and social learning theory." *Advances in Criminological Theory* 5: 85–102.

HARRIS, MARY B. (1996). "Aggressive experiences and aggressiveness: Relationship to ethnicity, gender, and age." *Journal of Applied Social Psychology* 26: 843–870.

HAYES, HENNESSEY D. (1997). "Using integrated theory to explain the movement into juvenile delinquency." *Deviant Behavior* 18: 161–184.

HEIMER, KAREN (1997). "Socioeconomic status, subcultural definitions, and violent delinquency." *Social Forces* 75: 799–834.

HOGHUGHI, M. S., and A. R. FORREST (1970). "Eysenck's theory of criminality: An examination with approved school boys." *British Journal of Criminology* 10: 240–254.

HOMANS, GEORGE C. (1961). *Social Behavior: Its Elementary Forms*. New York: Harcourt, Brace and World.

HOUTS, SANDRA, and CATHY KASSAB (1997). "Rotter's social learning theory and fear of crime: Differences by race and ethnicity." *Social Science Quarterly* 78: 122–136.

HOWELL, MARILYN, and KAREN PUGLIESI (1988). "Husbands who harm: Predicting spousal violence by men." *Journal of Family Violence* 3: 15–27.

JEFFERY, C. RAY (1965). "Criminal behavior and learning theory." *Journal of Criminal Law, Criminology and Police Science* 56: 294–300.

——— (1977). *Crime Prevention through Environmental Design*, 2nd ed. Beverly Hills, CA: Sage.

——— (1978). "Criminology as an interdisciplinary behavioral science." *Criminology* 16: 149–170.

——— (1980). "Sociobiology and criminology: The long, lean years of the unthinkable and the unmentionable." In E. Sagarin, ed., *Taboos in Criminology*, 115–124. Beverly Hills, CA: Sage.

——— (1989a). *Criminology: An Interdisciplinary Approach*. Englewood Cliffs, NJ: Prentice Hall.

——— (1989b). "An interdisciplinary theory of criminal behavior." In W. S. Laufer and F. Adler, eds., *Advances in Criminological Theory*, vol. 1, 69–87. New Brunswick, NJ: Transaction.

JOHNSON, RICHARD E., ANASTASIOS MARCOS, and STEPHEN J. BAHR (1987). "The role of peers in the complex etiology of adolescent drug use." *Criminology* 25: 323–340.

KROHN, MARVIN D., RONALD L. AKERS, MARCIA J. RADOSEVICH, and LONN LANZA-KADUCE (1982). "Norm qualities and adolescent drinking and drug behavior:

The effects of norm quality and reference group on using and abusing alcohol and marijuana." *Journal of Drug Issues* 4: 343–460.

KROHN, MARVIN D., LONN LANZA-KADUCE, and RONALD L. AKERS (1984). "Community context and theories of deviant behavior: An examination of social learning and social bonding theories." *Sociological Quarterly* 25: 353–371.

KROHN, MARVIN D., and WILLIAM F. SKINNER (1992). "Age and gender differences in a social process model of adolescent cigarette use." *Sociological Inquiry* 62: 56–82.

KROHN, MARVIN D., WILLIAM F. SKINNER, JAMES L. MASSEY, and RONALD L. AKERS (1985). "Social learning theory and adolescent cigarette smoking: A longitudinal study." *Social Problems* 32: 455–473.

KUNKEL, JOHN H. (1970). *Society and Economic Growth: A Behavioral Perspective of Social Change.* New York: Oxford University Press.

——— (1975). *Behavior, Social Problems, and Change.* Englewood Cliffs, NJ: Prentice Hall.

LANZA-KADUCE, LONN (1988). "Perceptual deterrence and drinking and driving among college students." *Criminology* 26: 321–341.

LANZA-KADUCE, LONN, RONALD L. AKERS, MARVIN D. KROHN, and MARCIA RADOSEVICH (1982). "Conceptual and analytical models in testing social learning theory." *American Sociological Review* 47: 169–173.

——— (1984). "Cessation of alcohol and drug use among adolescents: A social learning model." *Deviant Behavior* 5: 79–99.

LAUER, RONALD M., RONALD L. AKERS, JAMES MASSEY, and WILLIAM CLARKE (1982). "The evaluation of cigarette smoking among adolescents: The Muscatine study." *Preventive Medicine* 11: 417–428.

LOPEZ, JOSE MANUEL OTERO, LOURDES MIRON REDONDO, and ANGELES LUENGO MARTIN (1989). "Influence of family and peer group on the use of drugs by adolescents." *International Journal of the Addictions* 24: 1065–1082.

MARCOS, ANASTASIOS M., STEPHEN J. BAHR, and RICHARD E. JOHNSON (1986). "Test of bonding/association theory of adolescent drug use." *Social Forces* 65: 135–161.

McPHAIL, CLARK, and CYNTHIA REXROAT (1979). "Mead versus Blumer: The divergent methodological perspectives of social behaviorism and symbolic interactionism." *American Sociological Review* 44: 449–467.

——— (1980). "Ex cathedra Blumer or ex libris Mead?" *American Sociological Review* 45: 420–430.

MENARD, SCOTT (1992). "Demographic and theoretical variables in the age-period-cohort analysis of illegal behavior." *Journal of Research in Crime and Delinquency* 29: 178–199.

MILLER, SUSAN L., and LEEANN IOVANNI (1994). "Determinants of perceived risk of formal sanction for courtship violence." *Justice Quarterly* 11: 281–312.

MOFFITT, TERRI E. (1983). "The learning theory model of punishment: Implications for delinquency deterrence." *Criminal Justice and Behavior* 10: 131–158.

MOLM, LINDA D. (1981). "The legitimacy of behavioral theory as a sociological perspective." *American Sociologist* 16: 153–165.

NAGPAUL, HANS (1985). "Patterns of homicide in North India: Some sociological hypotheses." *International Journal of Offender Therapy and Comparative Criminology* 29: 147–158.

NEAPOLITAN, JERRY (1981). "Parental influences on aggressive behavior: A social learning approach." *Adolescence* 16: 831–840.

PATERNOSTER RAYMOND, LINDA E. SALTZMAN, GORDON P. WALDO, and THEODORE G. CHIRICOS (1983). "Perceived risk and social control: Do sanctions really deter?" *Law and Society Review* 17: 457–479.

PEARSON, FRANK, and NEIL ALAN WEINER (1985). "Toward an integration of criminological theories." *Journal of Criminal Law and Criminology* 76: 116–150.

Perry, D. G., and K. Bussey (1977). "Self-reinforcement in high and low aggressive boys following acts of aggression." *Child Development* 48: 653–658.

Rachman, Stanley, and John Teasdale (1970). *Aversion Therapy and Behavior Disorders.* Coral Gables, FL: University of Miami Press.

Rotter, Julian (1954). *Social Learning and Clinical Psychology.* Englewood Cliffs, NJ: Prentice Hall.

Rushton, O. Phillippe (1979). "Effects of prosocial television and film material on the behavior of viewers." In L. Berkowitz, ed., *Advances in Experimental Social Psychology,* 321–351. New York: Academic Press.

Schneider, Hans Joachim (1992). "The causation of crime in societal and interpersonal processes of learning and interaction." *EuroCriminology* 4: 5–13.

Sellers, Christine S., and L. Thomas Winfree, Jr. (1990). "Differential associations and definitions: A panel study of youthful drinking behavior." *International Journal of the Addictions* 25: 755–771.

Skinner, B. F. (1953). *Science and Human Behavior.* New York: Macmillan.

——— (1971). *Beyond Freedom and Dignity.* New York: Knopf.

Snyder, Scott (1991). "Movies and juvenile delinquency: An overview." *Adolescence* 26: 121–132.

Stafford, Mark C., and Sheldon Eckland-Olson (1982). "On social learning and deviant behavior: A reappraisal of the findings." *American Sociological Review* 47: 167–169.

Strickland, Donald E. (1982). "Social learning and deviant behavior: A comment and a critique." *American Sociological Review* 47: 162–167.

Tontodonato, Pamela (1992). "Dating violence, social learning theory, and gender: A multivariate analysis." *Violence and Victims* 7: 3–14.

Ullman, Leonard P., and Leonard Krasner (1969). *A Psychological Approach to Abnormal Behavior.* Englewood Cliffs, NJ: Prentice Hall.

Veneziano, Carol, and Louis Veneziano (1988). "Knowledge of social skills among institutionalized juvenile delinquents: An assessment." *Criminal Justice and Behavior* 15: 152–171.

Vreeland, R. G., and M. B. Waller (1979). *Personality Theory and Firesetting: An Elaboration of a Psychological Model.* University of North Carolina at Chapel Hill, U.S. National Bureau of Standards. Washington, DC: U.S. Government Printing Office.

Warr, Mark (1993). "Age, peers and delinquency." *Criminology* 31: 17–40.

Watson, John B. (1930). *Behaviorism,* 2nd ed. Chicago: University of Chicago Press.

Whitebeck, Les B., and Ronald L. Simons (1993). "A comparison of adaptive strategies and patterns of victimization among homeless adolescents and adults." *Violence and Victims* 8: 135–152.

Wiltfang, Gregory L., and John K. Cochran (1994). "The sanctuary movement and the smuggling of undocumented Central Americans into the United States: Crime, deviance, or defiance?" *Sociological Spectrum* 14: 101–128.

Winfree, L. Thomas Jr., Teresa V. Backstrom, and Larry G. Mays (1994). "Social learning theory, self-reported delinquency, and youth gangs: A new twist on a general theory of crime and delinquency." *Youth and Society* 26: 147–177.

Winfree, L. Thomas Jr., Finn-Aage Esbensen, and D. Wayne Osgood (1996). "Evaluating a school-based gang-prevention program." *Evaluation Review* 20: 181–203.

Winfree, L. Thomas, Jr., and Curt T. Griffiths (1983). "Social learning and adolescent marijuana use: A trend study of deviant behavior in a rural middle school." *Rural Sociology* 48: 219–239.

Winfree L. Thomas, Jr., Curt T. Griffiths, and Christine S. Sellers (1989). "Social learning theory, drug use, and American Indian youths: A cross-cultural test." *Justice Quarterly* 6: 395–417.

Winfree L. Thomas, Jr., Larry G. Mays, and Teresa V. Backstrom (1994). "Youth gangs and incarcerated delinquents: Exploring the ties between gang membership, delinquency, and social learning theory." *Justice Quarterly* 11: 229–256.

Winfree L. Thomas, Jr., Christine S. Sellers, and Dennis L. Clason (1993). "Social learning and adolescent deviance abstention: Toward understanding the reasons for initiating, quitting, and avoiding drugs." *Journal of Quantitative Criminology* 9: 101–125.

Winfree, L. Thomas, Jr., Harold E. Theis, and Curt T. Griffiths (1981). "Drug use in rural America: A cross-cultural examination of complementary social deviance theories." *Youth and Society* 12: 465–489.

Wood, Peter B., John K. Cochran, Betty Pfefferbaum, and Bruce J. Arneklev (1995). "Sensation-seeking and delinquent substance use: An extension of learning theory." *Journal of Drug Issues* 25: 173–193.

Wood, Peter B., Walter R. Gove, James A. Wilson, and John K. Cochran (1997). "Nonsocial reinforcement and habitual criminal conduct: An extension of learning theory." *Criminology* 35: 335–367.

12

RATIONAL THEORIES

INTRODUCTION

An entire group of contemporary theories is referred to as rational theories. Rational theories cover a range of psychological and sociological versions. The versions we cover in this chapter are sociological in orientation and are alternatively known as "lifestyle" or "routine activities" theories. One psychological variant, cognitive theory (Walters and White, 1989), was briefly examined in Chapter 3 on the Positive School. Another older perspective, deterrence, which is also directly associated with rationality and which has experienced a revival from the 1970s to the present, has already been discussed in Chapter 2 on the Classical School.

THE HERITAGE OF THE THEORY

The Social Heritage

The late 1970s and 1980s were a period of conservative thought, politics, and economic policies. Beginning with the oil crisis and Iranian hostage incident, Americans seemed to feel threatened, and they retreated to traditional values. Liberal policies were supplanted, and the term "liberal" even became an epithet to be used for political gain by conservatives. Reflecting the mood of the citizenry, politicians reinstated conservative governmental policies, increased defense budgets, removed restrictions on businesses, and attempted to trim welfare programs.

For criminal justice and crime, this was a time of crime control and punitive policies. Criminals were seen as people who were bad (Wilson, 1975) and who purposefully decided to commit criminal acts. They were to be punished because they "deserved it." Victims' rights were introduced into the criminal justice system, and victims were asked for their opinion about sentences. The country decided, as a whole, that more severe punishment would help to solve the crime problem. As a result, more prisons were built over a short period of time than ever before. The United States declared war on crime and shortly thereafter discovered the drug problem. The country then declared war on drugs and made drugs a problem to be handled by the criminal justice system. Drug users and sellers were targeted in a massive law enforcement effort, and the new prisons were soon filled to capacity.

All in all, the 1980s represented a time when U.S. society was punitively oriented and relatively intolerant. Several political and power groups emerged, each advocating their own position with little concern for others. Each group explained why others were not to be trusted, were doing bad things to the country, or had incorrect values. Indeed, all these things seemed to come together during the Republican Convention in 1992 and probably served as a major reason George Bush was not reelected. Against this backdrop, scholars were gaining ideas and reacting to popular positions.

The Intellectual Heritage

Throughout the 1980s some criminologists observed that the field was growing theoretically stagnant (Williams, 1984; Meier, 1985; Whitehead, 1986; Braithwaite, 1989). The 1970s were criticized as unimaginative and lacking creativity for criminological theory. The lone exception seemed to be the progressive theorizing present in radical and critical theory (Gordon, 1973; Chambliss, 1975; Spitzer, 1975; Quinney, 1977; Tifft, 1979). As the 1980s progressed, however, a concern with theoretical criminology seemed to grow. That effort seemed to be balanced with popular, antitheoretical positions taken by some writers on crime (Wilson, 1975) and administrators in government criminal justice circles. Just as rehabilitation was pronounced dead in the 1970s, so was criminological theorizing pronounced a waste of money and effort in the 1980s. It would suffice, we were told, that evil people would be held responsible for their actions and punished. Our needs were simple: more efficient criminal justice systems, more prisons, and more police officers on the street.

If people are indeed evil or self-centered, the problem was not how to explain the background factors of criminality, but instead to explain how criminals think differently. The criminal personality theory of Samuel Yochelson and Stanton Samenow (1976) began the period, but criminologists were still sociologically oriented enough to want a more social perspective. Thus, scholars returned to some of the central ideas of the old Classical School: rational humans, deterrence, and punishment. In fact, much of the new criminology has been called "neoclassical theory" by some criminologists (Brown, Esbensen, and Geis, 1991).

Finally, just as self-report studies had created a new form of evidence for crime theories, the emergence of national victimization studies in 1972 provided yet another set of facts to be explained. By 1980, victimization statistics had become a mainstay of criminological evidence about crime. And, as was probably inevitable, these statistics provided the fuel for the new rationalist theories and a new paradigm for criminology.

THE THEORETICAL PERSPECTIVE

With the late 1970s' emphasis on individual responsibility, criminologists realized no versions of theory contained an assumption of a rational, thinking individual. The closest theory to include such a criteria was David Matza's (1964) drift theory, which introduced the "will" as a predisposing factor in the decision to commit deviance. Matza did not mean to convey, however, that the individual had free will and made a calculated, rational decision to commit a delinquent act. Indeed, it is significant that Matza referred to the theory as "soft determinism" rather than as "soft free will." While sociologists were pondering how to introduce rationality, economists began discussing crime and, with their usual approach to behavior, assumed criminals make a rational decision to commit crime (Becker, 1974, 1976; Ehrlich, 1974). Borrowing from the economic approach, today's rational choice theorists talk in terms of opportunities, costs, and benefits when discussing offenders' decisions to commit crimes. In a sense, the economic approach brought us full circle to the two-hundred-year-old classical position that individual behavior is a calculation of gain and pain. Indeed, rationalist theories seem to share a common belief that criminal rationality is hedonistic and certain background factors lead to such a result.

The beginnings of rational theory were sociological in orientation and relied on the new victimization statistics. Variously called lifestyle theory (Hindelang, Gottfredson, and Garofalo, 1978), routine activities theory (Cohen and Felson, 1979), opportunity perspective (Mayhew et al., 1976), or the rational choice model (Cornish and Clark, 1986), the idea was to describe the factors one would expect to find in aggregate decisions to commit crime. Those decisions were expected to reflect ease of committing crime, the availability of worthwhile targets, and the anticipated presence of witnesses.

Routine Activities Theory

The routine activities perspective advanced by Larry Cohen and Marcus Felson (1979), initially viewed as a very practical look at crime, gained popularity and became a staple of the 1980s. One reason for its popularity was the easy connection with the burgeoning interest in victimology and a new ecological crime-prevention approach. The major reason, however, was the resurgence of assumptions about the nature of humans as rational beings. Either way, routine activity theory clearly has been an important contribution to criminology.

Routine activity theory basically states that the volume of criminal offenses is related to the nature of everyday patterns of social interaction. As the pattern of social interaction changes, so do the number of crimes. Cohen and Felson drew heavily from the work of Amos Hawley (1950), who had sketched out a popular theory of human ecology. Hawley emphasized the nature of routine activities as an essential part of everyday life. Routine activity means any commonly occurring social activity providing for basic needs. Examples include formal work, leisure pursuits, obtaining shelter, child rearing, grocery shopping, and sleeping. As social change disrupts or changes routine activities, social disorganization can occur. In emphasizing both social disorganization and ecology, routine activities theory can be considered a continuation of the work of the Chicago School.

Cohen and Felson's theory has three major areas of focus for a predatory criminal event, or, perhaps more appropriately, a victimization event. First, they said there must be a **motivated offender.** They were not particularly concerned with this factor, however. Existing criminological theories uniformly focus on the offender and the influences motivating him or her to an offense; Cohen and Felson wanted to examine the other pieces of the puzzle. Second, they speculated there must be a **suitable target:** that is, something worth stealing or taking, or that has the appearance of worth. Third, they said there must be an **absence of a capable guardian:** no one present who could prevent the occurrence of the crime.

In addition to these three elements, Cohen and Felson were concerned with **changes in society**, particularly those leading to social disorganization. As routine activities change, so does crime opportunity. In fact, they suggested that social changes since World War II led to routine activities taking place farther from the home, thus creating greater opportunities for crime. Indeed, under this reasoning, ecological and environmental factors suggest certain areas will be more prone to crime than others.

These ingredients come together as follows. Routine activities serve to bring offenders and victims into contact and create a convergence in time and space of motivated offenders, suitable targets, and absence of guardians. If one of these components is missing, crime is not likely to happen. However, if all components are present (and one element is even strengthened), the probability of crime increases. Because of routine activities, suitable victims (or targets) are found more frequently in some settings than in others. For example, work schedules present opportunities for burglary by presenting a suitable target (a house) with few guardians (people at home). Social changes such as an increased number of women in the work force have resulted in fewer people at home during work hours, thereby increasing the probability of a successful burglary. Moreover, Cohen and Felson argue that the changes that have taken place in American society have resulted in greater interaction with motivated offenders, more suitable targets, and a greater absence of guardians. Even if the number of motivated offenders does not increase, crime will be greater because of the increase in the latter two elements.

The theory can be used to explain rates of victimization for specific crimes. Based on differences in their routine activities, certain individuals will be more susceptible than others to robbery, burglary, rape, and homicide. Similarly, certain locations are more susceptible to crime because of the type of activities and the amount of social activity present. As areas gain a reputation for being crime "**hot spots**" (the most crime-ridden places in the city), feedback occurs, and fewer people go there at certain times. As a result, the absence of guardians is even greater, and offenders define more individuals in the area as suitable victims. Hot spots themselves can be determined empirically by finding their geographical centers and then mapping their boundaries (see Spring and Block, 1988; Sherman, Gartin, and Buerger, 1988; Roncek and Maier, 1991; Block and Block, 1995).

Routine activity theory has also been extended to offenders in an attempt to explain what may facilitate crime. Marcus Felson has explored the implications of routine activities for offenders (1986a, 1994), and others have discussed it as well (Riley, 1987; Gottfredson and Hirschi, 1990; Miethe and Meier, 1994). Wayne Osgood, Janet Wilson, and colleagues (1996) have proposed that unstructured and unsupervised socializing among young adults (a routine activity) can increase deviance. This happens because of an absence of authority figures, a reduction in social control responses, available unsupervised time, and an increase in the probability of reward for deviant behavior. Thus, the routine activities approach, which originally encompassed only victimization, is now a theory of offending as well.

Lifestyle Theory

The question of risk is central to the theoretical perspective developed by Michael Hindelang, Michael Gottfredson, and James Garofalo (1978). In short, they wanted to know why certain groups of people are at greater risk of being victims of crime than others. Their answer is that patterned activities, or lifestyles, of individuals lead to differential victimization rates. These lifestyles are characterized by daily functions involving both work and leisure activities.

Lifestyles are influenced by three basic elements. First, the **social roles** played by people in society. Based on the expectations of others, people conduct themselves in certain ways and construct lifestyles more or less conducive to victimization. For this reason, young persons are more frequently victimized because they have social roles that require frequent social activities outside the home, particularly at night. The second element is **position in the social structure.** Generally, the higher one's position, the lower the risk of victimization—largely because of the kind of activities in which one engages and the places one frequents. The third element is a **rational component,** in which decisions are made about which behaviors are desirable. Based on one's social role and structural position, decisions can be made to restrict routine behaviors to relatively safe ones or to accept risk. Young people tend to enhance their victimization probabilities by choosing to engage in activities in time and space with greater risk levels, such as going to nightclubs or attending sporting events.

When lifestyle variations are taken into account, victimization experiences and potential victimizations are relatively predictable. For those whose social and structural background creates greater interaction with offenders and places conducive to crime, there is indeed a greater risk of victimization. Similarly, individuals of higher social class engage in fewer routine activities (i.e., have a lifestyle) that involve crossing paths with fewer criminals (at least of the street-criminal variety). Such risks can be decreased, or increased, beyond the levels normally expected for one's group by the conscious decisions individuals make to engage in certain lifestyles.

The Rational Choice Perspective

A final approach to rational theory is a more generic one: rational choice theory. Identified most strongly with Derek Cornish and Ronald Clarke (1986, 1987), there are many criminologists who have embraced at least some part of the perspective, including Travis Hirschi (1986). Rational choice theory explains offender motivation to crime as an attempt to meet commonplace needs. Rationality is the decision-making process of determining the opportunities for meeting those needs, the potential costs of action, and the anticipated benefits. Full rationality is not required by the perspective, nor is the offender assumed to be sophisticated in his or her decision making. Adequate or accurate information is not even necessary. Thus, it is more precise to say the offender demonstrates limited rationality.

Rational choice theorists separate decision making into two different areas: involvement decisions and event decisions. *Involvement decisions* are those in which the choice is made to become involved in an offense, continue with an offense, or withdraw from an offense. These types of decisions are instrumental in the weighing of costs and benefits. The other form of decision making, *event decisions*, are those in which the tactics of carrying out an offense (the demands placed on the offender) are determined. If the tactics are easy, the involvement decision gains potential benefits. If the tactics are difficult, the involvement decision loses potential benefits.

The tactics issue also suggests that there are crime-specific decisions to be made. Because the demands of committing an offense vary by the offense itself, one can assume rational choices are themselves crime-specific. In addition, the needs of offenders vary—as do the needs offenses will meet.

Therefore, rational choice theorists view the needs/demands choices as crime-specific and focus on the prevention of individual crime types, rather than on a general approach to preventing crime (such as deterrence). Each form of crime offers different "choice-structuring properties" where a combination of availability and attractiveness can appeal to certain individuals at certain times.

Crime prevention under this model, then, is based on decreasing opportunity and attractiveness of specific crimes. Cornish and Clarke recommend drawing up lists of choice-structuring properties for various types of crime. Each list would be used to design greater cost into the offense and reduce its attractiveness. To build such lists, more information is needed about the ecological distribution of crimes and offenders' perceptions of opportunities, costs, and benefits. Because the theoretical perspective has obvious direct policy implications, rational choice theory has been popular within governmental circles, and particularly so within the criminological research centers of Great Britain.

CLASSIFICATION OF THE THEORY

As a whole, rational theories represent a return to some of the concerns of the old Classical School. They assume people have the capacity to make their own decisions, yet most of the theories also restrict those decisions by including the effects of the environment or social structure. Therefore, rational theories are primarily characterized by "**soft free will**" and are *classical.* They are also *consensus-oriented* because they assume an individual who decides to commit a crime chooses to behave in opposition to the established order of society. In addition, the approach tends to be more *process-oriented* and *microtheoretical,* with an emphasis on the individual making the decision. This is not always the case, however. Some versions are more concerned with the structural and environmental considerations that influence choices; thus, these are more macrotheoretical in character. In short, there are a number of variations within the general perspective of rational theory. As opposed to most earlier theories, however, the most distinctive feature of rational theory is the free-will, individualistic assumption.

Major Points of the Rational Theory Model

1. Humans live in a world in which behavior is partially determined and partially free will.
2. Social structures and institutions create the conditions of life for individuals in society.
3. Conditions of life are the chief determinants of social interactions between people in society and the social activities in which those people engage.
4. Social interactions and activities create generalized lifestyles, or routine activities, for groups in society. Those lifestyles are more conducive to some pursuits, and less so to others.

5. To the extent crime occurs in society, lifestyles are a critical element in placing people at risk of victimization and in generating needs that offenders wish to satisfy.
6. As changes in society produce changes in lifestyles, the general risk of victimization and probability of offending changes accordingly.
7. Individuals may introduce variation into their general victimization risk through conscious decisions to follow or avoid certain activities and areas. Similarly, offenders may increase or decrease their opportunities and costs.
8. Those individuals who make lifestyle choices with increased exposure are increasing their risk of victimization by enhancing the cost-benefit gains of potential offenders.

EPILOGUE: CURRENT DIRECTIONS AND POLICY IMPLICATIONS

Rational theories are very popular today. They combine elements from the old Chicago School, newer ways of looking at communities, and even concepts from environmental design. In one sense, they offer a promising approach to integrating knowledge and research findings on ecological areas with popular opinion stressing individual moral responsibility for one's actions. While we have introduced three different types of rational theories, the fact is most researchers and theorists have tended to combine both routine activities and lifestyle approaches into a generic rational choice model (see Ken Tunnell's *Choosing Crime* [1992] for one attempt to explain property crime).

One of the major advantages to rational theories is they are practical and relevant to policy. First, they give permission for punishment of offenders, because offenders are responsible for their actions and make purposeful decisions to commit crime. This, then, is a politically popular approach to crime causation. Criminals can be punished because they deserve it and they should have known better. Second, rational theories emphasize victims. Victim assistance programs help prepare victims for the criminal justice process, introduce victim testimony to assure just deserts for offenders, and increase the chances of conviction. They also place some responsibility on potential victims to recognize risk and take preventive measures to avoid being a target. This includes staying away from high-risk places, people, and activities, such as bars in "bad" neighborhoods or automated teller machines at night. Third, the concepts of capable guardians and suitable targets yield a number of environmental design options. Potential areas of change include increasing surveillance in neighborhoods (neighborhood watch programs, Guardian Angels, volunteer civilian patrols), target-hardening with deadbolt locks and burglar bars, and placing more lights in poorly lit areas.

BIBLIOGRAPHY

AGNEW, ROBERT (1990). "The origins of delinquent events: An examination of offender account." *Journal of Research in Crime and Delinquency* 27: 267–294.

AKERS, RONALD L. (1990). "Rational choice, deterrence, and social learning theory in criminology: The path not taken." *Journal of Criminal Law and Criminology* 81: 653–676.

AUSTIN, JAMES, and JOHN IRWIN (1993). Does Imprisonment Reduce Crime? A Critique of "Voodoo" *Criminology*. San Francisco: National Council on Crime and Delinquency.

BACHMAN, RONET, RAYMOND PATERNOSTER, and SALLY WARD (1992). "The rationality of sexual offending: Testing a deterrence/rational choice conception of sexual assault." *Law and Society Review* 26: 343–372.

BECKER, GARY S. (1968). "Crime and punishment: An economic approach." *Journal of Political Economy* 76: 169–217.

———— (1974). "Crime and punishment: An economic approach." In G. Becker and W. Landes, eds., *Essays in the Economics of Crime and Punishment*, 1–54. New York: Columbia University Press.

———— (1976). *The Economic Approach to Human Behavior*. Chicago: University of Chicago Press.

BECKER, GARY S., and WILLIAM M. LANDES (1974). *Essays in the Economics of Crime and Punishment*. New York: National Bureau of Economic Research.

BIRON, LOUISE L., and CAROL LADOUCEUR (1991). "The boy next door: Local teen-age burglars in Montreal." *Security Journal* 2: 200–204.

BLOCK, RICHARD, and CAROLYN R. BLOCK (1995). "Space, place and crime: Hot spot areas and hot places of liquor-related crime." In J. E. Eck and D. Weisburd, eds., *Crime and Place*, 145–184. Monsey, NY: Criminal Justice Press.

BRAITHWAITE, JOHN (1989). "The state of criminology: Theoretical decay or renaissance." *Australian and New Zealand Journal of Criminology* 22: 129–135.

BRANTINGHAM, PATRICIA L., and PAUL J. BRANTINGHAM (1993). "Environment, routine, and situation: Toward a pattern theory of crime." *Advances in Criminological Theory* 5: 259–294.

BROWN, STEPHEN E., FINN AAGE ESBENSEN, and GILBERT GEIS (1991). *Criminology: Explaining Crime and Its Context*. Cincinnati, OH: Anderson.

BUENO DE MESQUITA, BRUCE, and LAWRENCE E. COHEN (1995). "Self-interest, equity, and crime control: A game-theoretic analysis of criminal decision making." *Criminology* 33: 483–518.

CALHOUN, THOMAS C., and GREG WEAVER (1996). "Rational decision-making among male street prostitutes." *Deviant Behavior* 17: 209–227.

CANTOR, DAVID, and JAMES P. LYNCH (1988). "Empirical test of opportunity theories of victimization: Multi-level and domain-specific models." Draft of final report submitted to National Institute of Justice, Washington, DC.

CARROLL, JOHN S. (1982). "Committing a crime: The offender's decision." In V. J. Konecni and E. B. Ebbesen, eds., *The Criminal Justice System: A Social-Psychological Analysis*, 49–67. San Francisco: Freeman.

CHAMBLISS, WILLIAM J. (1975). "Toward a political economy of crime." *Theory and Society* 2: 149–169.

CLARKE, RONALD V. G. (1983). "Situational crime prevention: Its theoretical basis and practical scope." In M. Tonry and A. J. Reiss, Jr., eds., *Crime and Justice: An Annual Review of Research*, vol. 4, 225–256. Chicago: University of Chicago Press.

———— (1995). "Situational crime prevention." In M. Tonry and D. P. Farrington, eds., *Building a Safer Society: Strategic Approaches to Crime Prevention. Crime and Justice*, vol. 19, 91–150. Chicago: University of Chicago Press.

CLARKE, RONALD V. G., and DEREK B. CORNISH (1985). "Modeling offenders' decisions: A framework for research and policy." In M. Tonry and N. Morris, eds., *Crime and Justice: An Annual Review of Research,* vol. 6, 147–185. Chicago: University of Chicago Press.

CLARKE, RONALD V. G., and PATRICIA M. HARRIS (1992). "A rational choice perspective on the targets of automobile theft." *Criminal Behaviour and Mental Health* 2: 25–42.

COHEN, LAWRENCE E., and DAVID CANTOR (1980). "The determinants of larceny: An empirical and theoretical study." *Journal of Research in Crime and Delinquency* 17: 140–159.

—— (1981). "Residential burglary in the United States: Lifestyle and demographic factors associated with the probability of victimization." *Journal of Research in Crime and Delinquency* 18: 113–127.

COHEN, LAWRENCE E., and MARCUS FELSON (1979). "Social change and crime rate trends: A routine activities approach." *American Sociological Review* 44: 588–607.

COHEN, LAWRENCE E., JAMES KLUEGEL, and KENNETH LAND (1981). "Social inequality and predatory criminal victimization: An exposition and test of a formal theory." *American Sociological Review* 46: 505–524.

COHEN, LAWRENCE E., and KENNETH LAND (1987). "Age structure and crime: Symmetry versus asymmetry and the projection of crime rates through the 1990s." *American Sociological Review* 52: 170–183.

COHEN, LAWRENCE E., and RICHARD MACHALEK (1988). "A general theory of expropriative crime: An evolutionary ecological approach." *American Journal of Sociology* 94: 465–501.

COLLINS, JAMES J., BRENDA G. COX, and PATRICK A. LANGAN (1987). "Job activities and personal crime victimization: Implications for theory." *Social Science Research* 16: 345–360.

CORBETT, CLAIRE, and FRANCES SIMON(1992). "Decisions to break or adhere to the rules of the road, viewed from the rational choice perspective." *British Journal of Criminology* 32: 537–549.

CORNISH, DEREK, (1993). "Theories of action in criminology: Learning theory and rational choice approaches." *Advances in Criminological Theory* 5: 351–382.

CORNISH, DEREK B., and RONALD V. G. CLARKE, eds. (1986). *The Reasoning Criminal: Rational Choice Perspectives on Offending.* New York: Springer-Verlag.

—— (1987). "Understanding crime displacement: An application of rational choice theory." *Criminology* 25: 933–947.

CROMWELL, PAUL F., JAMES N. OLSON, D'AUNN W. AVARY and ALAN MARKS. (1991). "How drugs affect decisions by burglars." *International Journal of Offender Therapy and Comparative Criminology* 35: 310–321.

CUSSON, MAURICE (1993). "A strategic analysis of crime: Criminal tactics as responses to precriminal situations." *Advances in Criminological Theory* 5: 295–304.

EHRLICH, ISAAC (1973). "Participation in illegitimate activities: A theoretical and empirical investigation." *Journal of Political Economy* 81: 521–565.

—— (1974). "Participation in illegitimate activities: An economic analysis." In G. Becker and W. Landes, eds., *Essays in the Economics of Crime and Punishment,* 68–134. New York: Columbia University Press.

EIDE, ERLING (1994). *Economics of Crime: Deterrence and the Rational Offender.* North Holland: Elsevier.

FATTAH, EZZAT A. (1993). "The rational choice/opportunity perspectives as a vehicle for integrating criminological and victimological theories." *Advances in Criminological Theory* 5: 225–258.

FEENEY, FLOYD (1986). "Robbers as decision-makers." In D. Cornish and R. Clarke, eds., *The Reasoning Criminal: Rational Choice Perspectives on Offending,* 53–71. New York: Springer-Verlag.

FELSON, MARCUS (1986a). "Linking criminal choices, routine activities, informal control, and criminal outcomes." In D. Cornish and R. Clarke, eds., *The Reasoning Criminal: Rational Choice Perspectives on Offending*, 119–128. New York: Springer-Verlag.

———— (1986b). "Predicting crime potential at any point on the city map." In R. Figlio, S. Hakim, and G. Rengert, eds., *Metropolitan Crime Patterns*, 127–136. Monsey, NY: Criminal Justice Press.

———— (1987). "Routine activities and crime prevention in the developing metropolis." *Criminology* 25: 911–931.

———— (1990). "Preventing crime at Newark subway stations." *Security Journal* 1: 137–142.

———— (1994). *Crime and Everyday Life: Insights and Implications for Society*. Thousand Oaks, CA: Pine Forge Press.

FELSON, MARCUS, and LAWRENCE E. COHEN (1980). "Human ecology and crime: A routine activity approach." *Human Ecology* 4: 389–406.

FIGLIO, ROBERT M., SIMON HAKIM, and GEORGE F. RENGERT, eds. (1986). *Metropolitan Crime Patterns*. Monsey, NY: Criminal Justice Press.

GAROFALO, JAMES (1986). "Lifestyles and victimization: An update." In E. Fattah, ed., *From Crime Policy to Victim Policy: Reorienting the Justice System*, 135–155. New York: St. Martin's Press.

———— (1987). "Reassessing the lifestyle model of criminal victimization." In M. Gottfredson and T. Hirschi, eds., *Positive Criminology: Essays in Honor of Michael J. Hindelang*, 23–42. Beverly Hills, CA: Sage.

GAROFALO, JAMES, LESLIE SIEGEL, and JOHN LAUB (1987). "School-related victimizations among adolescents: An analysis of National Crime Survey (NCS) narratives." *Journal of Quantitative Criminology* 3: 321–338.

GORDON, DAVID M. (1973). "Capitalism, class and crime in America." *Crime and Delinquency* 19: 163–186.

GOTTFREDSON, MICHAEL (1986). "Substantive contributions of victimization surveys." In M. Tonry and N. Morris, eds., *Crime and Justice: An Annual Review of Research*, vol. 7, 251–287. Chicago: University of Chicago Press.

GOTTFREDSON, MICHAEL, and TRAVIS HIRSCHI, eds. (1987). *Positive Criminology: Essays in Honor of Michael J. Hindelang*. Beverly Hills, CA: Sage.

———— (1990). *A General Theory of Crime*. Stanford, CA: Stanford University Press.

GRASMICK, HAROLD G., and ROBERT J. BURSIK, JR. (1990). "Conscience, significant others, and rational choice: Extending the deterrence model." *Law and Society Review* 24: 837–861.

GRASMICK, HAROLD G., ROBERT J. BURSIK, JR., and BRUCE J. ARNEKLEV (1993). "Reduction in drunk driving as a response to increased threats of shame, embarrassment, and legal sanctions." *Criminology* 31: 41–67.

GRASMICK, HAROLD G., ROBERT J. BURSIK, JR., and JOHN K. COCHRAN (1991). "'Render unto Caesar what is Caesar's': Religiosity and taxpayers' inclinations to cheat." *Sociological Quarterly* 32: 251–266.

HARDING, RICHARD W. (1993). "Gun use in crime, rational choice, and social learning theory." *Advances in Criminological Theory* 5: 85–102.

HARTNAGEL, TIMOTHY, and G. LEE WON (1990). "Urban crime in Canada." *Canadian Journal of Criminology* 32: 591–606.

HAWLEY, AMOS (1950). *Human Ecology: A Theory of Community Structure*. New York: Ronald.

HINDELANG, MICHAEL J., MICHAEL GOTTFREDSON, and JAMES GAROFALO (1978). *Victims of Personal Crime: An Empirical Foundation for a Theory of Personal Victimization*. Cambridge, MA: Ballinger.

HIRSCHI, TRAVIS (1986). "On the compatibility of rational choice and social control theories of crime." In D. Cornish and R. Clarke, eds., *The Reasoning Criminal: Rational Choice Perspectives on Offending*, 105–118. New York: Springer-Verlag.

HOLZMAN, HAROLD R. (1983). "Rationalistic opportunity perspective on criminal behavior: Toward a reformulation of the theoretical basis for the notion of property crime as work." *Crime and Delinquency* 28: 233–246.

HOMEL, ROSS (1993). "Drivers who drink and rational choice: Random breath testing and the process of deterrence." *Advances in Criminological Theory* 5: 59–84.

HORNEY, JULIE, and INEKE HAEN MARSHALL (1992). "Risk perceptions among serious offenders: The role of crime and punishment." *Criminology* 23: 575–592.

HOUGH, MICHAEL (1987). "Offender's choice of targets: Findings from the Victims Survey." *Journal of Quantitative Criminology* 3: 355–369.

JACOB, HERBERT (1979). "Rationality and criminality." *Social Science Quarterly* 59: 584–585.

JEFFERY, C. RAY, and DIANE L. ZAHM (1993). "Crime prevention through environmental design, opportunity theory, and rational choice models." *Advances in Criminological Theory* 5: 323–350.

JENSEN, GARY F., and DAVID BROWNFIELD (1987). "Gender, lifestyles, and victimization: Beyond routine activity." *Violence and Victims* 1: 85–99.

JOHNSON, BRUCE D., MANGAI NATARAJAN, and HARRY SANABRIA (1993). "'Successful' criminal careers: Toward an ethnography within the rational choice perspective." *Advances in Criminological Theory* 5: 201–224.

JOHNSON, ERIC, and JOHN PAYNE (1986). "The decision to commit a crime: An information-processing analysis." In D. Cornish and R. Clarke, eds., *The Reasoning Criminal: Rational Choice Perspectives on Offending*, 170–185. New York: Springer-Verlag.

KENNEDY, DANIEL B. (1990). "Facility site selection and analysis through environmental criminology." *Journal of Criminal Justice* 18: 239–252.

KENNEDY, LESLIE, and DAVID FORDE (1990a). "Risky lifestyles and dangerous results: Routine activities and exposure to crime." *Sociology and Social Research* 74: 208–211.

——— (1990b). "Routine activities and crime: An analysis of victimization in Canada." *Criminology* 28: 137–152.

KENNEDY, LESLIE, and ROBERT SILVERMAN (1990). "The elderly victim of homicide: An application of the routine activities approach." *Sociological Quarterly* 31: 307–319.

LADOUCEUR, CAROL, and LOUISE L. BIRON (1993). "Disposing of stolen merchandise— A rational approach?" *Canadian Journal of Criminology* 35: 169–182.

LASLEY, JAMES R. (1989). "Drinking routines/lifestyles and predatory victimization: A causal analysis." *Justice Quarterly* 6: 529–542.

LASLEY, JAMES R., and JILL L. ROSENBAUM (1988). "Routine activities and multiple personal victimization." *Sociology and Social Research* 73: 47–50.

LEBEAU, JAMES L. (1986). "The linkages between routine activities, weather, and calls for police service." *Journal of Police Science and Administration* 14: 137–145.

LEBEAU, JAMES L., and WILLIAM CORCORAN (1990). "Changes in calls for police service with changes in routine activities and the arrival and passage of weather fronts." *Journal of Quantitative Criminology* 6: 269–291.

LESTER, DAVID (1991). "Crime as opportunity: A test of the hypothesis with European homicide rates." *British Journal of Criminology* 31: 186–191.

LEWISCH, PETER (1992). "A case study on the legal regulation of shoplifting in Austria and the 'criminal tourism' from the East." *International Review of Law and Economics* 12: 439–455.

LISKA, ALLEN, and BARBARA D. WARNER (1991). "Functions of crime: A paradoxical process." *American Journal of Sociology* 96: 1441–1463.

LYNCH, JAMES P. (1987). "Routine activity and victimization at work." *Journal of Quantitative Criminology* 3: 283–300.

LYNCH, JAMES P., and DAVID CANTOR (1992). "Ecological and behavioral influences on property victimization at home: Implications for opportunity theory." *Journal of Research in Crime and Delinquency* 29: 335–362.

MACY, MICHAEL W. (1993). "Backward-looking social control." *American Sociological Review* 58: 819–836.

MARONGIU, PIETRO, and RONALD V. G. CLARKE (1993). "Ransom kidnapping in Sardinia, subcultural theory and rational choice." *Advances in Criminological Theory* 5: 179–200.

MASSEY, JAMES, MARVIN KROHN, and LISA BONATI (1989). "Property crime and the routine activities of individuals." *Journal of Research in Crime and Delinquency* 26: 378–400.

MATZA, DAVID (1964). *Delinquency and Drift*. New York: John Wiley.

MAUME, DAVID J., JR. (1989). "Inequality and metropolitan rape rates: A routine activity approach." *Justice Quarterly* 6: 513–528.

MAXFIELD, MICHAEL (1987a). "Household composition, routine activity, and victimization: A comparative analysis." *Journal of Quantitative Criminology* 3: 301–320.

———— (1987b). "Lifestyle and routine activity theories of crime: Empirical studies of victimization, delinquency, and offender decision-making." *Journal of Quantitative Criminology* 3: 275–282.

MAYHEW, PAT M. (1991). "Displacement and vehicle theft: An attempt to reconcile some recent contradictory evidence." *Security Journal* 2: 233–239.

MAYHEW, PAT M., RONALD V. CLARKE, A. STURMAN, and J. M. HOUGH (1976). *Crime as Opportunity*. Home Office Research Study No. 24. London: H. M. Stationary Office.

MEIER, ROBERT F., ed. (1985). *Theoretical Methods in Criminology*. Beverly Hills, CA: Sage.

MENARD, SCOTT (1992). "Demographic and theoretical variables in the age-period-cohort analysis of illegal behavior." *Journal of Research in Crime and Delinquency* 29: 178–199.

MESSNER, STEVEN, and JUDITH BLAU (1987). "Routine leisure activities and rates of crime: A macro-level analysis." *Social Forces* 65: 1035–1052.

MESSNER, STEVEN, and KENNETH TARDIFF (1986). "The social ecology of urban homicide: An application of the 'routine activities' approach." *Criminology* 23: 241–267.

MIETHE, TERANCE D., MICHAEL HUGHES, and DAVID MCDOWALL (1991). "Social change and crime rates: An evaluation of alternative theoretical approaches." *Social Forces* 70: 165–185.

MIETHE, TERANCE D., and ROBERT F. MEIER (1990). "Opportunity, choice, and criminal victimization: A test of a theoretical model." *Journal of Research in Crime and Delinquency* 27: 243–266.

———— (1994). *Crime and Its Social Context: Toward an Integrated Theory of Offenders, Victims and Situations*. Albany: State University of New York Press.

MIETHE, TERANCE D., MARK C. STAFFORD, and J. SCOTT LONG (1987). "Social differentiation in criminal victimization: An application of routine activity/lifestyle theory using panel data." *American Sociological Review* 52: 184–194.

MIETHE, TERANCE D., MARK C. STAFFORD, and DOUGLAS SLOANE (1990). "Lifestyle changes and risks of criminal victimization." *Journal of Quantitative Criminology* 6: 357–376.

NAGIN, DANIEL S., and RAYMOND PATERNOSTER (1993). "Enduring individual differences and rational choice theories of crime." *Law and Society Review* 27: 467–496.

—— (1994). "Personal capital and social control: The deterrence implications of a theory of individual differences in criminal offending." *Criminology* 32: 581–606.

NATARAJAN, MANGAI (1995). "Victimization of women: A theoretical perspective on dowry deaths in India." *International Review of Victimology* 3: 297–308.

NIGGLI, MARCEL A. (1994). "Rational choice theory and crime prevention." *Studies on Crime and Crime Prevention* 3: 83–103.

O'BRIEN, ROBERT M. (1988). "Exploring the intersexual nature of violent crimes." *Criminology* 26: 151–170.

OSGOOD, D. WAYNE, JANET K. WILSON, PATRICK M. O'MALLEY, JERALD G. BACHMAN, and LLOYD D. JOHNSTON (1996). "Routine activities and individual deviant behavior." *American Sociological Review* 61: 635–655.

PALLONE, NATHANIEL J., and JAMES J. HENNESSY (1993). "Tinderbox criminal violence: Neurogenic impulsivity, risk-taking, and the phenomenology of rational choice." *Advances in Criminological Theory* 5: 127–158.

PARKER, ROBERT N. (1995). "Bringing 'booze' back in: The relationship between alcohol and homicide." *Journal of Research in Crime and Delinquency* 32: 2–38.

PARKER, ROBERT N., and ALLISON TOTH (1990). "Family, intimacy, and homicide: A macro-social approach." *Violence and Victims* 5: 195–210.

PATERNOSTER, RAYMOND (1989). "Absolute and restrictive deterrence in a panel of youth: Explaining the onset, persistence/desistance, and frequency of delinquent offending." *Social Problems* 36: 289–309.

PATERNOSTER, RAYMOND, and SALLY SIMPSON (1993). "A rational choice theory of corporate crime." *Advances in Criminological Theory* 5: 37–58.

—— (1996). "Sanction threats and appeals to morality: Testing a rational choice model of corporate crime." *Law and Society Review* 30: 549–583.

PHILIPSON, TOMAS J., and RICHARD A. POSNER (1996). "The economic epidemiology of crime." *Journal of Law and Economics* 39: 405–433.

PILIAVIN, IRVING, ROSEMARY GARTNER, CRAIG THORNTON, and ROSS L. MATSUEDA (1986). "Crime, deterrence, and rational choice." *American Sociological Review* 51: 101–119.

PIQUERO, ALEX, and STEPHEN TIBBETTS (1996). "Specifying the direct and indirect effects of low self-control and situational factors in offenders' decision making." *Justice Quarterly* 13: 481–510.

POLVI, NATALIE (1990). "Repeat break-and-enter victimization: Time course and crime prevention opportunity." *Journal of Police Science and Administration* 17: 8–11.

PYLE, DAVID J. (1995). *Cutting the Costs of Crime: The Economics of Crime and Criminal Justice.* London: Institute of Economic Affairs.

QUINNEY, RICHARD (1977). *Class, State, and Crime.* New York: Longman.

RILEY, DAVID (1987). "Time and crime: The link between teenager lifestyle and delinquency." *Journal of Quantitative Criminology* 3: 339–354.

RONCEK, DENNIS, and PAMELA A. MAIER (1991). "Bars, blocks and crimes revisited: Linking the theory of routine activities to the empiricism of 'hot spots.'" *Criminology* 29: 725–753.

ROSHIER, BOB (1989). *Controlling Crime: The Classical Perspective in Criminology.* Chicago: Lyceum Books.

SAMPSON, ROBERT J. (1987). "Personal violence by strangers: An extension and test of the opportunity model of predatory victimization." *Journal of Criminal Law and Criminology* 78: 327–356.

SAMPSON, ROBERT J., and JANET L. LAURITSEN (1990). "Deviant lifestyles, proximity to crime, and the offender-victim link in personal violence." *Journal of Research in Crime and Delinquency* 27: 110–139.

SAMPSON, ROBERT J., and JOHN D. WOOLDREDGE (1987). "Linking the micro- and macro-level dimensions of lifestyle, routine activity and opportunity models of predatory victimization." *Journal of Quantitative Criminology* 3: 371–394.

SCHNEIDER, ANNE L., and LAURIE ERVIN (1990). "Specific deterrence, rational choice, and decision heuristics: Applications in juvenile justice." *Social Science Quarterly* 71: 585–601.

SHERMAN, LAWRENCE, PATRICK GARTIN, and MICHAEL BUERGER (1988). "Hot spots of predatory crime: Routine activities and the criminology of place." *Criminology* 27: 27–55.

SHOVER, NEAL, and DAVID HONAKER (1992). "The socially bounded decision making of persistent property offenders." *Howard Journal of Criminal Justice* 31: 276–293.

SMITH, DOUGLAS, and G. R. JARJOURA (1989). "Household characteristics, neighborhood composition and victimization risk." *Social Forces* 68: 621–640.

SPITZER, STEVEN (1975). "Toward a Marxian theory of deviance." *Social Problems* 22: 638–651.

SPRING, JAMES W., and CAROLYN R. BLOCK (1988). "Finding crime hot spots: Experiments in the identification of high crime areas." Paper presented at the Annual Meeting of the Midwest Sociological Society, Minneapolis, MN.

STACK, STEVEN (1995). "The effect of temporary residences on burglary: A test of criminal opportunity theory." *American Journal of Criminal Justice* 19: 197–214.

STAHURA, JOHN, and RICHARD HOLLINGER (1988). "A routine activities approach to suburban arson rates." *Sociological Spectrum* 8: 349–369.

STAHURA, JOHN, and JOHN J. SLOAN III (1988). "Urban stratification of places, routine activities and suburban crime rates." *Social Forces* 66: 1102–1118.

STEINMETZ, CARL H. (1985). "Bystanders of crime: Some results from a national survey." *Victimology* 10: 441–460.

TANIOKA, ICHIRO, and DANIEL GLASER (1991). "School uniforms, routine activities, and the social control of delinquency in Japan." *Youth and Society* 23: 50–75.

TAYLOR, MAX (1993). "Rational choice, behavior analysis, and political violence." *Advances in Criminological Theory* 5: 159–178.

TIBBETTS, STEPHEN G., (1997). "Shame and rational choice in offending decisions." *Criminal Justice and Behavior* 24: 234–255.

TIBBETTS, STEPHEN G., and DENISE C. HERZ (1996). "Gender differences in factors of social control and rational choice." *Deviant Behavior* 17: 183–208.

TIFFT, LARRY (1979). "The coming redefinitions of crime: An anarchist perspective." *Social Problems* 26: 392–402.

TRASLER, GORDON (1993). "Conscience, opportunity, rational choice, and crime." *Advances in Criminological Theory* 5: 305–322.

TREMBLAY, PIERRE (1993). "Routine acts and rational choice." *Advances in Criminological Theory* 5: 17–36.

TUCK, MARY, and DAVID RILEY (1986). "The theory of reasoned action: A decision theory of crime." In D. Cornish and R. Clarke, eds., *The Reasoning Criminal: Rational Choice Perspectives on Offending*, 156–169. New York: Springer-Verlag.

TUNNELL, KENNETH D. (1992). *Choosing Crime: The Criminal Calculus of Property Offenders*. Chicago: Nelson Hall.

VAN DIJK, JAN J. M. (1994). "Understanding crime rates: On the interactions between the rational choices of victims and offenders." *British Journal of Criminology* 34: 105–121.

VOTEY, HAROLD L., JR. (1991). "Employment, age, race, and crime: A labor theoretic investigation." *Journal of Quantitative Criminology* 7: 123–153.

WALTERS, GLENN D. (1989). "Putting more thought into criminology." *International Journal of Offender Therapy and Comparative Criminology* 30: v–vii.

WALTERS, GLENN D., and THOMAS W. WHITE (1989). "The thinking criminal: A cognitive model of lifestyle criminality." *Criminal Justice Research Bulletin* 4: 1–10.

WEISBURD, DAVID, ELLEN WARING, and ELLEN CHAYET (1995). "Specific deterrence in a sample of offenders convicted of white-collar crimes." *Criminology* 33: 587–607.

WEISHEIT, RALPH A., and L. EDWARD WELLS (1996). "Rural crime and justice: Implications for theory and research." *Crime and Delinquency* 42: 379–397.

WHITEHEAD, JOHN T. (1986). "The criminological imagination: Another view." *Criminal Justice Review* 10: 22–26.

WIERSMA, ERIC (1996). "Commercial burglars in the Netherlands: Reasoning decision-makers?" *International Journal of Risk Security and Crime Prevention* 1: 217–225.

WIKSTROM, PER OLOF, RONALD V. G. CLARKE, and JOAN MCCORD, eds. (1995). *Integrating Crime Prevention Strategies: Propensity and Opportunity*. Stockholm, Sweden: National Council for Crime Prevention.

WILLIAMS, FRANK P. III (1984). "The demise of the criminological imagination: A critique of recent criminology." *Justice Quarterly* 1: 91–104.

WILSON, JAMES Q. (1975). *Thinking About Crime*. New York: Basic Books.

WILSON, JAMES Q., and RICHARD HERRNSTEIN (1985). *Crime and Human Nature*. New York: Simon and Schuster.

WOOLDREDGE, JOHN, FRANCIS T. CULLEN, and EDWARD LATESSA (1992). "Victimization in the workplace: A test of routine activities theory." *Justice Quarterly* 9: 325–335.

WORTLEY, RICHARD (1996). "Guilt, shame and situational crime prevention." In R. Homel, ed. *The Politics and Practice of Situational Crime Prevention*, 115–132. Monsey, NY: Criminal Justice Press.

WRIGHT, RICHARD T., and SCOTT H. DECKER (1994). *Burglars on the Job: Streetlife and Residential Break-Ins*. Boston: Northeastern University Press.

YOCHELSON, SAMUEL, and STANTON E. SAMENOW (1976). *The Criminal Personality*, Vol. I: *A Profile for Change*. New York: Jason Aronson.

ZAHM, DIANE, and PAUL CROMWELL, eds. (1993). *Proceedings of the International Seminar on Environmental Criminology and Crime Analysis*. Coral Gables: Florida Criminal Justice Executive Institute, University of Miami.

ZAHN, MARGARET (1975). "The female homicide victim." *Criminology* 13: 400–415.

13

GENDER-BASED THEORIES

INTRODUCTION

The gender theories comprise a diverse group of perspectives that specify gender as a critical variable in understanding crime. On the whole, they are designed to sensitize scholars to the relative "invisibility" of women in the field (in terms of offenders, workers, victims, and scholars). The perspective is largely based on a view of a patriarchal (male-based) society that empowers males in virtually all social interaction that matters. Males dominate government, make rules, define gender roles, and set the patterns for power in society. In short, males are dominant and females are subordinated. The most important point for virtually all feminist perspectives is males fail to understand the importance of gender and sex roles in society.

There are goals other than sensitizing. One is to produce a distinctly feminist perspective on society. Some feminist scholars (see Daly and Chesney-Lind, 1988) feel strongly that existing criminological knowledge is a product of "men's experiences" and therefore is a biased and power-centered view of the world. By analyzing and evaluating through female perspectives, it is assumed a different view will emerge of personal conflict, crime, and crime prevention.

THE HERITAGE OF THE THEORY

The Social Heritage

Although we have previously discussed the cultural and social climate of the 1960s and 1970s, there are a few things still worth mention in the context of feminist theory. The civil rights movement did more than sensitize some of the public to discriminatory practices affecting minorities, people began to realize females were also being treated unequally. One's gender became the subject of equal opportunity discussions and females ultimately fell under the equal opportunity statutes. The women's liberation movement was instrumental in bringing feminist issues to the surface and "women's lib" became a commonplace term. New magazines were devoted to the topic (e.g., *Cosmopolitan*) and many of society's cultural elite bandied the topic around. Television news shows and commentaries often reported "women's lib" issues. At the same time, criticism of government policies and emergent radical discussions served to highlight an overall sense of who was in power and who was being dominated. As minority groups began to get their discrimination message across, feminist concerns joined in the fray. A constitutional amendment guaranteeing equal rights ("ERA") was passed by Congress and just failed in ratification by the states. By the beginning of the 1990s, female themes had become so prevalent that catering to "the female vote" was intrinsic to national political campaigns.

The Intellectual Heritage

With the social turmoil, conflict-based theories became popular in academic circles. Because of their emphasis of power relationships, it was merely a matter of time before conflict theory discussions turned to the issue of gender. Indeed, the first gender-based article in criminology (Klein, 1973) was born out of a radical orientation. Even as late as the 1980s, a general mood of critique (and some degree of uneasiness about the dominant positivist model) in the social sciences contributed to, and was reflected in, feminist theorizing. In the 1980s, women's studies programs began to grow in universities and by the end of the decade had become commonplace. Feminist issues became part of the academic landscape. With that base, treatment of gender issues flourished and gender scholarship moved into virtually all academic disciplines. And this, perhaps more than anything, is the core intellectual heritage of feminist theory—it is not based in the traditional academic disciplines but is truly interdisciplinary.

THE THEORETICAL PERSPECTIVE

Many sources point to females as the forgotten population in criminology and criminal justice. Even when females have been included in theories of crime and delinquency, their behavior is explained by simple concepts and motives (Klein, 1973). There is, of course, no reason to suppose females are less complex in their behavior than males. A number of theorists have also found it unusual that, as a whole, females remain relatively noncriminal, yet gender is one of the least explored areas of criminology (Leonard, 1982). How, for instance, do we explain criminality is 80 percent male? Gender-based theories have attempted to do just that.

While we are oversimplifying here for convenience, the gender per-spective has two basic functions. One serves to criticize traditional male, *androcentric* (male-centered) approaches to studying crime and the tradi-tional operations of the criminal justice system. The second function is the development of gender-sensitive interpretations of deviance and a consider-ation of the nature of female criminality. Among these interpretations are a number of major works making up what is characterized as feminist theory.

Social Traits and Feminism

A feminist perspective on crime developed in criminology the same way the feminist view came to literature, art, politics, and science: one writer, one artist, one senator, and one astronaut at a time. Books such as Henrik Ibsen's *Doll's House*, Kate Chopin's *The Awakening*, and Virginia Woolfe's *A Room of One's Own* highlighted the struggle of women coming of age in a society rooted in **paternalism, chivalry,** and **sexism.** These social traits have become the cornerstones of several different approaches to studying female criminality.

Paternalism. Patriarchal (male-based) power relations are central to understanding the way we define and study crime. The roots of patriarchal power in our social system are dominant enough to explain why women are more likely to be victimized in the home, and by friends and intimates, than outside the home and by strangers. Paternalism suggests females need to be protected for their own good. A paternalistic society is organized around independence for males and dependence for females. A good example can be found in *Turner v. Safley,* in which the U.S. Supreme Court criticized the Missouri Department of Corrections for its paternalistic policies regarding the marriage of female inmates. While the marriages of male inmates were all routinely approved, the requests of females were carefully scrutinized and only rarely granted. It seems Missouri wardens were "protecting" their female inmates. The major impetus in granting a marriage request for a female prisoner was the presence of a child born out of wedlock. Calling the arbitrary policy unconstitutional, the court chastised the wardens for their discriminatory control of First Amendment rights. Meda Chesney-Lind (1988a, 1988b) argues paternalism is the major reason female juveniles are detained much more frequently for status offenses. The court was "protect-ing girls for their own good."

Chivalry. The notion of chivalry is tied up with old conceptions of men doing things for women, and, of course, is one way in which paternal-ism can be practiced. A classic example of chivalry is a man rushing ahead to open a door for a woman. Chivalry implies attitudes toward female offend-ers may account for differential processing in the criminal justice system. At each discretionary step from arrest to sentencing, women may benefit from the belief that males "just don't treat ladies badly" and thereby receive lenient dispositions. If police routinely chose not to arrest women, then female crime rates would appear to be quite low. If the system were to reduce its practice of chivalry, there would be a false perception that female criminality is increasing.

There is evidence chivalry does, indeed, exist within the criminal justice system, although the practice of chivalry appears to be complex. Christy Visher (1983) found chivalry in police encounters depended on the characteristics of the suspect. Older, white women who were calm and deferential were more likely to be granted leniency. Debra Curran (1983), however, failed to find support for chivalry at any decision point other than sentencing. In her research, judges seemed to be more lenient toward women when issuing sentences. Analyzing data from 1948 to 1976, Marvin Krohn, James Curry, and Shirley Nelson-Kilger (1983) found evidence of gender bias in the processing of juvenile status offenses. While girls were as likely to be referred to probation as boys who had committed misdemeanors (paternalism), they were still less likely to be referred for both misdemeanors and felonies (chivalry). Daly (1989b, 1994b) reports that there is substantial evidence females are treated more leniently than males by the criminal justice system.

Sexism. Sexism refers to attitudes or practices having the effect of producing inequality between the sexes. Over sixty years ago, a St. Louis official lamented that sexism created problems in the way illegitimate births were handled (Mangold, 1926). He claimed social service agencies were confronted with the prejudices of judges and prosecutors, as well as of the public, who believed that: (1) illegitimate babies should not be kept with their mothers but taken from them as soon as possible, (2) the parents of an illegitimate child should marry as soon as possible, (3) married men who father illegitimate children should not be exposed, and (4) the mothers of illegitimate children should wear the "scarlet letter." Much of the literature on the early juvenile justice system demonstrates the court's preoccupation with status offenses, particularly in sanctioning the sex-related behaviors of girls. Although girls were less likely than boys to be apprehended and adjudicated, they were more likely to be detained and institutionalized for status offenses (Chesney-Lind, 1977; Chesney-Lind and Sheldon, 1992). This was true even though self-report studies showed males as likely, if not more likely, to be involved in status offenses (Canter, 1982). Obviously, the juvenile courts were practicing a double standard for acceptable behavior.

Contemporary Theories of Female Criminality

The first of the modern gender-based perspectives on crime attempted to explain female criminality rather than offer a gender-sensitive approach to crime in general. Because of a lack of explanations of female crime, these perspectives were received with interest. With the advent of the feminist movement in the late 1960s, social observers began following changes in the role of women in society. By the mid-1970s, it appeared substantial changes were underway, and two criminologists, Freda Adler and Rita James Simon, proposed new theories of female criminality.

Liberation and Opportunity. Liberation/masculinity perspectives argue that as the gender gap narrows, the behavior, both legitimate and illegitimate, of women and men will become more alike. In *Sisters in Crime* (1975), Freda Adler developed the idea that changes in female criminality are the product of changes in the social roles of women in our society. This is an explanation of female crime based on the **women's liberation movement**. American society has grown progressively more receptive to women in the work force, and women have gained greater freedom. According to Adler, as women assume more assertive positions in society and adopt more traditionally "male" roles and statuses, they will experience a masculinizing of their own behaviors. This process will result in women committing more traditionally male crimes, such as violent crimes and white-collar crimes. The rate of female crime will also increase.

While Adler's ideas are logical and intriguing, research has yet to find much support for her position (Steffensmeier and Steffensmeier, 1980; Radosh, 1990). For example, Steven Cernkovich and Peggy Giordano (1979b) looked at delinquent activity and attitudes supporting "women's liberation" and failed to find a relationship. Instead, they found juveniles with the most liberated attitudes were less delinquent.

Rita James Simon (1975) presented a variation on this approach that focuses on **opportunities available to females.** She argued that the nature of female criminality has been molded by the social, familial, and occupational structures of the lives of women. Consequently, changes in the traditional roles of women are also a key to the hypothesis that, over time, women will be involved in more employment-related crimes. Instead of focusing on changes in the personal roles of women in society or on the consideration of behaviors as either feminine or masculine, however, this perspective simply looks at the opportunities women have available to participate in crime. Simon argues, in the past, limited participation in the labor force blocked women's access to opportunities to commit crimes such as fraud, embezzlement, and grand larceny. For example, as clerks and tellers, women in business and banking were too closely supervised to steal successfully. As women move into the ranks of executives, managers, and accountants, however, they gain greater access to more covert theft opportunities.

As an example, Italian police recently captured a key figure of one of the major branches of organized crime, Rosetta Cutolo. Although her prominent place in the organization was initiated by her brother, the founder of the gang, she was allegedly responsible for arranging the murder of a prison warden and the car bombing of a rival. The newspaper pointed out that seven of thirty-two leaders arrested from this organized crime gang have been women, and that the Camorra gang has "offered more equal opportunities for women than the Cosa Nostra, its Sicilian cousin."

Evidence for an opportunity-based version of female criminality is also lacking. It appears that the lower-class females who are most likely to engage in crime have had very little increase in opportunities. In a sense, Simon's theory could be called a theory of middle-class female criminality, and there is some question whether substantially greater opportunities exist or, if they do, whether female participation in white-collar crime has increased.

Economic Marginalization. Clarice Feinman (1986) and Ngaire Naffine (1987) have added a twist to the opportunity approach. In contrast to that approach, their economic marginalization theory argues that it is the *absence of real meaningful opportunities* for women that leads to increases in crime. Despite the strides made by some women in some areas of the business market, the majority of women remain underemployed and underpaid. This is supported by statistics showing that the bulk of female offenders are either unemployed or concentrated in a "pink-collar ghetto" where pay is low and work is unrewarding. Other evidence of economic marginalization can be found in figures that show female offenses are mostly oriented toward petty property crimes. Such crimes seem to indicate a rational response to the poverty and economic insecurity of the lower class.

Gender-based Theories of Criminality

Unlike theories explaining only female criminality, gender-based theories use the role of gender in explaining criminal and delinquent behavior of both males and females. John Hagan's power-control theory, while not a feminist theory, is an integrated theory that is feminist-informed. We include it here because gender is the most critical component of the theory. Feminist theories are also incorporated in this section. For two reasons, we doubt justice can be done to the perspective. First, too little space can be devoted to it, and second, there is still little agreement on the various directions of feminist criminological theory. We discuss this in greater detail in the next sections. [For those interested in reading about feminist criminology in greater detail, we suggest two excellent articles: Kathleen Daly and Meda Chesney-Lind (1988), and Kathleen Daly (1997).]

Power-control Theory. The work of John Hagan (1989a, 1989b) and colleagues in *Structural Criminology* (1989b) brings together a conflict-oriented theory with social control versions of family relationships to present a "power-control" theory of gender and delinquency. Hagan argues power relationships in larger society, especially in the workplace, are reflected in the family. In short, the relationships one learns in the work world, the methods of establishing authority and dominance over others, are carried home to the family. Members of different social classes experience different power relationships and therefore construct different family relationships. Similarly, because workplace relationships vary by gender, males and females experience different roles, expectations, and values. The combination of social class and gender experiences creates structured family relationships that help explain the social distribution of delinquency. As Hagan puts it (1991:130):

> The social reproduction of gender relations refers to the activities, institutions, and relationships that are involved in the maintenance and renewal of gender roles, in the family and elsewhere. These activities include the parenting involved in caring for, protecting and socializing children for the roles they will occupy as adults. According to power-control theory, family class structure shapes the social reproduction of gender relations, and in turn the social distribution of delinquency.

The critical components of gender relations in the patriarchal family, as they relate to delinquent behavior, include the way in which delinquency is defined, the amount and type of control parents exercise over children, and gender preferences for risk taking. First, delinquency (and criminality) reflects activities that are potentially fun, exciting, and pleasurable. All these are stratified by gender in the larger society such that males have greater access. Therefore, females are not as free to search out ways that lead to behaviors associated with delinquency. Second, reflecting the gender differences in the work world, males are less controlled and dominated than females are. This control is reproduced in the family, and females receive greater control than do males. Control can be achieved through close parental relations and domination, both of which are applied more thoroughly to females. Third, the form of control exercised over juveniles affects their preferences toward risk taking. Males are allowed greater freedom in both pleasure-seeking activity and in parental control; thus, they develop more taste for risk taking. Finally, because delinquency is allied with risk taking, delinquent behavior is stratified along gender lines, with males being more likely to commit delinquent acts.

Power-control theory then predicts the more patriarchal the family structure, the greater is the gender gap in delinquent behavior between sons and daughters. On the other hand, a more egalitarian family will reproduce relations that lead to sons and daughters participating more equally in delinquency. A final note from power-control theory is worthwhile. Because the gender roles in delinquency are shaped in the family by reflection from the workplace, power-control theory offers a potential explanation of the effect of the changing occupational roles of women. Clearly, as women gain more employment opportunities, or opportunities of a different nature, we should expect the gender distribution of delinquent behaviors to shift.

Crime as Structured Action. Another power-oriented theory, this one proposed by James Messerschmidt (1986, 1997), views sex, race, and class as created by social structure. By this, Messerschmidt means that a social structure defines the ways in which sex, race, and class are perceived and socially constructed. Once those perceptions are created, the next issue is how people *do* those categories—that is, how people in those roles act and interact according to their defined category. The social structure in a capitalist society helps determine these roles through economic competition and the validation of a white, male-dominated, patriarchal system. Typical "street" criminality, then, is a product of powerlessness for females and lower-class, nonwhite males. On the other hand, male power is also implicated in white-collar and corporate crime and sex crime. Messerschmidt is aware power can vary by role. For instance a male may exercise power as a husband, while being powerless as a factory worker (1997:9). Thus, he views masculinity and femininity as a fluid construct.

The Feminist Agenda: Four Perspectives for Criminologists. Over the last twenty years a growing body of literature has accumulated that represents feminist perspectives on crime and criminology. There is, however, no single feminist criminology. Approaches vary in how to develop a gender-sensitive perception of the problems and solutions for studying crime and justice. Perhaps mirroring the evolution of traditional criminological theory, feminist theorists have now developed a typology of specialized perspectives (liberal, radical, Marxist, and socialist feminism). This development has been applied to criminology, and recent attempts have been made to summarize existing criminological work into these perspectives (Daly and Chesney-Lind, 1988; Danner, 1989; Simpson, 1989; Radosh, 1990). An examination of the recent literature is important because of the growing popularity of both gender-based work and work that incorporates feminist conceptions of gender.

Despite early enthusiasm for the hypothesis that there is a link between liberation and crime, as we have noted, meaningful research support never materialized. Sally Simpson (1989) speculates the quest may have even distracted researchers from examining more productive variables such as economics, class, and opportunities. While Simpson believes the earlier liberal (quantitative and mainstream academic) contributions are now being answered with more radical critiques, she looks forward to work that emphasizes qualitative, historical, and more subjective approaches. In the face of debate about the precise role of the feminist perspective, writers such as Kathleen Daly and Meda Chesney-Lind (1988) call for integration of feminist thought in all areas of criminology. Mona Danner (1989) believes socialist feminism in particular, with its emphasis on the overlapping effects of class, race, and gender, will serve to strengthen critical criminological thought. In a recent article, Kathleen Daly (1997) identifies three major movements in contemporary gender scholarship as "class-race-gender," "doing gender," and "sexed bodies." She notes they critique each other and believes the discourse to be healthy. Finally, there is debate on whether to incorporate feminist thought into existing criminological theories or to throw out the old theories and begin fresh.

Liberal Feminism. Perhaps the first feminist perspective in criminology, liberal feminism focused on gender discrimination (Chapman, 1980; Datesman and Scarpitti, 1980; Feinman, 1986) and women's liberation. The general notion was that females deserve equal treatment in the criminal justice system. Concepts of paternalism and chivalry were the mainstay of liberal analyses. Gender-based laws were questioned, and criminal justice processing was examined for discriminatory and harmful practices. Perhaps as much as anything, liberal feminists challenged the prevailing assumptions that males and females have different roles in society. Females were said to have power in the domestic or private world and males to have power in the public world. Liberal feminists denounced the private/public division and demanded public power as well. This led to challenges of personnel policies and hiring in the various system agencies. The presumption was that, as females were more fully integrated into the work force, justice would be more evenly dispensed and discrimination would decrease. In addition, the work of Adler and Simon on liberation and opportunities characterizes liberal feminist criminology (Daly and Chesney-Lind, 1988:507).

Radical Feminism. While not exclusively so, the rise of radical feminist criminology is a product of two factors: the emergent radical criminology and a critique of liberal feminism. Its primary focus is on the way in which power is constructed and dominated by males in society (Griffin, 1971; Brownmiller, 1975; Smart, 1976, 1979; Dobash and Dobash, 1979). Rather than focus on roles, radical feminism deals with the way in which the capitalist economic system fosters crime through the creation of a patriarchal and sexist society. Patriarchy defines women as subjects, with men having the right of control. Sexism defines the value of women in terms of the family (unpaid housework as natural) and gives men control over reproduction. Thus, men generate legal concepts, such as marriage, that define women as property and de-emphasize the significance of assault on women (marital rape, domestic violence). Obviously, the radical feminist agenda includes changes in legal definitions of crime and the introduction of more gender-sensitive laws. Even more important, however, is the ability of women to exercise control over their own bodies and the restructuring of family relationships to eliminate male domination. And, as do the liberal feminists, radical feminists also want to eliminate the private/public division in gender roles.

Unlike some liberal feminists, however, radical feminists do not believe women's liberation will increase female crime rates. Dorie Klein and June Kress (1979:89) claim "if the women's movement develops a class analysis of women's oppression, and a program around which working class women can be organized, then we may witness a decrease in women's individualism, self-destruction, competitiveness and crime." Radical feminist theories of crime, then, suggest liberation can result in lower crime rates for women and should even precipitate a decrease in male violence against women.

Marxist Feminism. Ironically, early radical and Marxist theorists (including Marx himself) never addressed female criminality. Indeed, in many cases, crimes committed by females have been expressly excluded. In keeping with the general Marxist position, Marxist feminists see the capitalist system as exploiting subordinate groups (often based on race and gender) for capital production (profit). The emphasis on production and labor in Marxist thought results in a feminist focus on the sexual division of labor, which is literally a caste rather than a class (Radosh, 1990). Females are relegated to labor positions with little value and low occupational status. Further, acquisition and disbursement of capital is primarily restricted to males, with only token female participation. As a result, Polly Radosh (1990:113) describes the sexual division of labor as "the epitome of economic inequality." Crime, then, for women has two primary sources: a threat to the current distribution of property or a threat to the sexual division of labor. Under Marxist feminism, this explains why women are most frequently arrested for property crimes and sexually oriented offenses.

Another primary focus is on the status of women in the work force (Daly and Chesney-Lind, 1988). Females are viewed as secondary sources of labor, or as a surplus work force. This marginalization of their worth results in women being heavily dependent on males, or in the absence of a male in the family, dependent on welfare. The anger and frustration of such a position is another cause of crime. In fact, Radosh (1990:126) succinctly summarizes the Marxist feminist position when she says:

> Women's behavior is often labeled as criminal according to the moral implications of capitalism, but real criminal perpetration among women reflects the class differential of the economic system. Certain women occupy inter-generational positions outside of the legitimate system of rewards, which assures that a perpetual underclass, within the caste of women, suffers from alienation and frustration. This factor, more than any other social, psychological or physical characteristic, produces female crime.

As should be evident, the theories produced by Marxist feminists follow the radical and Marxist conflict approaches discussed in Chapter 9 and differ primarily in their inclusion of gender issues. Gender, however, is secondary to the concept of class in Marxist feminist analyses.

Socialist Feminism. Uniting radical and Marxist principles, socialist feminism identifies the oppression of women as a symptom of the patriarchal capitalist system (Danner, 1989). It considers criminality to be a product of the class-based system, and its discussions of female criminality are usually confined to property crimes. The social distribution of crime is derived from both the relationship to the production domain and the reproductive, or family, domain. Both domains are equally important. Patriarchal, capitalist society creates groups with different positions and opportunities in society. Females are exploited by the capitalist patriarchal system both for their labor and for their sexuality. James Messerschmidt (1986) notes crimes by powerless people reflect their resistance and accommodation to their position in society. Because of the way social organization is structured by gender, males commit crimes reflecting resistance; and females commit crimes characterized by accommodation. In other words, males are most likely to commit violent street crime; whereas females are most likely to commit property and vice crimes.

CLASSIFICATION OF THE PERSPECTIVE

Because there are so many variations of gender theory, there is no accurate classification system. For the same reason, we have not prepared a list of the major points of the theory; it would contain so many caveats as to be useless (but the box containing "Five Elements of Feminist Thought" serves a similar purpose). Some generalities, however, may be drawn.

On the whole, gender theories may be considered *structural* theories because they attempt to explain differences in rates of female crime or differences between the crimes of males and females. We can also, with reasonable accuracy, classify gender-based theories as *conflict-oriented*. Most of these theories have also attempted to explain crime from a determinist perspective, but conflict-oriented theorists resist the idea that conflict theories have anything in common with positivist theories. However, newer versions of feminist thought tend to share with postmodernism a rejection of the positivist approach.

FIVE ELEMENTS OF FEMINIST THOUGHT

- Gender is not a natural fact but a complex social, historical, and cultural product; it is related to, but not simply derived from, biological sex difference and reproductive capacities.
- Gender and gender relations order social life and social institutions in fundamental ways.
- Gender relations and constructs of masculinity and femininity are not symmetrical but are based on an organizing principle of men's superiority and social and political-economic dominance over women.
- Systems of knowledge reflect men's views of the natural and social world; the production of knowledge is gendered.
- Women should be at the center of intellectual inquiry, not peripheral, invisible, or appendages to men.

Source: Kathleen Daly and Meda Chesney-Lind, "Feminism and Criminology," *Justice Quarterly* 5(1988): 504.

POLICY IMPLICATIONS

Many of the changes that gender-based theories would introduce into crime control policy are not directly focused on crime. The general assumption is that reform of society to eliminate patriarchal domination would result in improved conditions for all, and that crime would lessen as a by-product of those improvements. Therefore, policies designed to equalize relationships between the genders are critical. Under the various feminist perspectives, this means increasing the role of women in most spheres of life, particularly the public ones. Feminists would provide greater access to educational opportunities, modify economic structures, socialize (or elevate the importance of) child care, eliminate or modify marriage laws, and emphasize the importance of gender relations in general. They expect the results of such changes to reduce social images of competition with and ownership of others, decrease aggressive behavior, and bolster self-esteem. Crime would then be affected in smaller numbers of female property and sexual offenses and a lessening of violence among males. Under power-control theory, policies would focus on relationships in the family (much as with low self-control theory), and children would be socialized in a more egalitarian fashion.

Other than child-rearing programs, gender-based theorists would propose programs to sensitize males and females about their gender roles in society. Such agendas are found in rape crisis centers, domestic abuse shelters, and the multicultural/gender diversity programs found in educational institutions. Similar programs are appearing in businesses as sexual harassment seminars. And, perhaps as important as any of the programmatic efforts, the victims' rights movement reflects many gender concerns and is the most extensive policy direction in criminal justice today.

BIBLIOGRAPHY

ADAMS, H. (1914). *Women and Crime*. London: T. Warner Laurie.

ADELBERG, E., and C. CURRIE (1987). *Too Few to Count: Canadian Women in Conflict with the Law*. Vancouver: Press Gang Publishers.

ADLER, FREDA (1975). *Sisters in Crime: The Rise of the New Female Criminal*. New York: McGraw-Hill.

———— (1981). *The Incidence of Female Criminality in the Contemporary World*. New York: New York University Press.

AGETON, SUZANNE S. (1983). "The dynamics of female delinquency, 1976–1980." *Criminology* 21: 555–584.

ALLEN, HILARY (1987). *Justice Unbalanced*. Milton Keynes, UK: Open University Press.

ALLEN, J. (1988). "The 'masculinity' of criminality and criminology: Interrogating some impasses." In M. Findlay and R. Hogg, eds., *Understanding Crime and Criminal Justice*, 1–23. Sydney, Australia: Law Book Company.

AUSTIN, ROY (1982). "Women's liberation and increases in minor, major, and occupational offenses." *Criminology* 20: 407–430.

BARON, LARRY, and MURRAY STRAUS (1984). "Sexual stratification, pornography, and rape in the United States." In N. Malamuth and E. Donnerstein, eds., *Pornography and Sexual Aggression*, 185–209. Orlando, FL: Academic Press.

Berger, Ronald, Lawrence Newman, and Patricia Searles (1991). "The social and political context of rape law reform: An aggregate analysis." *Social Science Quarterly* 72: 221–238.

Berger, Ronald, Patricia Searles, and Lawrence Neuman (1988). "The dimensions of rape reform legislation." *Law and Society Review* 22: 329–357.

Bertrand, Marie-Andree. (1994). "1893–1993: From La Donna Delinquente to a postmodern deconstruction of the 'woman question' in social control theory." *Journal of Human Justice* 5: 43–57.

Bosworth, Mary (1996). "Resistance and compliance in women's prisons: Towards a critique of legitimacy." *Critical Criminology* 7: 5–19.

Boutellier, Johannes. (1991). "Prostitution, criminal law and morality in the Netherlands." *Crime, Law and Social Change* 15: 201–211.

Bowker, Lee K (1978). *Women, Crime, and the Criminal Justice System*. Lexington, MA: Lexington.

——— (1981). *Women and Crime in America*. New York: Macmillan.

Brown, B. (1986). "Women and crime: The dark figures of criminology." *Economy and Society* 15: 355–402.

Browne, Angela (1987). *When Battered Women Kill*. New York: Free Press.

Brownmiller, Susan (1975). *Against Our Will: Men, Women and Rape*. New York: Simon and Schuster.

Cain, Maureen (1990). "Towards transgression: New directions in feminist criminology." *International Journal of the Sociology of Law* 18: 1–18.

———, ed. (1989). *Growing up Good: Policing the Behavior of Girls in Europe*. Newbury Park, CA: Sage.

Cameron, Deborah, and Elizabeth Frazer (1987). *Lust to Kill*. New York: Columbia University Press.

Campbell, Anne (1981). *Girl Delinquents*. New York: St. Martin's Press.

——— (1984). *The Girls in the Gang: A Report from New York City*. New York: Basil Blackwell.

——— (1990). "Female participation in gangs." In G. R. Huff, ed., *Gangs in America*, 163–182. Newbury Park, CA: Sage.

Canter, Rachelle J. (1982). "Sex differences in self-report delinquency." *Criminology* 20: 373–393.

Caringella-MacDonald, Susan (1988). "Marxist and feminist interpretations on the aftermath of rape reforms." *Contemporary Crises* 12: 125–144.

Carlen, Pat (1983). *Women's Imprisonment: A Study in Social Control*. Boston: Routledge and Keagan Paul.

——— (1990). "Women, crime, feminism, and realism." *Social Justice* 17: 107–123.

——— (1994). "Gender, class, racism, and criminal justice: Against global and gender-centric theories, for poststructuralist perspectives." In G. S. Bridges and M. A. Myers, eds., *Inequality and Social Control*, 134-144. Boulder, CO: Westview.

Carlen, Pat, D. Christina, J. Hicks, J. O'Dwyer, and C. Tchaikowsky (1985). *Criminal Women*. Oxford: Polity Press.

Carlen Pat, and Anne Worrall (1987). *Gender, Crime and Justice*. Philadelphia: Open University Press.

Carrington, Kerry (1994). "Postmodern and feminist criminologies: Disconnecting discourses?" *International Journal of the Sociology of Law* 22: 261–277.

Cernkovich, Stephen, and Peggy C. Giordano (1979a). "A comparative analysis of male and female delinquency." *Sociological Quarterly* 20: 131–145.

——— (1979b). "Delinquency, opportunity and gender." *Journal of Criminal Law and Criminology* 70: 145–151.

Chapman, Jane R. (1980). *Economic Realities and the Female Offender*. Lexington, MA: Lexington.

CHESNEY-LIND, MEDA (1977). "Judicial paternalism and the female status offender: Training women to know their place." *Crime and Delinquency* 23: 121–130.

——— (1986). "Women and crime: The female offender." *Signs: Journal of Women in Culture and Society* 12: 78–96.

——— (1987). "Girls and violence: An exploration of the gender gap in serious delinquent behavior." In D. Crowell, I. Evans, and C. O'Donnell, eds., *Childhood Aggression and Violence: Sources of Influence, Prevention, and Control,* 207–229. New York: Plenum Press.

——— (1988a). "Doing feminist criminology." *Criminologist* 13(4): 1, 3, 16–17.

——— (1988b). "Girls and status offenses: Is juvenile justice still sexist?" *Criminal Justice Abstracts* 20: 144–165.

CHESNEY-LIND, MEDA, and RANDALL G. SHELDEN (1992). *Girls, Delinquency and Juvenile Justice.* Belmont, CA: Wadsworth

CONWAY, A., and C. BOGDAN (1977). "Sexual delinquency: The persistence of a double standard." *Crime and Delinquency* 23: 131–135.

CRITES, LAURA (1976). *The Female Offender.* Lexington, MA: Lexington.

CRITES, LAURA, and WINIFRED L. HEPPERLE, eds. (1976). *Women, the Courts and Equality.* Newbury Park, CA: Sage.

CULLIVER, CONCHETTA A., ed. (1993). *Female Criminality: The State of the Art.* New York: Garland.

CURRAN, DEBRA (1983). "Judicial discretion and defendant's sex." *Criminology* 21: 41–58.

——— (1984). "The myth of the new female delinquent." *Crime and Delinquency* 30: 386–399.

CURRIE, DAWN (1990). "Battered women and the state: From the failure of theory to a theory of failure." *Journal of Human Justice* 1: 77–96.

DALY, KATHLEEN (1987a). "Discrimination in the criminal courts: Family, gender, and the problem of equal treatment." *Social Forces* 66: 152–175.

——— (1987b). "Structure and practice of familial-based justice in a criminal court." *Law and Society Review* 21: 267–290.

——— (1988). "The social control of sexuality: A case study of the criminalization of prostitution in the Progressive era." In S. Spitzer and A. Scull, eds., *Research in Law, Deviance and Social Control,* vol. 9, 171–206. Greenwich, CT: Jai Press.

——— (1989a). "Criminal justice ideologies and practices in different voices: Some feminist questions about justice." *International Journal of the Sociology of Law* 17: 1–18.

——— (1989b). "Neither conflict nor labeling nor paternalism will suffice: Intersections of race, ethnicity, gender and family in criminal court decisions." *Crime and Delinquency* 35: 136–168.

——— (1993). "Class-race-gender: Sloganeering in search of meaning." *Social Justice* 20: 56–71.

——— (1994a). "Criminal law and justice system practices as racist, white and racialized." *Washington & Lee Law Review* 51: 431–464.

——— (1994b). *Gender, Crime and Punishment.* New Haven, CT: Yale University Press.

——— (1997). "Different ways of conceptualizing sex/gender in feminist theory and their implications for criminology." *Theoretical Criminology* 1: 25–51.

DALY, KATHLEEN, and MEDA CHESNEY-LIND (1988). "Feminism and criminology." *Justice Quarterly* 5: 497–538.

DALY, KATHLEEN, and DEBORAH STEPHENS (1995). "The 'dark figure' of criminology: Toward a black and multi-ethnic feminist agenda for theory and research." In N. H. Rafter and F. Heidensohn, eds., *International Feminist Perspectives in Criminology,* 189–215. Philadelphia: Open University Press.

DANNER, MONA (1989). "Socialist feminism: A brief introduction." *Critical Criminologist* 1: 1–2.

—— (1991). "Socialist feminism: A brief introduction." In B. D. MacLean and D. Milovanovic, eds., *New Directions in Critical Criminology*, 51–54. Vancouver: Collective Press.

—— (1996). "Gender inequality and criminalization: A socialist feminist perspective on the legal social control of women." In M. D. Schwartz and D. Milovanovic, eds., *Race, Gender, and Class in Criminology*, 29–48. New York: Garland.

DANNER, MONA, and JEAN LANDIS (1990). "Carpe diem (seize the day!): An opportunity for feminist connections." In B. D. MacLean and D. Milovanovic, eds., *Racism, Empiricism and Criminal Justice*, 109–112. Vancouver: Collective Press.

DATESMAN, SUSAN, and FRANK R. SCARPITTI (1980). *Women, Crime and Justice*. New York: Oxford University Press.

DAVIS, NANETTE (1988). "Battered women: Implications for social control." *Contemporary Crises* 12: 345–372.

DOBASH, R. EMERSON, and RUSSELL P. DOBASH (1979). *Violence against Wives: The Case against Patriarchy*. New York: Free Press.

DRIVER, EMILY, and AUDREY DROISEN, eds. (1989) *Child Sexual Abuse: Feminist Perspectives*. Hampshire and London: Macmillan.

DUGDALE, RICHARD (1895). *The Jukes: A Study in Crime, Pauperism, Disease and Heredity*. New York: Putnam.

EDWARDS, ANNE R. (1989). "Sex/gender, sexism and criminal justice: Some theoretical considerations." *International Journal of the Sociology of Law* 17: 165–184.

FARNWORTH, MARGARET (1984). "Male-female differences in delinquency in a minority group sample." *Journal of Research in Crime and Delinquency* 21: 191–212.

FEINMAN, CLARICE (1979). "Sex role stereotypes and justice for women." *Crime and Delinquency* 25: 87–94.

—— (1986). *Women in the Criminal Justice System*. New York: Praeger.

FIGUEIRA-MCDONOUGH, JOSEFINA, and ELAINE SELO (1980). "A reformulation of the 'equal opportunity' explanation of female delinquency." *Crime and Delinquency* 26: 333–343.

FLOWERS, R. B. (1987). *Women and Criminality*. New York: Greenwood Press.

FOSSATI, THOMAS E., and JAMES W. MEEKER (1997). "Evaluations of institutional legitimacy and court system fairness: A study of gender differences." *Journal of Criminal Justice* 25: 141–154.

FREEDMAN, ESTELLE (1981). *Their Sisters' Keepers: Women's Prison Reform in America, 1830–1930*. Ann Arbor: University of Michigan Press.

GEIS, GILBERT, and ROBLEY GEIS (1978). "Rape reform: An appreciative-critical review." *Bulletin of the American Academy of Psychiatry and the Law* 6: 301–312.

GELSTHORPE, LORAINE, and ALLISON MORRIS (1988). "Feminism and criminology in Britain." *British Journal of Criminology* 28: 223–240.

—— (1990). *Feminist Perspectives in Criminology*. Buckingham, England: Open University Press.

GIORDANO, PEGGY, C., STEPHEN CERNKOVICH, and M. PUGH (1978). "Girls, guys, and gangs: The changing social context of female delinquency." *Journal of Criminal Law and Criminology* 69: 126–132.

GLUECK, ELEANOR, and SHELDON GLUECK (1934). *Five Hundred Delinquent Women*. New York: Knopf.

GONDOLF, EDWARD (1985). "Anger and oppression in men who batter: Empiricist and feminist perspectives and their implications for research." *Victimology* 10: 311–324.

GORA, JOANN (1982). *The New Female Criminal: Empirical Reality or Social Myth?* New York: Praeger.

GRIFFIN, SUSAN (1971). "Rape: The all-American crime." *Ramparts* 10(3): 26–35.

GRIFFITHS, A. (1895). "Female criminals." *North American Review* 161: 141–152.

Hagan, John (1989a). "Micro- and macro-structures of delinquency causation and a power-control theory of gender and delinquency." In S. F. Messner, M. D. Krohn, and A. E. Liska, eds., *Theoretical Integration in the Study of Deviance and Crime: Problems and Prospects,* 213–227. Albany: State University of New York Press.

——— (1989b). *Structural Criminology.* New Brunswick, NJ: Rutgers University Press.

——— (1991). "A power-control theory of gender and delinquency." In R. Silverman, J. Teevan, and V. Sacco, eds., *Crime in Canadian Society,* 4th ed., 130–136. Toronto: Butterworths.

Hagan, John, A. R. Gillis, and John Simpson (1985). "The class structure of gender and delinquency: Toward a power-control theory of common delinquent behavior." *American Journal of Sociology* 90: 1151–1178.

Hagan, John, John Simpson, and A. R. Gillis (1987). "Class in the household: A power-control theory of gender and delinquency." *American Journal of Sociology* 92: 788–816.

Harris, Anthony R. (1977). "Sex and theories of deviance: Toward a functional theory of deviant type-scripts." *American Sociological Review* 42: 3–16.

Harris, M. Kay (1991). "Moving into the new millennium: Toward a feminist vision of justice." In H. Pepinsky and R. Quinney, eds., *Criminology as Peacemaking,* 83–97. Bloomington: Indiana University Press.

Heidensohn, Frances (1968). "The deviance of women: A critique and an enquiry." *British Journal of Sociology* 19: 160–176.

——— (1985). *Women and Crime: The Life of the Female Offender.* New York: New York University Press.

Hill, Gary D., and Maxine P. Atkinson (1988). "Gender, familial control, and delinquency." *Criminology* 26: 127–149.

Howe, Adrian (1994). *Punish and Critique: Towards a Feminist Analysis of Penality.* London, UK: Routledge.

James, Jennifer, and William Thornton (1980). "Women's liberation and the female delinquent." *Journal of Research in Crime and Delinquency* 17: 230–244.

Jenness, Valerie (1990). "From sex as sin to sex as work: COYOTE and the reorganization of prostitution as a social problem." *Social Problems* 37: 403–420.

Jensen, Gary, and R. Eve (1976). "Sex differences in delinquency." *Criminology* 13: 427–448.

Jensen, Gary F., and David Brownfield (1987). "Gender, lifestyles, and victimization: Beyond routine activity." *Violence and Victims* 1: 85–99.

Jensen, Gary, and K. Thompson (1990). "What's class got to do with it? A further examination of power-control theory." *American Journal of Sociology* 95: 1009–1023.

Karras, Ruth M. (1996). *Common Women: Prostitution and Sexuality in Medieval England.* Oxford, UK: Oxford University Press

Kerstetter, Wayne (1990). "Gateway to justice: Police and prosecutorial response to sexual assaults against women." *Journal of Criminal Law and Criminology* 81: 267–313.

Klein, Dorie (1973). "The etiology of female crime: A review of the literature." *Issues in Criminology* 8: 3–30.

Klein, Dorie, and June Kress (1979). "Any woman's blues: A critical overview of women, crime, and the criminal justice system." In F. Adler and R. Simon, eds., *Criminality of Deviant Women,* 82–90. Boston: Houghton Mifflin.

Konopka, Gisela (1966). *The Adolescent Girl in Conflict.* Englewood Cliffs, NJ: Prentice Hall.

Krohn, Marvin, James P. Curry, and Shirley Nelson-Kilger (1983). "Is chivalry dead? An analysis of changes in police dispositions of males and females." *Criminology* 21: 417–437.

KRUTTSCHNITT, CANDACE (1982). "Women, crime and dependency: An application of the theory of law." *Criminology* 19: 495–513.

—— (1984). "Sex and criminal court dispositions: The unresolved controversy." *Research in Crime and Delinquency* 21: 213–232.

—— (1996). "Contributions of quantitative methods to the study of gender and crime, or bootstrapping our way into the theoretical thicket." *Journal of Quantitative Criminology* 12: 135–161.

LABERGE, DANIELLE (1990). "Women's criminality, criminal women, criminalized women? Questions in and for a feminist perspective." *Journal of Human Justice* 2: 37–56.

LASTER, KATHY (1989). "Infanticide: A litmus test for feminist criminological theory." *Australian and New Zealand Journal of Criminology* 22: 151–166.

LAUB, JOHN, and M. J. MCDERMOTT (1985). "An analysis of serious crime by young black women." *Criminology* 23: 81–98.

LEONARD, EILEEN (1982). *Women, Crime and Society: A Critique of Theoretical Criminology.* New York. Longman.

LOMBROSO, CESARE, and G. FERRERO (1899). *The Female Offender.* New York: Appleton.

MADRIZ, ESTER I. (1997). "Images of criminals and victims: A study on women's fear and social control." *Gender and Society* 11: 342–356.

MAHER, LISA (1990). "Criminalizing pregnancy: The downside of a kinder, gentler nation?" *Critical Criminologist* 2: 1, 2, 8.

MAHER, LISA, and KATHLEEN DALY (1996). "Women in the street-level drug economy: Continuity or change?" *Criminology* 34: 465–491.

MANGOLD, GEORGE (1926). "Illegitimacy in St. Louis." *Annals of the American Academy of Political and Social Science* 125: 63–67.

MANN, CORAMAE RICHEY (1984). *Female Crime and Delinquency.* Tuscaloosa: University of Alabama Press.

MARTIN, SUSAN E., and NANCY D. JURIK (1996). *Doing Justice, Doing Gender: Women in Law and Criminal Justice Occupations.* Thousand Oaks, CA: Sage.

MESSERSCHMIDT, JAMES (1986). *Capitalism, Patriarchy and Crime: Toward a Socialist Feminist Criminology.* Totowa, NJ: Rowan and Littlefield.

—— (1987). "Feminism, criminology and the rise of the female sex 'delinquent,' 1880–1930." *Contemporary Crises* 11: 243–264.

—— (1993). *Masculinities and Crime: Critique and Reconceptualization of Theory.* Lanham, MD: Rowman and Littlefield.

—— (1997). *Crime as Structured Action: Gender, Race, Class, and Crime in the Making.* Thousand Oaks, CA: Sage.

MILLMAN, MARCIA (1975). "She did it all for love: A feminist view of the sociology of deviance." In M. Millman and R. Kanter, eds., *Another Voice: Feminist Perspectives on Social Life and Social Science*, 251–279. Garden City, NY: Anchor Doubleday.

MONAHAN, FLORENCE (1941). *Women in Crime.* New York: Washbum.

MORRIS, ALLISON (1987). *Women, Crime and Criminal Justice.* New York: Blackwell.

MORRIS, ALLISON, and LORAINE GELSTHORPE (1991). "Feminist perspectives in criminology: Transforming and transgressing." *Women and Criminal Justice* 2: 3–26.

MOYER, IMOGENE L., ed. (1985). *The Changing Roles of Women in the Criminal Justice System.* Prospect Heights, IL: Waveland.

MUSHENO, MICHAEL, and KATHRYN SEELEY (1987). "Prostitution policy and the women's movement: Historical analysis of feminist thought and organization." *Contemporary Crises* 10: 237–255.

NAFFINE, NGAIRE (1987). *Female Crime: The Construction of Women in Criminology.* Boston: Allen and Unwin.

—— (1994). *Gender, Crime and Feminism.* Brookfield, VT: Dartmouth.

NOBLIT, G. W., and J. M. BURKHART (1976). "Women and crime: 1960–1970." *Social Science Quarterly* 56: 650–657.

O'BRIEN, ROBERT M. (1991). "Sex ratios and rape rates: A power-control theory." *Criminology* 29: 99–114.

ODEM, MARY. E., and STEVEN SCHLOSSMAN (1991). "Guardians of virtue: The juvenile court and female delinquency in early 20th century Los Angeles." *Crime and Delinquency* 37: 186–203.

OGLE, ROBBIN S., DANIEL MAIER-KATKIN, and THOMAS J. BERNARD (1995). "A theory of homicidal behavior among women." *Criminology* 33: 173–193.

PIKE, L. (1876). *A History of Crime in England.* London: Smith, Edler.

POLLAK, OTTO (1961). *The Criminality of Women.* New York: A. S. Barnes.

POLLOCK-BYRNE, JOYCELYN M. (1990). *Women, Prison, and Crime.* Pacific Grove, CA: Brooks/Cole.

PRICE, BARBARA R., and NATALIE J. SOKOLOFF, eds. (1982). *The Criminal Justice System and Women: Offenders, Victims, and Workers,* 2nd ed. New York: McGraw-Hill.

RADOSH, POLLY (1990). "Women and crime in the United States: A Marxian explanation." *Sociological Spectrum* 10: 105–131.

RAFTER, NICOLE H. (1985). *Partial Justice: Women in State Prisons, 1800–1935.* Boston: Northeastern University Press.

RAFTER, NICOLE H. and FRANCES HEIDENSOHN, eds. (1995). *International Feminist Perspectives in Criminology.* Philadelphia: Open University Press.

RAFTER, NICOLE H., and ELENA M. NATALIZIA (1982). "Marxist feminism: Implications for criminal justice." In B. Price and N. Sokoloff, eds., *The Criminal Justice System and Women,* 465–484. New York: Clark Boardman.

RAFTER, NICOLE H., and ELIZABETH STANKO (1982). *Judge, Lawyer, Victim, Thief: Women, Gender Roles and Criminal Justice.* Boston: Northeastern University Press.

RIFKIN, JANET (1980). "Toward a theory of law and patriarchy." In P. Beirne and R. Quinney, eds., *Marxism and Law,* 295–302. New York: Wiley.

RUSSELL, KATHERYN K. (1992). "Development of a black criminology and role of the black criminologist." *Justice Quarterly* 9: 667–683.

SCHLOSSMAN, STEVEN, and STEPHANIE WALLACH (1978). "The crime of precocious sexuality: Female juvenile delinquency in the progressive era." *Harvard Educational Review* 48: 65–94.

SCHUR, EDWIN M. (1984). *Labeling Women Deviant: Gender, Stigma, and Social Control.* New York: Random House.

SCHWARTZ, MARTIN D. (1988). "Ain't got no class: Universal risk theories of battering." *Contemporary Crises* 12: 373–392.

SCHWARTZ, MARTIN D., and DRAGAN MILOVANOVIC, eds. (1996). *Race, Gender, and Class in Criminology: The Intersections.* New York: Garland.

SCHWENDINGER, JULIA, and HERMAN SCHWENDINGER (1983). *Rape and Inequality.* Newbury Park, CA: Sage.

SECOMBE, WALLY (1973). "The housewife and her labour under capitalism." *New Left Review* (Jan.–Feb.): 3–24.

SHOVER, NEAL, STEPHEN NORLAND, JENNIFER JAMES, and WILLIAM THORNTON (1979). "Gender roles and delinquency." *Social Forces* 58: 162–175.

SIMON, RITA J. (1975). *Women and Crime.* Lexington, MA: Lexington Books.

SIMON, RITA J., and M. BENSON (1980). "Evaluating changes in female criminality." In M. W. Klein and K. S. Teilmann, eds., *Handbook of Criminal Justice Evaluation,* 549–571. Beverly Hills, CA: Sage.

SIMON, RITA J., and JEAN LANDIS (1991). *The Crimes Women Commit, the Punishments They Receive.* Lexington, MA: Lexington.

SIMPSON, SALLY S. (1989). "Feminist theory, crime and justice." *Criminology* 27: 605–632.

—— (1991). "Caste, class, and violent crime: Explaining differences in female offending." *Criminology* 29: 115–136.

SIMPSON, SALLY S., and LORI ELIS. (1994). "Is gender subordinate to class? An empirical assessment of Colvin and Pauly's structural Marxist theory of delinquency." *Journal of Criminal Law and Criminology* 85: 453–480.

—— (1995). "Doing gender: Sorting out the caste and crime conundrum." *Criminology* 29: 115–135.

SMART, B., and CAROL SMART (1978). *Women, Sexuality and Social Control.* London: Routledge and Kegan Paul.

SMART, CAROL (1976). *Women, Crime and Criminology: A Feminist Critique.* Boston: Routledge and Kegan Paul.

—— (1979). "The new female criminality: Reality or myth?" *British Journal of Criminology* 19: 50–59.

—— (1995). *Law, Crime and Sexuality: Essays in Feminism.* London, UK: Sage.

SMITH, DOUGLAS A., and RAYMOND PATERNOSTER (1987). "The gender gap in theories of deviance: Issues and evidence." *Journal of Research in Crime and Delinquency* 24: 140–172.

SMITH, MICHAEL D. (1988). "Women's fear of violent crime: An exploratory test of a feminist hypothesis." *Journal of Family Violence* 3: 29–38.

—— (1990). "Patriarchal ideology and wife beating: A test of a feminist hypothesis." *Violence and Victims* 5: 257–274.

SPOHN, CASSIA, JOHN GRUHL, and SUSAN WELCH (1987). "The impact of the ethnicity and gender of defendants on the decision to reject or dismiss felony charges." *Criminology* 25: 175–191.

SPOHN, CASSIA C., and JEFFREY W. SPEARS (1997). "Gender and case processing decisions: A comparison of case outcomes for male and female defendants charged with violent felonies." *Women and Criminal Justice* 8: 29–59.

SPOHN, CASSIA, SUSAN WELCH, and JOHN GRUHL (1985). "Women defendants in court: The interaction between sex and race in convicting and sentencing." *Social Science Quarterly* 66: 178–185.

STEFFENSMEIER, DARRELL, and EMILIE A. ALLAN (1988). "Sex disparities in arrests by residence, race, and age: An assessment of the gender convergence/crime hypothesis." *Justice Quarterly* 5: 53–80.

STEFFENSMEIER, DARRELL, and JOHN H. KRAMER (1982). "Sex-based differences in the sentencing of adult criminal defendants." *Sociology and Social Research* 66: 289–304.

STEFFENSMEIER, DARRELL, and R. H. STEFFENSMEIER (1980). "Trends in female delinquency." *Criminology* 18: 62–85.

THOMAS, WILLIAM I. (1907). *The Unadjusted Girl.* New York: Harper and Row.

THORTON, WILLIAM E., and JENNIFER JAMES (1979). "Masculinity and delinquency revisited." *British Journal of Criminology* 19: 225–241.

VAN DE WARKER, E. (1975–1976). "The relations of women to crime." *Popular Science Monthly* 8: 1–16.

VEDDER, CLYDE, and DORA SOMERVILLE (1970). *The Delinquent Girl.* Springfield, IL: Charles C. Thomas.

VISHER, CHRISTY A. (1983). "Gender, police arrest decisions, and notions of chivalry." *Criminology* 21: 5–28.

WALKER, GILLIAN A. (1990). *Family Violence and the Women's Movement: The Conceptual Politics of Struggle.* Toronto: University of Toronto Press.

WALSH, ANTHONY (1984). "Gender-based differences: A study of probation officers' attitudes about, and recommendations for, felony sexual assault cases." *Criminology* 22: 371–388.

WEIS, JOSEPH (1976). "Liberation and crime: The invention of the new female criminal." *Social Justice* 1: 17–27.

WEISHEIT, RALPH, and SUE MAHAN (1988). *Women, Crime, and Criminal Justice.* Cincinnati, OH: Anderson.

WIDOM, CATHY S. (1979). "Female offenders: Three assumptions about self-esteem, sex-role identity, and feminism." *Criminal Justice and Behavior* 6: 365–382.

WIDOM, CATHY S., and A. J. STEWART (1986). "Female criminality and the status of women." *International Annals of Criminology* 24: 137–162.

WILLIAMS, JOYCE, and KAREN HOLMES (1981). *The Second Assault: Rape and Public Attitudes.* Westport, CT: Greenwood Press.

WILLIAMS, LARRY, L., THOMAS WINFREE, and HAROLD THEIS (1984). "Women, crimes, and judicial dispositions: A comparative examination of the female offender." *Sociological Spectrum* 4: 249–273.

WITT, DAVID (1987) "A conflict theory of family violence." *Journal of Family Violence* 2: 291–301.

WONDERS, NANCY A. (1996). "Determinate sentencing: A feminist and postmodern story." *Justice Quarterly* 13: 611–648.

YLLO, KERSTI (1984). "The impact of structural inequality and sexist family norms on rates of wife beating." *Journal of International and Comparative Social Welfare* 1: 16–29.

YLLO, KERSTI, and MICHELE BOGRAD, eds. (1988). *Feminist Perspectives on Wife Abuse.* Newbury Park, CA: Sage.

YOUNG, ALLISON (1996). *Imagining Crime.* London, UK: Sage.

THE FUTURE OF CRIMINOLOGICAL THEORY

INTRODUCTION

One of the hazards of presenting theories one after the other is that the differences among them become magnified. Too often students (and criminologists) see the various theories as separate from each other. By providing a brief look at the heritage of each theory, we have tried to show that this is really not the case. Even this, though, cannot adequately suggest the ways in which theories are related. As long as people see each theory as separate and distinct, there will be little real progress in criminology. Fortunately, several criminologists are beginning to work on the integration of theories. This final chapter discusses some of the things that have happened in criminological theory in the last decade, points out the effect that we think they will have, and makes some observations about the future of criminological theory.

THE HERITAGE OF CONTEMPORARY THEORY

The events and influences that will affect current theoretical direction are difficult to see because of their close proximity to us. A few influences, however, should have a bearing on the ways theorists think. The social influences are political and economic conservatism. The intellectual influences include a new discipline specializing in criminal justice and an emphasis on quantification.

Social Influences

Since the early 1970s, society has been moving in a decidedly conservative direction. With the Iranian hostage crisis, it seemed that public attitudes came together and a conservative majority opinion developed. Political and religious factions claim to speak for the "silent majority," an ostensibly large group of strongly religious, conservative citizens. Whether or not this silent majority exists, there has indeed been a movement toward religious fundamentalism, even to the extent of political involvement. A further impetus for this conservative direction has been the economic depression of the 1980s. Responding to fiscal necessity, many governmental programs have been cut and a pragmatic approach to expenditures in the criminal justice system has been taken. In some instances people have recognized that a pure punishment-oriented approach does not work, and intervention strategies more closely allied with treatment are now being tried. The drug war, while still focused on law enforcement approaches, has also begun to encourage education and treatment efforts. However, the Clinton administration seems to be squarely in the law-and-order camp and it seems clear that liberal ideologies are not ready for a comeback.

The most important implication for criminology of this continuing conservative movement has been in the way criminals are viewed. The appreciative and sympathetic portrayal of criminals in the 1960s disappeared in favor of a view of the criminal as a rational being. A rational criminal, of course, chooses to commit crimes and is not particularly amenable to expensive rehabilitation programs. Thus, other approaches are necessary. The expansion of research and literature on deterrence, just deserts, and rational theories exemplifies the direction many criminologists are choosing.

In previous editions of this book we suggested there would be little immediate future for structural theories. However, the new strain theory proposed by Robert Agnew (1992) runs against this tide. Indeed, there is now room for structural theories under the social disorganization and ecology framework of the new victimology studies (see Bursik, 1988). Further, both the new gender-informed theories and new variations on conflict theories demonstrate a greater degree of vitality than was the case just eight years ago. Nonetheless, it still seems that rational choice and process-oriented theories will be dominant. This means that criminological theory will probably tend toward explaining the various processes of how one becomes criminal. These processes, given a conservative bent, will most likely be explained by emphasizing traditional values and institutions: schools, family, friends, and work. Indeed, the most popular direction in new theories is a focus on the family and child-rearing practices. Social control theories, and integrative theories that incorporate social control ideas, should remain popular.

The Rise of Criminal Justice

While criminology has never been the only discipline responsible for the study of crime, the years after 1965 saw the emergence of a new discipline with a singular focus on crime and the criminal justice system. This new discipline, criminal justice, arose during a period of increased federal activity in the area of crime control—mostly as a result of the 1967 President's Commission on Law Enforcement and the Administration of Justice. That commission strongly advocated that a "war against crime" be launched and that those working in the criminal justice system be professionalized. The federal agency that evolved from the work of the commission, the Law Enforcement Assistance Administration, not only spent funds to upgrade various criminal justice departments and programs but also provided educational funding for college courses. Many colleges thus began offering criminal justice courses as a way to tap this unexpected new source of tuition funds.

The discipline of criminal justice expanded throughout the 1970s. By the end of the decade, a good portion of criminology had become part of criminal justice, with criminologists teaching and doing research within academic criminal justice departments. This movement was not without its problems, however. Between the research funding of the federal government and the practitioner-oriented focus of criminal justice departments, much theoretical work was left behind. The 1970s represented the only decade since 1920 in which no major new theory was developed. Theory was largely put aside in favor of pragmatic descriptions of the system and research on increasing the effectiveness of system processing. Thus, theoretical criminology suffered from a lack of creative interest.

Quantitative Methodology and Theory

During the same period, the widespread employment of computers in criminological research assisted in the development of statistically-oriented forms of data analysis. More and more attention was spent on the development of research skills and techniques, until the training of most graduate students in criminology incorporated more statistics courses than theoretical materials. This movement, in and of itself, was not particularly undesirable; extended into other areas, however, the overemphasis on quantification represented a limited view of the world.

Since statistical analysis depends on transforming the world around us into numbers, the use of numbers often became more important than the quality of information. Mathematical formulas were developed to represent models of reality, personal characteristics were assumed from a few questions on a survey instrument, and aggregate social data were derived from the statistics collected by various governmental agencies. In short, criminologists often used data that were unsuited to the task of conveying the complexity of life, especially where deviance was concerned. They did this because those data were convenient for the statistical tools at hand.

Even this, though, did not present a particularly difficult problem for criminological theorizing. The problem arose when quantitative methodology was extended into guidelines for theory construction. Since methodology of this type is intensely concerned with the ability to measure, the major criteria for a "good" theory was that it should contain easily measured concepts. In fact, advocates of this position held that the most appropriate theory construction was a series of highly specific, objective, and mathematically formulated statements (see, for instance, Reynolds, 1971; Gibbs, 1972, 1987; Dubin 1978).

The problem with this approach is that it continues to prevent the creation of theories about larger issues and results in a series of unconnected explanations of some very specific behavior. Many theoretical concepts are not directly measurable (for example, the notions of social structure, values, and norms, which are all common to criminological literature). Further, such an approach almost precludes structural theories in favor of processual ones. However, the approach does strongly encourage the testing of theory, and this is exactly what the field has been doing in the last twenty years.

Braithwaite's Critique of Criminology

In an article in the *Australian and New Zealand Journal of Criminology* (1989c), John Braithwaite argues that theory became unpopular because it was allegedly nonproductive. The major reasons critics advance for this lack of productivity are (1) the difficulty of defining crime and (2) a belief that individual differences among criminals are so great that general theories of crime are impossible. Braithwaite suggests that there are indeed universalities by which crimes can be brought together in a general explanation. He believes that this is the case even in the face of myriad other causes of crime and makes the astute observation that "to be useful, a general theory is not required to explain all of the variance in all types of cases, but some of the variance in all types of cases" (1989c:130). In other words, the fact that there are many causal factors involved in criminality does not rule out the possibility that some factors may be present in all cases.

Concerning relativistic definitions of crime, Braithwaite notes that just as there are those who have a vested interest in clarifying crime, there are those with vested interests in keeping definitions of crime vague. That this is particularly the case with corporate and governmental crimes is self-evident; thus, it makes sense for criminologists to study the process by which offenders (or prospective offenders) come to rationalize behaviors by keeping those behaviors out of criminal definitions. In this way, there is room under the framework of a general explanatory theory for interpretative theory.

Braithwaite also finds a destructiveness in contemporary criminology. Citing Charles Tittle's (1985) earlier work, Braithwaite suggests that there is a tendency to test and discard rather than reconstruct theory if some part of the theory is found wanting. He argues that theories are built in a piecemeal fashion rather than created whole. Thus, from his viewpoint, a failure to attempt reconstruction after testing is a failure to nurture explanation. As a result, criminology has been relatively atheoretical and lacks convincing evidence that it has anything to say to policymakers. Finally, he believes that the "mission of criminology as a science should be to build theories of as general a scope as we can manage" (1989c:134). With this position, Braithwaite clearly believes it is the job of policymakers, not necessarily criminologists, to derive the policy implications from theory. In short, Braithwaite calls for a cooperative criminology.

THE NEW ERA OF THEORY PRODUCTION

As if the restraints on theory building had created a pent-up demand, criminologists began exploring new theoretical constructs during the 1980s. Slowly at first, and then with great rapidity, theoretical efforts began to emerge. Some of the first efforts included a "crime-as-self-help" theory proposed by Donald Black (1983), the routine activity theory of Lawrence Cohen and Marcus Felson (1979), and Hal Pepinsky and Paul Jesilow's (1985) argument for a recognition of diversity in lifestyles. A new burst of theoretical energy seemed to occur about 1987 with the publication of a special theory issue of the journal *Criminology*. Since that time, new theories, or adaptations of older theories, have been rapidly emerging. The previous two chapters explored some of major contemporary efforts in rational and feminist theory, and the adaptations of older theories have been noted at the end of each of the respective theory chapters. We examine four theoretical directions in this concluding chapter: integrative theories, subjective theories, metatheories, and postmodern theories.

THE INTEGRATION OF THEORY

Perhaps as much as anything, criminology needs to take stock of the theories it has already developed. The same variables have been used time and again to explain crime and delinquency, yet each time the claim was that a new theory was being developed, although not necessarily by the authors themselves. It may even be that we have enough theories and just need to determine exactly what they explain and the contexts in which they work best. At this point, it makes sense to begin to determine exactly how and where existing theories fit together, something we have tried to do in this book by classifying the theories as we have discussed them. Macrotheories obviously do not compete with microtheories. Structural theories may be compatible with and explain the society in which processual theories operate. Thus, a good starting point might be to integrate some of these theories.

Directions for Integrative Theories

At the same time an interest in new theorizing began expanding, other criminologists concerned with the state of existing mainstream theories began to search for ways to return to criminological truisms. The easiest way to accomplish this, some argued, was to begin the process of integrating theories. The two most popular theories of the 1970s and 1980s, social control and social learning, were among the first candidates for integration (see the epilogue to Chapter 11). Thus, Elliott and colleagues (1979, 1985) and Edwards (1992) contributed a theory derived from social control, strain, and social learning perspectives (Edwards also added labeling to the mix). Others attempted integration of social learning with biological traits (Wilson and Herrnstein, 1985), conflict with subculture (Schwendinger and Schwendinger, 1985) and, perhaps the most popular integration, social control with deterrence (Meier and Johnson, 1977; Minor, 1977; Williams, 1985; Paternoster, 1989a).

In addition, some theorists noted that theories do not necessarily compete with each other and advanced an argument that theories speak to varied levels of explanation (Short, 1985, 1989). Thus, as long as assumptions are compatible, there is no need to cast out one theory to accept another. In fact, if most theories speak to different levels, then one task of criminology is to determine how theories might be organized into a coherent whole.

Not everyone is in favor of integration, and some theorists have claimed that the process of integration is doomed to failure. Travis Hirschi (1979), for example, argues that the assumptions of most major theories are fundamentally incompatible. Accordingly, he discourages integration and suggests instead that effort be put into the creation of new theory. Whether Hirschi is correct remains to be seen, but those doing integrative work today clearly seem to disagree.

The way in which theories are integrated is also of interest. It is possible to put theories together in a sequential, straight-line fashion, referred to as an **end-to-end model** (Hirschi, 1979). In this model, a structural, macrolevel theory would precede a middle-level theory (bridging theory), and a microtheory might conclude the process. Thus, social structure might produce social disorganization (anomie theory), disorganization might affect the quality of general relationships of groups in urban areas (differential opportunity), and those relationships might result in inadequate child-rearing practices leading to greater levels of delinquency (low self-concept theory). Another approach is to borrow concepts from several theories without regard to either the assumptions or the general thrust of the theories. These concepts are then put together in a new fashion. This approach is called a **fully-integrated model.** For example, one such model might put together gender roles, social disorganization, attachment to the family, and differential association. This tentative model might suggest that males and females react to social disorganization differently by relying more or less on the family for primary relationships. Social disorganization might push males to spend more time outside of the family, while females might react with greater family attachment. The associations thus built provide differential definitions for delinquent behavior, with males having proportionately higher numbers of delinquent definitions. We do not suggest that either of these two integrative examples are necessarily useful as a theory of delinquency, but they illustrate the difference between the two approaches.

This process of integration is well under way. We have noted that some of the theories discussed here are really integrations of two or more previous theories. Albert Cohen, and Richard Cloward and Lloyd Ohlin, for example, integrated Chicago School approaches with the anomie tradition. The subculture of violence theory proposed by Marvin Wolfgang and Franco Ferracuti attempted to synthesize most of the theoretical work of its day. More recent work has focused on combining the theories of social control and social learning (Conger, 1976; Hayes, 1997) or both of these with anomie theory (Elliott, Huizinga, and Ageton, 1985). Even conflict and consensus versions of theory may prove to be more compatible than the field has thought (Schwendinger and Schwendinger, 1985). We briefly explore seven examples of integrative theories here.

An Integrated Theory of Patterned Delinquent Behavior

Delbert Elliott, Suzanne Ageton, and Rachelle Canter (1979) have created an example of an end-to-end integrated theory model. They use social control theory, strain theory, and social learning theory to explain patterns of delinquent activity. First, they discuss social control variables, such as Hirschi's attachment, involvement, commitment, and belief, as well as the ways in which children are socialized. Their argument is that the childhood socialization process is critical to the strength of each of these elements of the bond. A well-socialized child is integrated into conventional society (attached to the family, involved with school and church, and committed to conventional activities). Second, they claim that as the child grows older, he or she gains exposure to a wide variety of social institutions and experiences. These experiences are both successful and unsuccessful. To the extent they are unsuccessful, the bonds to conventional society begin to weaken; that is, strain reduces the strength of the social control bonds.

Along with their life experiences, children are also introduced to larger networks of peers. This expanded peer network, or peer group, contains other children with various definitions about delinquent acts and reinforces attitudes toward delinquency. The greater the exposure to delinquent peers, the weaker the conventional bonds become and the more reinforcement is given to delinquency, creating a higher probability of committing delinquent acts.

The model also suggests that various factors interact together in producing delinquency. For instance, if bonds are weak to begin with because of poor socialization, little strain and delinquent reinforcement may be required for delinquent acts to take place. On the other hand, good childhood socialization may be overcome by the effects of poor experiences and poor associations. Indeed, the combination of the three theories means that a number of possible paths to delinquency (or conformity) can take place. The advantage of this integrated model is that it adds to the predictive power of each of the individual theories and helps account for cases in which the individual theory might incorrectly predict delinquency or conformity.

Adolescent Subcultures

A good example of a fully integrated and complex theory is the one proposed by Herman and Julia Schwendinger (1985), which attempts to explain subcultural delinquency. The theory is constructed on the concepts of conflict, subcultures, and peer networks. Other than the updated labeling approach expounded by Mark Colvin and John Pauley, the Schwendinger's theory is the only delinquency theory (of which we are aware) that uses conflict as the major integrating structure. The theorists reject mainstream approaches because those theories have problems explaining middle-class delinquency. Only social control theory can deal effectively with middle-class delinquency, but it requires that delinquents be poorly socialized. The Schwendingers claim their research shows that middle-class delinquents are reasonably socialized. Thus, they feel there is a crisis in criminology in that no theory adequately explains delinquency.

They propose a theory built around the effects of capitalist modes of production. The means of production in a society govern the types of relations present between social groups. While social groups may differ, capitalism also uniformly generates economic individualism by encouraging competition with others. Economic individualism makes social interests secondary to personal interests, thus leading to the development of ethical principles based on indifference. That is, adolescents in a capitalist society learn to put their needs above the needs of others. This serves to free youths from the anxieties and ethical problems posed by potential victims and others in society and leaves them mainly with a concern for maximizing their own self-interested behavior.

The Schwendingers found class-stratified adolescent subcultures characterized by the names "socialites" (upper classes), "intermediaries" (middle and working classes), and "street-corner youths" (lower classes). These subcultures vary in the form of the delinquencies in which they engage. In order to compare similar forms of behavior, the Schwendingers use a broad definition of delinquency that includes socialite hazing, date rape, and auto insurance fraud. Indeed, they note that socialite hazing is similar to street-corner gang violence. Within the continuum of subcultures from socialite to street-corner youth, the form of delinquency varies, though the largest amounts of delinquency occur at each end of this continuum. Finally, the generalized subcultures have local peer networks and social types (changing from time to time in the youth's life) that further dictate the membership of delinquent groups and the types of delinquency in which they engage.

Shaming

One relatively novel integrated theory based on a fully integrative model has been developed by John Braithwaite (1989a, 1989b). He incorporates opportunity, subcultural, control, learning, and labeling theories to produce a theory that relies on the notion of differential shaming. Beginning with opportunity theory, Braithwaite notes that there are aspirations and means, both legitimate and illegitimate. For criminality or delinquency to occur, blocked legitimate opportunities must be replaced by available illegitimate ones. With this background, Braithwaite borrows from subcultural theories the concept of organization for learning and transmission of law-breaking values. Here he notes the contrast with social control theory. Social control creates conformity with the law, whereas differential learning and value transmission create conformity with the subculture and nonconformity with the law. However, the direction an individual takes is not explained by these concepts; a "tipping point" is needed.

Differential shaming is posited as that tipping point. Many forms of shaming are available both to conventional and subcultural groups. To the extent that an offender is exposed to shaming or anticipates shaming, a tipping point is reached. Two forms of shaming are presented: disintegrative shaming and integrative shaming. The former fails to reunite a shamed offender with the community or subgroup, thus resulting in an outcast status and greater deviance. The latter returns a shamed offender to the group with conciliatory gestures and separates the evil act from the character of the offender. The obvious policy implications are that acts can be strongly sanctioned, but a reformed offender can be treated in a forgiving fashion. Since subcultures have power to shame (as does the conventional moral order), the theoretical problem is to overcome the subcultural effect by a network of communities operating under a reintegrative shaming modality. Braithwaite's article on organizational crime (1989b) makes just such an attempt. As noted in Chapter 8, shaming has been reintroduced as a labeling theory concept, and Braithwaite's approach may yet become popular.

Evolutionary Ecology Theory

The most complex theory in recent theorizing is Lawrence Cohen and Richard Machalek's (1988) evolutionary ecology perspective (with contributions by Bryan Vila, 1993, 1994). Ignoring the problem of crime committed by truly deviant individuals, they examine crime committed by otherwise normal people. The theory, which is drawn primarily from concepts in the fields of behavioral ecology and evolutionary biology, focuses on the diversity of "behavioral strategies" derived from social and personal interactions. Factors contributing to criminality are variously sociocultural, constitutional, developmental, environmental, situational (opportunities), and psychological. If this perspective gains in popularity, it will clearly create a new paradigm by which we view reality.

Life-course Theory

Life-course theory, an integrative theory derived from social control, ecology, and a new perspective on an old dataset, has been developed by Robert Sampson and John Laub (1990, 1992, 1993). Based on an analysis of the Gluecks' (1950) old data on a thousand juveniles followed until age thirty-two, Sampson and Laub found that traditional delinquency experiences predicted criminality in adult life. Thus, they conclude change over time is a critical component in explaining crime: the criminal experience is a dynamic one. However, informal social control also seems to have an effect on the likelihood of delinquent experiences. Events after becoming an adult, such as job stability, were important in decreasing adult criminality. In other words, various forms of social bonds (particularly work, education, and the family) change the life trajectory of crime (1990:618) and at different points in life have different effects. Just as they serve to reduce criminal activity, these bonds can also be broken and then act as a destabilizing force over the affected portion of the life course. The focus on a dynamic approach to life events is crucial to the theory (particularly the effects of social and biological-aging, stability and change, human agency, cohort, and historical period.) Sampson and Laub's life-course theory has already gained popularity as a way of arguing for dynamic theory and longitudinal research.

Crime and Social Context

A different approach to integrative theory comes from Terance Miethe and Robert Meier (1994). Rather than line up a list of theories for integration, they look instead at the overall picture of crime. They argue that three base components exist in crime: the offender, the victim, and facilitating contexts (situations). Miethe and Meier bring these components together by using concepts from theories of rationally motivated offenders, routine activities perspectives related to victimization, and ecological concepts in order to structure social contexts. They achieve an integrative theory resembling a social disorganization perspective. A social context with low socioeconomic status, population mobility, ethnic heterogeneity, and family disruption facilitates both offender motivation and criminal opportunity. These factors influence youths' ties to conventional institutions of social control, the level of community supervision, and the ability to articulate and achieve communal goals. Thus, crime rates are primarily a function of a socially-disorganized area's effect on social control and criminal opportunities. Such an area produces and brings together offenders and victims in the same time and space.

Control Balance Theory

Charles Tittle (1995) has developed a general theory of crime to compete with Gottfredson and Hirschi's version. Called control balance theory, it combines ideas from control and deterrence theories, some "propensity" theories, and subjective theories. Its major concept is that of "balancing" control—the amount of control people exercise as opposed to the amount of control to which they are subjected. Tittle refers to the amount of control from these two sources as the "control ratio." When there is a control imbalance, either a deficit or surplus, deviance is more likely to occur.

Rather than pointing to the "causes" of crime, Tittle refers to the *probability* of deviance (or a specific form of it) occurring. The theory does not merely balance the two forms of control, however. Tittle recognizes the complexity of deviance and incorporates several other concepts: basic human impulses or preferences, desire for autonomy, predisposition toward deviant motivation, feelings of debasement, situational risk, seriousness, and opportunity.

Control balance theory states that deviant behavior is designed to alter the individual's control ratio. As a result, examining only the form of deviance may not directly explain the deviant's motivation because the control-ratio motivation serves a specific purpose for the individual that may not otherwise be apparent. When the control-ratio is unbalanced, counter-control (the control one is subjected to) is important in preventing deviance.

SUBJECTIVE THEORIES

Subjective theories differ from most of the theories we discuss in this book in their emphasis on understanding the motives and intents of the people involved in committing crime. This perspective is often referred to as a **phenomenological** one. Rather than predict criminality or focus on differences in crime rates, subjective theories shun statistics and focus on describing the *essence* of behavior or why people do certain things. In keeping with this tradition, perhaps the most controversial, and original, recent theoretical position is found in *Seductions of Crime: Moral and Sensual Attractions in Doing Evil,* by Jack Katz (1988). Katz offers a critique of positivist criminology, largely by noting that many of the people predicted to commit crime do not actually do so. On the other hand, many of those who are not predicted to commit crime end up becoming criminals. In addition, he points out that the people predicted to become criminals often do not commit crimes for long periods of time, even though the **background factors** (social class, race, employment) remain the same. Katz's final critique, and the one most central to his theory, is that the standard background factors (the variables of anomie, differential association, etc.) cannot predict which individuals will engage in crime.

Katz's theory of violent crime revolves around the notion that the **experiential foreground** (what is happening at the moment) is crucial to the choice to engage in criminal action. Perhaps the term "choice" is not exactly correct here, because Katz really means that certain events and situations are "given" the power to seduce an individual into action. Different crimes have different forms of seduction, but they are all passionate, exciting, and relevant to the current personal identity of the offender. In a sense, crime is as Chicago School researcher Frederic Thrasher (1927) once described gang delinquency—it can be fun.

But the essence of violent forms of crime is more than just fun, in that the offender transcends normal life by becoming a "badass," or becoming tough, mean, and chaotic. By being unpredictable and chaotic, the robber establishes him- or herself as beyond the normal experience of victims and uses the threat of chaos to usurp the orderly lifestyle of victims. By being "alien," the badass generates a posture that transcends abnormal morality and demonstrates that he or she comes from a "morally alien place" (Katz, 1988:88). In addition, the offender becomes "hard," thereby denying others' attempts at reestablishing control over the situation. Thus, the individual creates "an angle of moral superiority over the intended victim" (Katz, 1988:169) and the system at large. Regarding murder, the killer is moved from the "eternally humiliating situation" to passionate rage and, finally, to a "righteous slaughter." Katz describes the humiliating situation as not simply a humiliation of the individual (the potential killer), but as an affront to his or her "eternal human value." Rage, then, is less unbridled than it is a focused effort to redeem oneself, generate power, and defend the eternal value. Thus, the term "righteous slaughter" is used to mean that the murder has been undertaken as a last stand to correct a wrong. Katz makes similar observations about shoplifting and youth gangs.

Katz's phenomenological perspective requires that one understand the situation from the view of the offender. Without this focus, the offense appears irrational. The problem is that Katz not only has to understand and appreciate these offenses from the perspective of the offender, but that he also has to assume the motives and intents of the offenders he has studied are essentially the same for other offenders. This is the problem of generalizability, and we do not know whether all, most, or only a few offenders share these meanings. The advantage of Katz's position is that it sensitizes criminologists to alternative meanings of deviance. Rationality from the point of view of the offender can be vastly different from the things that the observer (or victim) believes about the offender. Moreover, this perspective adds a spiritual flavor to the gains of crime: offenders attempt to construct their own worlds, at least temporarily. Because most criminologists prefer objective and deterministic perspectives, Katz's theory, although novel and interesting, will probably not become too popular.

Peacemaking Criminology

Harold Pepinsky and Richard Quinney have separately and jointly worked to create an emerging form of criminological theory called "peacemaking" (Pepinsky, 1988, 1991; Quinney, 1988, 1989; Pepinsky and Quinney, 1991; Quinney and Wildeman, 1991). The perspective looks at the entire enterprise of criminal justice and argues that we are going about things the wrong way. The focus should be on relieving suffering, and as a product of that, crime can be reduced. Indeed, peacemaking criminologists want to shift crime control emphasis from the way in which offenders behave and methods of punishment to the way in which people's motives interact. If the motives are self-interested rather than cooperative, crime occurs and "war" is made. In short, they believe that contemporary conceptions of crime should be changed from a social problem to an integral part of the problem of how to make peace. For peacemaking theory, then, crime is created when a society encourages or creates relationships among its citizens that destroy interpersonal cohesiveness (the bonds between people) and makes citizens unresponsive to each other.

Perhaps the most important part of refocusing from offenders to citizens is the form of social interactions that people have with each other. As community members gain the ability to interact and cooperate in order to meet each other's needs, the theory assumes that members of a community will generate greater compassion. This is the mainstay of interpersonal cohesion, which serves to restrain violence.

Peacemaking criminology encourages a transformation in human interaction in the areas of social, economic, and authority structures. Not only do people have to become more concerned with the welfare of others, but social institutions must also be modified to emphasize the same concerns. In addition, the makeup of the economic structure has to be changed to discourage competition and ego-centered behavior. People need to work for and with each other rather than against each other.

Finally, peacemaking theorists argue that the criminal justice system has to integrate the community much more thoroughly into policing, judicial systems, and forms of correction. The new community-policing orientation is a step in that direction. Interpersonal cohesiveness is the only way to bring together police and citizens in conflict management to ward off violence and crime. The peacemaking approach thus provides a way for citizens and police to work together to give citizens more control over their own disputes.

METATHEORY

As with sociology proper, criminology has recently become concerned with metatheory. Metatheories tell us how to put unit theories together, or they specify the things that should be included in unit theories about a particular subject. As noted in Chapter 1, unit theories are explanations of specific phenomena; therefore, all of the theories we have discussed are unit theories.

In general, metatheory is concerned with the organization of principles that can be used to make sense of theories. Metatheory is not directly testable and for that reason is rejected by some critics (for example, Gibbs, 1989b). It does, however, have its uses, particularly in the identification of levels of explanation of various theories (Short, 1989). Unless theoretical assumptions and points of focus are clearly identified, there is little to prevent improper tests and integration of those theories. Some theories, for instance, focus on either crime or criminal behavior, two rather different phenomena that are often treated as if they were identical.

Some writers, such as Joan McCord (1989), view metatheories as approaches that meld together existing theories. Her concern, however, is that we may integrate theories without having the criteria needed to measure their adequacy. Because integrative theorizing appears to be in vogue, McCord's concern may be valid. In one documentation of this trend, Steven Messner, Marvin Krohn, and Allan Liska (1989) have published a collection of papers presented at a 1987 conference on theoretical integration. The authors of the various papers represent most of the major criminological theoreticians and they discuss microlevel, macrolevel, and cross-level integration. On the whole, there seems to be a consensus that there are too many problems for successful integration to take place (see, especially, the papers by Hirschi, Thornberry, Swigert, Gibbs, Meier, Short, and Giordano). If so, perhaps a metatheory or two is needed that will provide organizing principles for the integration of theories. We present one such metatheory in the following discussion of postmodern theories.

POSTMODERN THEORIES

New alternatives to conventional theories are emerging under the general rubric of *postmodern theory*. While it is many things, recent work seems to focus on two major directions: the use of linguistic theory, or semiotics, and chaos-based theory. The semiotic version (see Milovanovic, 1997a, and Arrigo, 1996) trades primarily on the writings of Jacques Lacan (1981), a French psychoanalyst. This approach defines reality as the subjective way in which people understand the world about them. The "understanding" is primarily formed by the concepts and metaphors in language. For instance, one's role and place in society is structured by the language concepts of that society. Similarly, the reality of the criminal justice system is created by the metaphors and linguistic concepts essential to the workings of the criminal justice system. These theorists note that the created reality is such that those accused of crime are inherently disadvantaged in the legal process. This happens, for example, through the association of evil with crime, irrationality with criminality, and good with the prosecution. An appreciation of the subjective reality of legal structures and concepts adds to an understanding of crime, particularly the structuring of responses to crime. As has been the case with most critical theory, however, there seems to be little likelihood that mainstream criminology will see fit to incorporate these postmodern concepts.

The other form of postmodern theory (see Milovanovic, 1997b) is just beginning to emerge and, in one sense, shows more promise in being reflected in mainstream criminology. This is primarily because chaos theories offer a radically different view of the world, yet they do not have the intellectual and conceptual baggage left over from radical/critical theory. As far as the conflict/consensus debate goes, chaos theories are relatively uninterested. Another name for the perspective, at least from physics and related fields, is complexity theory. The general idea is that highly complex systems are difficult to model in rather simplistic, but common, linear analyses and the interaction of hundreds (perhaps millions) of variables makes static analysis virtually worthless. Thus, chaotic systems are nonlinear, dynamic representations of reality (which is why the general approach is called complexity theory). In addition, there are no ideological positions that require variables from only one discipline (actually, multidisciplinary models are common). The main problem with such theories is that traditional analytical techniques are virtually worthless, making the approach a challenge to the dominant analytical paradigm.

Critical-incident Metatheory

One version of chaos-based postmodern theory proposed by Frank Williams (1998) is called *critical-incident metatheory*. Rather than proposing a theory of behavior, Williams proposes a way to view and structure reality, thus a way to "understand" the existing evidence on crime and criminals. The metatheory basically says, because reality is highly complex, so are the concepts of crime and criminality. Behavior is a product of the interplay of genetics, neurochemistry, physical environment, psychological tendencies, and social environment. These factors come together in an individual's background, with new events either adding to or subtracting from the accumulating pile of factors. At some time, a critical point is reached and the individual reacts to relieve stress with some behavior. The problem is that the exact release of a critical point is unpredictable, as is the type of behavior emitted. Further, the last addition to the background pile of factors is no more the "cause" of the critical point and subsequent behavior than any other individual factor in the pile.

Once the problem of "emitting" a behavior is potentially resolved, there are other difficulties in predicting criminal behavior. First, the individual interacts with his or her environment, so being "ready" to commit a crime (or other similar behavior) is not sufficient. For instance, one cannot commit a purse-snatching without a victim with a purse being in the environment. Similarly, a barricade between the potential offender and victim serves the same preventive purpose. Moreover, there is substantial evidence demonstrating that the presence of people to react to a behavior is crucial to the emitting of a behavior and, perhaps, even the form of behavior emitted. That is, potential witnesses are sufficient to discourage much would-be criminality.

All of the "objective" factors above do not yet constitute the whole story. An important but often-forgotten ingredient in the crime picture is subjectivity. For instance, do all potential offenders (or potential reactors) interpret a situation in the same way? Regardless of the objective ingredients of a crime situation, each person's perception of reality governs the way he or she will respond and act. Both potential criminals and potential reactors must combine their subjective viewpoints with the objective situation to create a "crime."

As a metatheory, then, the critical-incident perspective reminds us to be aware of the complex nature of reality and to incorporate that complexity into our understanding of action and reaction. Thus, the position holds that (1) explanations based on variables from a single discipline probably overlook most of what precipitates behavior; (2) "causes" of behavior occurring just prior to the behavior are probably not a cause, just more additions to a set of factors already headed toward a critical point; (3) crime is not a particularly unique form of behavior and may be only one of a number of behaviors capable of relieving the stress of a critical point (thereby making the prediction of a single type of behavior, such as crime, somewhat unreliable); and (4) the composite of factors in an individual's background, the environment of the moment, the individual's subjective interpretation of events and the reaction behaviors of others are all necessary parts of the crime/criminality puzzle.

A BRIEF SUMMARY OF CRITICAL-INCIDENT METATHEORY

1. Chaos approaches emphasize the presence of seemingly random information that under certain dimensions of observation yield rather systematic patterns. Dimensions of observation involve moving up to larger views of phenomena, or moving down to smaller ones. They also involve changing the position of observation and the period of time.
2. A certain offshoot of chaos theory, self-organized criticality theory, suggests that various, otherwise random, events and factors accumulate into recognizable shapes and patterns. Moreover, these ultimately result in similar processes, like the analogy of dropping grains of sand to form a sandpile.
3. A criminological critical-incident perspective focuses on the "accumulation" of variables over time to produce behavior. The variables being accumulated are biological, social, environmental, and psychological. Some are obviously deposited prior to others, and it is

also possible to "take away" some variables. That is, both addition and subtraction are possible, as well as interaction (actually any function is theoretically possible), and all affect the composite weight of the system.

4. No particular order is required for the accumulating variables. All that is necessary is that the pile begins to assume a particular shape. These accumulated variables ultimately achieve enough weight to reach a critical point where something (a behavior) is waiting to happen. The next variable (perhaps one with a tiny addition to the pile) may be enough to create the behavior.

5. Once a behavior is at the critical point, the effect of adding a new variable does not assure that a particular behavior (such as theft) will occur. This is because the emission of behavior is a weakly random function. Over a large number of critical points or over a large group of individuals, however, behavior becomes patterned and more predictable.

6. Predicting specific behavior is a problem. Any of a similar class of behaviors remains possible, or even a nonclass behavior may occur.

7. If the critical point randomly remains for an extreme period of time, it becomes supercritical. Under these conditions, the addition of each new variable is more and more likely to produce behavior. Such supercritical stress-relieving behavior is more likely to be seen as spontaneous and potentially more harmful behavior.

8. Once a behavior relieves the stress, the "accumulation" of variables begins again. If only accretion takes place, things will build toward the critical point once again. Because of this, where there are segments of society in which social, environmental, and biological variables routinely build toward critical points, behaviors are aggregately repetitive and predictability increases.

9. Criminal behavior itself is only one of a class of behaviors. There are many different forms of behavior that serve to relieve the stress of a critical point. Thus, the task is not to explain criminal behavior per se, but the class of behavior. At aggregated levels, however, rates of crime should increase given accumulations of certain variables for certain groups. Crime rate predictions, then, are more possible.

10. Social reaction is governed by similar rules. Additionally, the behavior of social reaction interacts with criminal behavior to make the scenario quite complex. Not only is a critical incident required to produce a critical point for behavior, but public/agency reaction interacts with and affects the form of emitted behavior.

11. Behavior is also a function of subjective reality, both for the individual acting and those reacting to the response. Therefore, the interpretation of various conditions and stimuli present at any given time affects the nature of the life-shape (the slope) and whether a particular factor is a critical incident or not.

Source: Frank P. Williams III, *Imagining Criminology: An Alternative Paradigm* (New York: Garland, 1998).

CONCLUSIONS

The Rise of a New Criminology?

The relative theoretical quiet represented by the 1970s may have simply been the end of a paradigm (Kuhn, 1970). Buoyed by new evidence produced by environmental design and victimization research, some criminologists began to conceive of criminals as rational individuals who made their own behavioral choices from a patchwork of opportunity. Others, informed by advances in feminist thought, used age-old evidence on male/female crime to create gender-based explanations of socialization, power, and lifestyle differentials as they affect criminality. Still others, tired of the orderly way in which mainstream theories relegated deviance to objective existence, insisted that crime is best understood as a subjective experience, a "seduction into evil" (Katz, 1988). Even the concept of crime itself has been questioned, and terrorism became a topic worthy of treatment by two prominent theorists (Gibbs, 1989a; Turk, 1989). Finally, some attempted to find new ways to reconstruct the old versions of criminological theories (Cullen, 1984; Bursik, 1988, 1989; Braithwaite, 1989b; Farnworth and Leiber, 1989; Hagan, 1989; Link et al., 1989; Luckenbill and Doyle, 1989; Paternoster and Iovanni, 1989; Gottfredson and Hirschi, 1990; Agnew, 1992) and work on deterrence became more sophisticated (Paternoster, 1989a, 1989b).

While the Kuhnian paradigm may not quite describe the happenings at the end of this decade (some argue that it does not fit the social sciences anyway), it seems reasonable to use it as a way of analyzing the experience (see Williams, 1998, for an explanation of paradigms in criminology). The emergence of a single paradigm has always been questionable in criminology, yet reference to "mainstream" criminology is common. This mainstream criminology, whatever form it may take, has largely been consensus-based, and through the 1950s and 1960s, it was a combination of structural-functionalist and Chicago School thought. Arguably, these mainstream theories at least had social determinism in common. The 1960s brought new forms of social determinist theories, such as labeling, conflict, social learning, and social control; all of which (except for radical versions of conflict) became mainstream criminology by the 1980s.

Perhaps because of the massive effort to test theory, the 1980s produced a period of doubt. No one theory seemed to hold up very well to evidence, although some were declared to be superior to others. Thus, some degree of confusion set in. If we borrow from Kuhn's ideas, the period was one of crisis. Criminology was not sure if it was supposed to explain crime, criminal behavior, or some subset of crime; in fact, criminologists were not even sure if they had the right questions (Farrington, Ohlin, and Wilson, 1986), let alone the right answers. Much of the criminological literature of the 1980s reflects this problem, as well as a groping for new directions.

While it is difficult to say that Kuhn's revolutionary phase has been reached, new theoretical insights have clearly begun to challenge the old paradigm of social determinism. The assumption of rationalism and the return of "natural propensities" allow the introduction of psychological and biological concepts into the explanation of criminality. At the same time, traditional notions of socially-structured crime conditions can be interpreted to mean that there are persistent patterns of rationality, personality traits, or biological properties in the population. Thus, the older perspectives do not necessarily die out; instead, they may be reworked to mesh with the new ideas.

We now have a relatively large number of theories being proposed. While the forms and types of theory are diverse, it is also true that there are alternative dependent variables. Theorists are busy explaining crime in general, victim events, and fear of crime. Variety is also evident from the number of "minitheories" proposing to explain singular forms of crime (from fraud to rape to serial murder to property crime). While all this has been going on, some criminologists have returned to notions that general theory is possible and are busy explaining crime as an overall phenomena.

If this analysis is correct, contemporary criminology is now fermenting nicely. Theorists are entertaining new evidence on criminality while at the same time reconceptualizing and reassessing old evidence. The direction the new theories will take is still in doubt. Nonetheless, the field appears to be on the verge of a paradigm revolution as energetic and far-reaching as that which precipitated the labeling movement of the early 1960s.

What Does This Mean to Students of Criminology?

All these different theories, and the current attempts to integrate them, often leave students of criminology puzzled: how can there be so many different explanations of the same thing? One answer lies in the fact that crime is a very complex phenomenon. Even the determination of whether behavior is criminal is difficult. Further, if an act occurs without the knowledge of anyone other than the perpetrator, has a crime really occurred? If a legislature passes a law that makes an act a crime, was the same act a criminal one before the passing of the law? This complexity means that scholars look at the reality of crime and see different things. In part what they see is a product of what they are prepared to see, and what they propose as an answer or cause is a product of what they are prepared to propose.

A second answer is that theories attempt to explain different pieces of the crime puzzle. This is the level-of-explanation problem we discussed in Chapter 1. Some theories attempt to explain how rates of crime differ from one group to another, others deal with the making of laws, and still others try to account for individual propensities toward crime. One of the reasons for the classification schemes at the end of each chapter is to make readers aware of the varying foci of the theories.

Yet another reason for the number of theories is embedded in the assumptions we make about human nature and the way the world functions. If you believe that people are basically self-interested (as Hirschi does), then deviance requires no real explanation and conformity needs explaining. On the other hand, if you believe that people are basically social creatures and conformity is natural (as Cohen does), then conformity needs no explanation and deviance needs explaining. Other assumptions about the nature of society, whether crime largely belongs to the lower class, and whether gender is an important factor lead to certain constructions of theory and not others.

The fact is that we will never all see the world the same way. Nevertheless, these theories of crime and delinquency are worth understanding. They help us see various facts about the crime problem and give us ammunition to create policy-related proposals to reduce crime. Without these theories, logical policies are much more difficult to produce, and there is the danger that atheoretical policies might cause unanticipated negative consequences. Most of our crime policies, of course, are a product of political expediency, and the danger of negative consequences is very real. Clearly, there are enough policy implications in the criminological theories we have discussed here to create a wide range of programs to suit almost any need. Through your acquaintance with these theories, perhaps you will be able to influence the direction of crime policy in your community.

BIBLIOGRAPHY

AGNEW, ROBERT (1992). "Foundation for a general strain theory of crime and delinquency." *Criminology* 30: 47–66.

AKERS, RONALD L. (1989). "A social behaviorist's perspective on integration of theories of crime and deviance." In S. F. Messner, M. D. Krohn, and A. E. Liska, eds., *Theoretical Integration in the Study of Deviance and Crime: Problems and Prospects,* 23–36. Albany: State University of New York Press.

ARRIGO, BRUCE (1993). *Madness, Language and the Law.* Albany, NY: Harrow and Heston.

——— (1994). "The insanity defense." In R. Kevelson, ed., *The Eyes of Justice,* 57–83. New York, NY: Peter Lang.

——— (1995a). "The peripheral core of law and criminology: On postmodern social theory and conceptual integration." *Justice Quarterly* 12: 447–72.

——— (1995b). "Deconstructing classroom instruction: Theoretical and methodological contributions of the postmodern sciences for crimino-legal education." *Social Pathology* 1: 115–148.

——— (1996). "The behavior of law and psychiatry: Rethinking knowledge construction and the guilty-but-mentally-ill verdict." *Criminal Justice and Behavior* 23: 572–592.

BAKER, PATRICK (1993). "Chaos, order and sociological theory." *Sociological Inquiry* 63: 123–149.

BALKIN J. M. (1987). "Deconstructive practice and legal theory." *Yale Law Journal* 96: 743–786.

BANKSTON, CARL L., III, and STEPHEN J. CALDAS (1996). "Adolescents and deviance in a Vietnamese American community: A theoretical synthesis." *Deviant Behavior* 17: 159–181.

BANNISTER, SHELLEY, and DRAGAN MILOVANOVIC (1990). "The necessity defense, substantive justice, and oppositional linguistic praxis." *International Journal of the Sociology of Law* 18: 179–198.

BENDA, BRENT B., and LEANNE WHITESIDE (1995). "Testing an integrated model of delinquency using LISREL." *Journal of Social Science Research* 21: 1–32.

BENNET, LANCE, and MARTHA FELDMAN (1981). *Reconstructing Reality in the Courtroom.* New Brunswick, NJ: Rutgers University Press.

BERNARD, THOMAS J. (1989). "A theoretical approach to integration." In S. F. Messner, M. D. Krohn, and A. E. Liska, eds., *Theoretical Integration in the Study of Deviance and Crime: Problems and Prospects,* 137–159. Albany: State University of New York Press.

BLACK, DONALD (1983). "Crime as social control." *American Sociological Review* 48: 34–45.

BRACHER, MARK (1988). "Lacan's theory of the four discourses." *Prose Studies* 11: 32–49.

——— (1993). *Lacan, Discourse and Social Change.* Ithaca, NY. Cornell University Press.

BRAITHWAITE, JOHN (1989a). *Crime, Shame, and Reintegration.* Cambridge: Cambridge University Press.

——— (1989b). "Criminological theory and organizational crime." *Justice Quarterly* 6: 333–358.

——— (1989c). "The state of criminology: Theoretical decay or renaissance?" *Australian and New Zealand Journal of Criminology* 22: 129–135.

BURSIK, ROBERT J., JR. (1988). "Social disorganization and theories of crime and delinquency." *Criminology* 26: 519–545.

——— (1989). "Political decisionmaking and ecological models of delinquency: Conflict and consensus." In S. F. Messner, M. D. Krohn, and A. E. Liska, eds., *Theoretical Integration in the Study of Deviance and Crime: Problems and Prospects,* 105–117. Albany: State University of New York Press.

CHAMBLISS, WILLIAM J. (1975). "Toward a political economy of crime." *Theory and Society* 2: 149–169.

COHEN, LAWRENCE E., and MARCUS FELSON (1979). "Social change and crime rates: A routine activity approach." *American Sociological Review* 44: 588–607.

COHEN, LAWRENCE E., and RICHARD MACHALEK (1988). "A general theory of expropriative crime: An evolutionary ecological approach." *American Journal of Sociology* 94: 465–501.

COHEN, LAWRENCE E., BRYAN J. VILA, and RICHARD MACHALEK (1995). "Expropriative crime and crime policy: An evolutionary ecological analysis." *Studies on Crime and Crime Prevention* 4: 197–219.

CONGER, RAND (1976). "Social control and social learning models of delinquent behavior: A synthesis." *Criminology* 14: 17–40.

CULLEN, FRANCIS T. (1984). *Rethinking Crime and Deviance Theory: The Emergence of a Structuring Tradition.* Totowa, NJ: Rowman and Allanheld.

DALY, KATHLEEN, and MEDA CHESNEY-LIND (1988). "Feminism and criminology." *Justice Quarterly* 5: 497–538.

DUBIN, ROBERT (1978). *Theory Building,* rev. ed. New York: Free Press.

EBERT, TEREA (1991). "Writing in the political: Resistance (post)modernism." *Legal Studies Forum* 15: 291–303.

EDWARDS, WILLIE J. (1992). "Predicting juvenile delinquency: A review of correlates and a confirmation by recent research based on an integrated theoretical model." *Justice Quarterly* 9: 553–583.

ELLIOTT, DELBERT S. (1985). "The assumption that theories can be combined with increased explanatory power: Theoretical integrations." In R. Meier, ed., *Theoretical Methods in Criminology,* 123–149. Beverly Hills, CA: Sage.

ELLIOTT, DELBERT S., SUZANNE S. AGETON, and RACHELLE J. CANTER (1979). "An integrated theoretical perspective on delinquent behavior." *Journal of Research in Crime and Delinquency* 16: 3–27.

ELLIOTT, DELBERT S., DAVID HUIZINGA, and SUZANNE S. AGETON (1985). *Explaining Delinquency and Drug Use.* Beverly Hills, CA: Sage.

FARNWORTH, MARGARET, and MICHAEL J. LEIBER (1989). "Strain theory revisited: Economic goals, educational means and delinquency." *American Sociological Review* 54: 263–274.

FARRINGTON, DAVID, LLOYD OHLIN, and JAMES Q. WILSON (1986). *Understanding and Controlling Crime.* New York: Springer-Verlag.

GIBBS, JACK P. (1972). *Sociological Theory Construction.* Hinsdale, IL: Dryden.

——— (1987). "The state of criminological theory." *Criminology* 25: 821–840.

——— (1989a). "Conceptualization of terrorism." *American Sociological Review* 54: 329–340.

——— (1989b) "Three perennial issues in the sociology of deviance." In S. F. Messner, M. D. Krohn, and A. E. Liska, eds., *Theoretical Integration in the Study of Deviance and Crime: Problems and Prospects,* 179–198. Albany: State University of New York Press.

GIORDANO, PEGGY C. (1989). "Confronting control theory's negative cases." In S. F. Messner, M. D. Krohn, and A. E. Liska, eds., *Theoretical Integration in the Study of Deviance and Crime: Problems and Prospects,* 261–278. Albany: State University of New York Press.

GLUECK, SHELDON and ELEANOR GLUECK (1950). *Unraveling Juvenile Delinquency.* New York: The Commonwealth Fund.

GOTTFREDSON, DON M. (1989). "Criminological theories: The truth as told by Mark Twain." In W. S. Laufer and F. Adler, eds., *Advances in Criminological Theory,* vol. 1, 1–16. New Brunswick, NJ: Transaction.

GOTTFREDSON, MICHAEL, and TRAVIS HIRSCHI (1990). *A General Theory of Crime.* Stanford, CA: Stanford University Press.

GREGERSEN, HAL, and LEE SAILER (1993). "Chaos theory and its implications for social science research." *Human Relations* 46: 777–802.

HAGAN, JOHN (1989). "Micro- and macro-structures of delinquency causation and a power-control theory of gender and delinquency." In S. F. Messner, M. D. Krohn, and A. E. Liska, eds., *Theoretical Integration in the Study of Deviance and Crime: Problems and Prospects,* 213–227. Albany: State University of New York Press.

——— (1989b). *Structural Criminology.* New Brunswick, NJ: Rutgers University Press.

HAYES, HENNESSEY D. (1997). "Using integrated theory to explain the movement into juvenile delinquency." *Deviant Behavior* 18: 161–184.

HENRY, STUART, and DRAGAN MILOVANOVIC (1996). *Constitutive Criminology.* London: Sage.

HIRSCHI, TRAVIS (1979). "Separate and unequal is better." *Journal of Research in Crime and Delinquency* 16: 34–38.

——— (1989). "Exploring alternatives to integrated theory." In S. F. Messner, M. D. Krohn, and A. E. Liska, eds., *Theoretical Integration in the Study of Deviance and Crime: Problems and Prospects,* 37–49. Albany: State University of New York Press.

HIRSCHI, TRAVIS and MICHAEL R. GOTTFREDSON (1995). "Control theory and life-course perspective." *Studies on Crime Prevention* 4: 131–142.

HOWE, ADRIAN (1994). *Punish and Critique.* London: Routledge.

KATZ, JACK (1988). *Seductions of Crime: Moral and Sensual Attractions in Doing Evil.* New York: Basic Books.

———— (1991). "The motivation of the persistent robber." In M. Tonry, ed., *Crime and Justice: A Review of Research*, vol. 14, 277–306. Chicago: University of Chicago Press.

KUHN, THOMAS (1970). *The Structure of Scientific Revolutions*, 2nd ed. Chicago: University of Chicago Press.

LACAN, JAQUES (1981). *The Four Fundamental Concepts of Psycho-Analysis*. New York: Norton.

LINK, BRUCE, FRANCIS T. CULLEN, ELMER STRUENING, PATRICK E. SHROUT, and BRUCE P. DOHREWEND (1989). "A modified labeling theory approach to mental disorders: An empirical assessment." *American Sociological Review* 54: 400–423.

LUCKENBILL, DAVID F., and DANIEL P. DOYLE (1989). "Structural position and violence: developing a cultural explanation." *Criminology* 27: 419–433.

MACMILLAN, ROSS (1995). "Changes in the structure of life courses and the decline of social capital in Canadian society: A time series analysis of property crime rates." *Canadian Journal of Sociology* 20: 51–79.

MCCARTHY, BILL (1995). "Not just 'for the thrill of it': An instrumentalist elaboration of Katz's explanation of sneaky thrill property crimes." *Criminology* 33: 519–538.

MCCORD, JOAN (1989). "Theory, pseudotheory, and metatheory." In W. S. Laufer and F. Adler, eds., *Advances in Criminological Theory*, vol. 1, 127–145. New Brunswick, NJ: Transaction.

MEIER, ROBERT F. (1989). "Deviance and differentiation." In S. F. Messner, M. D. Krohn, and A. E. Liska, eds., *Theoretical Integration in the Study of Deviance and Crime: Problems and Prospects*, 199–212. Albany: State University of New York Press.

MEIER, ROBERT F., and WELDON JOHNSON (1977). "Deterrence as social control: The legal and extra-legal production of conformity." *American Sociological Review* 42: 292–304.

MEIER, ROBERT F., and TERANCE D. MIETHE (1993). "Understanding theories of criminal victimization." In M. Tonry, ed., *Crime and Justice: A Review of Research*, vol. 17, 459–499. Chicago: University of Chicago Press.

MENARD, SCOTT, and DELBERT S. ELLIOTT (1994). "Delinquent bonding, moral beliefs, and illegal behavior: A three-wave panel model." *Justice Quarterly* 11: 173–188.

MESSNER, STEVEN F., MARVIN D. KROHN, and ALLEN E. LISKA, eds. (1989). *Theoretical Integration in the Study of Deviance and Crime: Problems and Prospects*. Albany: State University of New York Press.

MESSNER, STEVEN F., and RICHARD ROSENFELD (1994). *Crime and the American Dream*. Belmont, CA: Wadsworth.

MIETHE, TERANCE D., and ROBERT F. MEIER (1994). *Crime and Its Social Context: Toward an Integrated Theory of Offenders, Victims, and Situations*. Albany: State University of New York Press.

MILOVANOVIC, DRAGAN (1990). "Repressive formalism." In B. MacLean and D. Milovanovic, eds., *Racism, Empiricism and Criminal Justice*, 81–88. Vancouver: Collective Press.

———— (1992). *Postmodern Law and Disorder: Psychoanalytic Semiotics, Chaos and Juridic Exegeses*. Liverpool, UK: Deborah Charles.

———— (1993a). "Lacan's four discourses." *Studies in Psychoanalytic Theory* 2: 3–23.

———— (1993b). "Borromean knots and the constitution of sense in juridico-discursive production." *Legal Studies Forum* 17: 171–192.

———— (1994a). "The decentered subject in law." *Studies in Psychoanalytic Theory* 3: 93–127.

———— (1995). "Dueling paradigms: Modernist vs. postmodernist." *Humanity and Society* 19: 1–22.

———— (1996). "Postmodern criminology: Mapping the terrain." *Justice Quarterly* 13: 567–610.

———— (1997a). *Postmodern Criminology.* New York: Garland.

————, ed. (1997b). *Chaos, Criminology and Social Justice: The New Orderly (Dis)Order.* Westport, CT: Praeger.

MILOVANOVIC, DRAGAN, and JIM THOMAS (1989). "Overcoming the absurd: Legal struggle as primitive rebellion." *Social Problems* 36: 48–60.

MINOR, WILLIAM (1977). "A deterrence-control theory of crime." In R. Meier, ed., *Theory in Criminology: Contemporary Views,* 117–137. Beverly Hills, CA: Sage.

MORRISON, WAYNE (1995). *Theoretical Criminology: From Modernity to Post-Modernism.* London, UK: Cavendish

NELKEN, DAVID, ed. (1994). *The Futures of Criminology.* London: Sage

O'MALLEY, PATRICK, and STEPHEN MUGFORD (1994). "Crime, excitement, and modernity." In G. Barak, ed., *Varieties of Criminology,* 189–121. Westport, CT: Praeger.

PATERNOSTER, RAYMOND (1989a). "Absolute and restrictive deterrence in a panel of youth: Explaining the onset, persistence/desistence and frequency of delinquent offending." *Social Problems* 36: 289–308.

———— (1989b). "Decisions to participate in and desist from four types of common delinquency: Deterrence and the rational choice perspective." *Law and Society Review* 23: 7–40.

PATERNOSTER, RAYMOND, and LEE IOVANNI (1989). "The labeling perspective and delinquency: An elaboration of the theory and assessment of the evidence." *Justice Quarterly* 6: 359–394.

PEPINSKY, HAROLD E. (1986). "This can't be peace: A pessimist looks at punishment." In W. B. Groves and G. Newman, eds., *Punishment and Privilege,* 119–130. Albany, NY: Harrow and Heston.

———— (1988). "Violence as unresponsiveness: Toward a new conception of crime." *Justice Quarterly* 5: 539–563.

———— (1989). "Issues of citizen involvement in policing." *Crime and Delinquency* 35: 458–470.

———— (1991). *The Geometry of Violence and Democracy.* Bloomington: Indiana University Press.

PEPINSKY, HAROLD E., and PAUL JESILOW (1985). *Myths That Cause Crime,* 2nd ed., Cabin John, MD: Seven Locks Press.

PEPINSKY, HAROLD E., and RICHARD QUINNEY, eds. (1991). *Criminology as Peace-Making.* Bloomington: University of Indiana Press.

QUINNEY, RICHARD (1988). "Crime, suffering, service: Toward a criminology of peacemaking." *Quest* 1: 66–75.

———— (1989). "The theory and practice of peacemaking in the development of radical criminology." *Critical Criminologist* 1(5): 5.

QUINNEY, RICHARD, and JOHN WILDEMAN (1991). *The Problem of Crime: A Peace and Social Justice Perspective,* 3rd ed. Mountain View, CA: Mayfield.

REYNOLDS, PAUL D. (1971). *A Primer in Theory Construction.* Indianapolis, IN: Bobbs-Merrill.

RODRIGUEZ, ORLANDO, and DAVID WEISBURD (1991). "The integrated social control model and ethnicity: The case of Puerto Rican American delinquency." *Criminal Justice and Behavior* 18: 464–479.

SALECI, RENALDO (1993). "Crime as a mode of subjectivization: Lacan and the law." *Law and Critique* 4: 2–20.

SAMPSON, ROBERT J., and JOHN H. LAUB (1990). "Crime and deviance over the life course: The salience of adult social bonds." *American Sociological Review* 55: 609–627.

———— (1992). "Crime and deviance in the life course." *Annual Review of Sociology* 58: 63–84.

—— (1993). *Crime in the Making: Pathways and Turning Points through Life.* Cambridge, MA: Harvard University Press.

—— (1994). "Urban poverty and the family context of delinquency: A new look at structure and process in a classic study." *Child Development* 65: 523–540.

—— (1995). "Understanding variability in lives through time: Contributions of life-course criminology." *Studies on Crime and Crime Prevention* 4: 143–158.

SCHWARTZ, MARTIN D., and DAVID O. FRIEDRICHS (1994). "Postmodern thought and criminological discontent: New metaphors for understanding violence." *Criminology* 32: 221–246.

SCHWENDINGER, HERMAN, and JULIA S. SCHWENDINGER (1985). *Adolescent Subcultures and Delinquency.* New York: Praeger.

SHORT, JAMES F., JR. (1985). "The level of explanation problem in criminology." In R. F. Meier, ed., *Theoretical Methods in Criminology,* 51–72. Beverly Hills, CA: Sage.

—— (1989). "Exploring integration of theoretical levels of explanation: Notes on gang delinquency." In S. F. Messner, M. D. Krohn, and A. E. Liska, eds., *Theoretical Integration in the Study of Deviance and Crime: Problems and Prospects,* 243–259. Albany: State University of New York Press.

SMART, CAROL (1990). "Feminist approaches to criminology or postmodern woman meets atavistic man." In L. Geisthorpe and A. Morris, eds., *Feminist Perspectives in Criminology,* 70–88. London: Open University Press.

SWIGERT, VICTORIA L. (1989). "The discipline as data: Resolving the theoretical crisis in criminology." In S. F. Messner, M. D. Krohn, and A. E. Liska, eds., *Theoretical Integration in the Study of Deviance and Crime: Problems and Prospects,* 129–135. Albany: State University of New York Press.

THORNBERRY, TERRENCE P. (1989). "Reflections on the advantages and disadvantages of theoretical integration." In S. F. Messner, M. D. Krohn, and A. E. Liska, eds., *Theoretical Integration in the Study of Deviance and Crime: Problems and Prospects,* 51–60. Albany: State University of New York Press.

THRASHER, FREDERIC M. (1927). *The Gang: A Study of 1,313 Gangs in Chicago.* Chicago: University of Chicago Press.

TITTLE, CHARLES R. (1985). "The assumption that general theories are not possible." In R. F. Meier, ed., *Theoretical Methods in Criminology,* 93–121. Beverly Hills, CA: Sage.

—— (1989). "Prospects for synthetic theory: A consideration of macro-level criminological activity." In S. F. Messner, M. D. Krohn, and A. E. Liska, eds., *Theoretical Integration in the Study of Deviance and Crime: Problems and Prospects,* 161–178. Albany: State University of New York Press.

—— (1995). *Control Balance: Toward a General Theory of Deviance.* Boulder, CO: Westview.

TURK, AUSTIN T. (1989). "Notes on criminology and terrorism." In W. S. Laufer and F. Adler, eds., *Advances in Criminological Theory,* vol. 1, 17–29. New Brunswick, NJ: Transaction.

VILA, BRYAN J. (1994). "A general paradigm for understanding criminal behavior: Extending evolutionary ecological theory." *Criminology* 32: 311–359.

VILA, BRYAN J., and LAWRENCE E. COHEN (1993). "Crime as strategy: Testing an evolutionary ecological theory of expropriative crime." *American Journal of Sociology* 98: 873–912.

WILLIAMS, FRANK P. III (1981). "The sociology of criminological theory: Paradigm or fad." In G. F. Jensen, ed., *Sociology of Delinquency: Current Issues,* 20–28. Beverly Hills, CA: Sage.

—— (1985). "Deterrence and social control: Rethinking the relationship." *Journal of Criminal Justice* 13: 141–151.

—— (1998). *Imagining Criminology: An Alternative Paradigm.* New York: Garland.

WILSON, JAMES Q., and RICHARD HERRNSTEIN (1985). *Crime and Human Nature.* New York: Simon and Schuster.

WOLFGANG, MARVIN E., and FRANCO FERRACUTI (1967). *The Subculture of Violence: Towards an Integrated Theory in Criminology.* London: Tavistock.

WONDERS, NANCY A. (1996). "Determinate sentencing: A feminist and postmodern story." *Justice Quarterly* 13: 611–648.

YOUNG, T. R. (1991). "Chaos and crime: Nonlinear and fractal forms of crime." *Critical Criminologist* 3: 3-4, 10–11, 13–14.

——— (1992). "Chaos theory and human agency." *Humanity and Society* 16: 441–460.

INDEX

Benson, Bruce, 25
Benson, Michael, 202, 204, 266
Bentham, Jeremy, 14, 16-19, 21, 24-29
Berger, Ronald, 261
Berk, Richard A., 25, 30, 178, 201, 207
Bernard, Thomas J., 12, 101, 105, 109, 128, 163, 165,
    178, 186, 190, 195, 201, 204, 214, 266, 289
Bernstein, Ilene N., 152
Bierstedt, Robert, 105
Binder, Arnold, 150, 152
Biological theory, 32-43, 46, 75, 95, 188, 219, 220,
    274, 277, 287
    anomaly, 36
    atavism, 37
    brain, 35, 42, 43, 192, 220, 223
    body types, 38
    born criminal, 36, 37
    concordance, 38
    criminal personality, 44
    degeneracy, 36
    diet, 42, 48, 220
    epilepsy, 36
    evolutionary theories, 32, 34, 43
    feeblemindedness, 37, 49, 56, 76
    genetic studies, 38
    heredity, 37, 58
    intelligence, 37, 43, 76, 197
    occasional criminal, 36
    phrenology, 35
    physiognomy, 35
    somatotypes, 38
    twin studies, 38
Biosocial theory, 42, 51
Biron, Louise, 241, 244
Bishop, Donna, 159
Blackburne, R., 47
Blalock, Hubert M., 3, 13
Blankenship, Ralph, 159
Blaske, David M., 204
Block, Carolyn R., 129, 237, 241, 247
Bloch, Herbert, A., 128
Block, Richard, 88, 237, 241
Blomberg, Thomas G., 150, 152
Bloom, Diana M., 178
Blumer, Herbert, 59, 67, 230
Blumstein, Alfred, 25, 27, 204
Bock, Gregory, 47
Bogdan, C., 262
Bograd, Michele, 268
Bohannon, Stephen R., 210
Bohlander, Edward W., 169, 184
Bohlke, Robert H., 105
Bohm, Robert M., 168, 169, 171, 178, 185
Bohman, M., 47
Bohmer, S., 229
Bonati, Lisa, 245
Bookin-Weiner, Hedy, 128
Booth, Alan, 47
Bordua, David J., 105, 115, 128
Boris, Steven B., 67
Bornstein, Philip H., 227
Bortner, M. A., 178
Bosworth, Mary, 178, 261
Bottoms, Anthony E., 65, 67
Boundary maintenance, 191
Boutellier, Johannes, 261
Bowers, William, 25
Bowker, Lee K., 261
Box, Steven, 52, 178
Boyer, Debra, 128
Braithwaite, John, 28, 88, 105, 125, 126, 128, 132, 148,
    152, 204, 210, 234, 241, 272, 273, 277, 286, 289

Brantingham, Patricia L., 67, 241
Brantingham, Paul J., 67, 241
Brass, Paul, 178
Breault, Kevin, 70, 131
Breed, Warren, 105
Brennan, P. A., 47
Brezin, Timothy, 105
Brezitz, T., 204
Briar, Scott, 194, 204
Brier, S. S., 25
Britt, Chester L., 52, 204
Britt, David, 182
Brittain, R. P., 50
Bromley, Rosemary, 71
Brooks, John, 47
Brower, Sidney, 73
Brown, B., 261
Brown, David, 178
Brown, M. Craig, 178
Brown, Marjorie, 128
Brown, Stephen E., 103, 105, 125, 127, 128, 234, 241
Brown, Waln K., 153
Browne, Angela, 261
Brownfield, David, 125, 128, 204, 205, 208, 227, 244,
    264
Brownmiller, Susan, 257, 261
Bruinsma, Gerben J. N., 86
Brunton, M. M., 50
Bryce-Smith, D., 47
Buerger, Michael, 237, 247
Buffalo, M. D., 158, 212
Bulmer, Martin, 56, 57, 67
Bung, W. L., 131
Burak, Cynthia, 210
Burger, William, 86, 105, 128, 178
Burgess, Ernest W., 57, 60, 67, 71, 77
Burgess, Robert L., 84, 86, 216, 217, 220, 227
Burgos, William, 228
Burke, Mary Jean, 85, 91
Burkett, Steven R., 25, 205, 210, 227, 228
Burkhart, J. M., 266
Bursik, Robert J., Jr., 26, 27, 65-67, 69, 148, 155, 207,
    243, 270, 286, 289
Bustamante, Jorge A., 153
Buttell, Alan J., 67
Buzawa, Eve, 25
Buzawa, Carl, 25
Byrne, James M., 67, 72, 266

Cain, Maureen, 159, 261
Caldas, Stephen, 152, 227, 288
Calhoun, Thomas, 241
Calvin, Lyle, 132
Cameron, Deborah, 261
Campbell, Alec, 25
Campbell, Anne, 128, 129, 205, 261
Canela-Cacho, Josea, 25
Canter, Rachelle J., 130, 201, 205, 206, 228, 252, 261,
    275, 290
Cantor, David, 70, 241, 242, 245
Caringella-MacDonald, Susan, 247
Cao, Liqun, 129
Caplan, Aaron, 209
Cardarelli, Albert, 179
Carlen, Pat, 179, 261
Carmichael, Benjamin, 105
Carothers, Linn E., 210
Carrington, Kerry, 261
Carroll, John S., 241
Carter, David, 108, 132
Carter, Timothy J., 110

O'Brien, Robert M., 246, 266
O'Connell, Brian, 109
O'Day, Patrick, 131
Odem, Mary. E., 266
O'Donnell, C., 262
O'Donnell, J., 133
O'Dwyer, J., 261
Official statistics, 5, 7, 76, 138, 140
Ogle, Robin, 109, 266
Ohlin, Lloyd E., xii, 64, 84, 86, 101, 106, 112, 113, 117-121, 124, 127, 129, 130, 132, 133, 219, 275, 286, 290
Ohm, Rose Marie, 71
Olsen, Marvin, 109
O'Malley, Patrick, 146, 192
O'Malley, Patrick M., 184
O'Maolchatha, Aogan, 175, 186
Opp, Karl-Dieter, 89, 158
Opportunity (*see* Anomie theory; Gender theory; Subculture theory)
Orcutt, James D., 7, 13, 89, 140, 158, 211
Oropesa, Ralph S., 70
Osborn, S. G., 154
Osborne, Lynne, 158
Osgood, D. Wayne, 47, 52, 231, 237, 246
Otto, Luther, 211

Pabon, Edward, 206, 228
Palacios, Wilson, 133
Palamara, Frances, 158
Palamore, Erdman B., 110
Pallone, Nathaniel, 49, 52, 246
Palloni, Alberto, 155, 207
Paradigm, 190, 235, 278, 283, 286, 287
Park, Robert E., 57, 60, 67, 68, 70, 71, 73, 77
Parker, Jerry, 29,
Parker, Robert N., 133, 184, 246
Parsons, Talcott, 94, 110, 114
Passas, Nikos, 110
Pate, Antony M., 29
Paternoster, Raymond, 29, 30, 90, 102, 110, 111, 158, 159, 211, 230, 241, 245, 246, 267, 274, 286, 292
Patterned delinquent behavior, 275
Patterson, Gerald R., 211
Pauly, John, 106, 170, 179
Payne, John, 244
Payne, William D., 158
Peacemaking criminology, 176, 281
Pearce, Frank, 184
Pearson, Frank, 9, 13, 230
Pease, Susan, 48
Pedi, Stephen J., 160
Pelletier, G., 52
Pepinsky, Harold E., xii, 168, 177, 184, 264, 273, 281, 292
Perkins, Douglas, 71
Perkovich, Joseph, 24
Petchesky, R. P., 184
Petee, Thomas A., 71, 131
Peters, Helge, 158
Peters, Ardith, 204
Peterson, Ruth D., 24, 29, 181
Petrunik, Michael, 158
Pfau-Vicent, B. A., 205
Pfefferbaum, Betty, 214, 232
Pfohl, Stephen J., 127, 133
Philipson, Thomas, 246
Phillips, Charles D., 158
Phillips, David P., 29
Phillips, Howard, 129
Phillips, John C., 211

Phillips, Lorne, 108, 110
Pierce, Glenn, 25
Pihl, R. O., 52
Piliavin, Irving, 29, 194, 204, 246
Pincus, J. H., 50
Pink, William T., 209
Piper, Elizabeth, 130
Piquero, Alex, 29, 246
Pisciotta, Alexander W., 183
Platt, Tony, 168, 169, 172, 181, 184
Pogrebin, Mark, 71
Polakowski, Michael, 211
Polder, Wim, 108
Polk, Kenneth, 133, 202, 211
Pollock-Byrne, Joycelyn M., 266
Polsky, Ned, 133
Polvi, Natalie, 246
Pomersheim, Frank, 185
Poole, Eric D., 71, 110, 158, 211, 212
Porter, Sheila, 47, 211
Positive School, 32–46, 60, 233
    determinism, 62, 286, 287
    evolution, 32, 34, 256
    natural crime, 36
    pathology, 9, 45, 62, 64, 94, 98, 100, 288
    treatment, 3, 9, 18, 32, 40, 41, 45, 46, 62, 85, 127, 151, 216, 222, 225, 270
Posner, Richard, 246
Postmodern theory, 282, 283
Poverty, 42, 56, 102, 113, 126, 133, 172, 203, 219, 220, 254
Powell, Elwin H., 110
Powell, Kenneth, 52
Power-control theory, 254, 255, 260
Price, Barbara R., 266
Psychological theory, 38, 43–45
    criminal personality, 44, 234
    emotional trauma, 38, 177
    extroversion, 45
    insanity, 36, 288
    introversion, 38
    MMPI, 39
    neuroticism, 45
    personality, 38, 39, 42–45, 102, 124, 188, 191, 192, 224, 234, 287
    psychopathology, 39
    psychoticism, 45
    unconscious conflict, 38
Pyle, David, 246

Quantitative methodology, 271
Quetelet, Adolphe, 35, 39, 47, 52
Quicker, John C., 133
Quinney, Richard, xii, 5, 13, 71, 87, 163, 166-171, 174, 177, 183, 185, 217, 228, 234, 246, 264, 266, 281, 292

Radical theory, 172 (*see* Conflict theory)
Radosevich, Marcia J., 226, 229, 230
Radosh, Polly, 253, 256, 258, 266
Rafky, David M., 158
Rafter, Nicole H., 262, 266
Rahav, Giora, 71, 89, 110, 159
Raine, Adrian, 52
Rains, Prudence, 158
Rankin, Bruce, 68
Rankin, Joseph H., 29, 110, 160, 211
Rasmussen, David, 25
Rathus, Spencer A., 134
Rational theory, 233–240

cognitive theory, 44, 46, 233
  guardians, 236, 237, 240
  lifestyle, 235, 237, 238, 240
  motivated offenders, 236, 237, 278
  routine activities, 235–240, 278
  targets, 235–237, 240
Rattner, Arye, 212
Raushenbush, Winifred, 71
Ray, Marsh, 158
Raymond, Frank B., 89, 110
Reasons, Charles E., 178
Reckless, Walter C., 154, 189, 190, 192, 205, 210-213
Recreation, 66
Reddon, John, 47
Redondo, Lourdes Miron, 230
Reed, Gary, 202, 212
Reed, Mark D., 200, 209
Reed-Sanders, D., 212
Regoli, Robert M., 110, 158, 211, 212
Reiman, Jeffrey, 185
Reinarman, Craig, 80, 89
Reisig, Michael, 210
Reiss, Albert J., Jr., xii, 2, 13, 52, 65-67, 71-73, 89, 110,
       133, 189-191, 212, 241
Relative deprivation, 102
Rengert, George F., 68, 71–73, 243
Renneville, Marc, 52
Rennie, Ysabel, 52
Retzinger, Suzanne M., 158
Rexroat, Cynthia, 230
Rhodes, Albert Lewis, 2, 13, 89, 110, 133, 212
Rice, Kent, 107
Rice, Tom, 133
Rich, Richard, 71
Richard, Wayne C., 158
Richards, Pamela J., 201, 207
Richmond, F. Lynn, 133, 211
Rifkin, Janet, 266
Riley, David, 237, 246, 347
Ritzer, George, 13
Robbins, C., 208
Roberts, Mary K., 200, 214
Robertson, Joan, 153
Robin, Gerald D., 89, 133
Robins, Lee, 53
Robinson, William S., 72
Rock, Paul, 158
Rodgers, J. L., 52
Rodman, Hyman, 134
Rodriquez, Orlando, 292
Roebuck, Julian B., 134, 153
Rogan, Dennis, 30
Rogers, Patrice, 29
Rogers, Joseph W., 158, 212
Rohe, William, 69
Roncek, Dennis, 237, 246
Rosanoff, Aaron J., 52
Rosanoff, Isabel Avis, 52
Rose, Robert M., 108
Rosenbaum, Dennis, 72, 206
Rosenbaum, Jill Leslie, 212, 244
Rosenberg, Bernard, 110, 228
Rosenfeld, Richard, 103, 109, 110, 291
Rosenhan, D. L., 158
Roshier, Bob, 29, 246
Ross, H. Laurence, 23, 29, 30
Rossi, Peter H., 178
Roth, Loren H., 52, 53
Rothman, David, 33, 52
Rothstein, Edward, 134
Routine-activity theory, 235–237, 273 (*see* Rational
       theory)

Rowe, Allan, 30
Rowe, David C., 52, 212
Ruppert, Carol Ann, 134
Rushing, William A., 110, 251
Rushton, J. Philippe, 52
Rushton, O. Philippe, 231
Russell, Katheryn, 266
Rust, James, 106
Rytina, Steve, 27

Sabol, W. J., 184
Sadler, Jay, 159
Sailer, Lee, 290
Saleci, Renaldo, 292
Saltzman, Linda E., 29, 30, 230 (*see* Anderson,
       Linda)
Samenow, Stanton E., 43, 44, 53, 234, 248
Sampson, Robert J., 50, 58, 66-68, 72, 88, 102, 110,
       134, 148, 158, 181, 202, 205, 209, 212, 246,
       247, 278, 293
Sanabria, Harry, 244
Savitz, Leonard D., 34, 52
Scarpitti, Frank R., 129, 212, 257, 263
Scaturo, L. A., 180
Scheff, Thomas J., 148, 158
Schiraldi, Vincent, 24, 26
Schlesinger, Louis, 52
Schlossman, Steven, 72, 266
Schmeidler, James, 228
Schmidt, Janell, 30, 49
Schneider, Hans, 231
Schneider, Anne, 247
Schneller, Donald, 159
Schoen, Donald F., 152
Schoenthaler, Stephen, 53
Schrag, Clarence C., 89
Schuerman, Leo, 65, 69, 72
Schuessler, Karl F., 53, 76, 77, 81, 86, 89, 90
Schulsinger, Fini, 38, 53
Schulz, Barbara, 152
Schumann, Karl F., 185
Schur, Edwin M., 144, 147, 150, 151, 159, 266
Schwartz, Gary, 131
Schwartz, Joseph E., 73, 134
Schwartz, Martin D., 180, 185, 263, 266, 293
Schwartz, Michael, 212, 213
Schwartz, Richard D., 142, 143, 159
Schweitzer, Robert D., 208
Schwendinger, Herman, 126, 134, 169, 185, 266,
       274–276, 293
Schwendinger, Julia S., 126, 134, 169, 185, 266,
       274–276, 293
Scott, Joseph J., 129
Scraton, Phil, 185
Scull, Andrew T., 151, 159, 262
Searles, Patricia, 261
Secombe, Wally, 266
Sedlak, Michael, 72
Seeley, Kathryn, 265
Seeman, M., 110
Segrave, Jeffrey O., 201, 212
Seidman, Robert B., 168, 179
Self-concept, 59, 144, 147, 192, 274 (*see also* Control
       theory; Labeling theory)
Self-control, 192, 196-199, 202, 203, 260 (*see* Self con-
       trol theory; Psychological theories)
Self-control theory, 196, 198, 199, 202, 203, 260
  child-rearing practices, 197, 198, 270, 274
  propensity-event, 202
  socialization, 188, 198, 191, 198–200
Self-help theory, 273

305